コンプレックス・エイジ

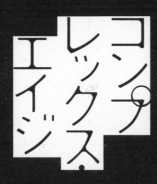

Complex age

Yui Sakuma

4

C O N T E N T S
C o m p l e x   a g e

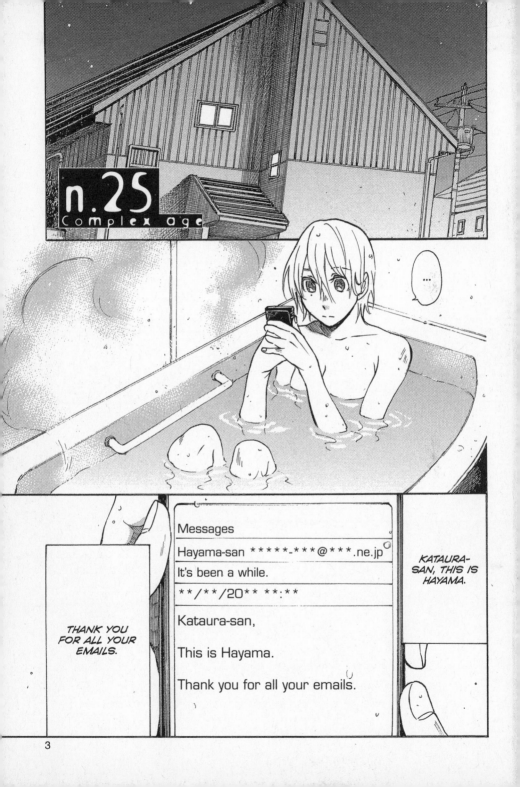

n.25
Complex age

...

Messages
Hayama-san *****-***@***.ne.jp
It's been a while.
//20** **:**
Kataura-san,
This is Hayama.
Thank you for all your emails.

THANK YOU
FOR ALL YOUR
EMAILS.

KATAURA-
SAN, THIS IS
HAYAMA.

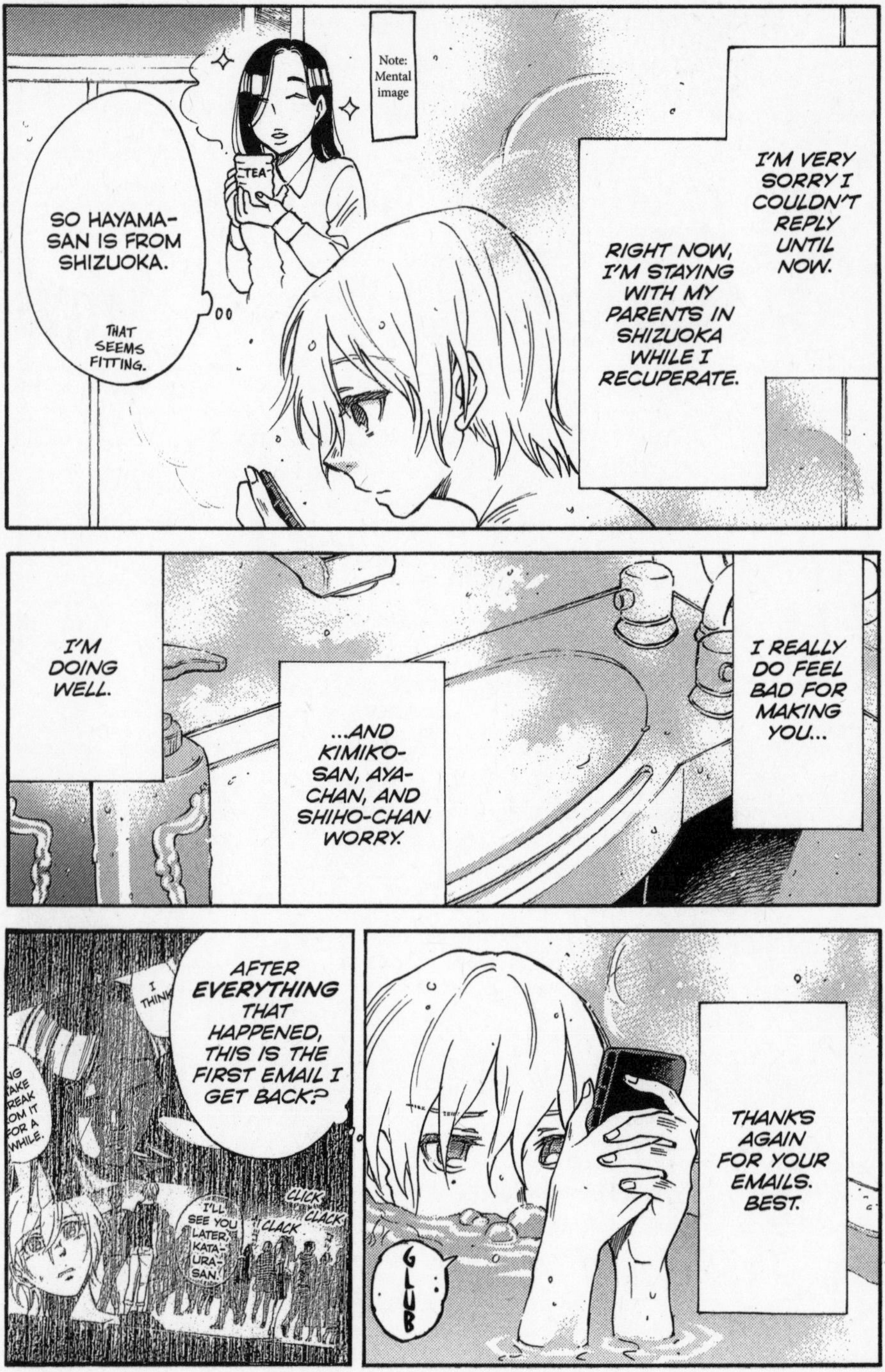

I'M VERY SORRY I COULDN'T REPLY UNTIL NOW.
RIGHT NOW, I'M STAYING WITH MY PARENTS IN SHIZUOKA WHILE I RECUPERATE.
Note: Mental image
TEA
SO HAYAMA-SAN IS FROM SHIZUOKA.
THAT SEEMS FITTING.
I REALLY DO FEEL BAD FOR MAKING YOU...
...AND KIMIKO-SAN, AYA-CHAN, AND SHIHO-CHAN WORRY.
I'M DOING WELL.
THANKS AGAIN FOR YOUR EMAILS. BEST.
GLUB
AFTER EVERYTHING THAT HAPPENED, THIS IS THE FIRST EMAIL I GET BACK?
I THINK
I'LL SEE YOU LATER, KATA-URA-SAN.
CLICK
CLACK
CLACK

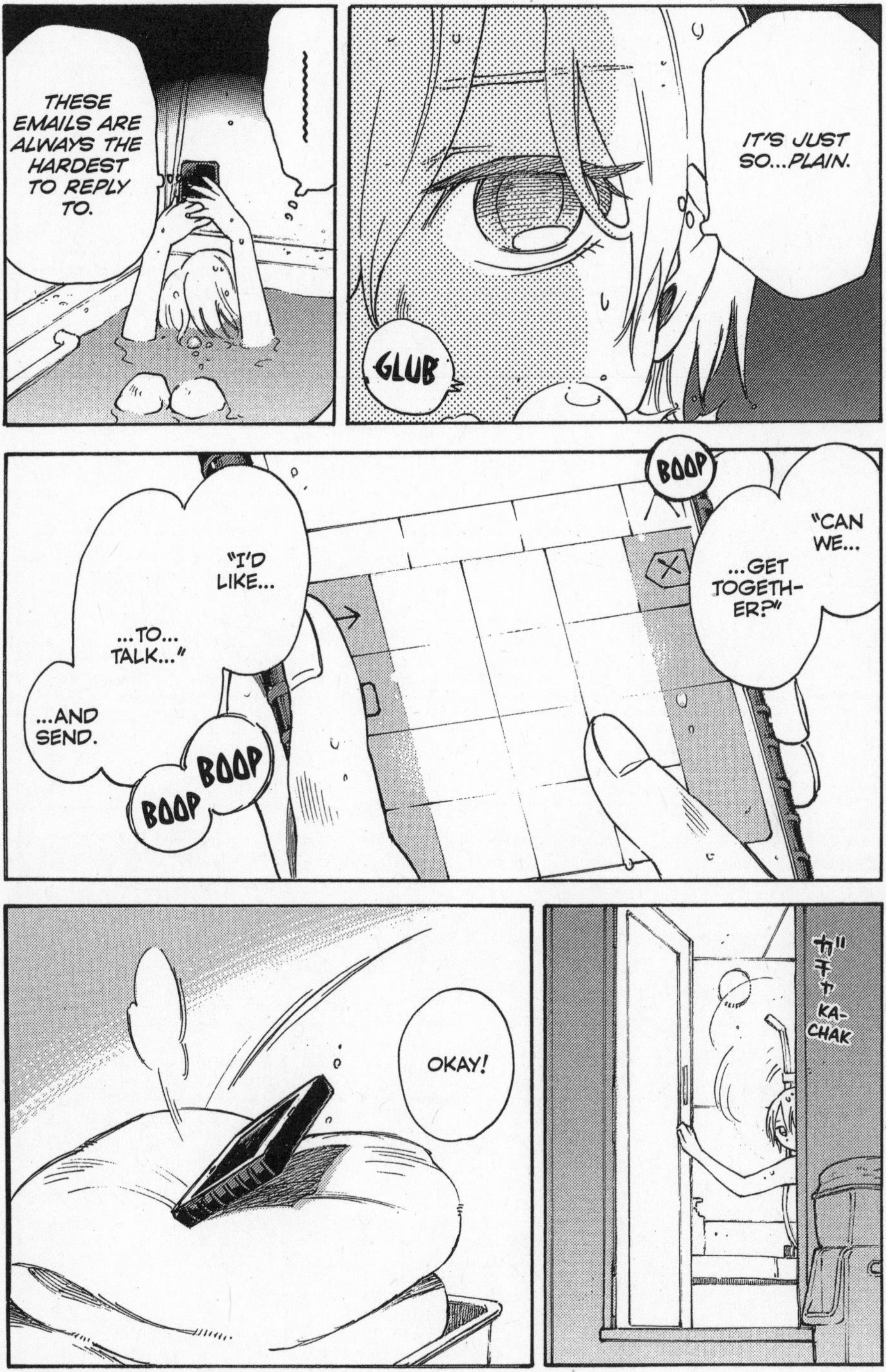
IT'S JUST SO...PLAIN.
GLUB
THESE EMAILS ARE ALWAYS THE HARDEST TO REPLY TO.
BOOP
"CAN WE...
...GET TOGETHER?"
"I'D LIKE...
...TO... TALK..."
...AND SEND.
BOOP
BOOP
ガチャ
KA-CHAK
OKAY!

WHEW.

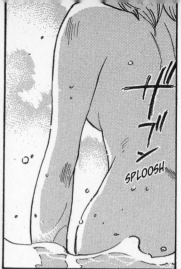

SPLOOSH

I GUESS...

I HAVE A LOT TO THINK ABOUT.

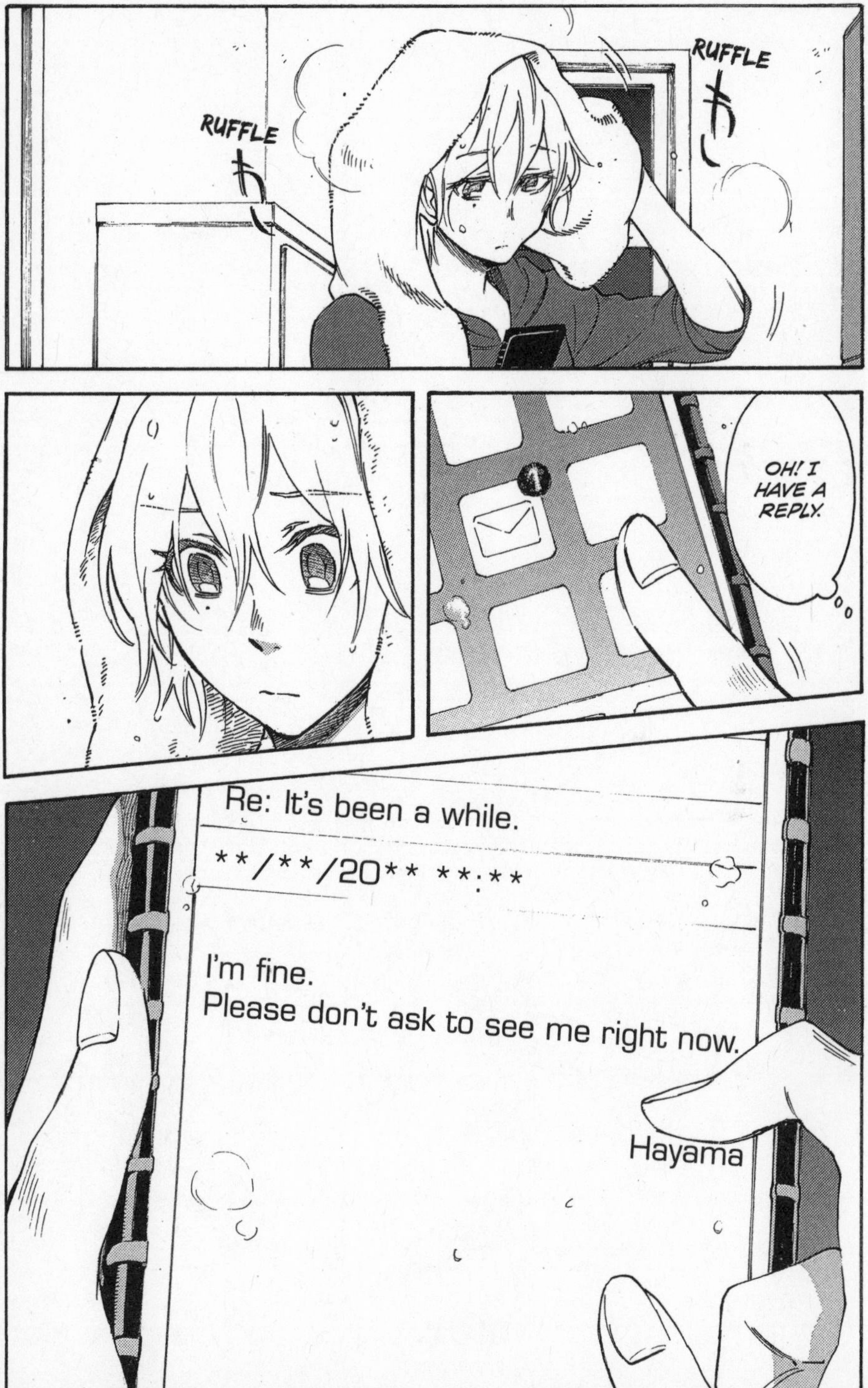
RUFFLE
RUFFLE
OH! I HAVE A REPLY.
Re: It's been a while.
//20** **:**
I'm fine.
Please don't ask to see me right now.
Hayama

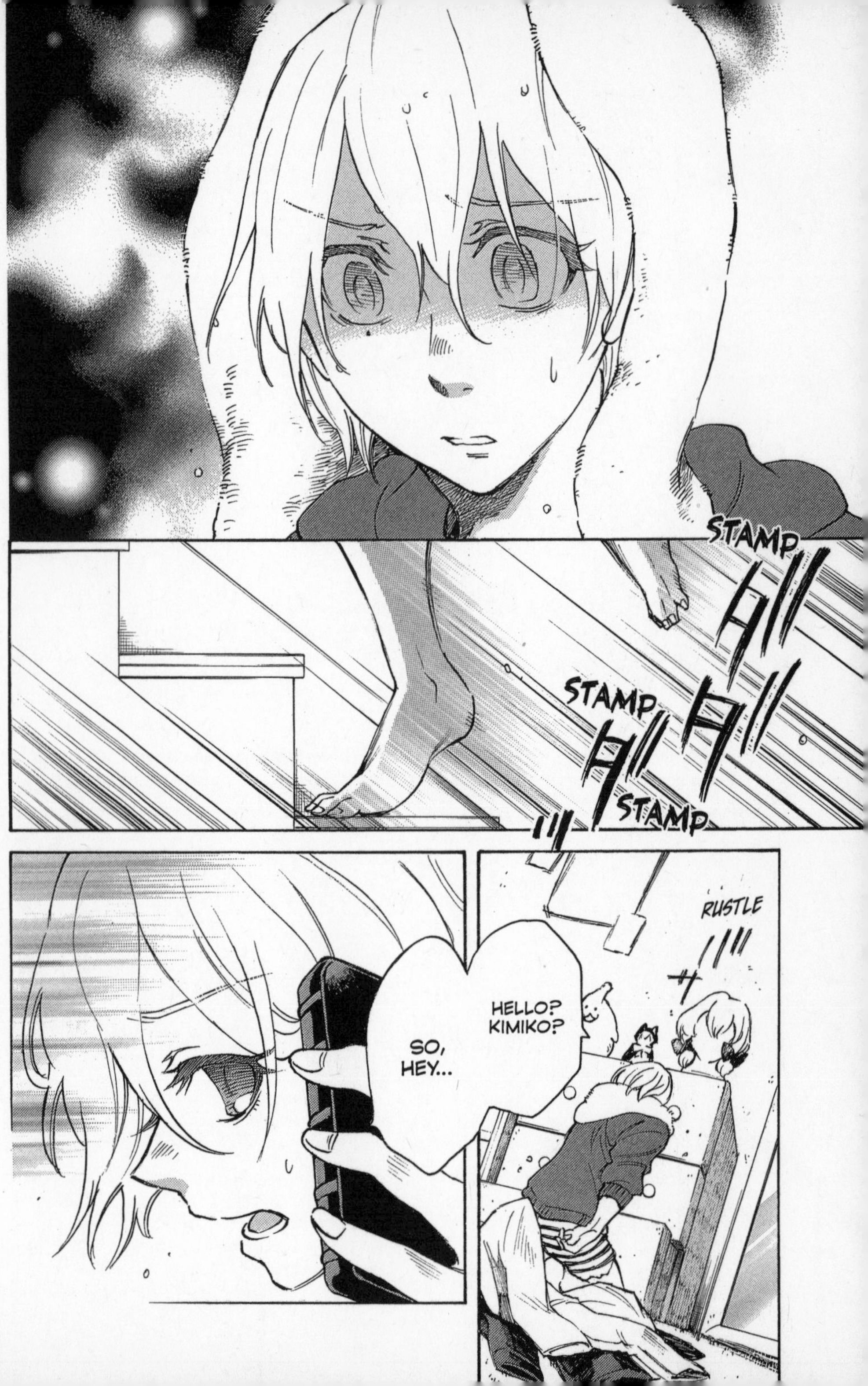
STAMP
STAMP
STAMP
RUSTLE
HELLO? KIMIKO?
SO, HEY...

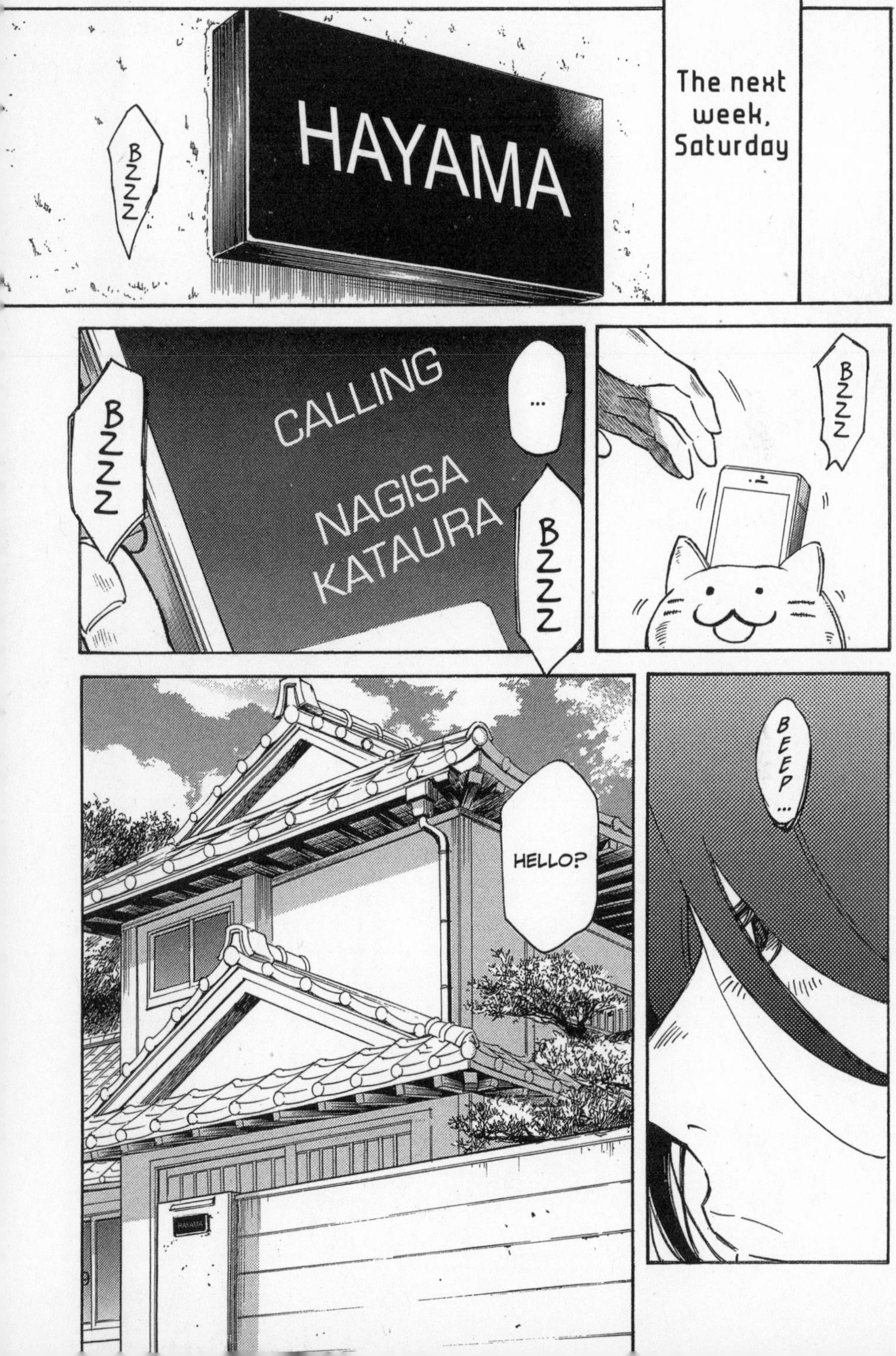
The next week, Saturday
HAYAMA
BZZZ
BZZZ
...
BZZZ
CALLING
NAGISA KATAURA
BZZZ
BEEP...
HELLO?
HAYAMA

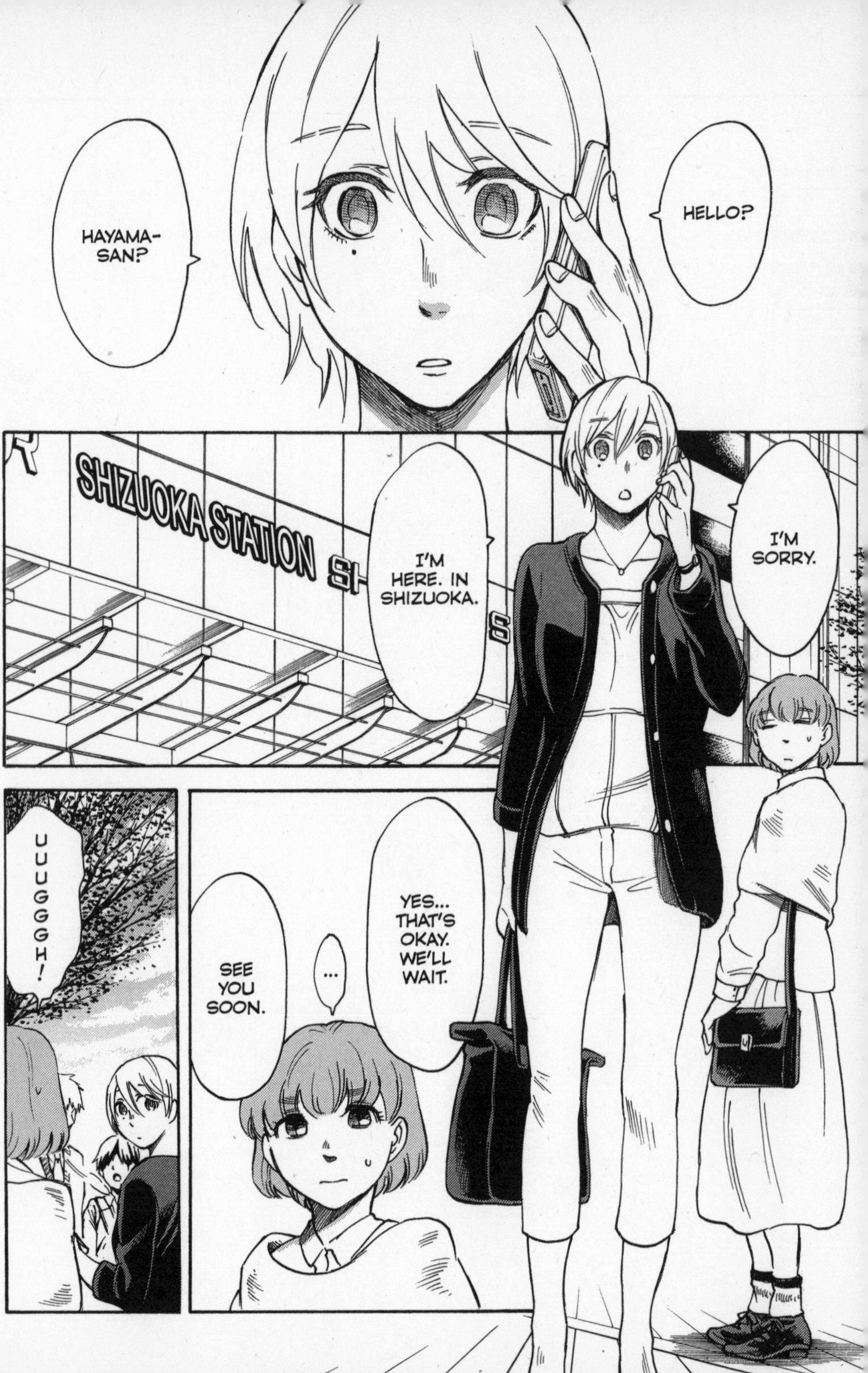
HELLO?
HAYAMA-SAN?
I'M SORRY.
I'M HERE. IN SHIZUOKA.
SHIZUOKA STATION
YES... THAT'S OKAY. WE'LL WAIT.
...
SEE YOU SOON.
UUUGGGH!

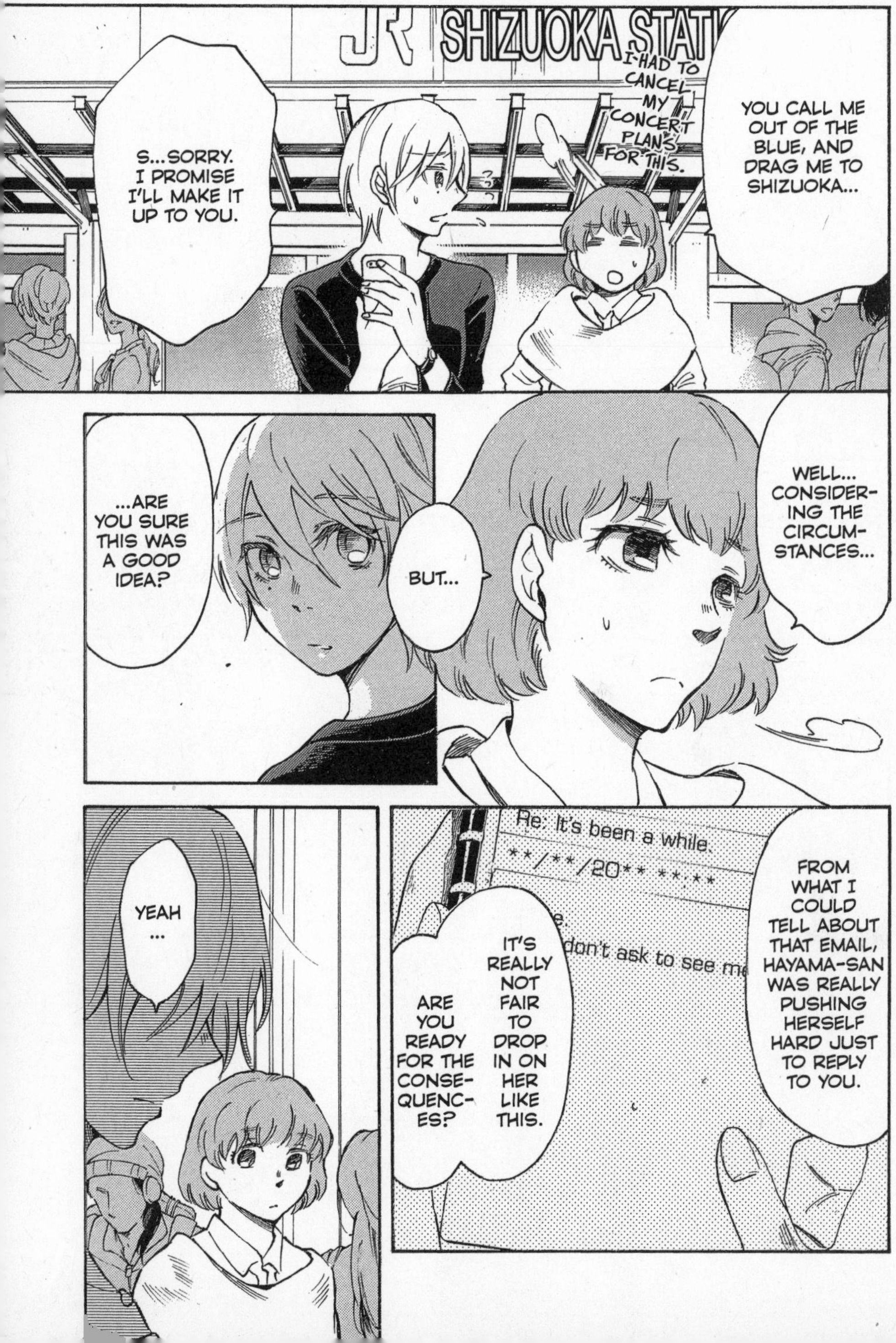
JR
SHIZUOKA STATI
YOU CALL ME OUT OF THE BLUE, AND DRAG ME TO SHIZUOKA...
I HAD TO CANCEL MY CONCERT PLANS FOR THIS.
S...SORRY. I PROMISE I'LL MAKE IT UP TO YOU.
WELL... CONSIDERING THE CIRCUMSTANCES...
BUT...
...ARE YOU SURE THIS WAS A GOOD IDEA?
FROM WHAT I COULD TELL ABOUT THAT EMAIL, HAYAMA-SAN WAS REALLY PUSHING HERSELF HARD JUST TO REPLY TO YOU.
Re: It's been a while.
//20** **:**
don't ask to see me
IT'S REALLY NOT FAIR TO DROP IN ON HER LIKE THIS.
ARE YOU READY FOR THE CONSEQUENCES?
YEAH ...

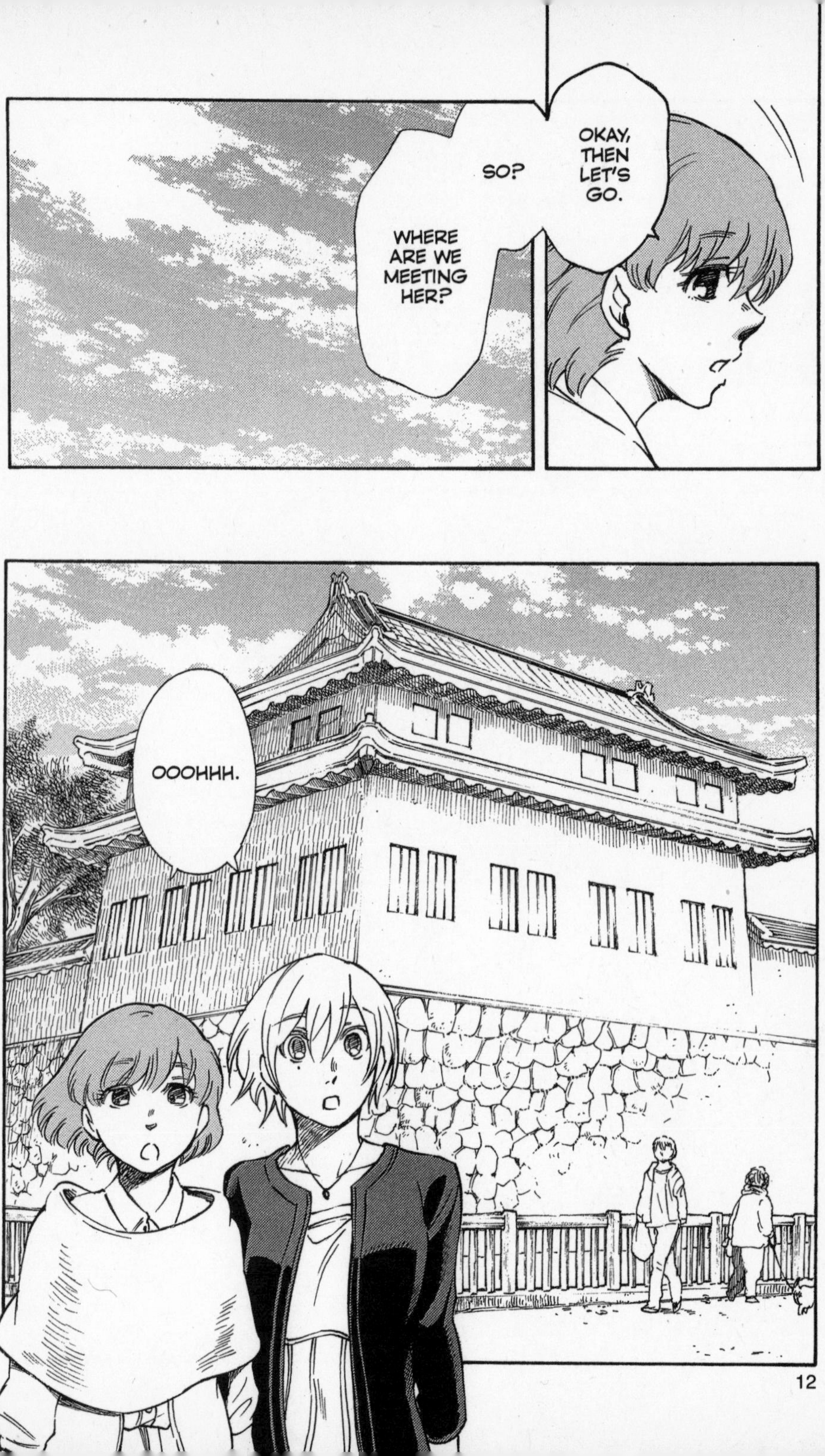
OKAY, THEN LET'S GO.
SO?
WHERE ARE WE MEETING HER?
OOOHHH.

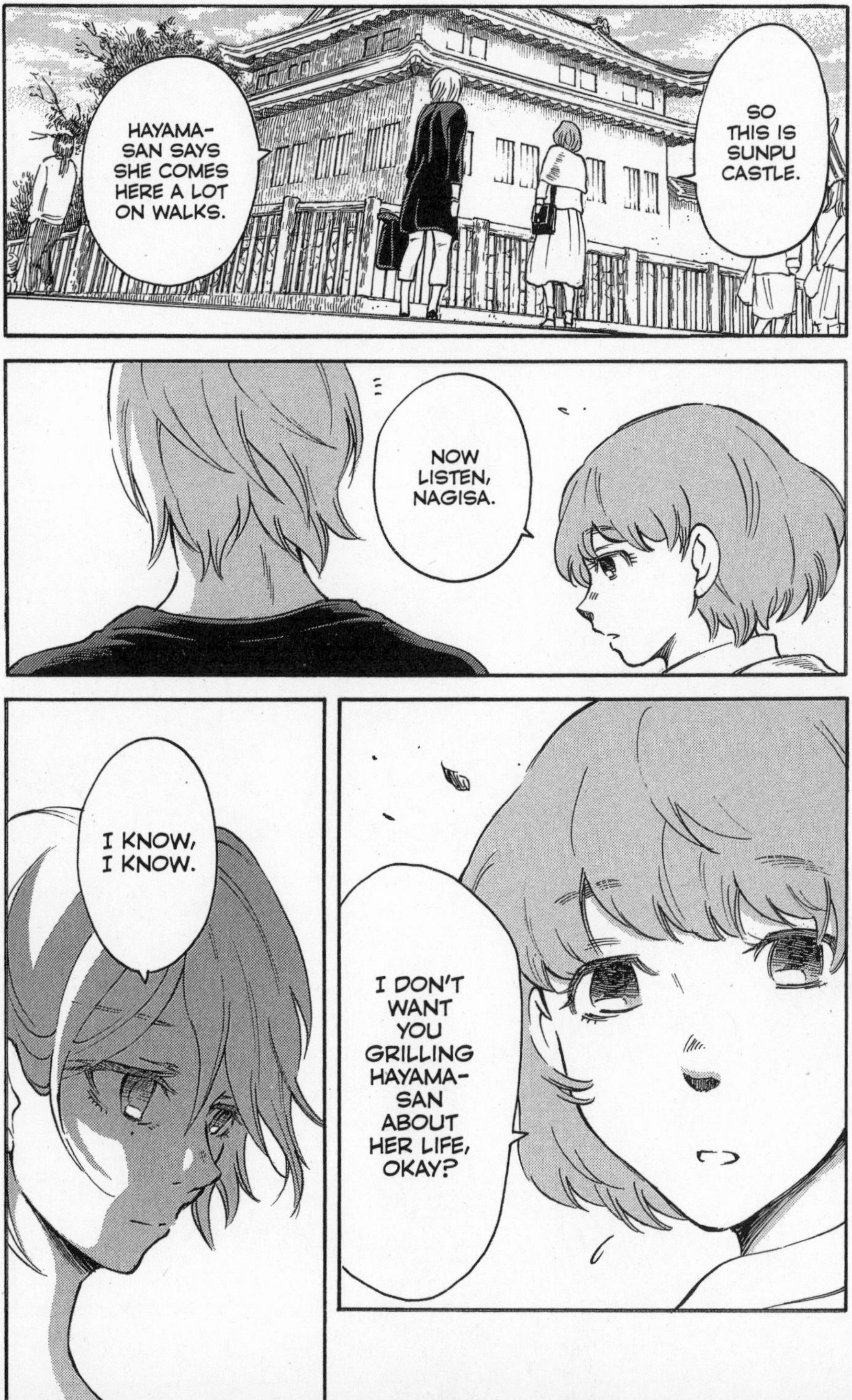
SO THIS IS SUNPU CASTLE.
HAYAMA-SAN SAYS SHE COMES HERE A LOT ON WALKS.
NOW LISTEN, NAGISA.
I DON'T WANT YOU GRILLING HAYAMA-SAN ABOUT HER LIFE, OKAY?
I KNOW, I KNOW.

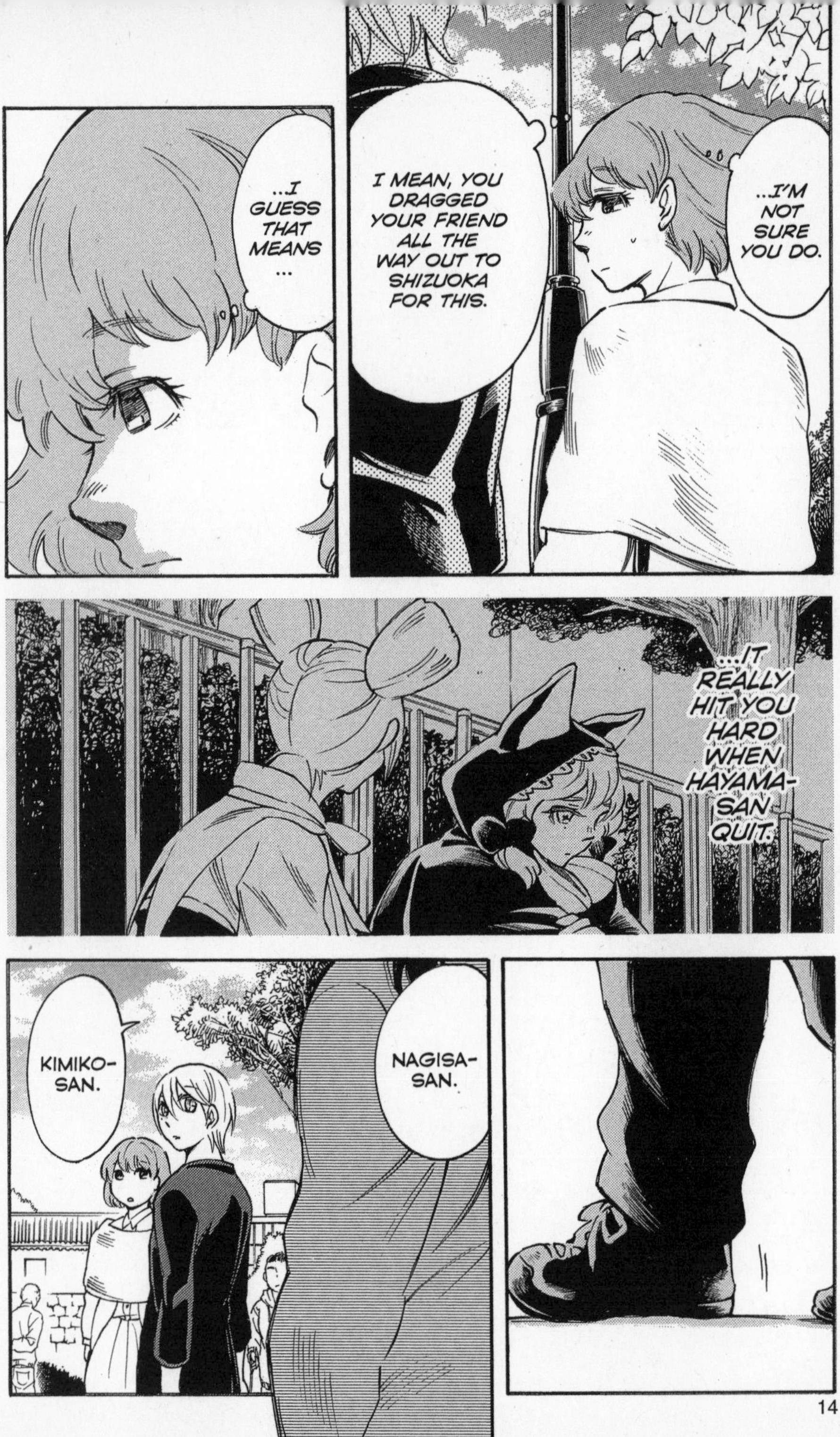
...I'M NOT SURE YOU DO.
I MEAN, YOU DRAGGED YOUR FRIEND ALL THE WAY OUT TO SHIZUOKA FOR THIS.
...I GUESS THAT MEANS ...
...IT REALLY HIT YOU HARD WHEN HAYAMA-SAN QUIT.
NAGISA-SAN.
KIMIKO-SAN.

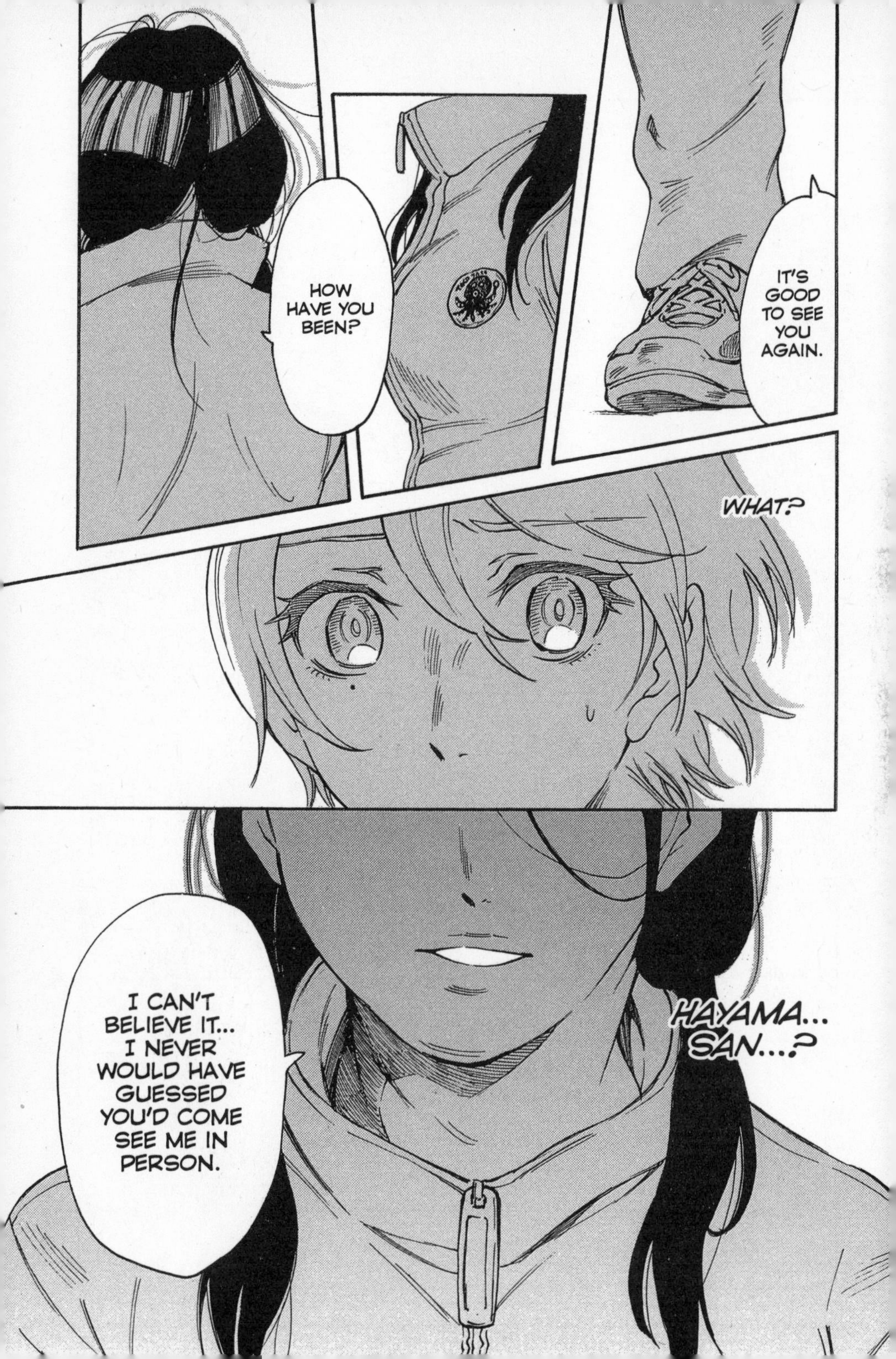
IT'S GOOD TO SEE YOU AGAIN.
HOW HAVE YOU BEEN?
WHAT?
HAYAMA... SAN...?
I CAN'T BELIEVE IT... I NEVER WOULD HAVE GUESSED YOU'D COME SEE ME IN PERSON.

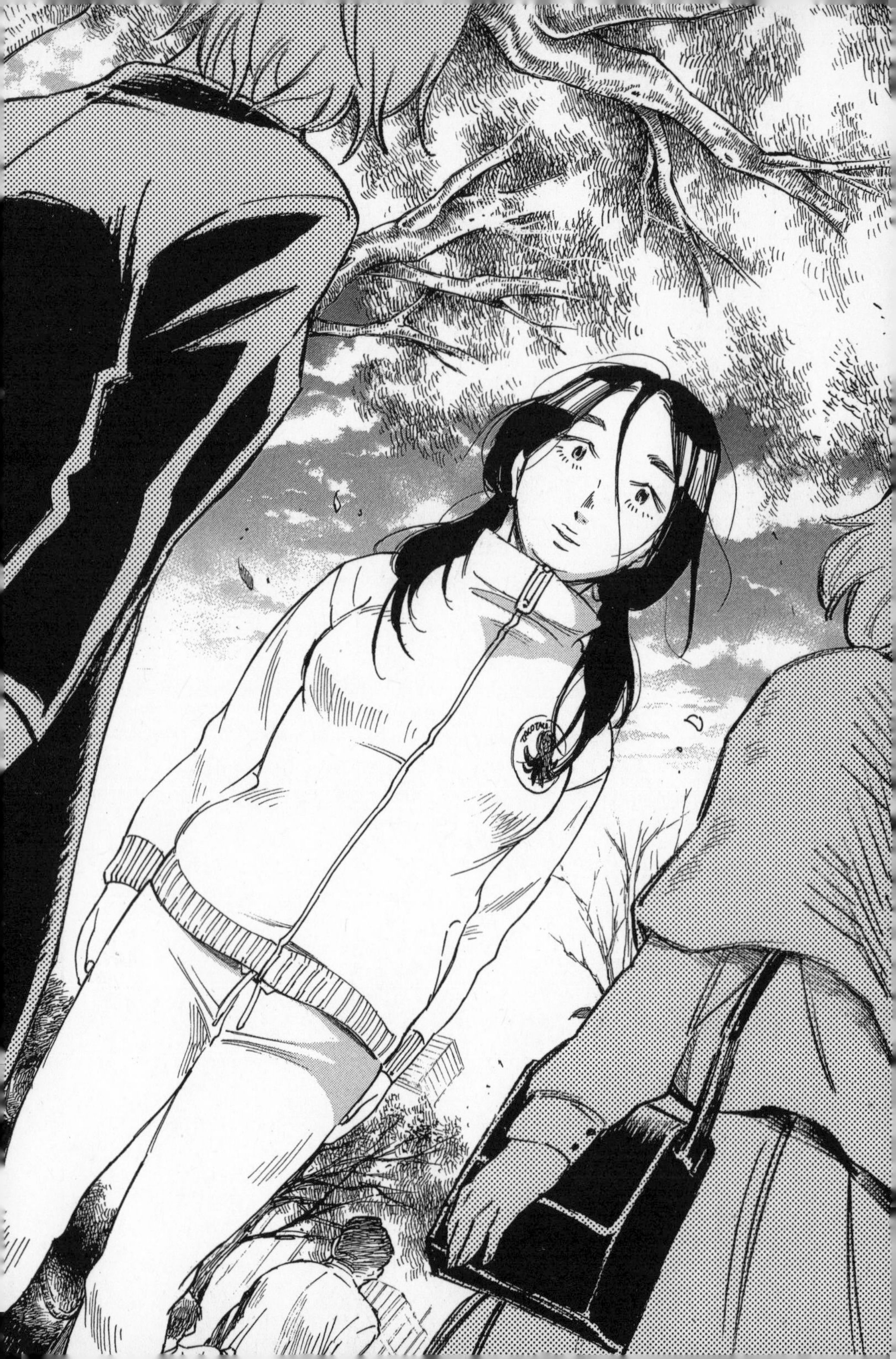

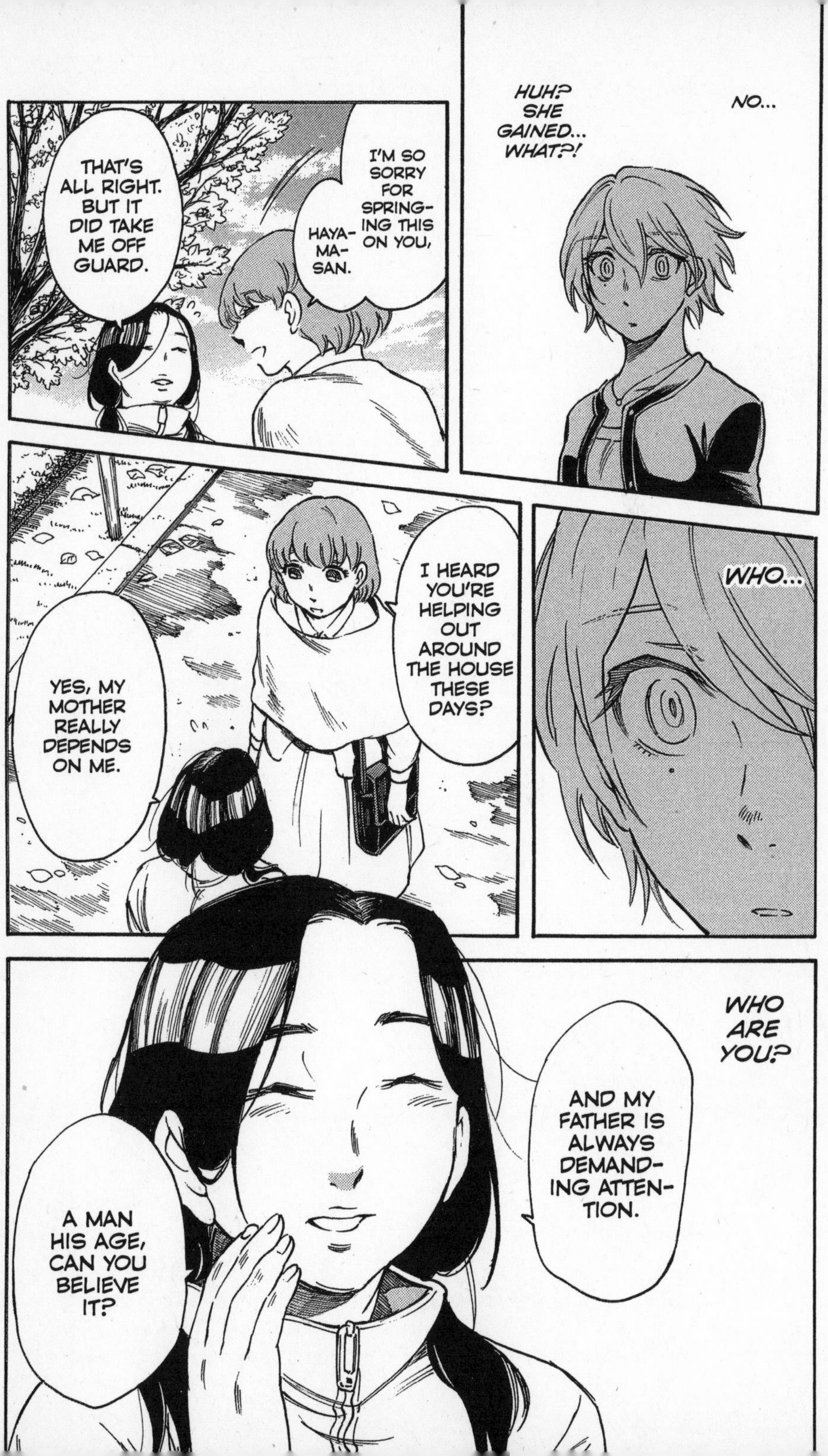
NO...
HUH? SHE GAINED... WHAT?!
I'M SO SORRY FOR SPRINGING THIS ON YOU, HAYAMA-SAN.
THAT'S ALL RIGHT. BUT IT DID TAKE ME OFF GUARD.
WHO...
I HEARD YOU'RE HELPING OUT AROUND THE HOUSE THESE DAYS?
YES, MY MOTHER REALLY DEPENDS ON ME.
WHO ARE YOU?
AND MY FATHER IS ALWAYS DEMANDING ATTENTION.
A MAN HIS AGE, CAN YOU BELIEVE IT?

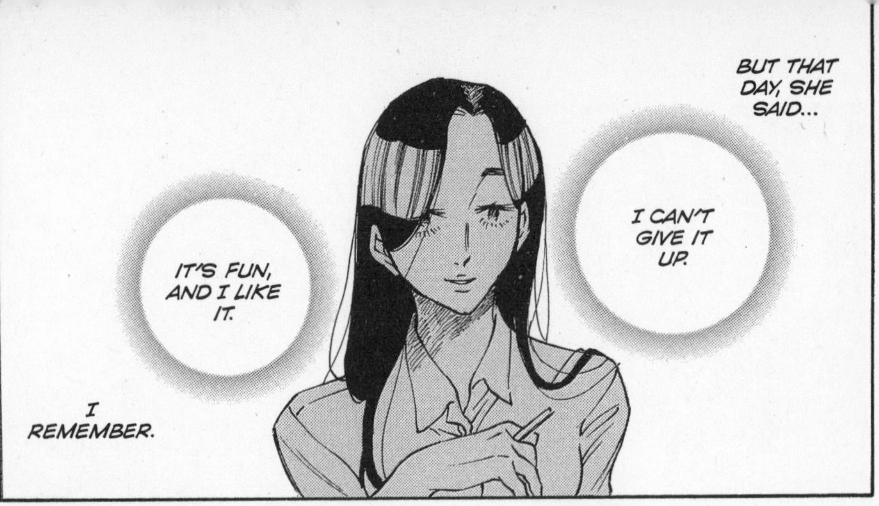
BUT THAT DAY, SHE SAID...
I CAN'T GIVE IT UP.
IT'S FUN, AND I LIKE IT.
I REMEMBER.

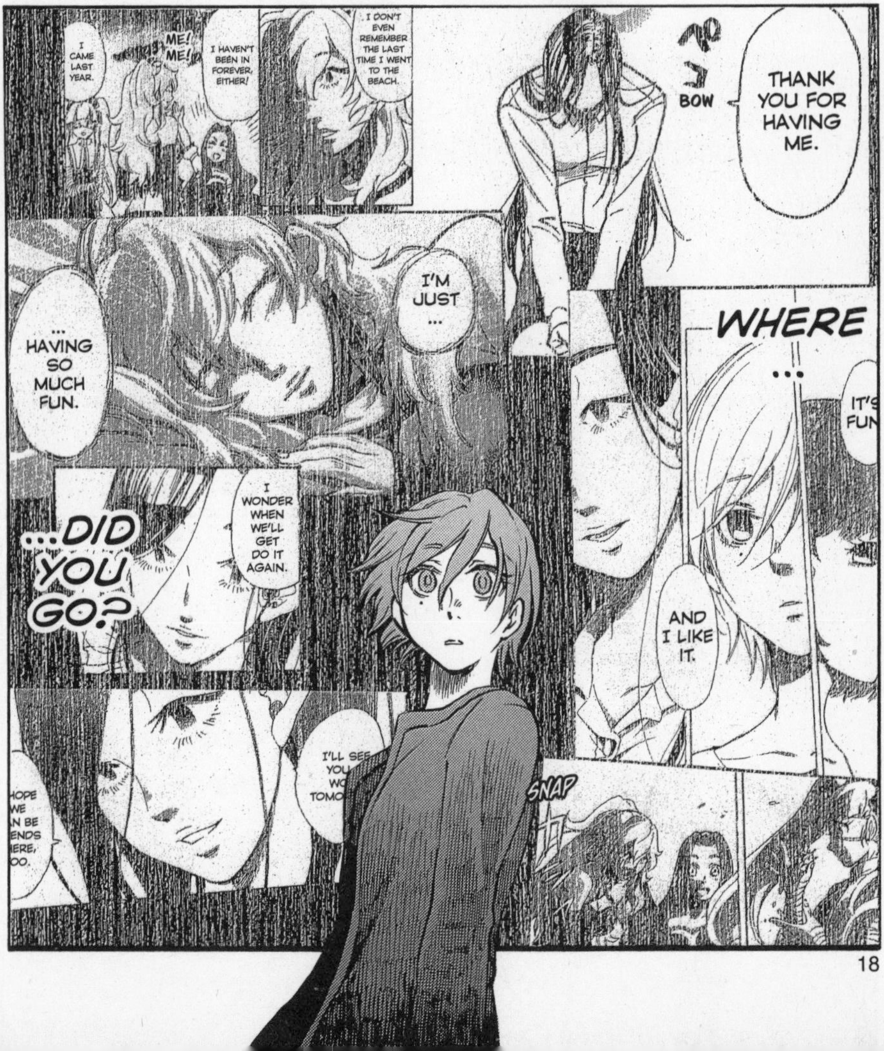
BOW
THANK YOU FOR HAVING ME.
I DON'T EVEN REMEMBER THE LAST TIME I WENT TO THE BEACH.
I HAVEN'T BEEN IN FOREVER, EITHER!
ME! ME!
I CAME LAST YEAR.
WHERE...
IT'S FUN
AND I LIKE IT.
I'M JUST...
...HAVING SO MUCH FUN.
...DID YOU GO?
I WONDER WHEN WE'LL GET DO IT AGAIN.
SNAP

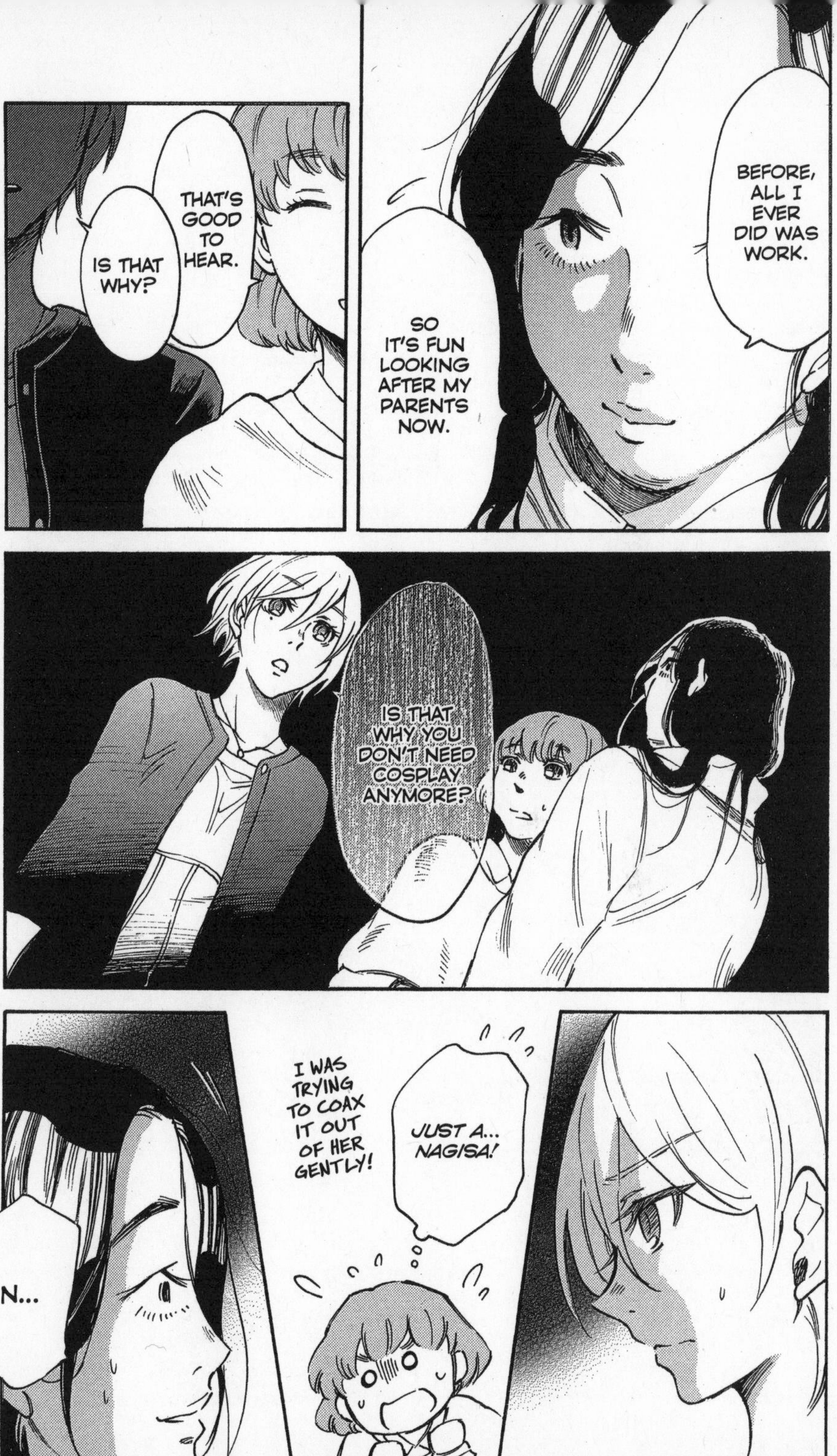
BEFORE, ALL I EVER DID WAS WORK.
SO IT'S FUN LOOKING AFTER MY PARENTS NOW.
THAT'S GOOD TO HEAR.
IS THAT WHY?
IS THAT WHY YOU DON'T NEED COSPLAY ANYMORE?
JUST A... NAGISA!
I WAS TRYING TO COAX IT OUT OF HER GENTLY!
N...

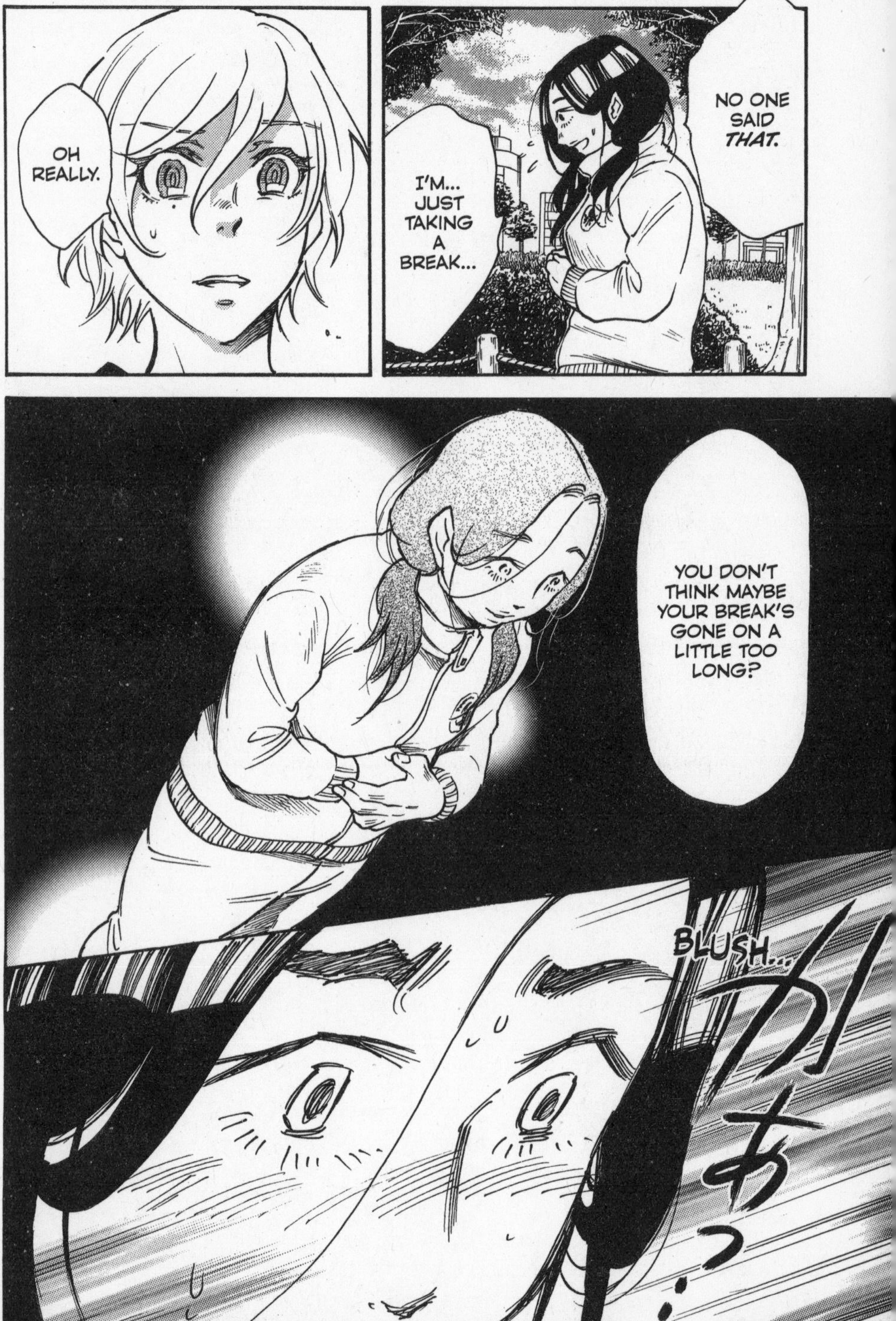
NO ONE SAID *THAT.*
I'M... JUST TAKING A BREAK...
OH REALLY.
YOU DON'T THINK MAYBE YOUR BREAK'S GONE ON A LITTLE TOO LONG?
BLUSH...

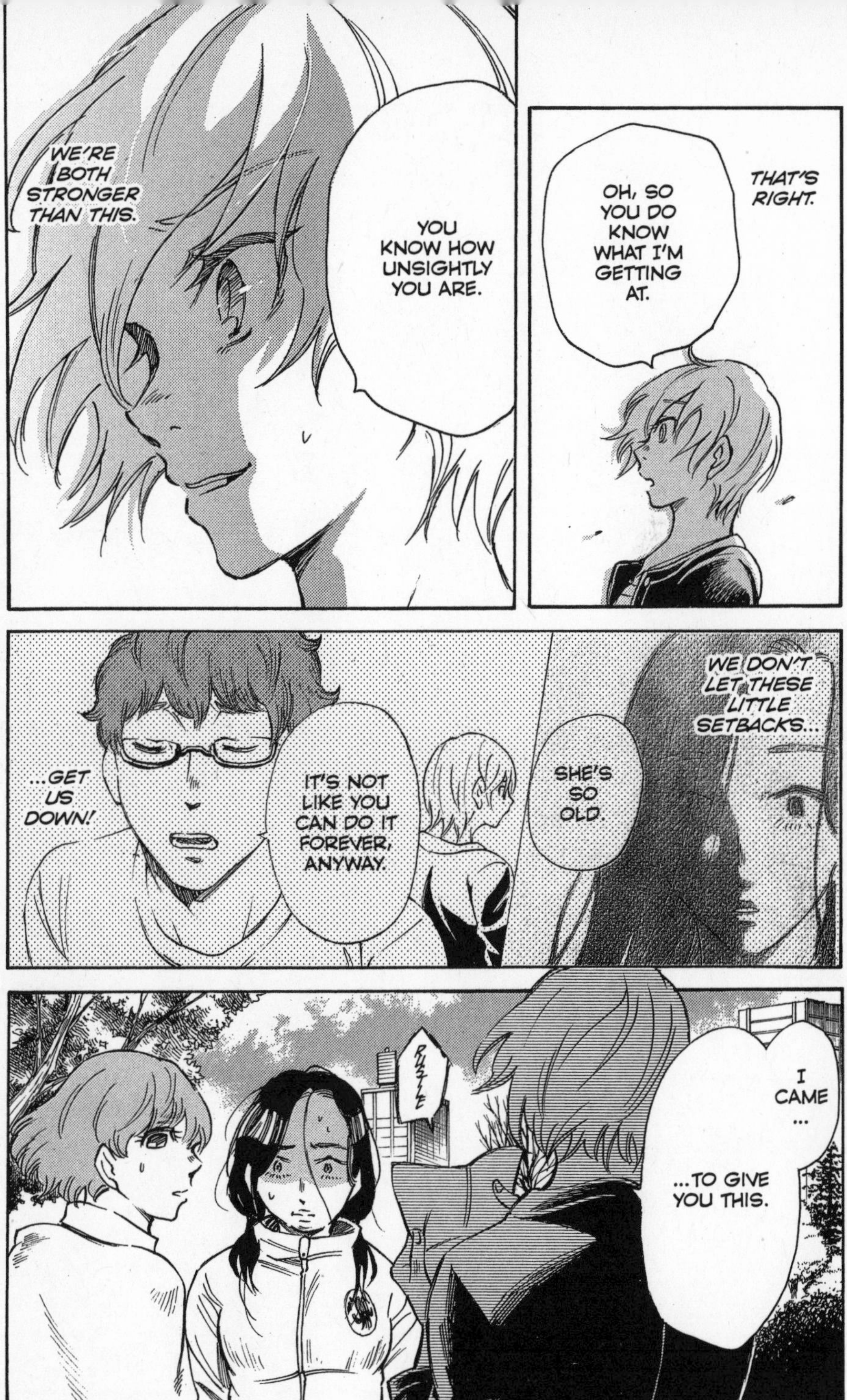
OH, SO YOU DO KNOW WHAT I'M GETTING AT.
THAT'S RIGHT.
YOU KNOW HOW UNSIGHTLY YOU ARE.
WE'RE BOTH STRONGER THAN THIS.
WE DON'T LET THESE LITTLE SETBACKS...
SHE'S SO OLD.
IT'S NOT LIKE YOU CAN DO IT FOREVER, ANYWAY.
...GET US DOWN!
I CAME ...
...TO GIVE YOU THIS.
RUSTLE

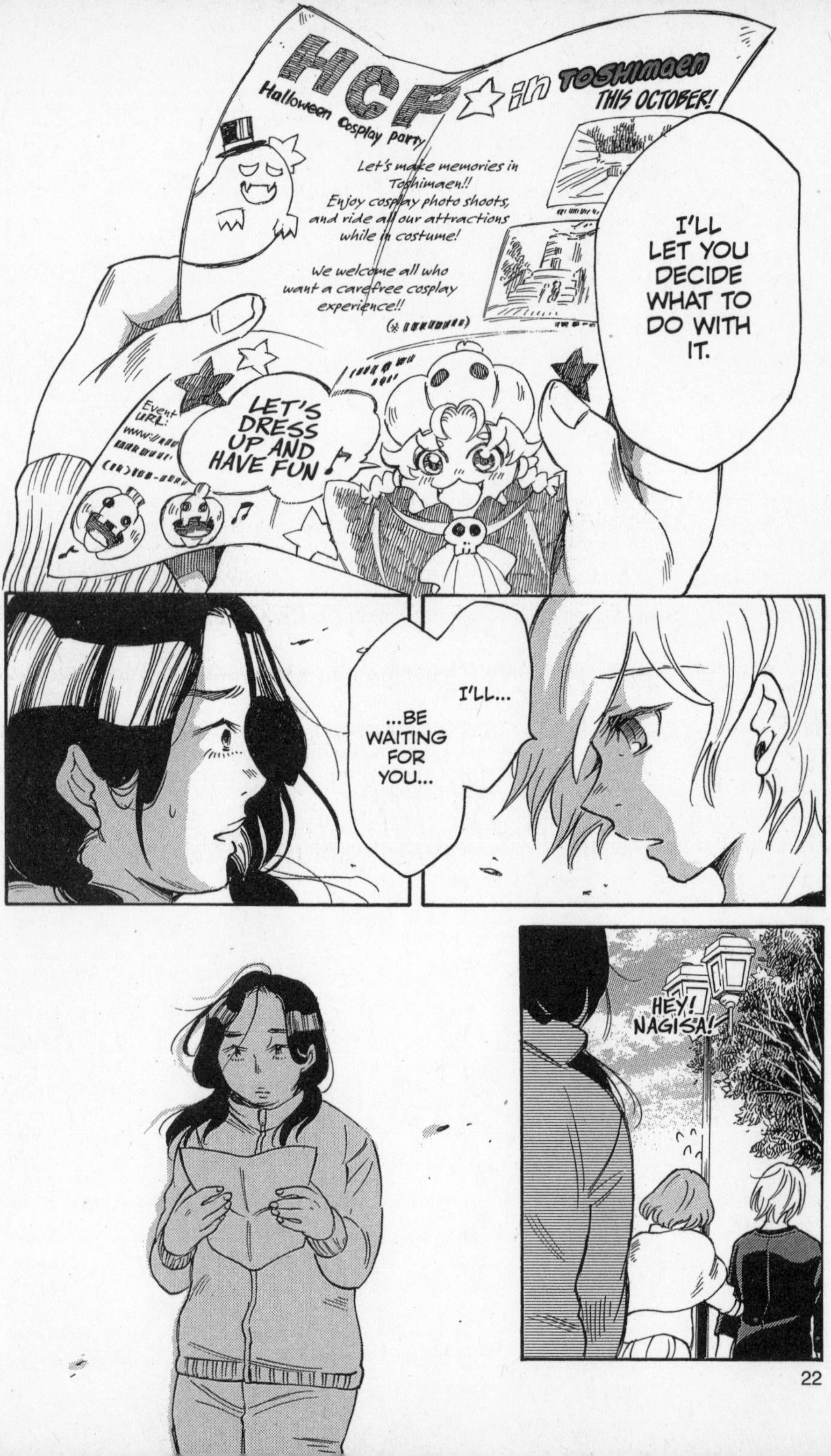
HCP in TOSHIMAEN
THIS OCTOBER!
Halloween Cosplay party
Let's make memories in Toshimaen!! Enjoy cosplay photo shoots, and ride all our attractions while in costume!
We welcome all who want a carefree cosplay experience!!
Event URL:
LET'S DRESS UP AND HAVE FUN
I'LL LET YOU DECIDE WHAT TO DO WITH IT.
I'LL...
...BE WAITING FOR YOU...
HEY! NAGISA!

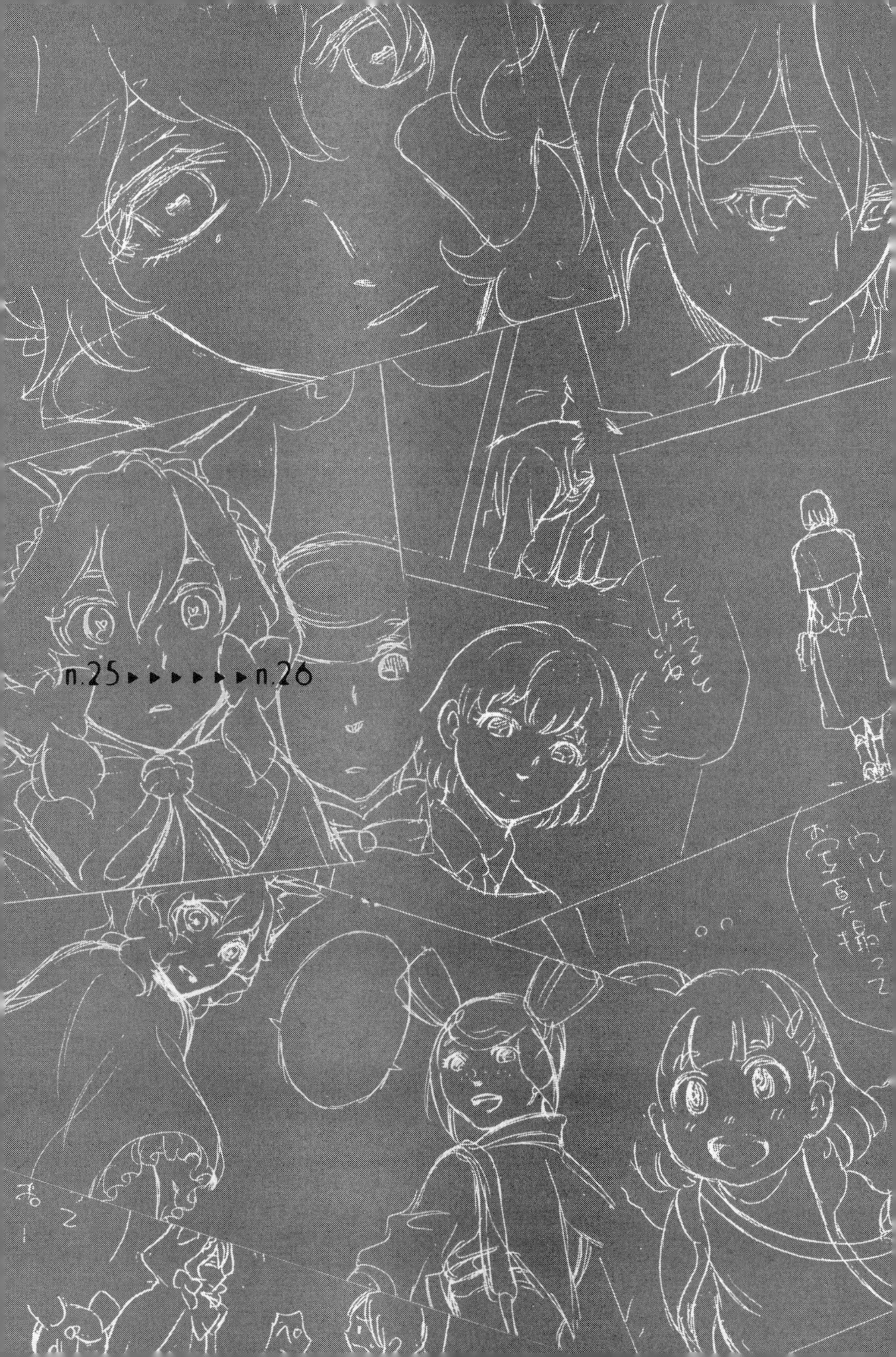
n.25▸▸▸▸▸▸▸n.26

HELLO, SAKUMA HERE.

IT SEEMS SO FAST, BUT HERE'S VOLUME FOUR. I ALWAYS DREAMED OF A DAY WHEN I COULD DRAW FOUR VOLUMES' WORTH OF A MANGA, BUT I NEVER ACTUALLY EXPECTED IT TO HAPPEN.

I REALLY AM LUCKY.

I WANT TO KEEP DRAWING, PAGE BY PAGE, AS IF EACH ONE IS MY LAST CHANCE.

THIS VOLUME'S BONUS PAGES FEATURE COSPLAY CARDS!!

LATELY, I'LL OCCASIONALLY SPOT SOMEBODY IN URURU COSPLAY. IT MAKES ME VERY HAPPY.

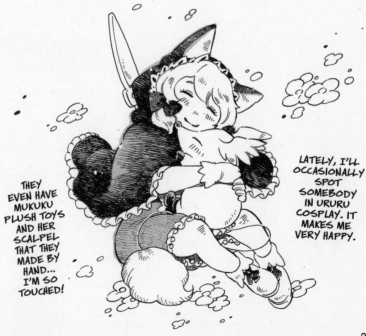

THEY EVEN HAVE MUKUKU PLUSH TOYS AND HER SCALPEL THAT THEY MADE BY HAND... I'M SO TOUCHED!

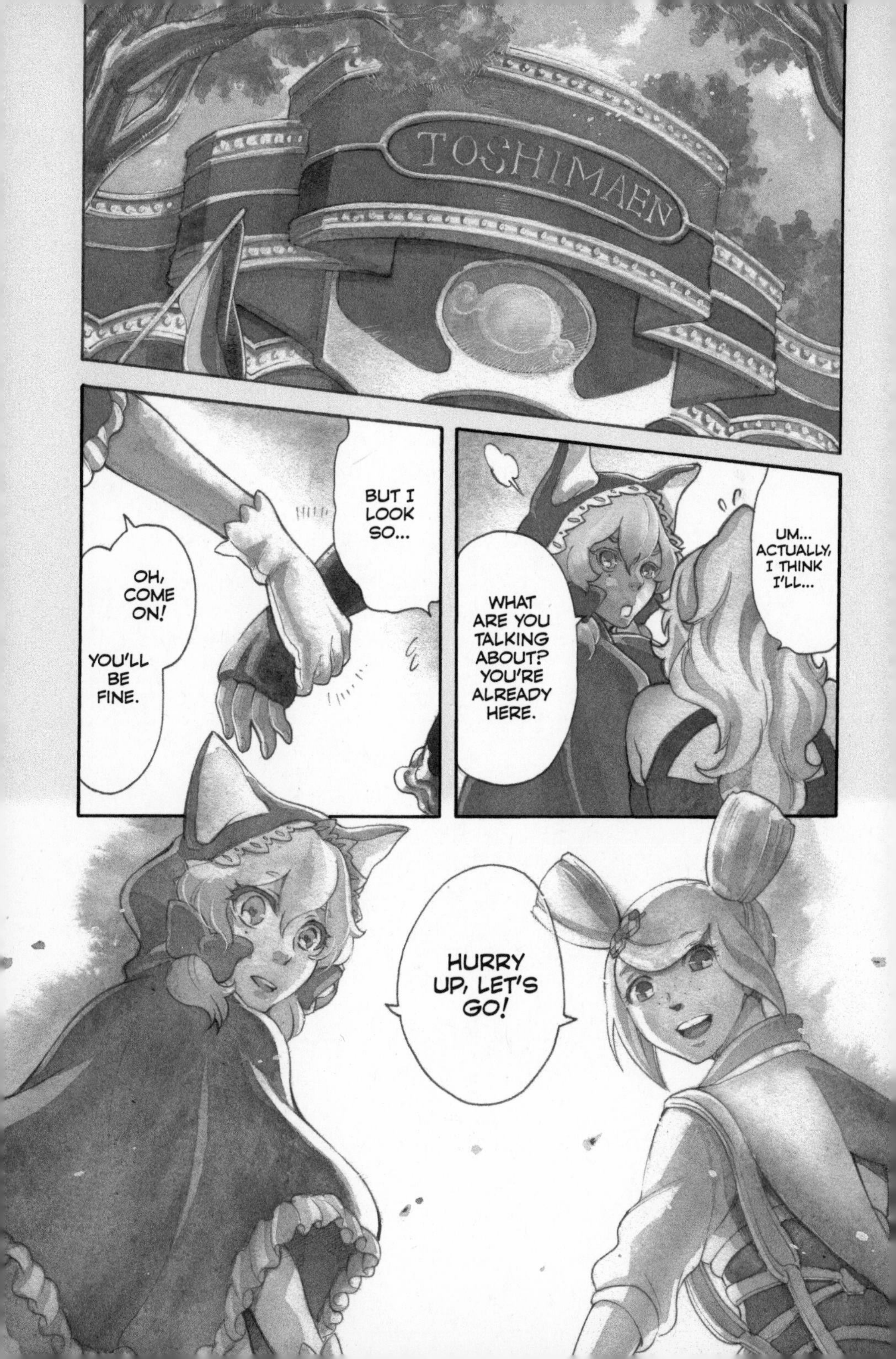
TOSHIMAEN
UM... ACTUALLY, I THINK I'LL...
WHAT ARE YOU TALKING ABOUT? YOU'RE ALREADY HERE.
BUT I LOOK SO...
OH, COME ON!
YOU'LL BE FINE.
HURRY UP, LET'S GO!

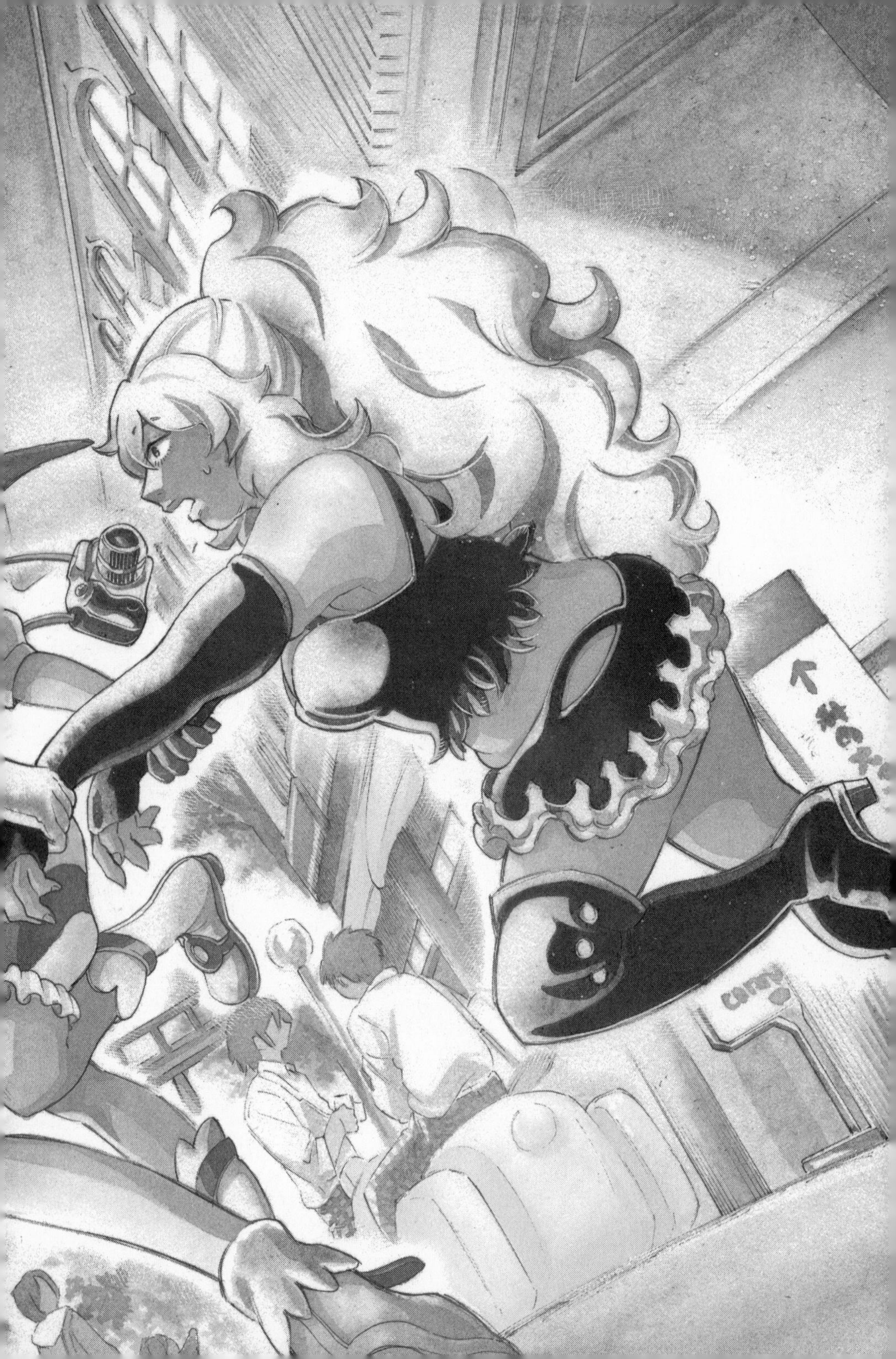

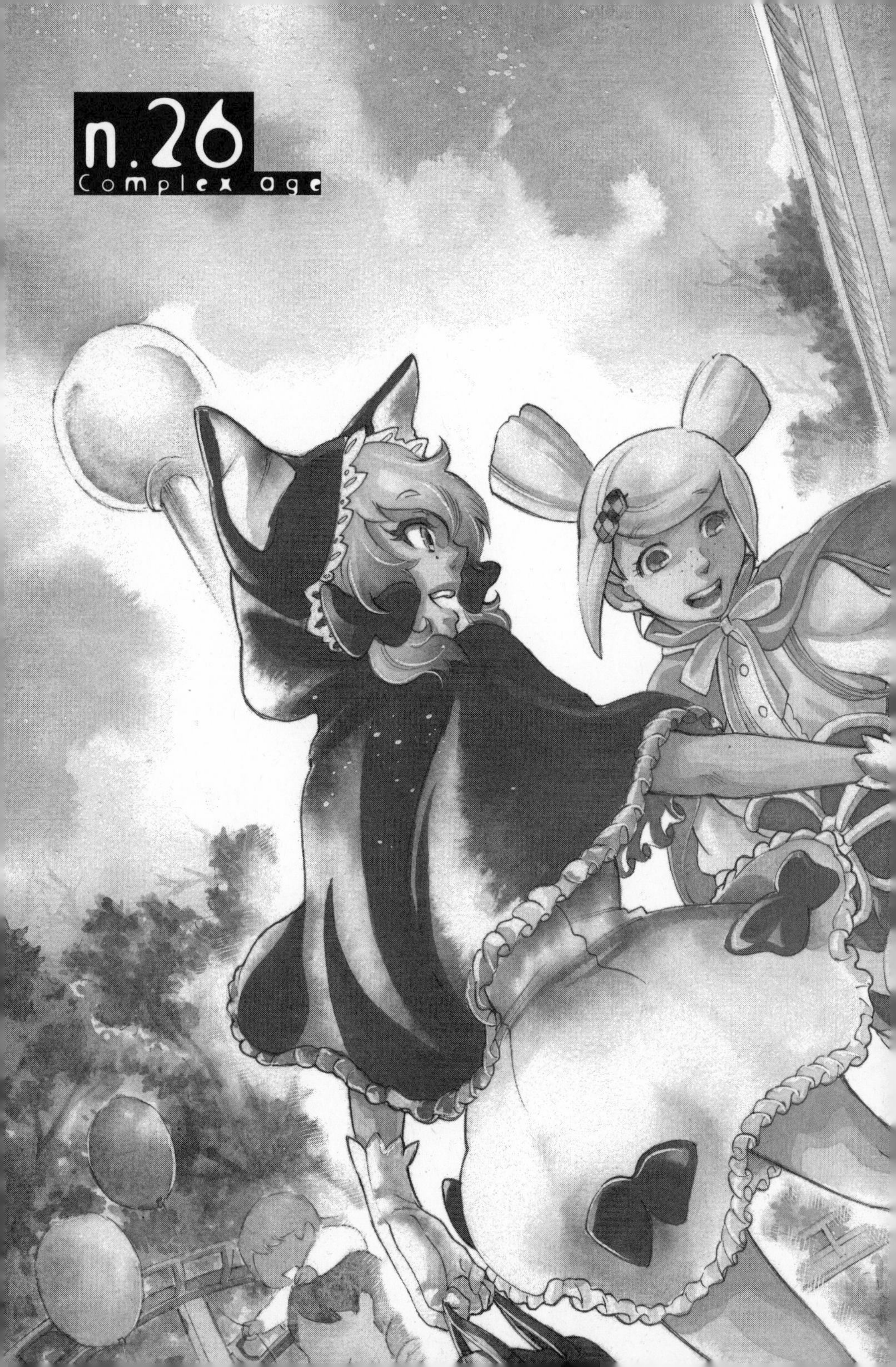
n.26
Complex age

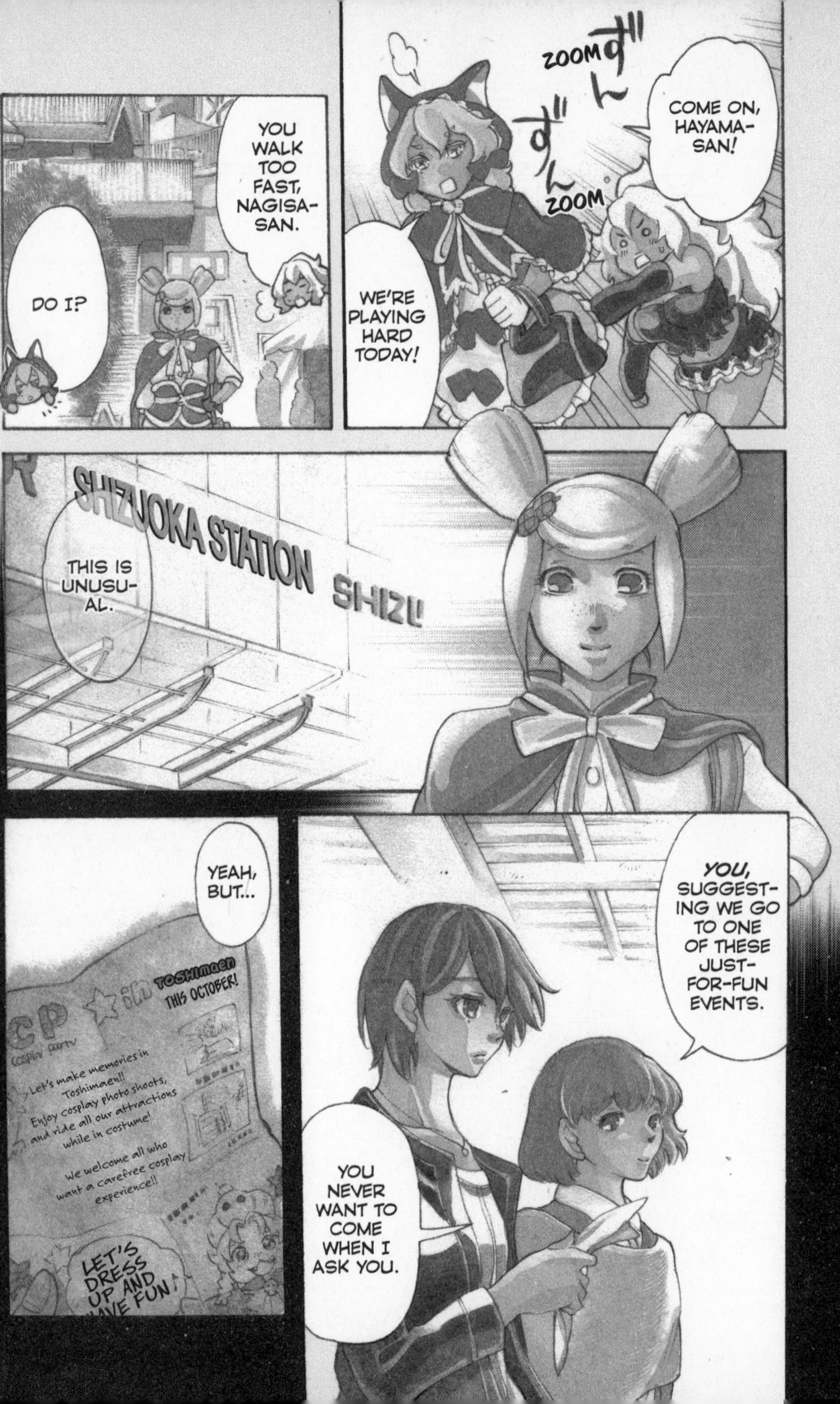
ZOOM ずん
COME ON, HAYAMA-SAN!
ずん ZOOM
WE'RE PLAYING HARD TODAY!
YOU WALK TOO FAST, NAGISA-SAN.
DO I?
SHIZUOKA STATION
SHIZU
THIS IS UNUSUAL.
YOU, SUGGESTING WE GO TO ONE OF THESE JUST-FOR-FUN EVENTS.
YOU NEVER WANT TO COME WHEN I ASK YOU.
YEAH, BUT...
CP ☆ in TOSHIMAEN THIS OCTOBER!
Cosplay party
Let's make memories in Toshimaen!! Enjoy cosplay photo shoots, and ride all our attractions while in costume!
We welcome all who want a carefree cosplay experience!!
LET'S DRESS UP AND HAVE FUN

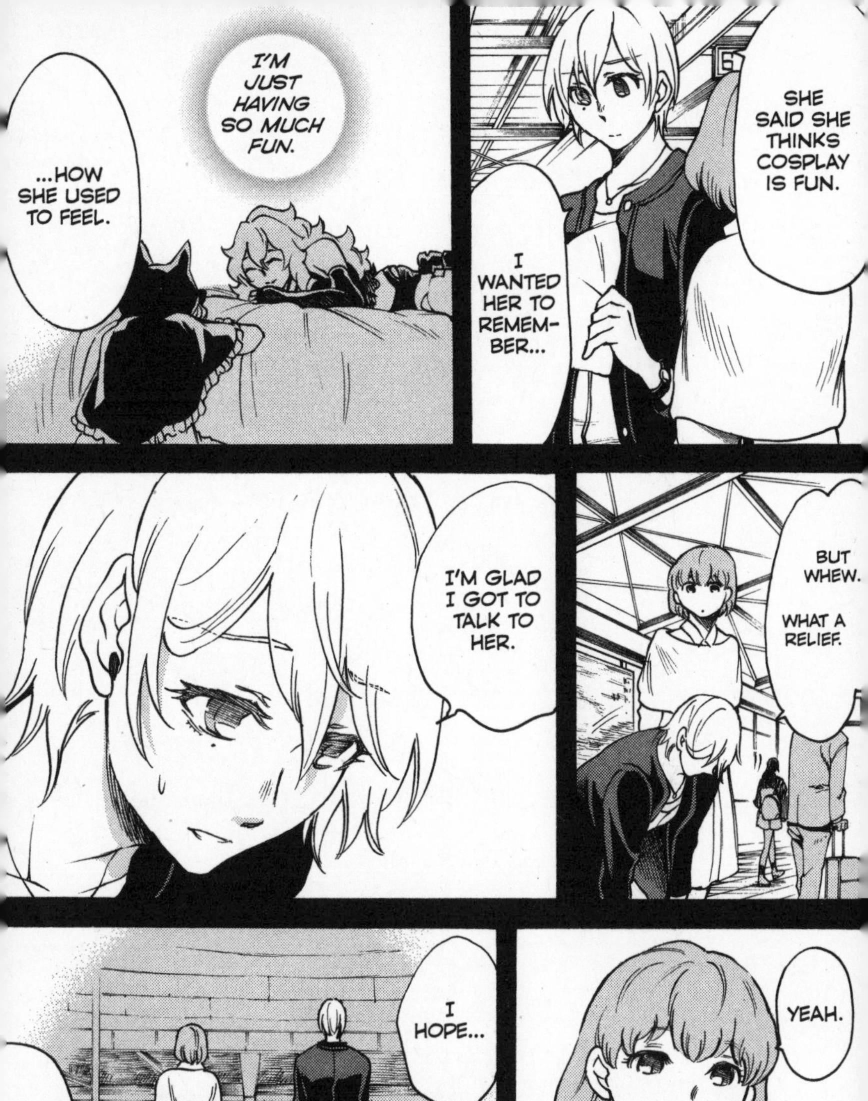
SHE SAID SHE THINKS COSPLAY IS FUN.
I WANTED HER TO REMEMBER...
I'M JUST HAVING SO MUCH FUN.
...HOW SHE USED TO FEEL.
BUT WHEW.
WHAT A RELIEF.
I'M GLAD I GOT TO TALK TO HER.
YEAH.
I HOPE...
SHE IDES OME.

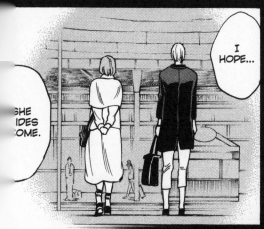

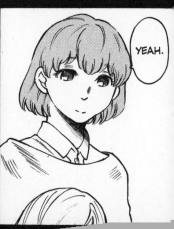

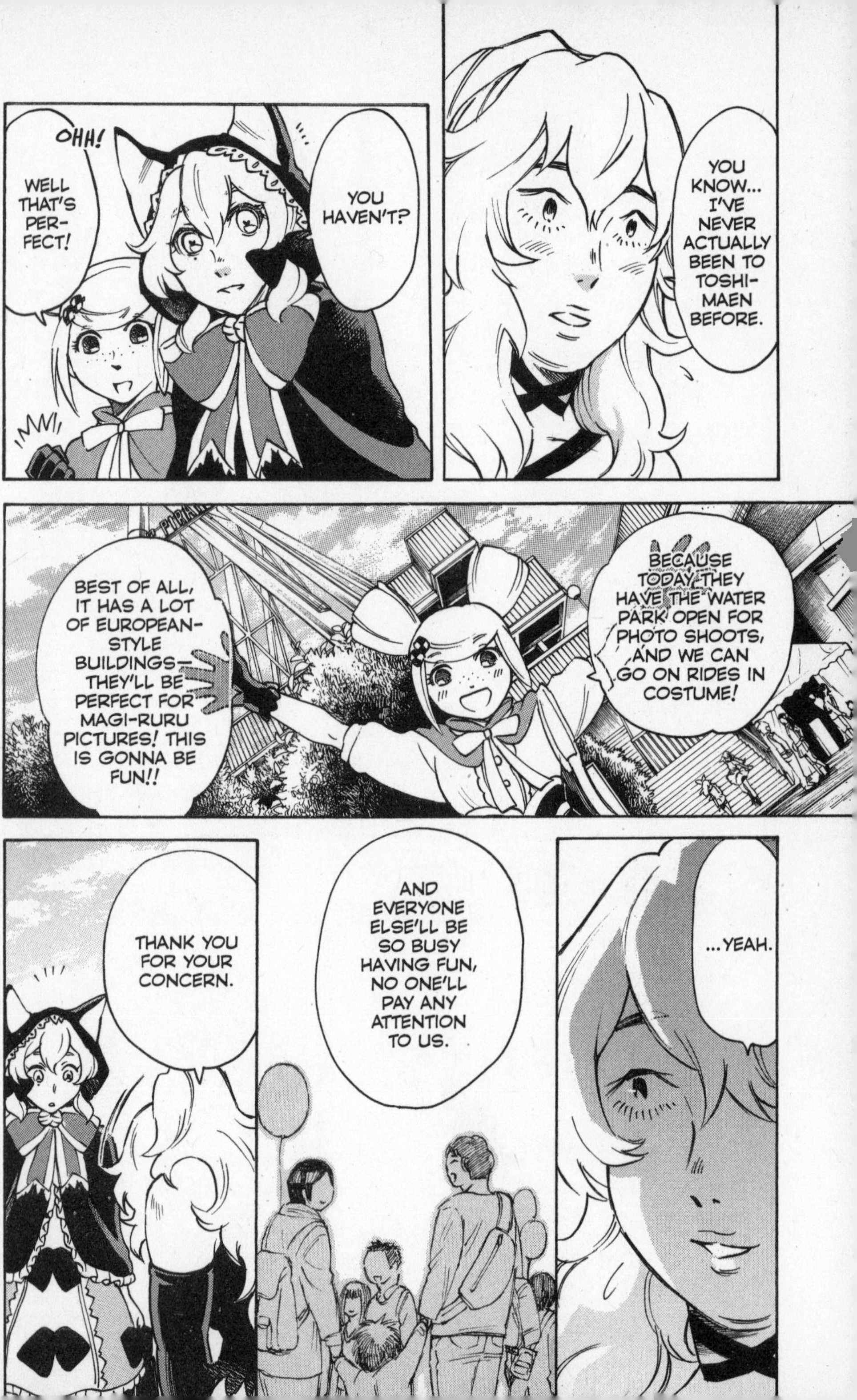
YOU KNOW... I'VE NEVER ACTUALLY BEEN TO TOSHIMAEN BEFORE.
YOU HAVEN'T?
OHH!
WELL THAT'S PERFECT!
BECAUSE TODAY THEY HAVE THE WATER PARK OPEN FOR PHOTO SHOOTS, AND WE CAN GO ON RIDES IN COSTUME!
BEST OF ALL, IT HAS A LOT OF EUROPEAN-STYLE BUILDINGS—THEY'LL BE PERFECT FOR MAGI-RURU PICTURES! THIS IS GONNA BE FUN!!
...YEAH.
AND EVERYONE ELSE'LL BE SO BUSY HAVING FUN, NO ONE'LL PAY ANY ATTENTION TO US.
THANK YOU FOR YOUR CONCERN.

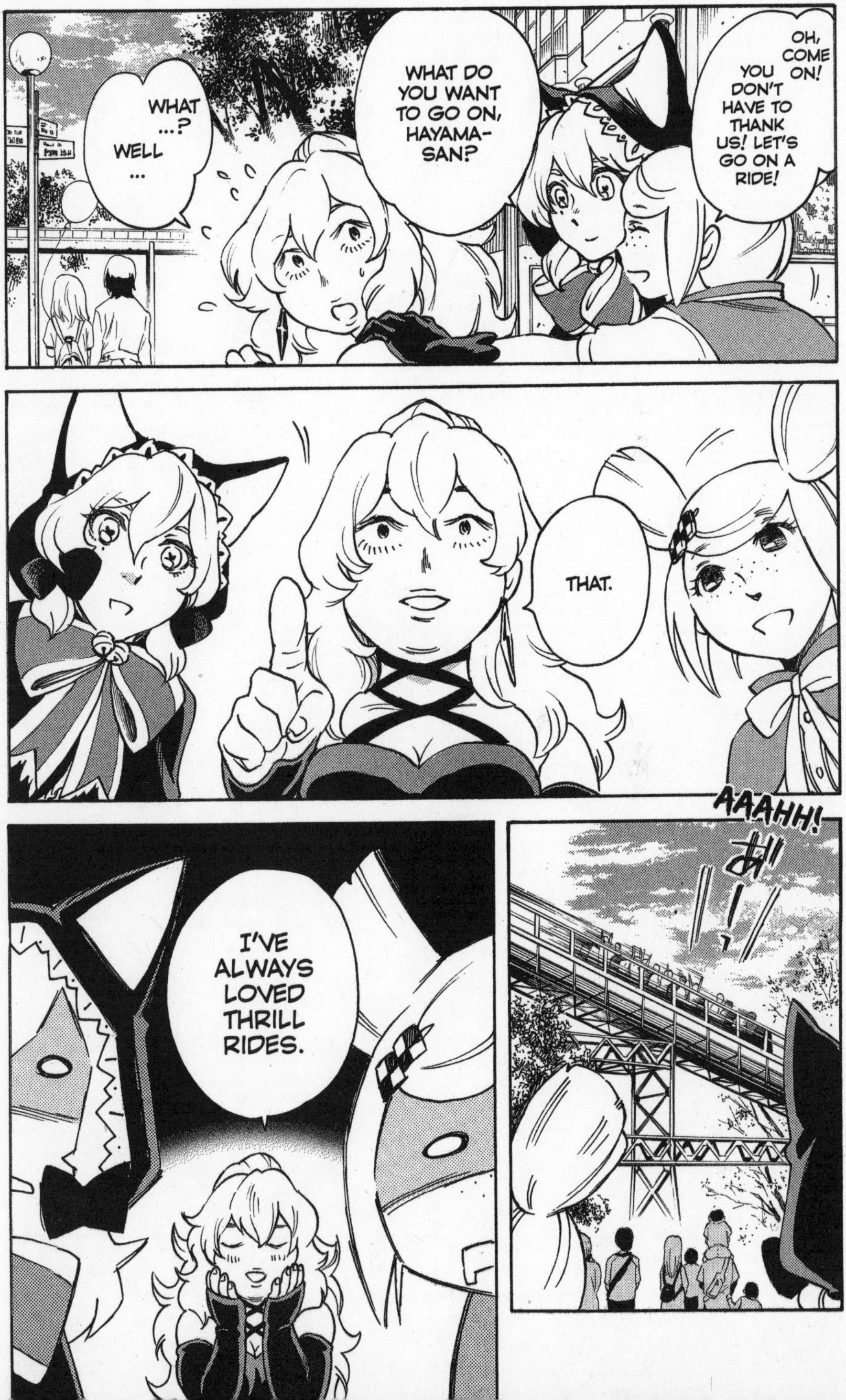
OH, COME ON! YOU DON'T HAVE TO THANK US! LET'S GO ON A RIDE!
WHAT DO YOU WANT TO GO ON, HAYAMA-SAN?
WHAT ...? WELL ...
THAT.
AAAHH!
I'VE ALWAYS LOVED THRILL RIDES.

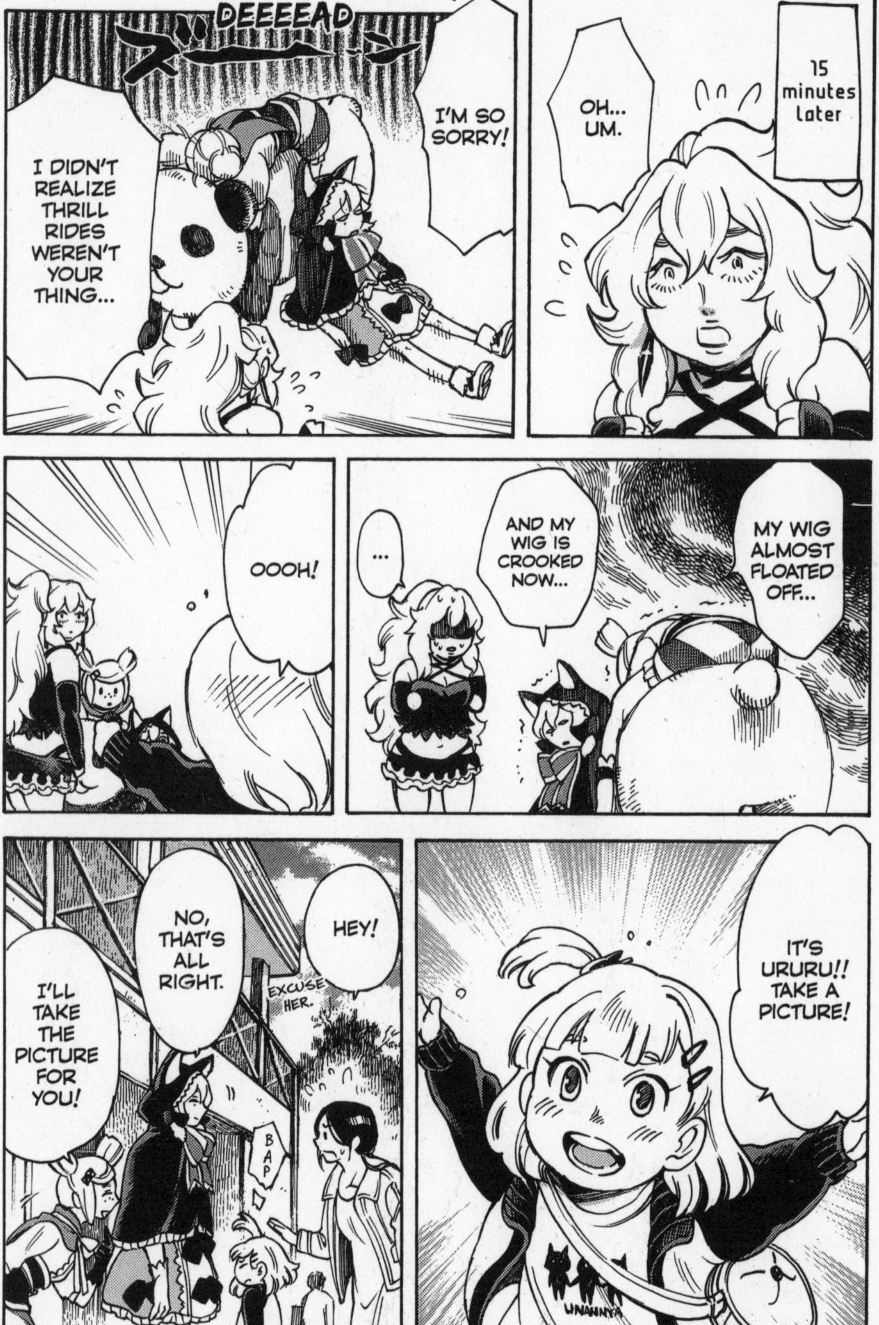
15 minutes later
OH... UM.
I'M SO SORRY!
DEEEEAD
I DIDN'T REALIZE THRILL RIDES WEREN'T YOUR THING...
MY WIG ALMOST FLOATED OFF...
AND MY WIG IS CROOKED NOW...
...
OOOH!
IT'S URURU!! TAKE A PICTURE!
UNANNYA
HEY!
NO, THAT'S ALL RIGHT.
EXCUSE HER.
BAP
I'LL TAKE THE PICTURE FOR YOU!

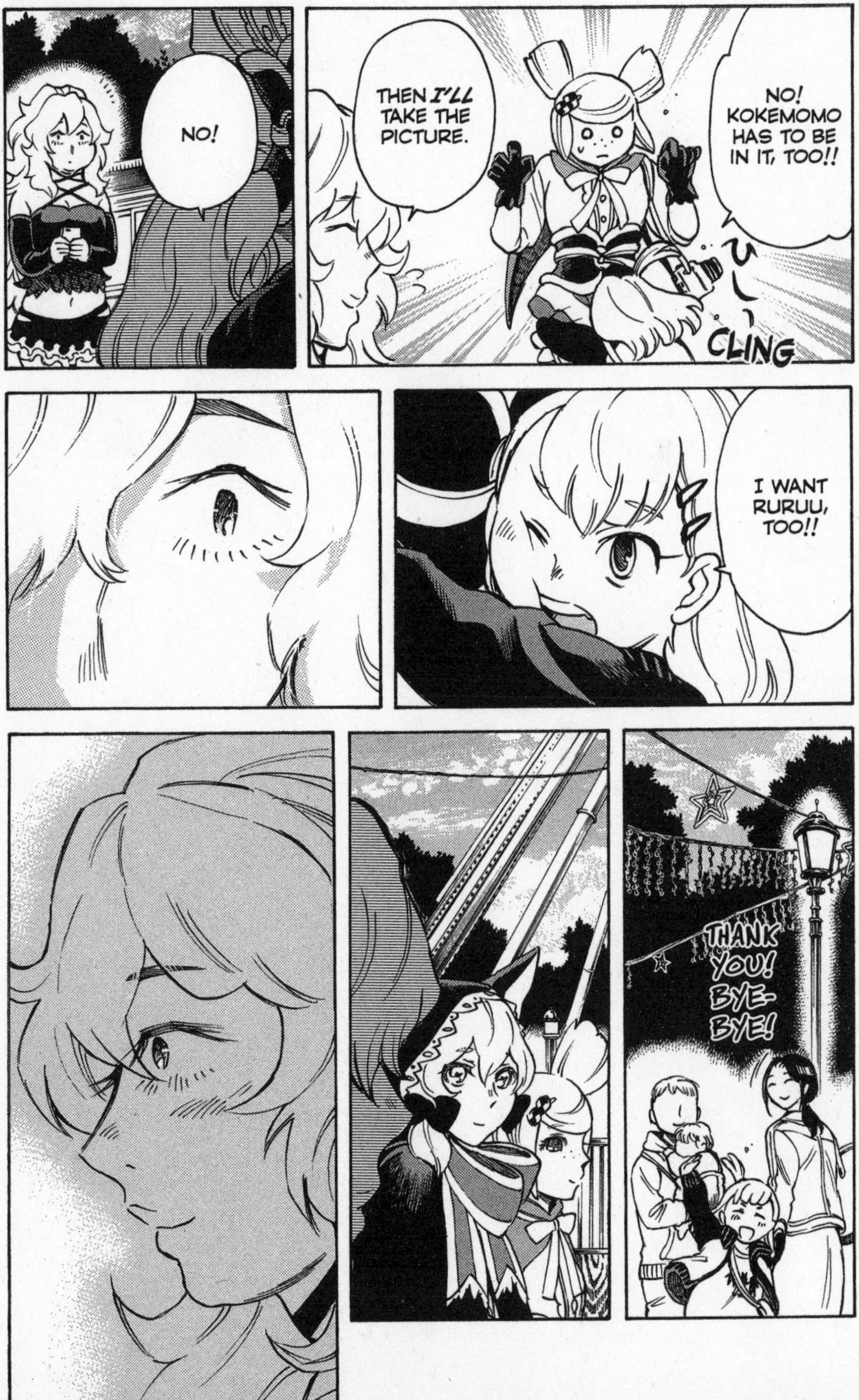
NO! KOKEMOMO HAS TO BE IN IT, TOO!!
THEN *I'LL* TAKE THE PICTURE.
CLING
NO!
I WANT RURUU, TOO!!
THANK YOU! BYE-BYE!

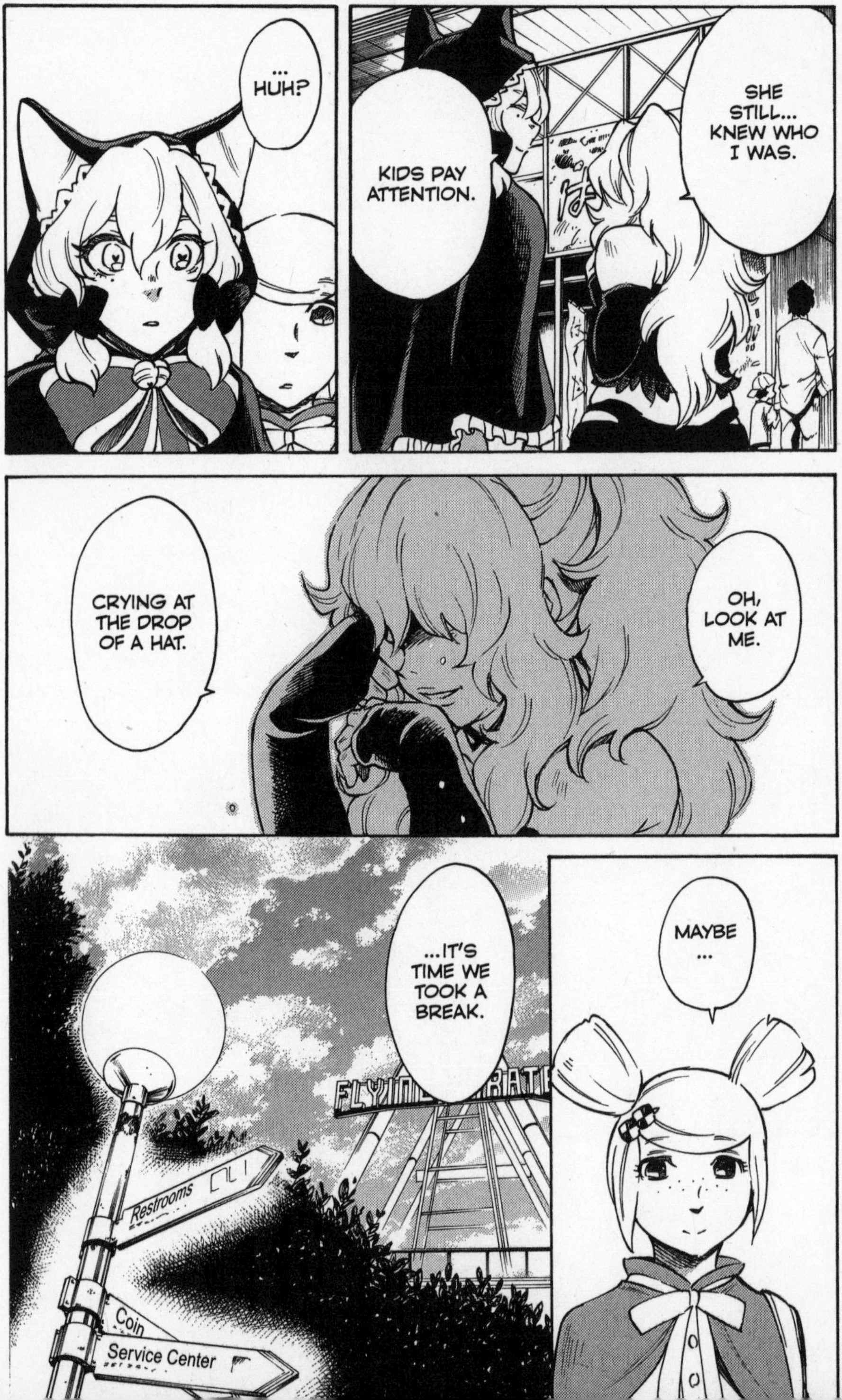
SHE STILL... KNEW WHO I WAS.
KIDS PAY ATTENTION.
... HUH?
OH, LOOK AT ME.
CRYING AT THE DROP OF A HAT.
MAYBE ...
...IT'S TIME WE TOOK A BREAK.
Restrooms
Coin
Service Center

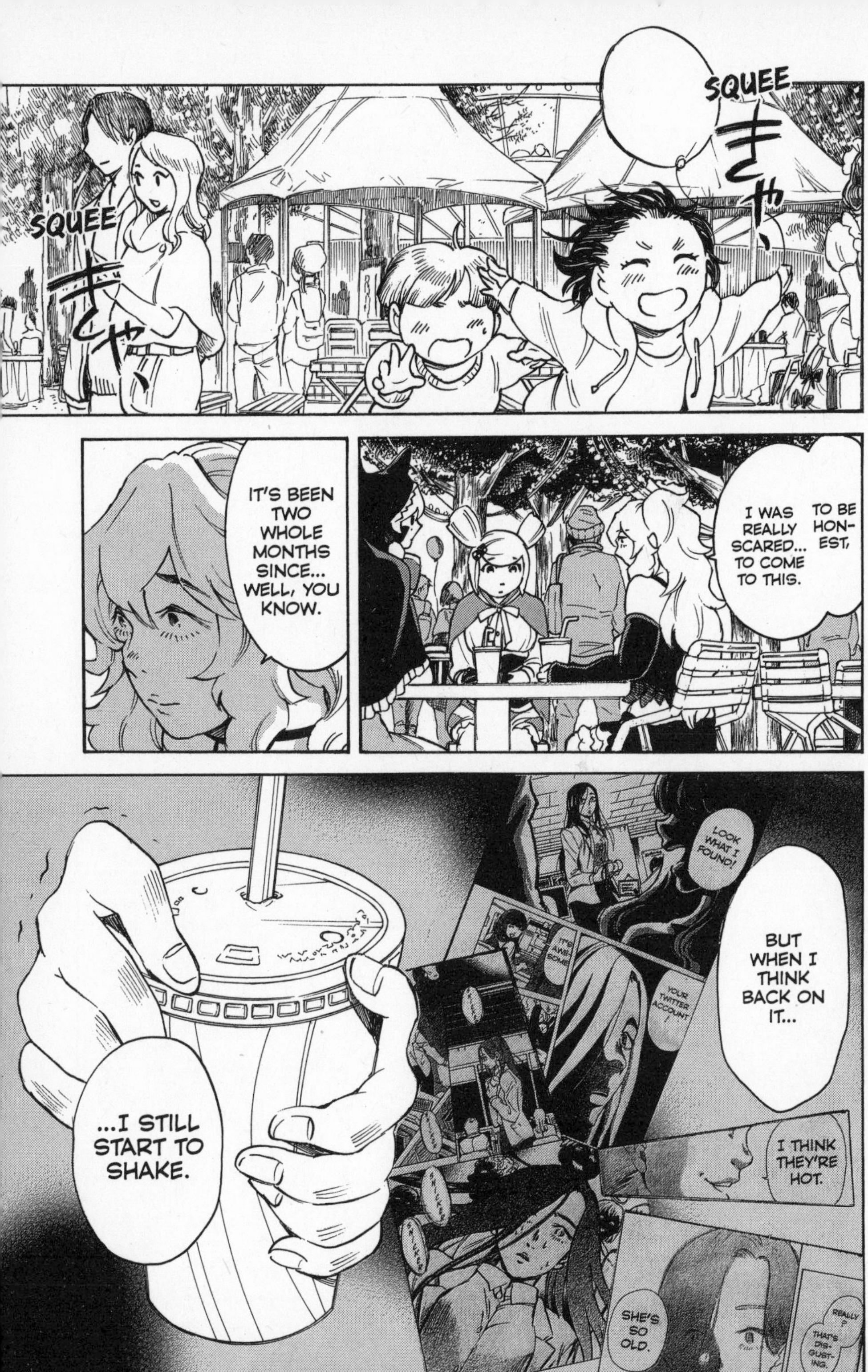
SQUEE
きゃ、
SQUEE
きゃ、
TO BE HONEST, I WAS REALLY SCARED... TO COME TO THIS.
IT'S BEEN TWO WHOLE MONTHS SINCE... WELL, YOU KNOW.
LOOK WHAT I FOUND!
BUT WHEN I THINK BACK ON IT...
IT'S AWESOME!
YOUR TWITTER ACCOUNT!
I THINK THEY'RE HOT.
REALLY? THAT'S DISGUSTING.
SHE'S SO OLD.
...I STILL START TO SHAKE.

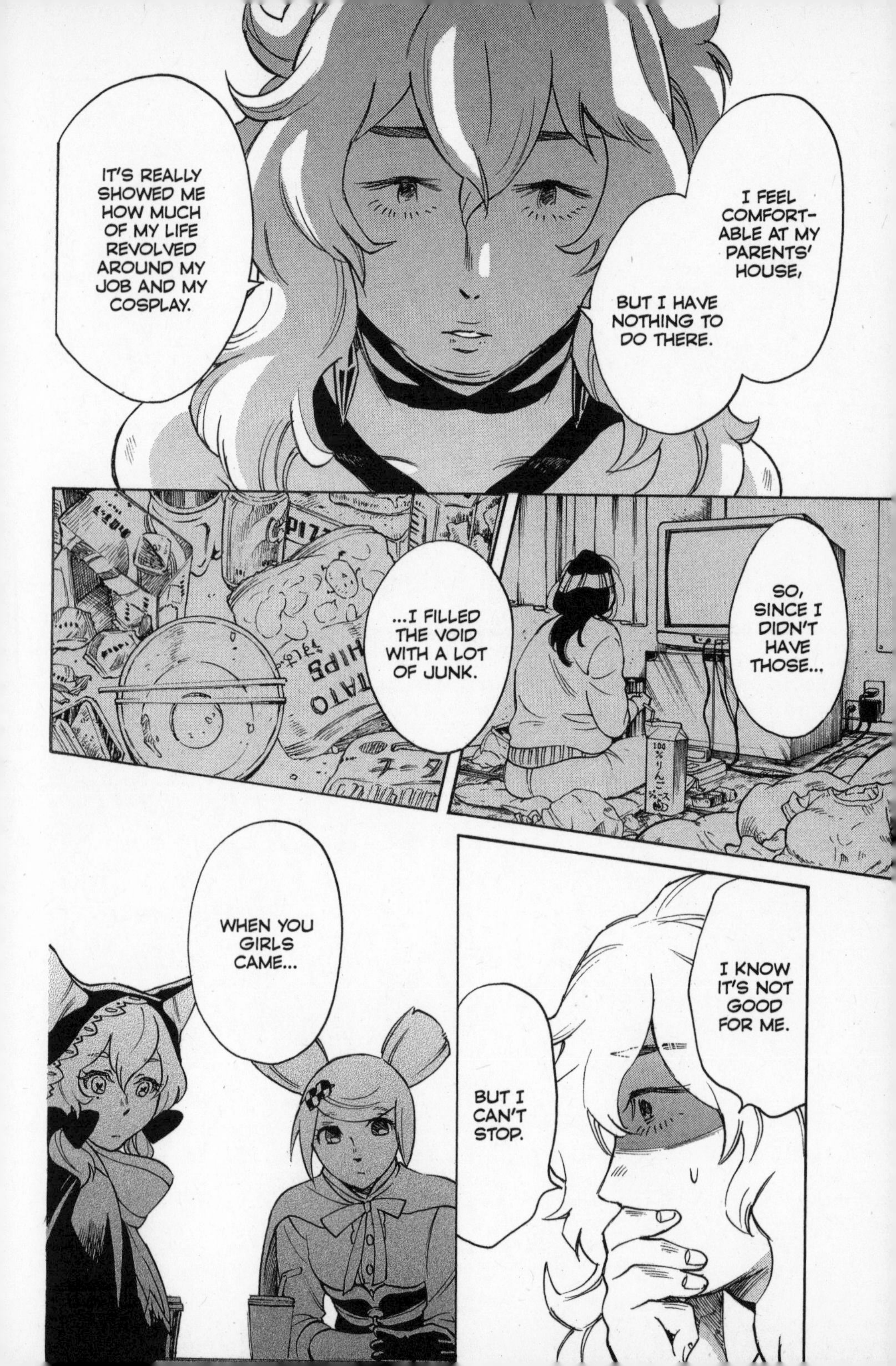
I FEEL COMFORTABLE AT MY PARENTS' HOUSE,
BUT I HAVE NOTHING TO DO THERE.
IT'S REALLY SHOWED ME HOW MUCH OF MY LIFE REVOLVED AROUND MY JOB AND MY COSPLAY.
SO, SINCE I DIDN'T HAVE THOSE...
...I FILLED THE VOID WITH A LOT OF JUNK.
I KNOW IT'S NOT GOOD FOR ME.
BUT I CAN'T STOP.
WHEN YOU GIRLS CAME...

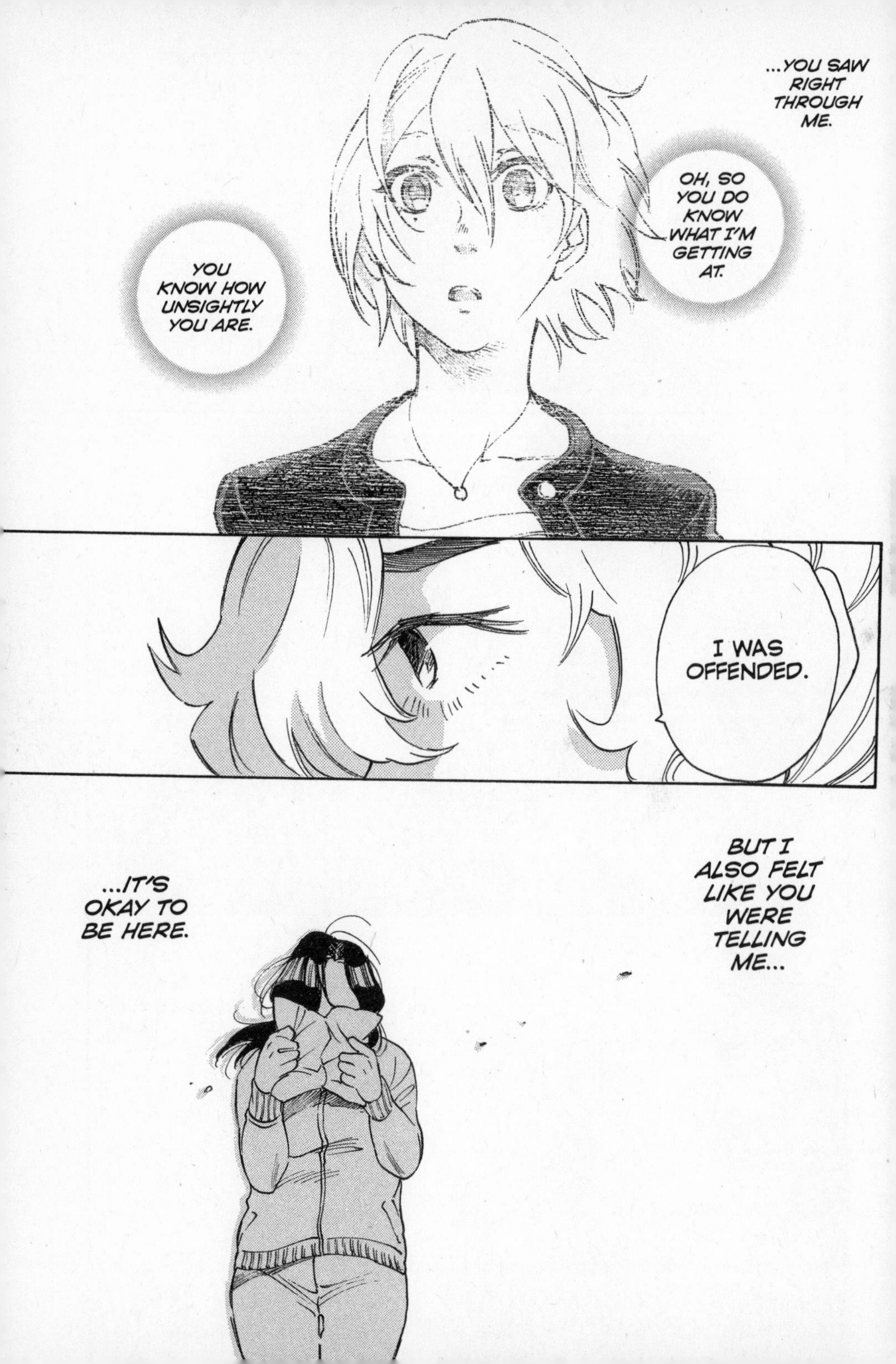
...YOU SAW RIGHT THROUGH ME.
OH, SO YOU DO KNOW WHAT I'M GETTING AT.
YOU KNOW HOW UNSIGHTLY YOU ARE.
I WAS OFFENDED.
BUT I ALSO FELT LIKE YOU WERE TELLING ME...
...IT'S OKAY TO BE HERE.

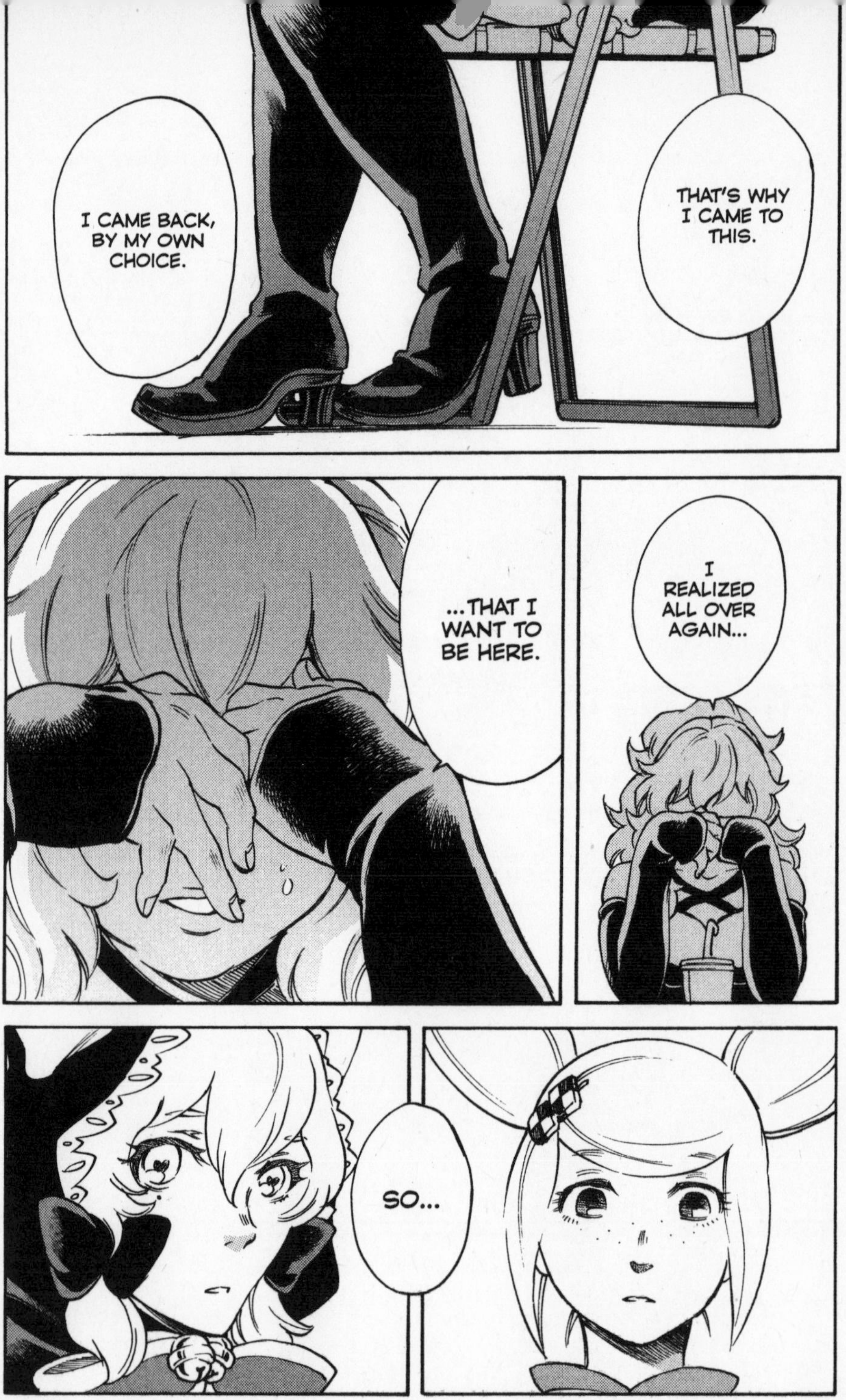
THAT'S WHY I CAME TO THIS.
I CAME BACK, BY MY OWN CHOICE.
I REALIZED ALL OVER AGAIN...
...THAT I WANT TO BE HERE.
SO...

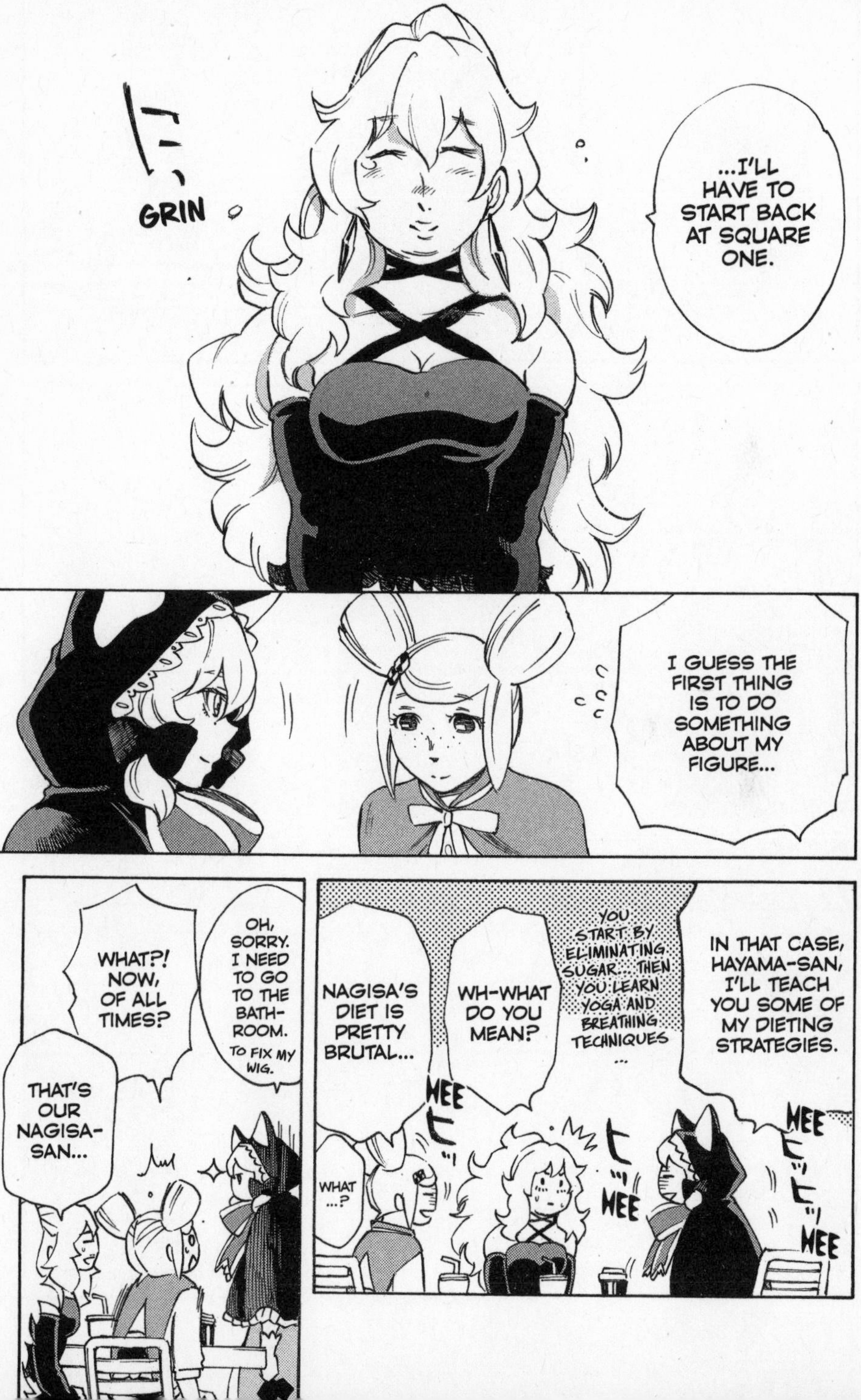
...I'LL HAVE TO START BACK AT SQUARE ONE.
GRIN
I GUESS THE FIRST THING IS TO DO SOMETHING ABOUT MY FIGURE...
IN THAT CASE, HAYAMA-SAN, I'LL TEACH YOU SOME OF MY DIETING STRATEGIES.
YOU START BY ELIMINATING SUGAR... THEN YOU LEARN YOGA AND BREATHING TECHNIQUES...
WH-WHAT DO YOU MEAN?
NAGISA'S DIET IS PRETTY BRUTAL...
HEE
HEE
HEE
HEE
WHAT...?
OH, SORRY. I NEED TO GO TO THE BATH-ROOM.
TO FIX MY WIG.
WHAT?! NOW, OF ALL TIMES?
THAT'S OUR NAGISA-SAN...

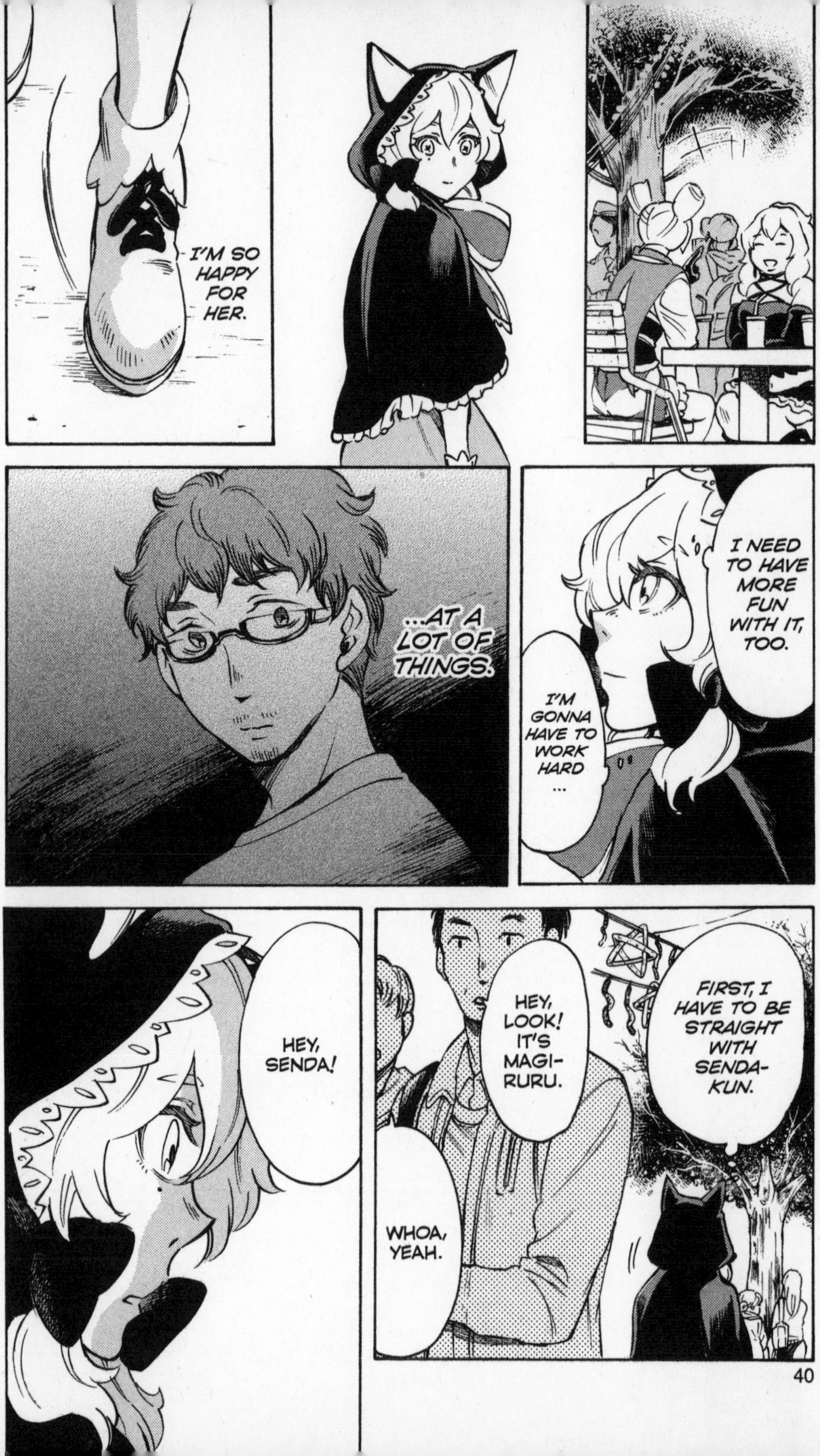
I'M SO HAPPY FOR HER.
I NEED TO HAVE MORE FUN WITH IT, TOO.
I'M GONNA HAVE TO WORK HARD ...
...AT A LOT OF THINGS.
FIRST, I HAVE TO BE STRAIGHT WITH SENDA-KUN.
HEY, LOOK! IT'S MAGI-RURU.
WHOA, YEAH.
HEY, SENDA!

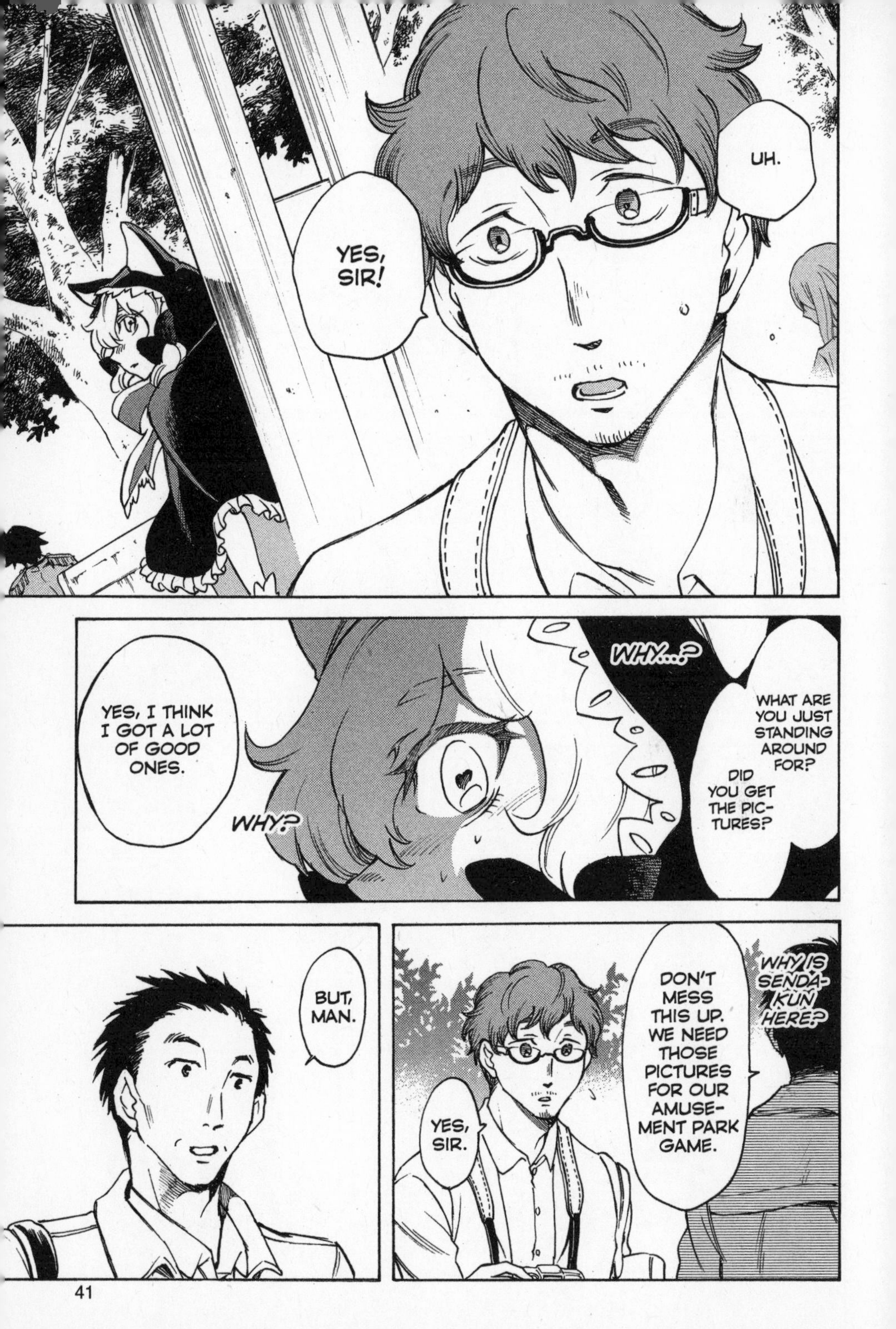
UH.
YES, SIR!
WHAT ARE YOU JUST STANDING AROUND FOR?
DID YOU GET THE PIC-TURES?
WHY...?
YES, I THINK I GOT A LOT OF GOOD ONES.
WHY?
WHY IS SENDA-KUN HERE?
DON'T MESS THIS UP. WE NEED THOSE PICTURES FOR OUR AMUSE-MENT PARK GAME.
YES, SIR.
BUT, MAN.

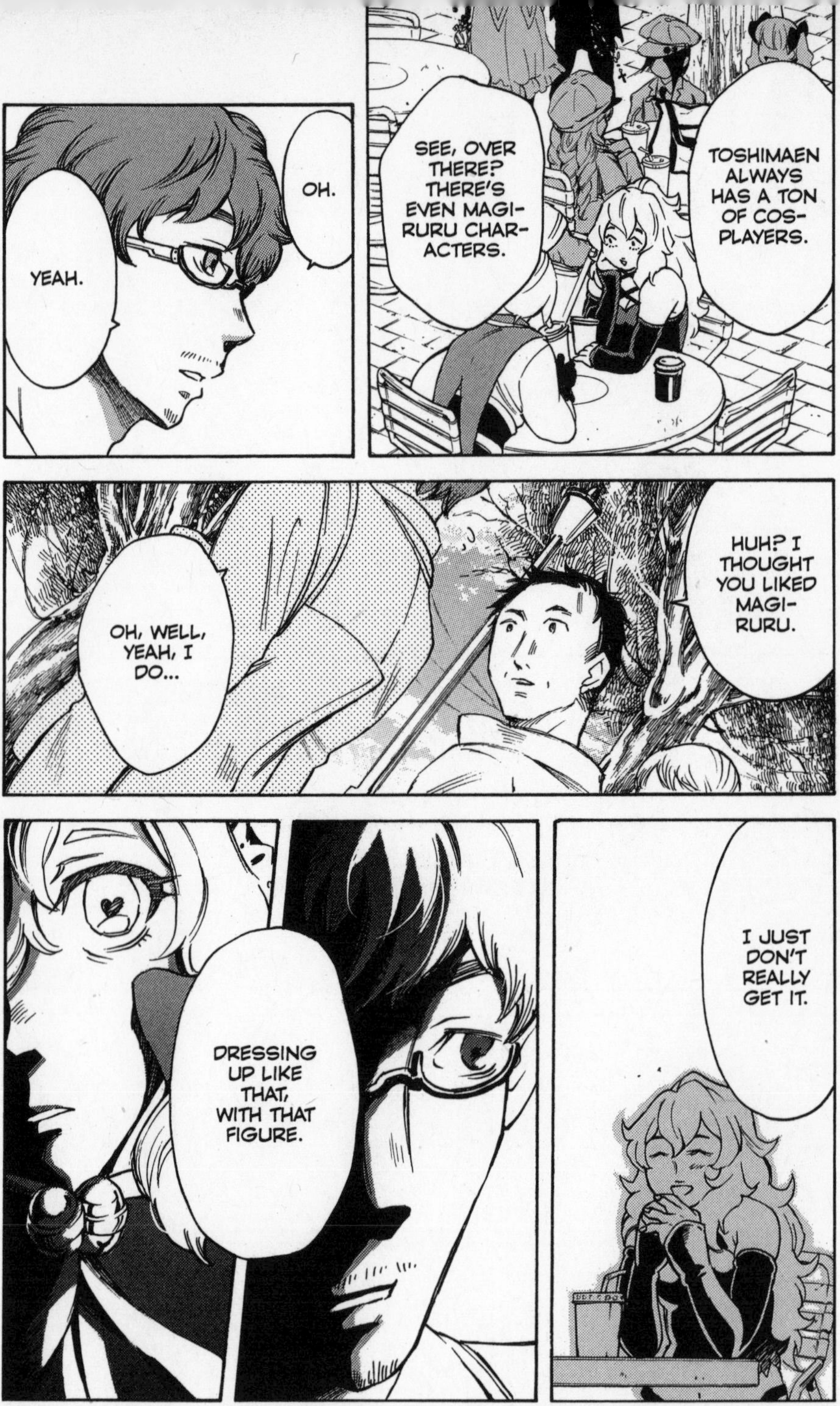
TOSHIMAEN ALWAYS HAS A TON OF COS-PLAYERS.
SEE, OVER THERE? THERE'S EVEN MAGI-RURU CHAR-ACTERS.
OH.
YEAH.
HUH? I THOUGHT YOU LIKED MAGI-RURU.
OH, WELL, YEAH, I DO...
I JUST DON'T REALLY GET IT.
DRESSING UP LIKE THAT, WITH THAT FIGURE.

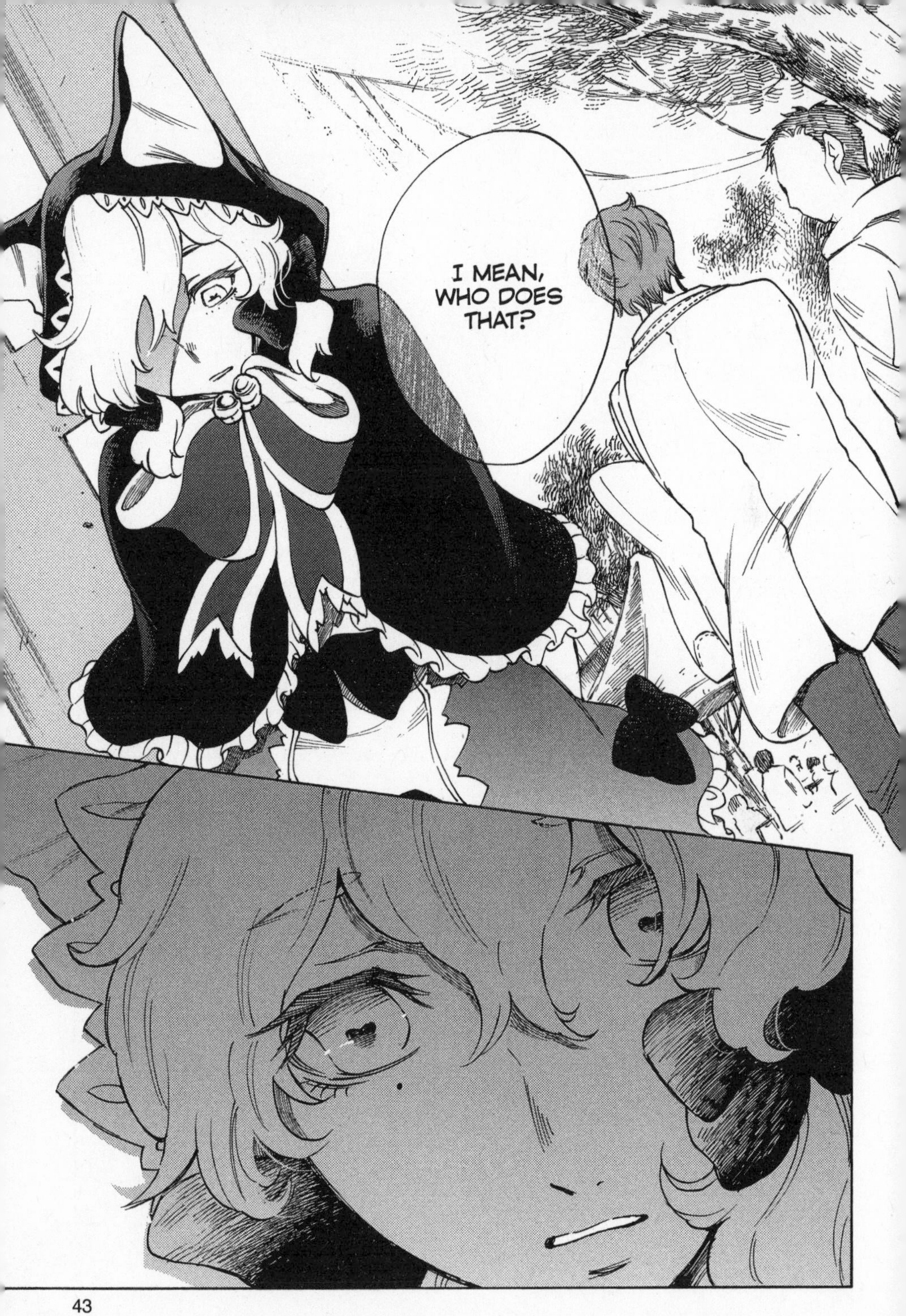
I MEAN, WHO DOES THAT?

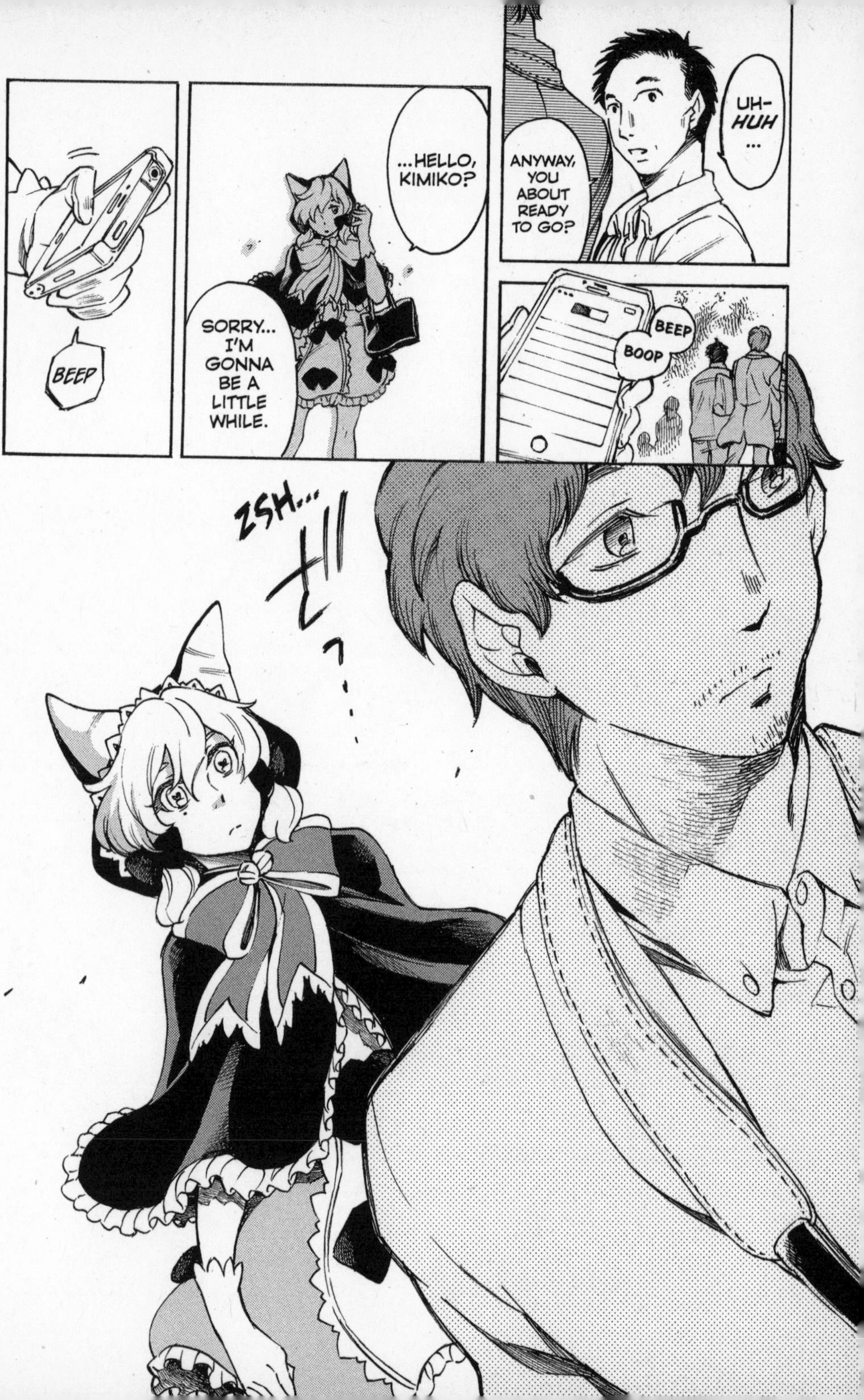
UH-HUH...
ANYWAY, YOU ABOUT READY TO GO?
BEEP
BOOP
...HELLO, KIMIKO?
SORRY... I'M GONNA BE A LITTLE WHILE.
BEEP
ZSH...

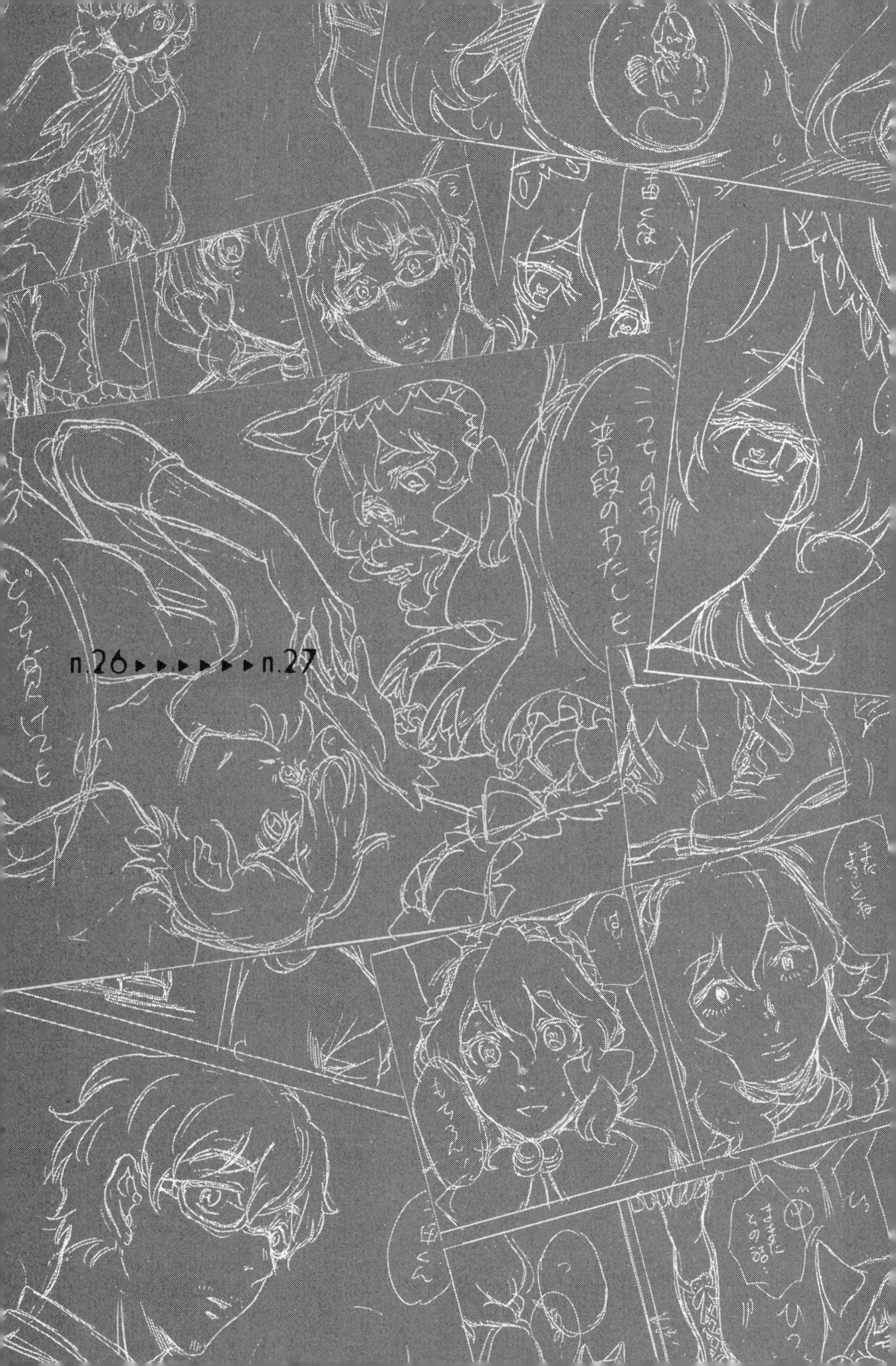
普段のわたしも
n.26▶▶▶▶▶▶▶▶n.27

COSPLAY CARD
COLLECTION
①

凪 Nagi

cure: xxxxx
archive: xxxx

NAGISA AS URURU

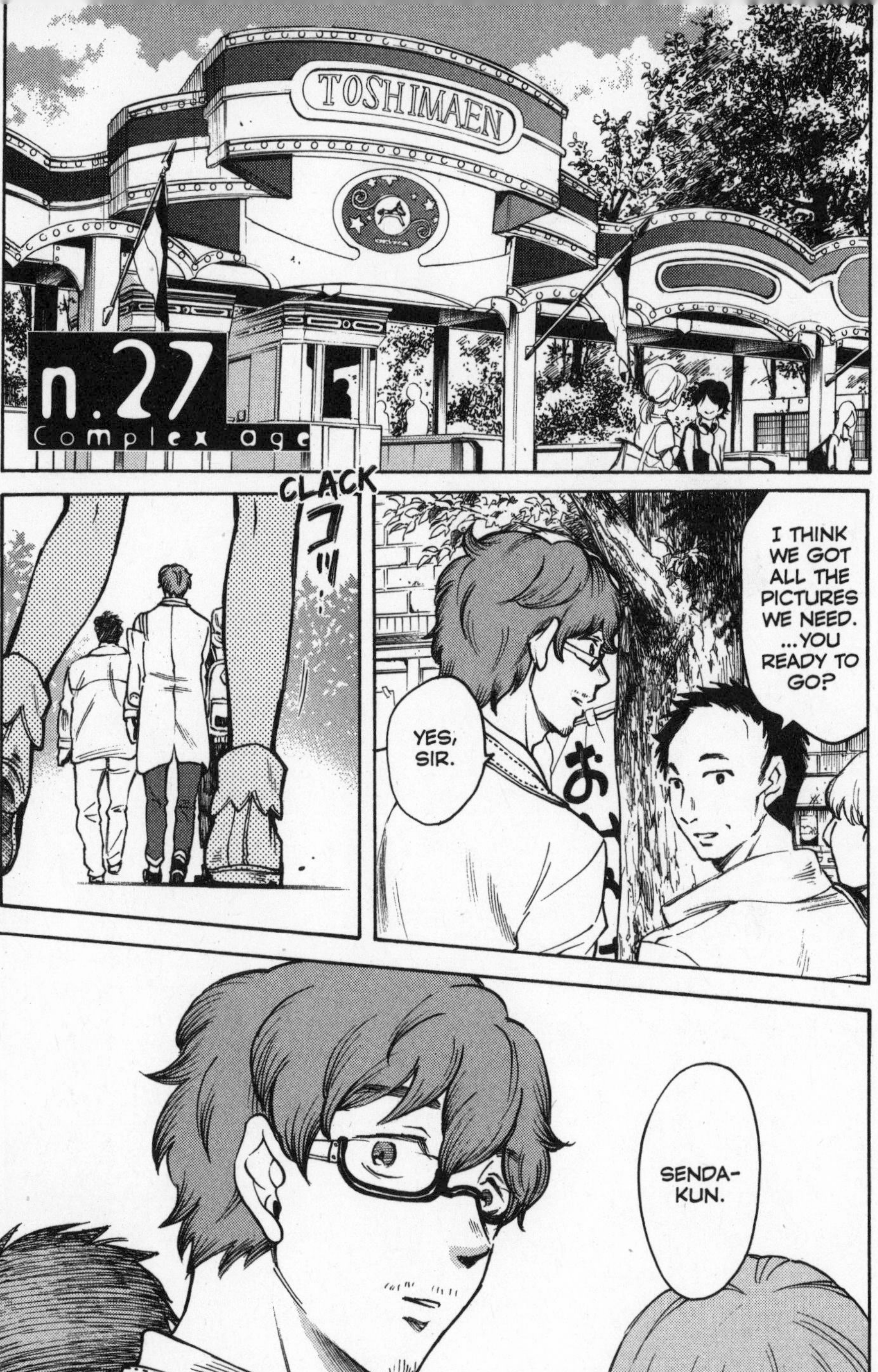
TOSHIMAEN
n.27
Complex age
I THINK WE GOT ALL THE PICTURES WE NEED. ...YOU READY TO GO?
YES, SIR.
CLACK
コッ
SENDA-KUN.

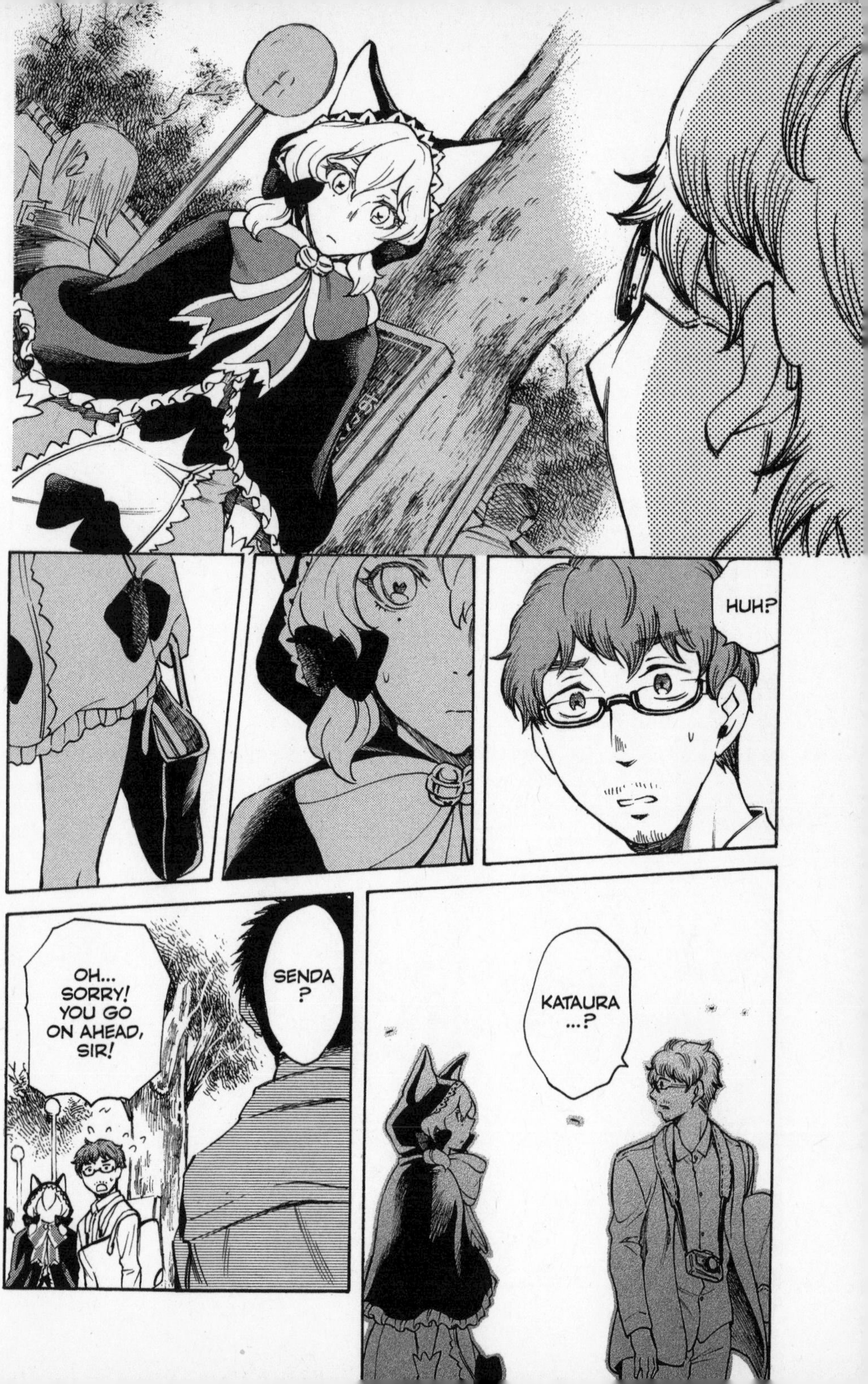
HUH?
KATAURA ...?
SENDA ?
OH... SORRY! YOU GO ON AHEAD, SIR!

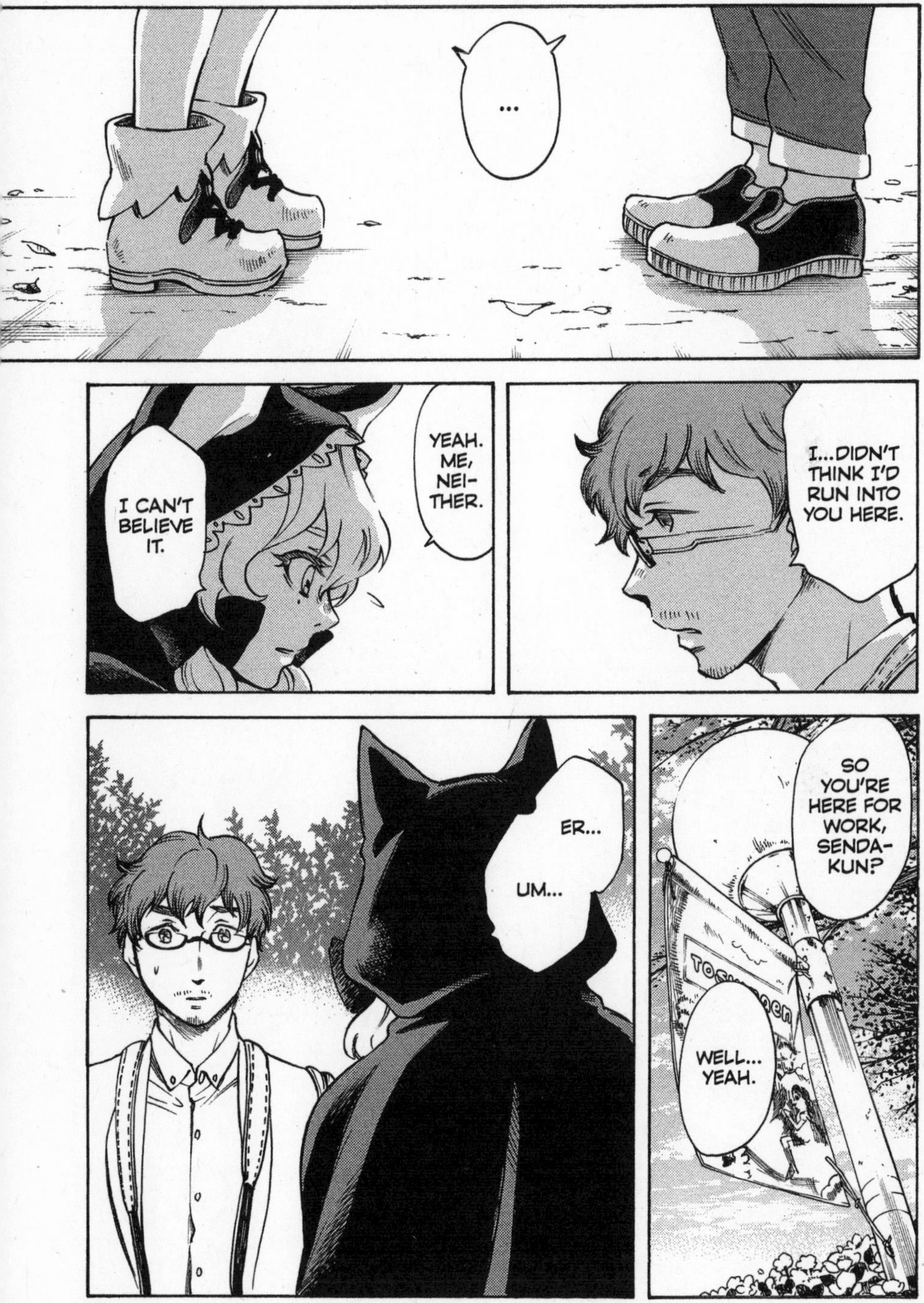
...
I...DIDN'T THINK I'D RUN INTO YOU HERE.
YEAH. ME, NEI-THER.
I CAN'T BELIEVE IT.
SO YOU'RE HERE FOR WORK, SENDA-KUN?
WELL... YEAH.
ER...
UM...

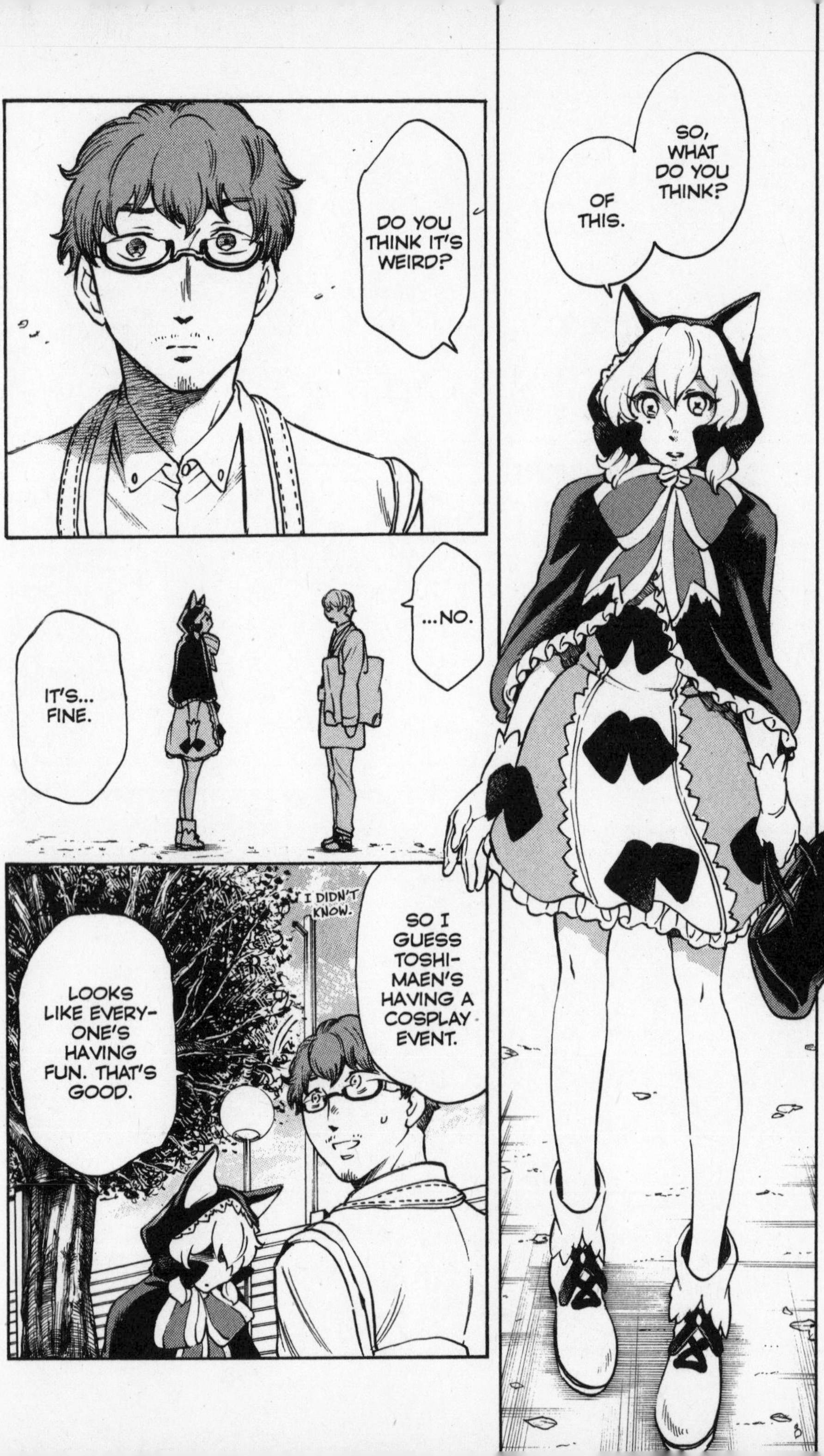
SO, WHAT DO YOU THINK?
OF THIS.
DO YOU THINK IT'S WEIRD?
...NO.
IT'S... FINE.
SO I GUESS TOSHI-MAEN'S HAVING A COSPLAY EVENT.
I DIDN'T KNOW.
LOOKS LIKE EVERY-ONE'S HAVING FUN. THAT'S GOOD.

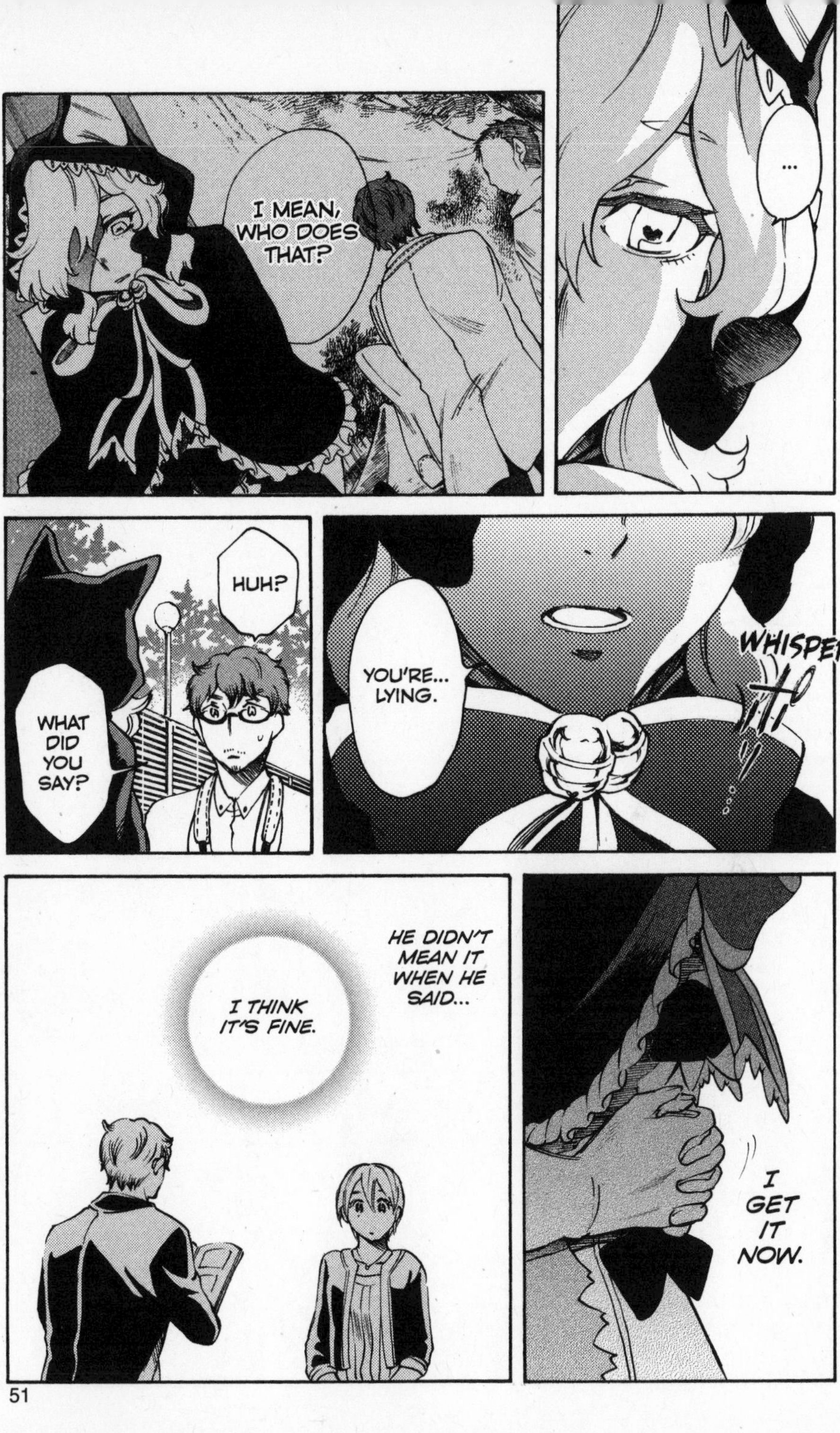
...
I MEAN, WHO DOES THAT?
YOU'RE... LYING.
WHISPER...
HUH?
WHAT DID YOU SAY?
I GET IT NOW.
HE DIDN'T MEAN IT WHEN HE SAID...
I THINK IT'S FINE.

I GET IT.

WE WERE NEVER...

...GOING TO WORK OUT.

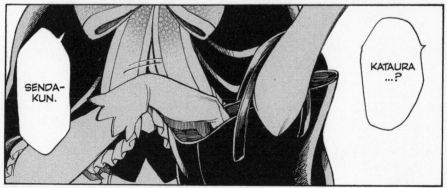

SENDA-KUN.

KATAURA ...?

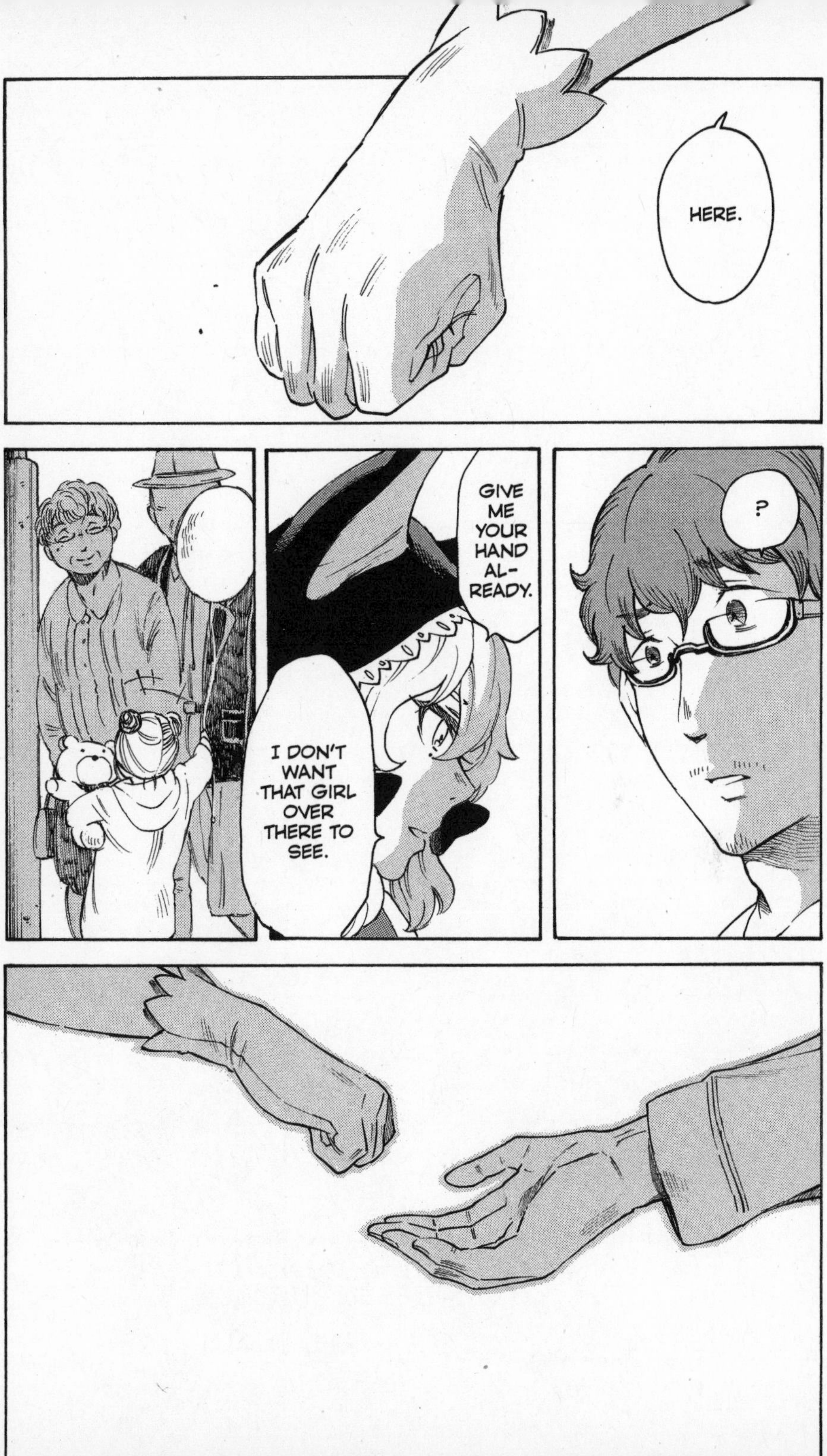
HERE.
?
GIVE ME YOUR HAND AL- READY.
I DON'T WANT THAT GIRL OVER THERE TO SEE.

WHAT...? THIS IS MY APARTMENT KEY.

BUT... WHY?

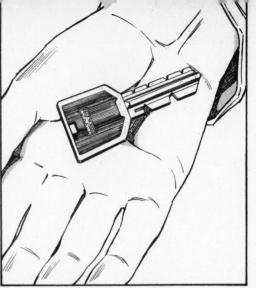

DID I DO SOMETHING?

YOU DON'T WANT *THIS* NAGISA.

BECAUSE SENDA-KUN...

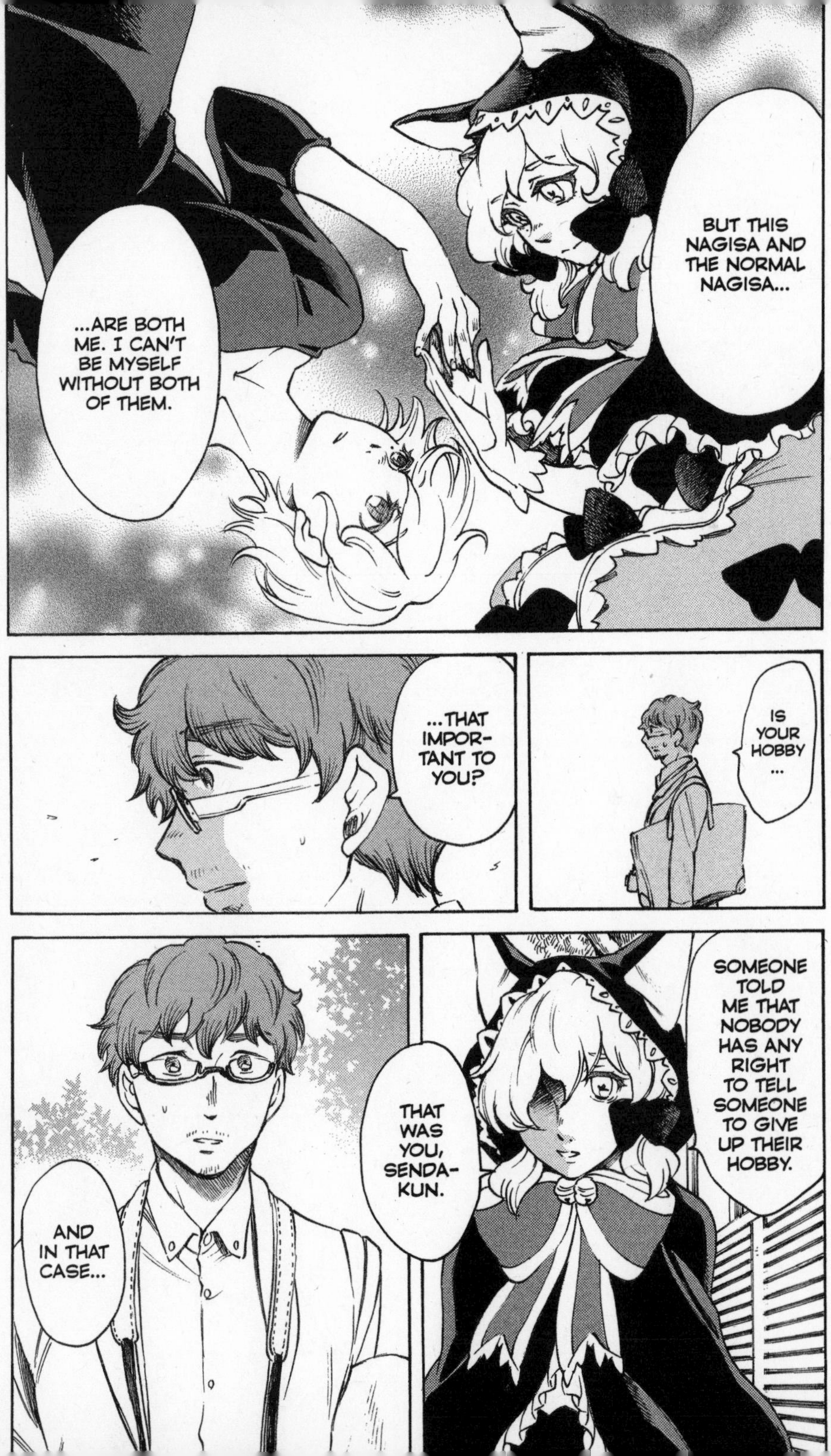
BUT THIS NAGISA AND THE NORMAL NAGISA...
...ARE BOTH ME. I CAN'T BE MYSELF WITHOUT BOTH OF THEM.
IS YOUR HOBBY ...
...THAT IMPORTANT TO YOU?
SOMEONE TOLD ME THAT NOBODY HAS ANY RIGHT TO TELL SOMEONE TO GIVE UP THEIR HOBBY.
THAT WAS YOU, SENDA-KUN.
AND IN THAT CASE...

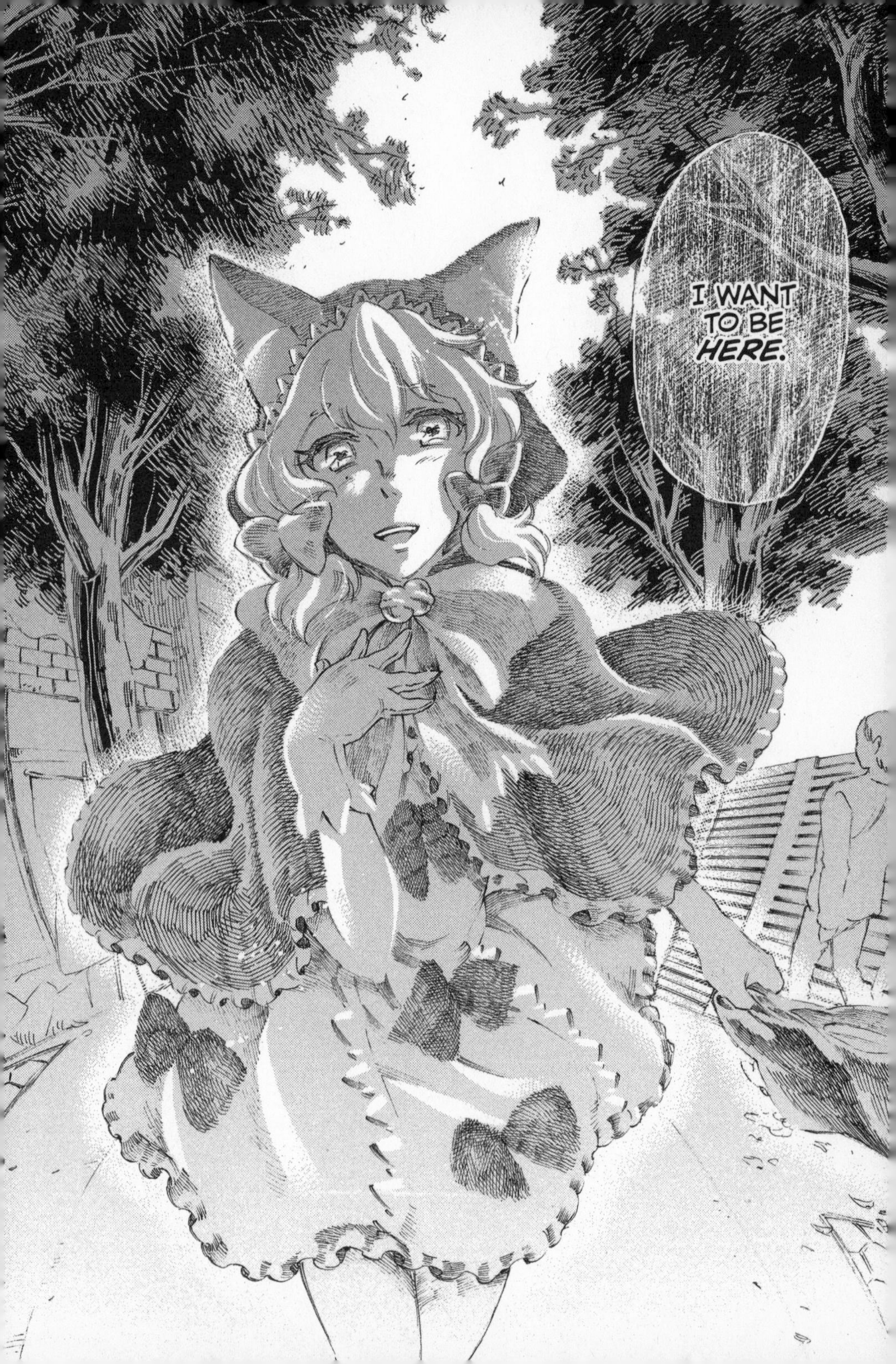
I WANT TO BE HERE.

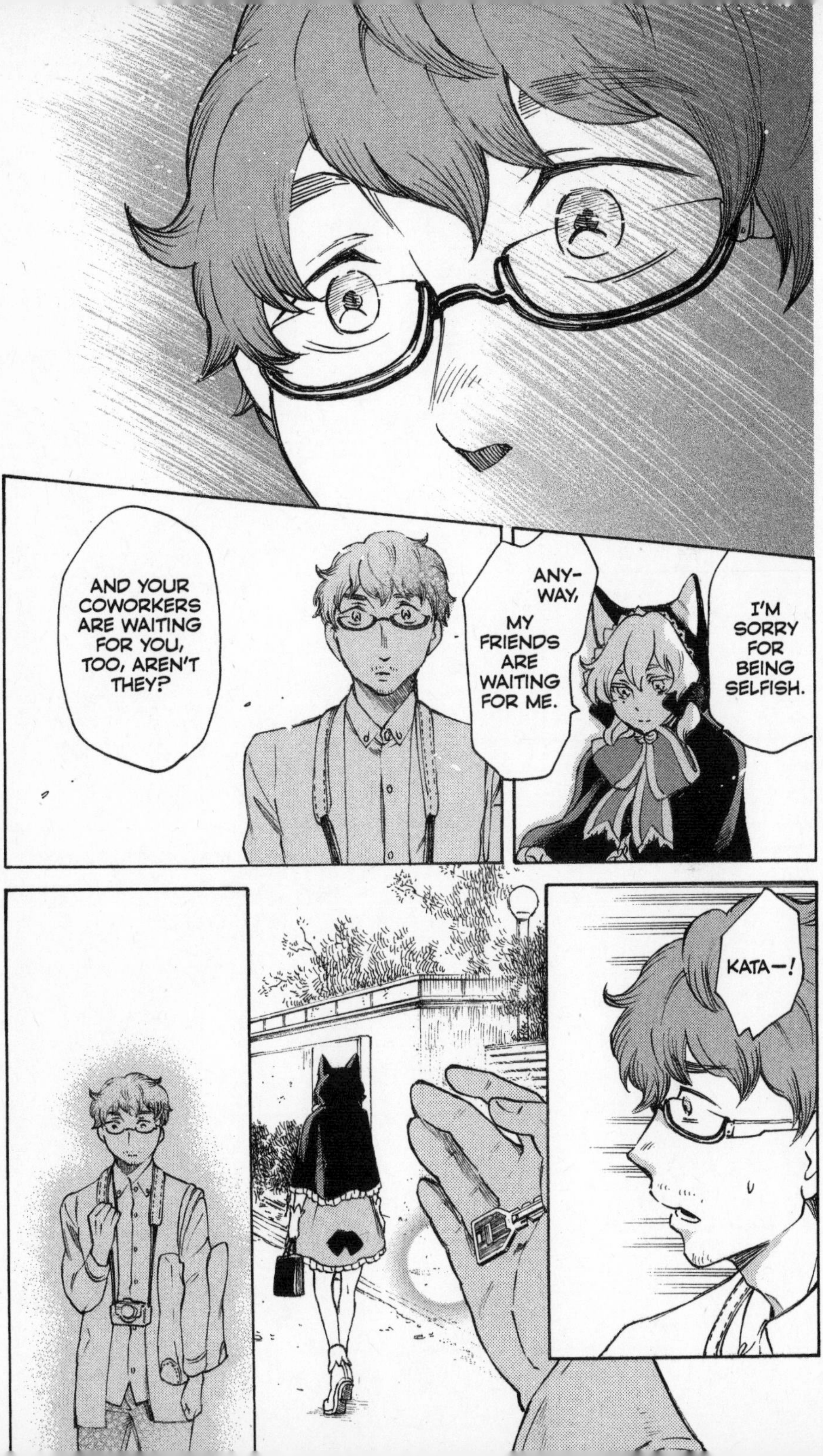
I'M SORRY FOR BEING SELFISH.
ANY-WAY, MY FRIENDS ARE WAITING FOR ME.
AND YOUR COWORKERS ARE WAITING FOR YOU, TOO, AREN'T THEY?
KATA—!

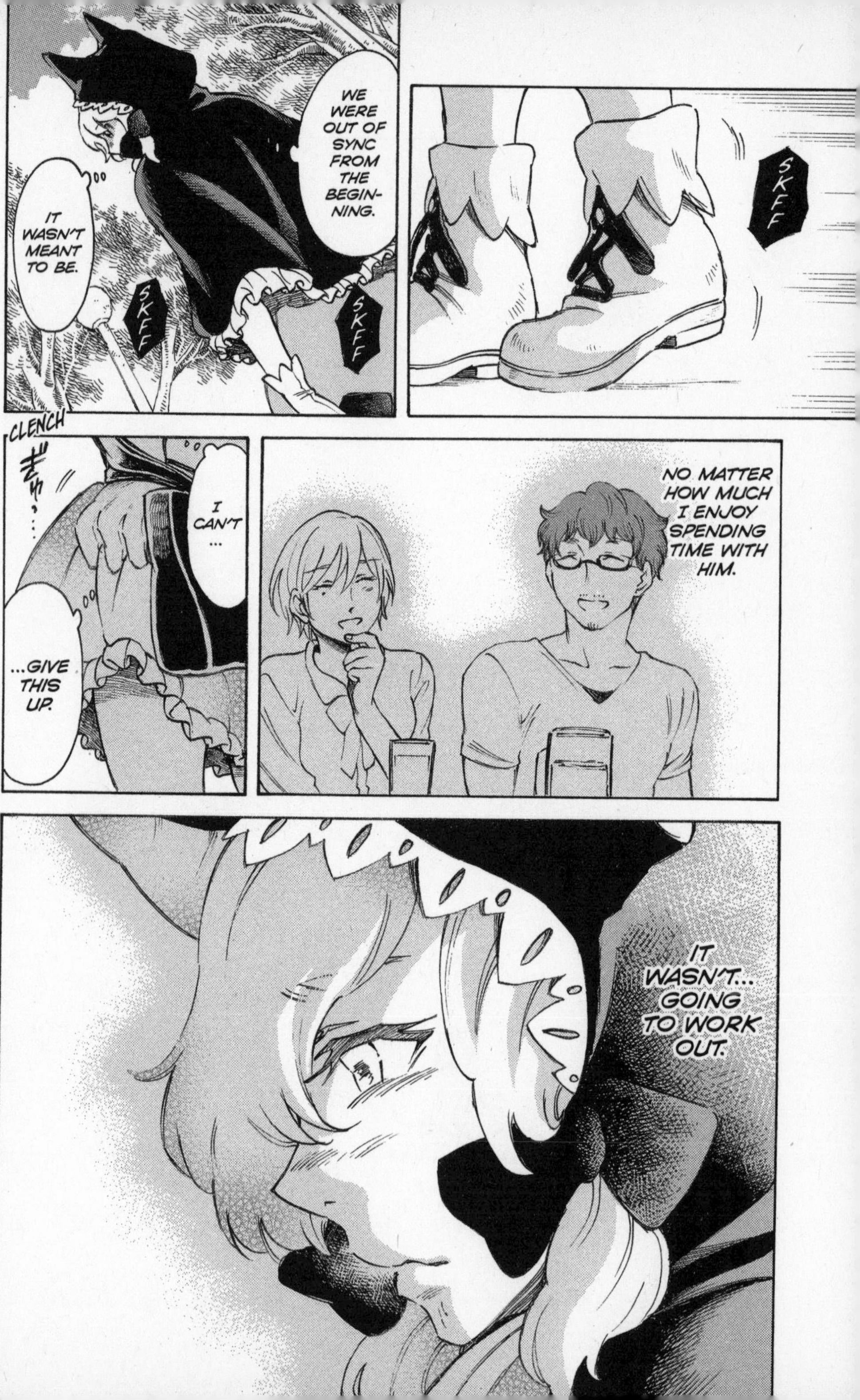
SKFF
WE WERE OUT OF SYNC FROM THE BEGINNING.
IT WASN'T MEANT TO BE.
SKFF
SKFF
NO MATTER HOW MUCH I ENJOY SPENDING TIME WITH HIM.
CLENCH
I CAN'T ...
...GIVE THIS UP.
IT WASN'T... GOING TO WORK OUT.

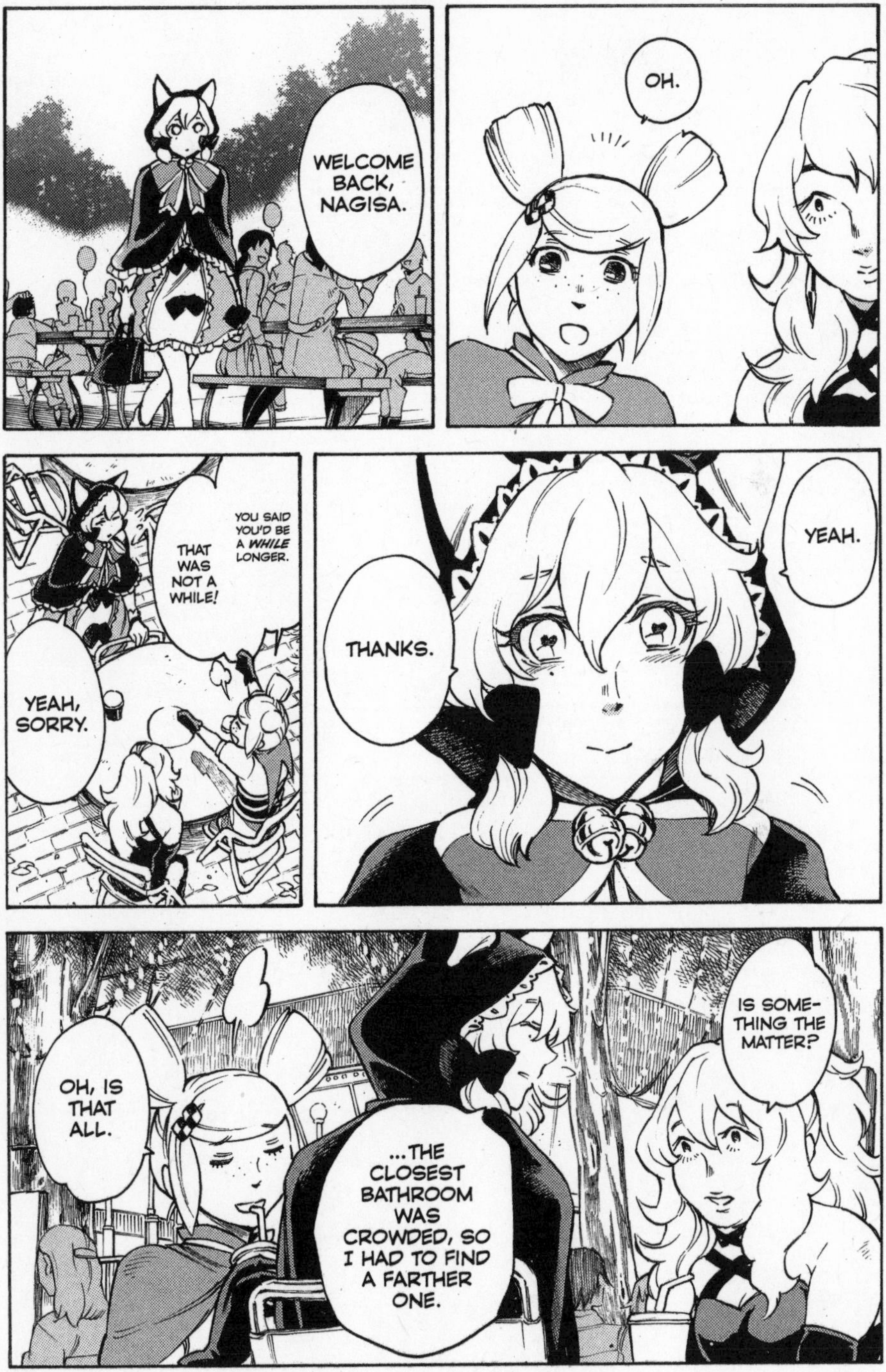
OH.
WELCOME BACK, NAGISA.
YEAH.
THANKS.
YOU SAID YOU'D BE A *WHILE* LONGER.
THAT WAS NOT A WHILE!
YEAH, SORRY.
IS SOME-THING THE MATTER?
...THE CLOSEST BATHROOM WAS CROWDED, SO I HAD TO FIND A FARTHER ONE.
OH, IS THAT ALL.

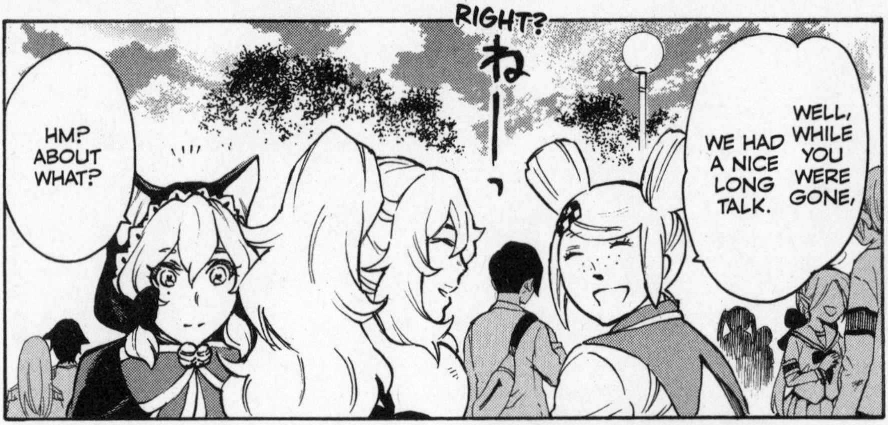
WELL, WHILE YOU WERE GONE,
WE HAD A NICE LONG TALK.
RIGHT?
ねー
HM? ABOUT WHAT?

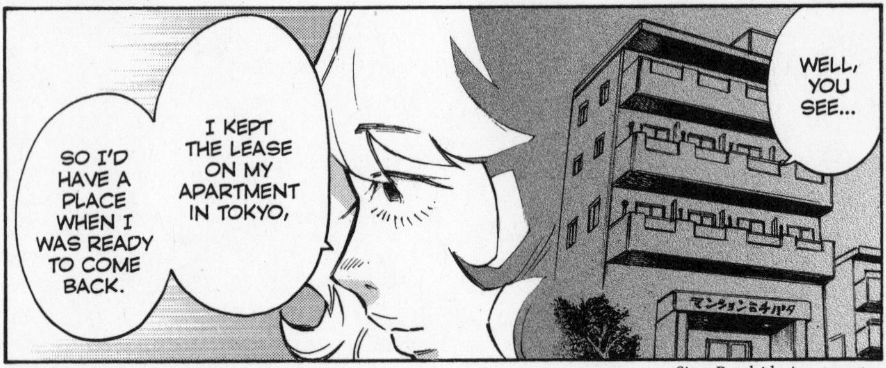
WELL, YOU SEE...
I KEPT THE LEASE ON MY APARTMENT IN TOKYO,
SO I'D HAVE A PLACE WHEN I WAS READY TO COME BACK.

Sign: Roadside Apartments

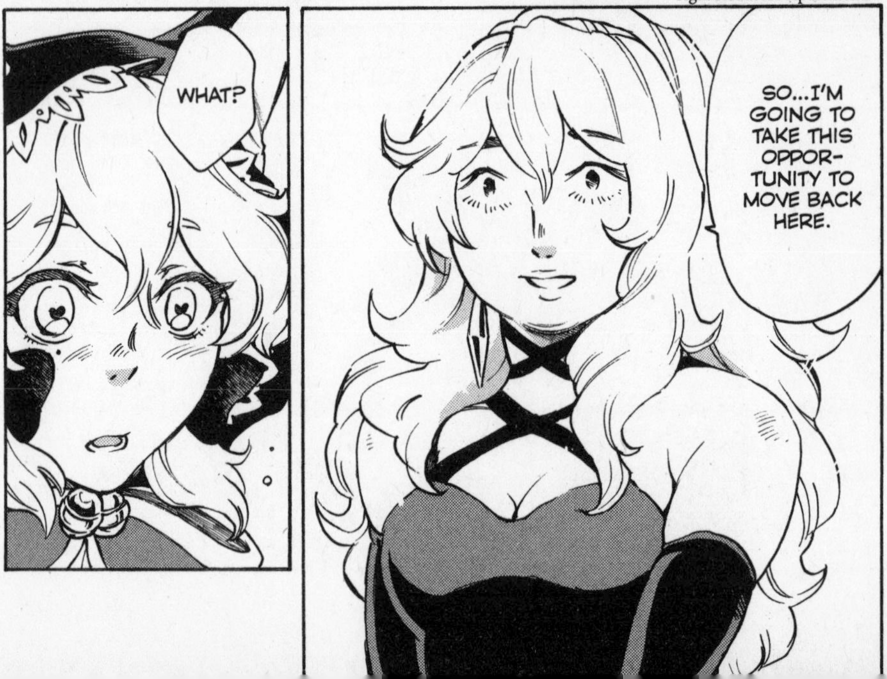
SO...I'M GOING TO TAKE THIS OPPOR-TUNITY TO MOVE BACK HERE.
WHAT?

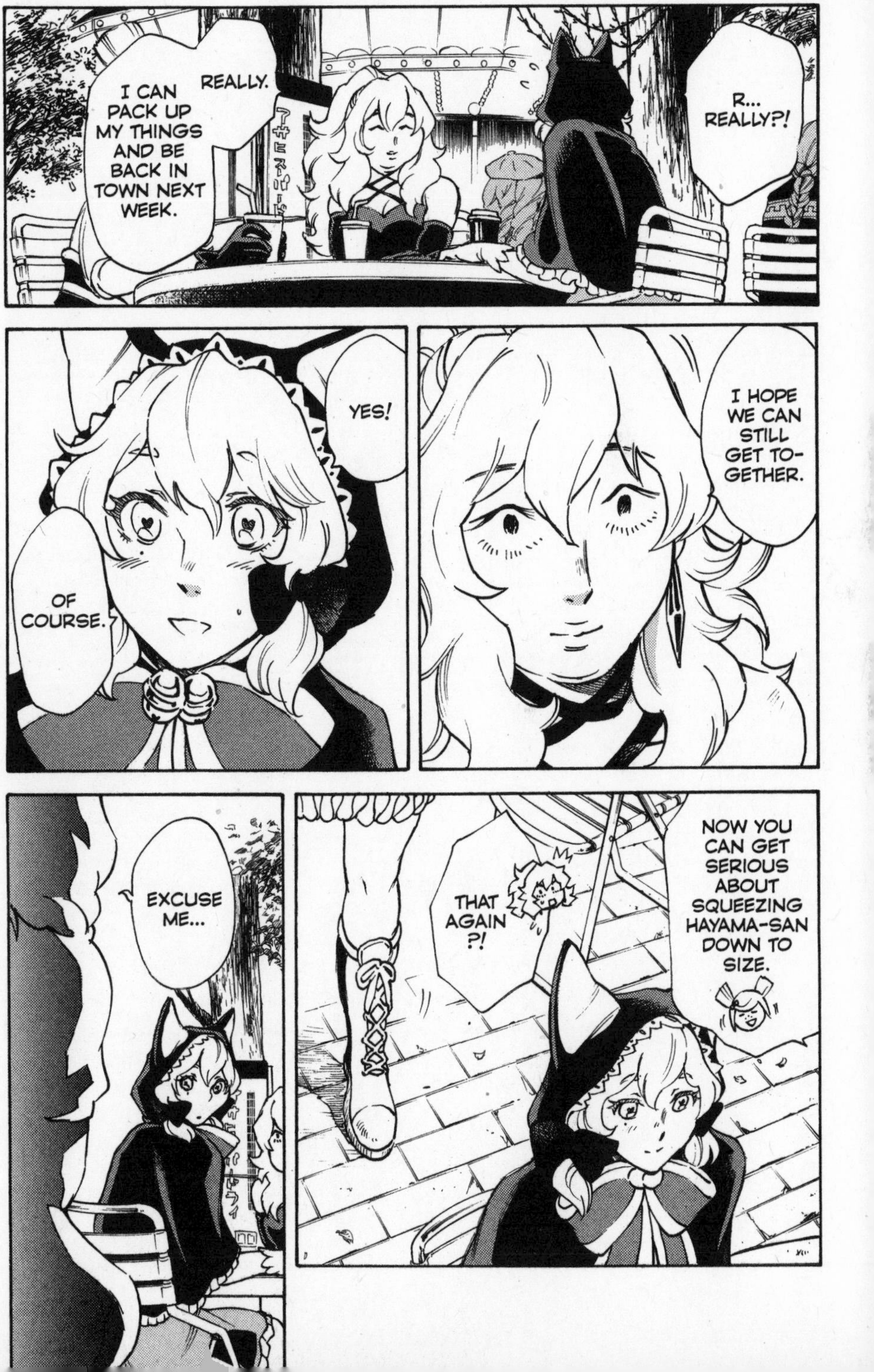
R... REALLY?!
REALLY.
I CAN PACK UP MY THINGS AND BE BACK IN TOWN NEXT WEEK.
I HOPE WE CAN STILL GET TO-GETHER.
YES!
OF COURSE.
NOW YOU CAN GET SERIOUS ABOUT SQUEEZING HAYAMA-SAN DOWN TO SIZE.
THAT AGAIN?!
EXCUSE ME...

UM.

YOU'RE... NAGI-SAN, RIGHT?

I'M SORRY TO BE SO FORWARD...

OH... UM.

GASP

UH... YES?

OH, RIGHT!

OF COURSE.

AND YOU ARE?

YES ...

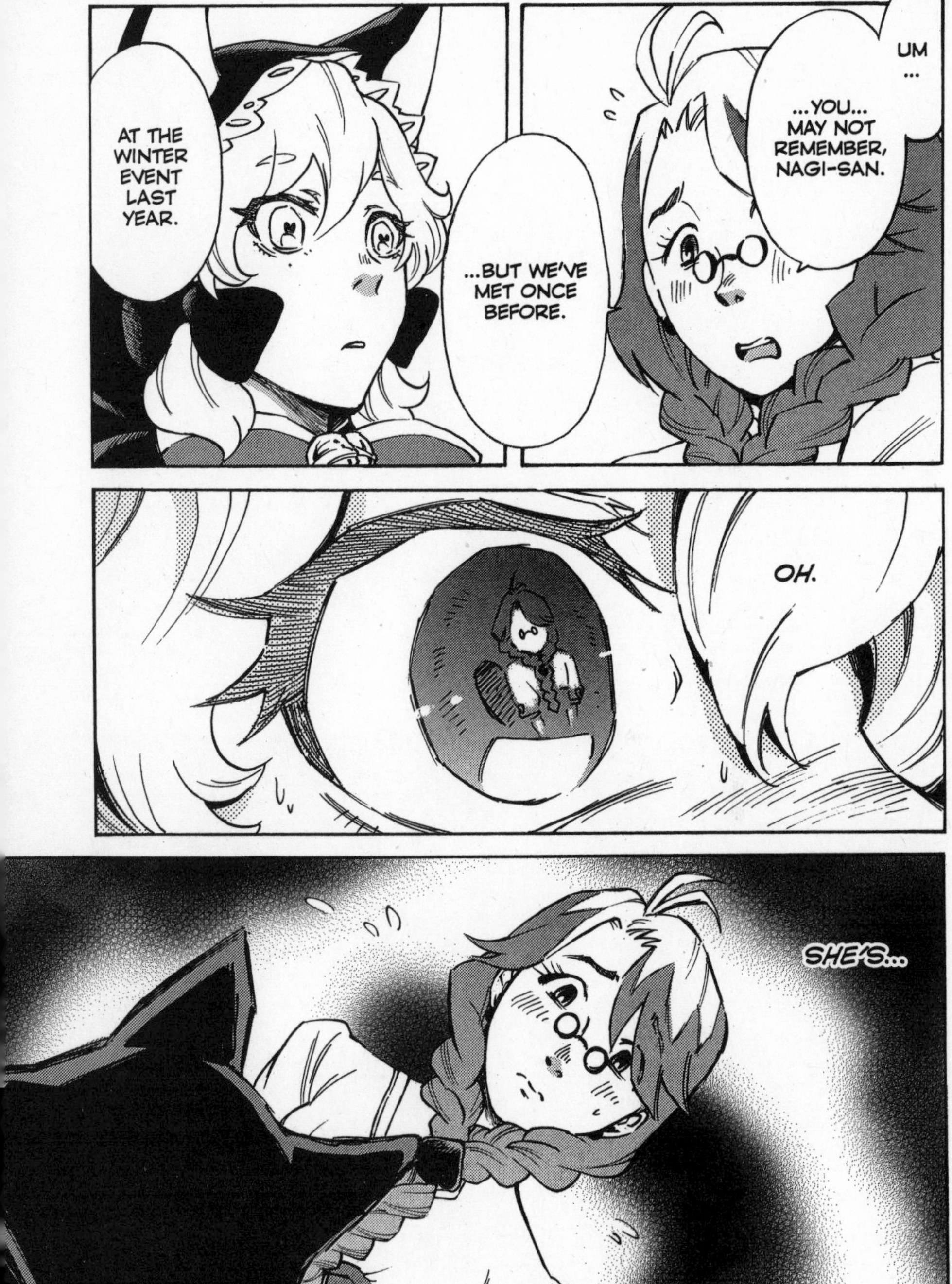
UM ...
...YOU... MAY NOT REMEMBER, NAGI-SAN.
...BUT WE'VE MET ONCE BEFORE.
AT THE WINTER EVENT LAST YEAR.
OH.
SHE'S...

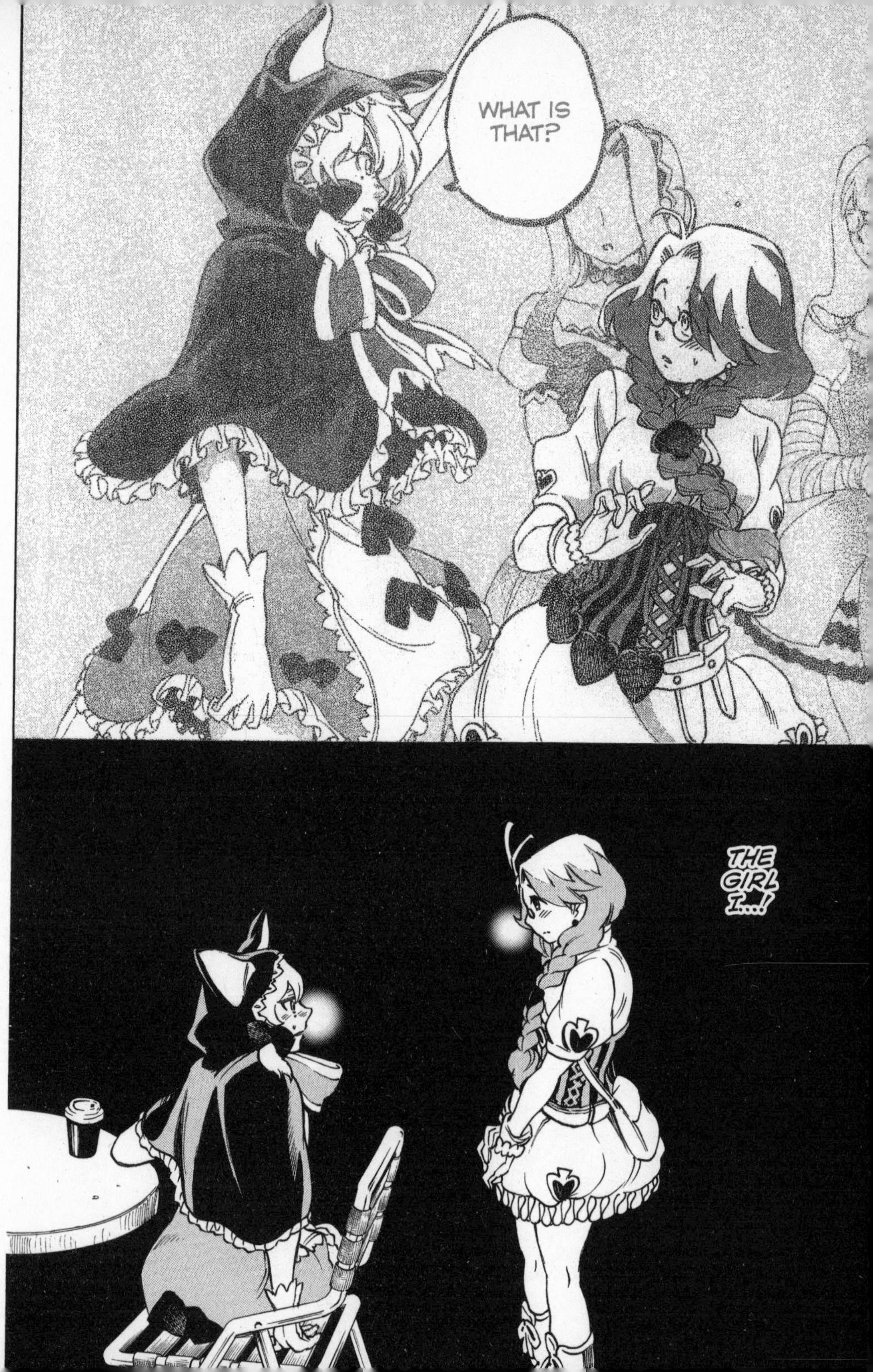
WHAT IS THAT?
THE GIRL I...!

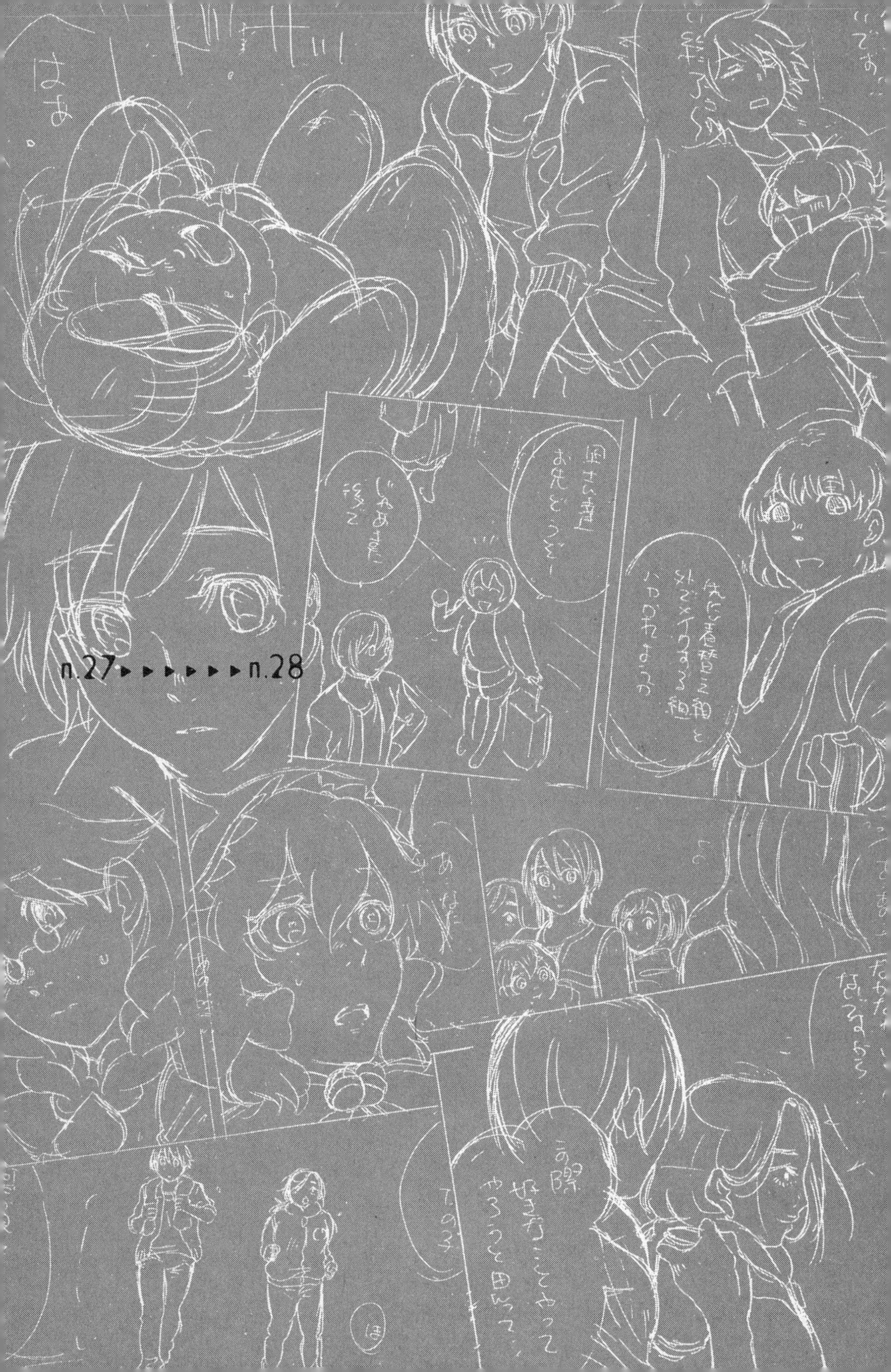
n.27▸▸▸▸▸▸▸n.28

COSPLAY CARD

COLLECTION

2

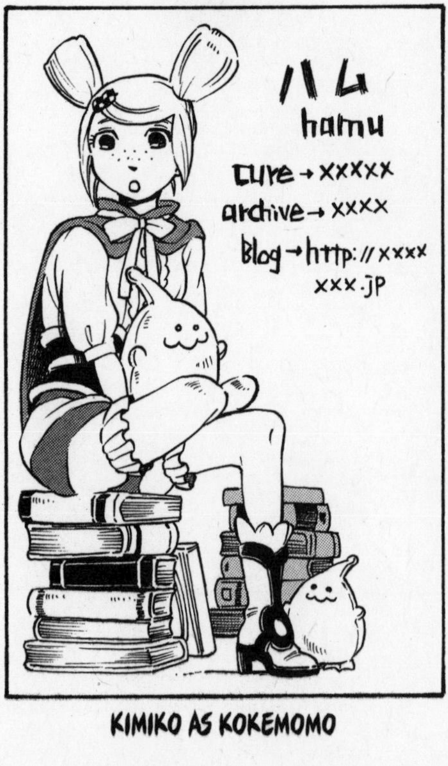
ハム
hamu
cure→xxxxx
archive→xxxx
Blog→http://xxxx
xxx.jp

KIMIKO AS KOKEMOMO

n.28 Complex age

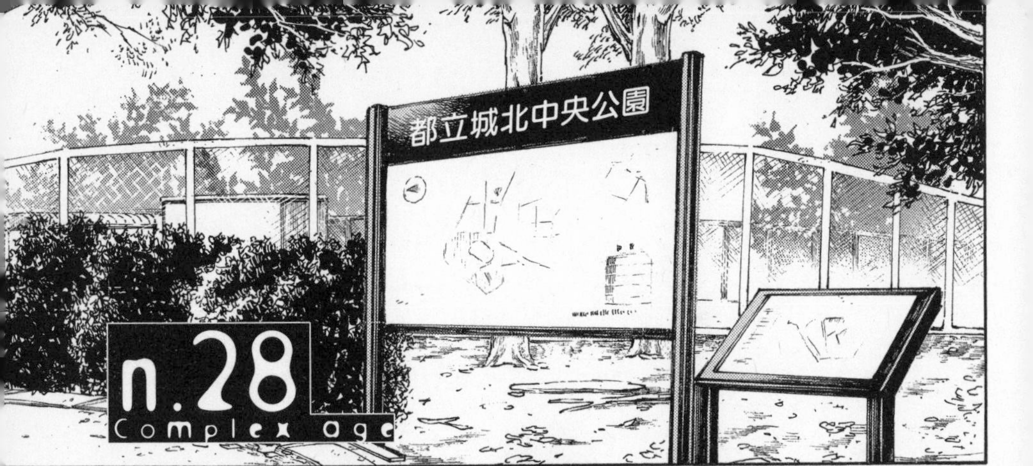
都立城北中央公園

Sign: Toritsu Jōhoku Central Park

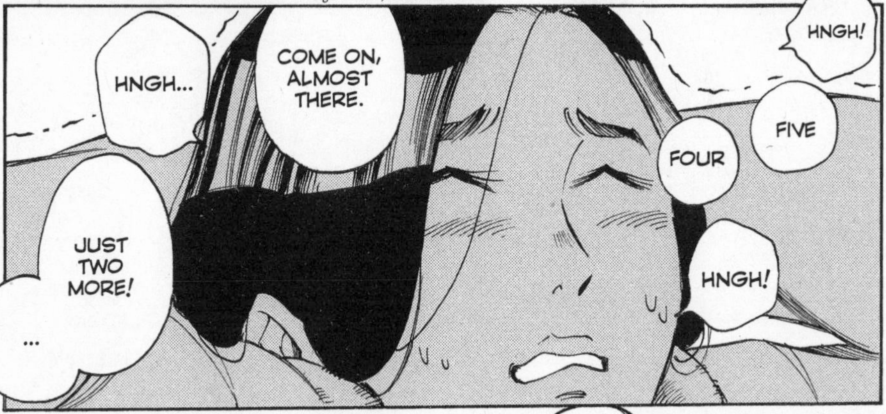
HNGH!
FIVE
FOUR
HNGH!
COME ON, ALMOST THERE.
HNGH...
JUST TWO MORE!
...

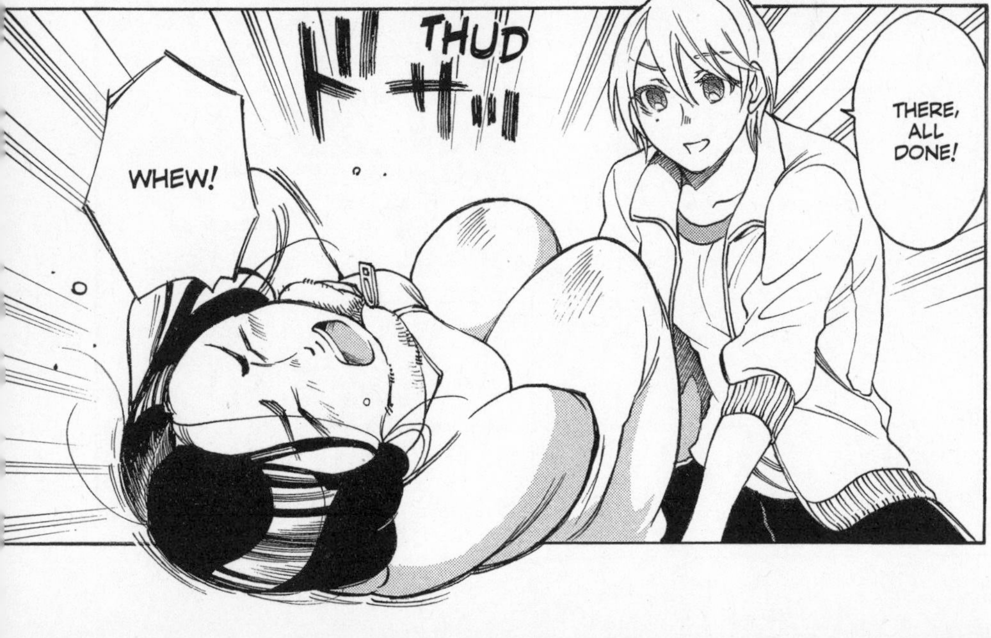
THERE, ALL DONE!
THUD
WHEW!

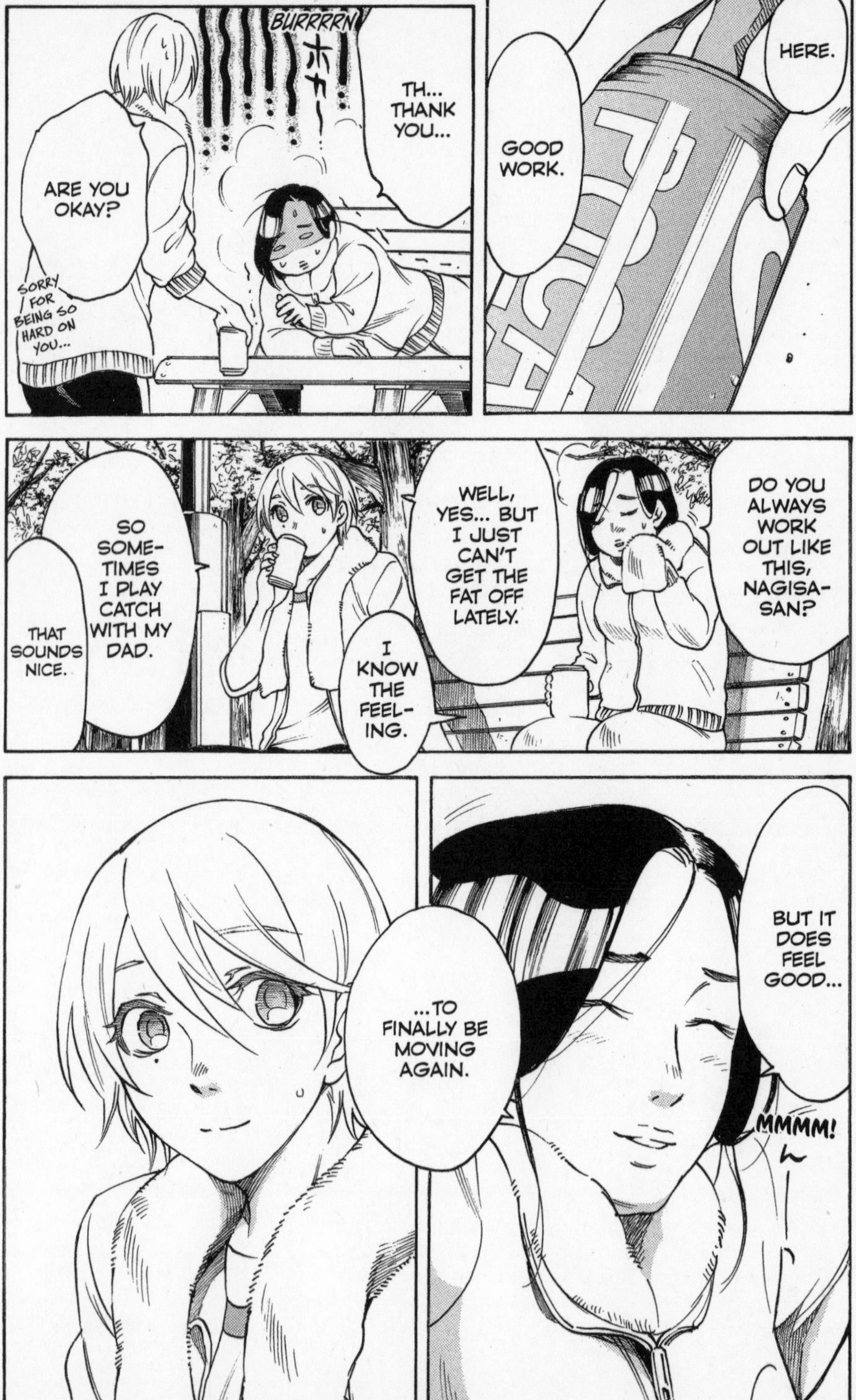
HERE.
GOOD WORK.
BURRRRN ホカ～
TH... THANK YOU...
ARE YOU OKAY?
SORRY FOR BEING SO HARD ON YOU...
DO YOU ALWAYS WORK OUT LIKE THIS, NAGISA-SAN?
WELL, YES... BUT I JUST CAN'T GET THE FAT OFF LATELY.
I KNOW THE FEELING.
SO SOMETIMES I PLAY CATCH WITH MY DAD.
THAT SOUNDS NICE.
BUT IT DOES FEEL GOOD...
MMMM! ん
...TO FINALLY BE MOVING AGAIN.

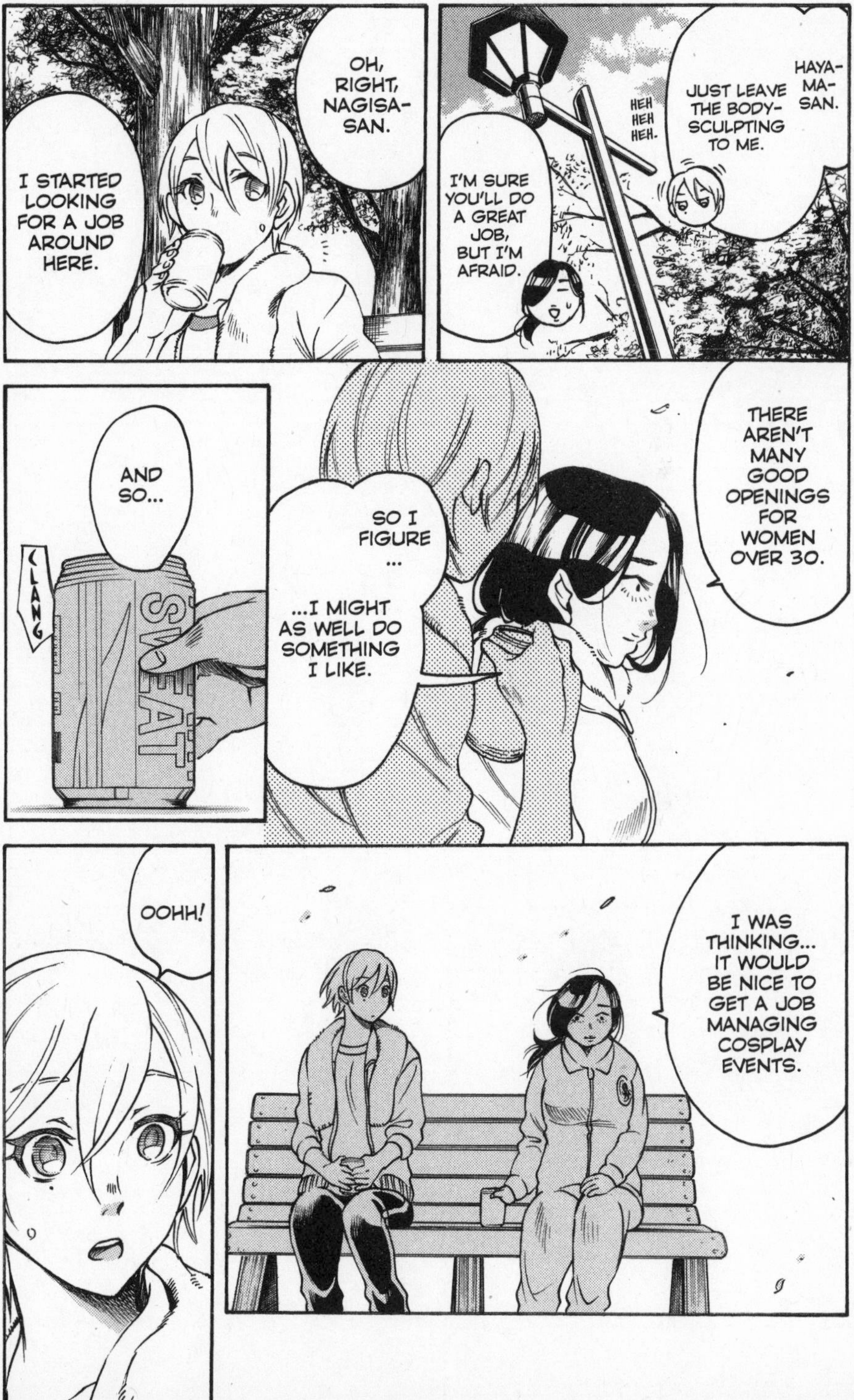

HAYA-MA-SAN.
JUST LEAVE THE BODY-SCULPTING TO ME.
HEH HEH HEH.
I'M SURE YOU'LL DO A GREAT JOB, BUT I'M AFRAID.
OH, RIGHT, NAGISA-SAN.
I STARTED LOOKING FOR A JOB AROUND HERE.
THERE AREN'T MANY GOOD OPENINGS FOR WOMEN OVER 30.
SO I FIGURE ...
...I MIGHT AS WELL DO SOMETHING I LIKE.
AND SO...
CLANG
SWEAT
I WAS THINKING... IT WOULD BE NICE TO GET A JOB MANAGING COSPLAY EVENTS.
OOHH!

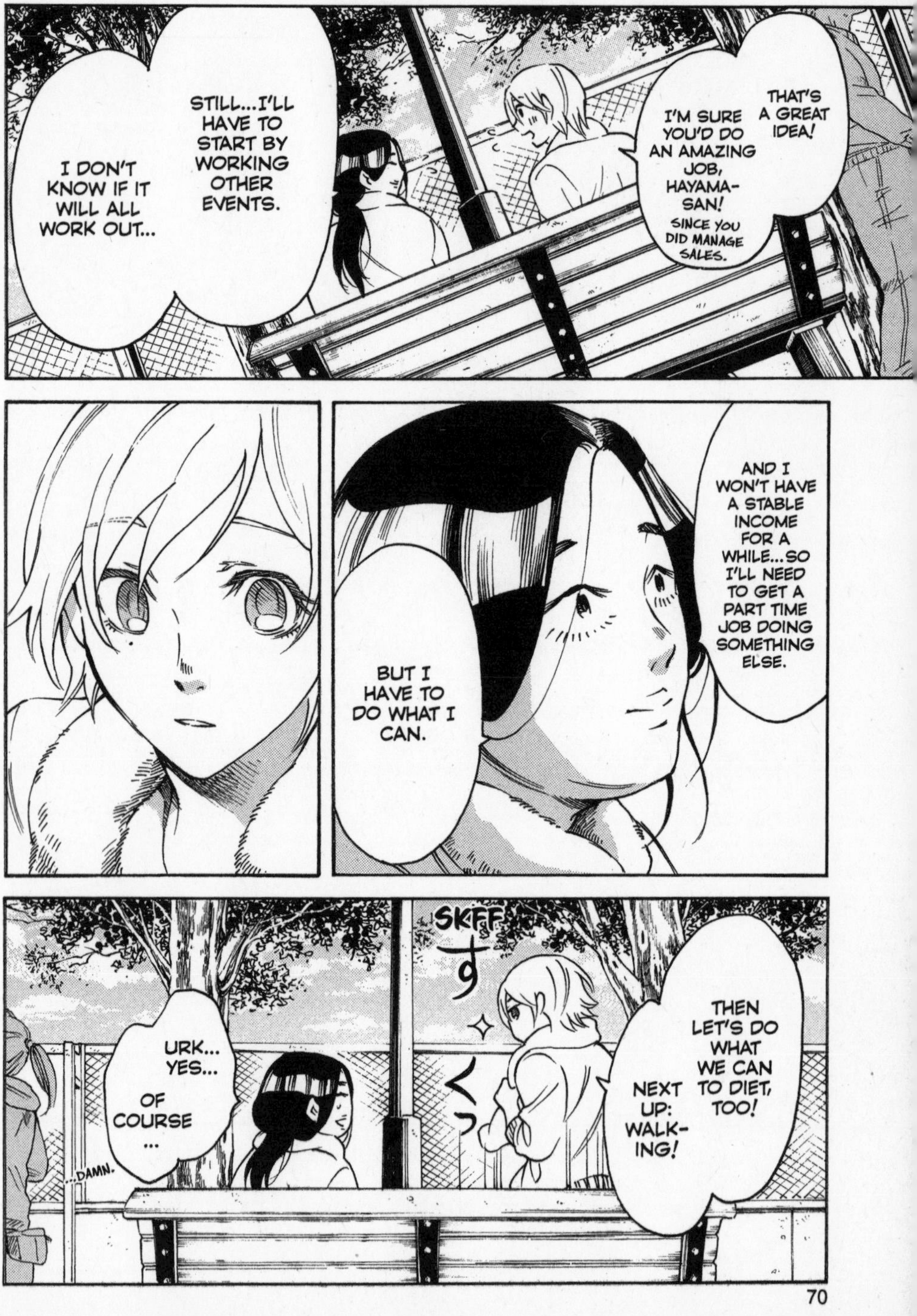
THAT'S A GREAT IDEA!
I'M SURE YOU'D DO AN AMAZING JOB, HAYAMA-SAN!
SINCE YOU DID MANAGE SALES.
STILL...I'LL HAVE TO START BY WORKING OTHER EVENTS.
I DON'T KNOW IF IT WILL ALL WORK OUT...
AND I WON'T HAVE A STABLE INCOME FOR A WHILE...SO I'LL NEED TO GET A PART TIME JOB DOING SOMETHING ELSE.
BUT I HAVE TO DO WHAT I CAN.
SKFF
す
THEN LET'S DO WHAT WE CAN TO DIET, TOO!
NEXT UP: WALKING!
くっ
URK... YES...
OF COURSE ...
...DAMN.

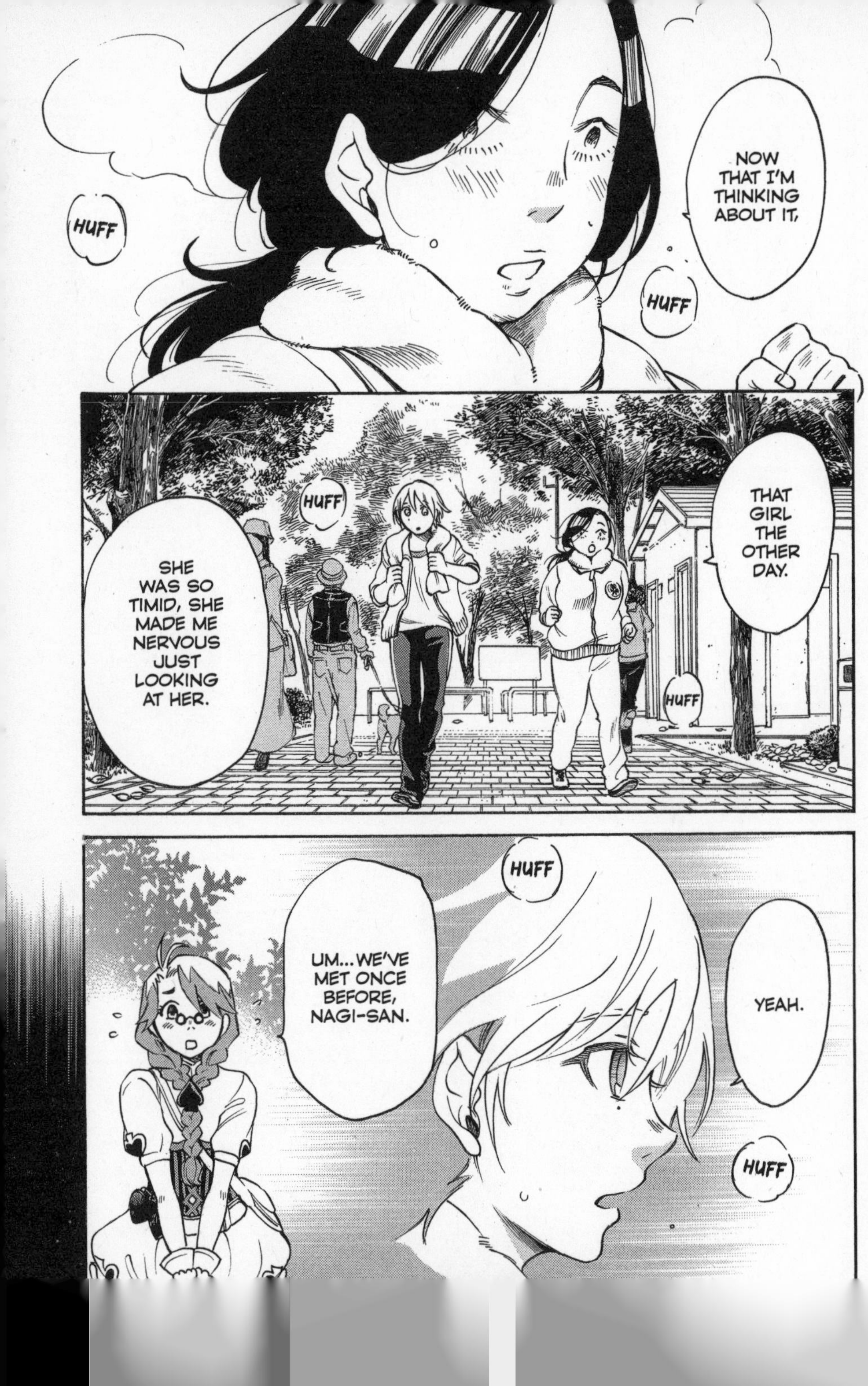
NOW THAT I'M THINKING ABOUT IT,
HUFF
HUFF
THAT GIRL THE OTHER DAY.
HUFF
HUFF
SHE WAS SO TIMID, SHE MADE ME NERVOUS JUST LOOKING AT HER.
HUFF
YEAH.
UM...WE'VE MET ONCE BEFORE, NAGI-SAN.
HUFF

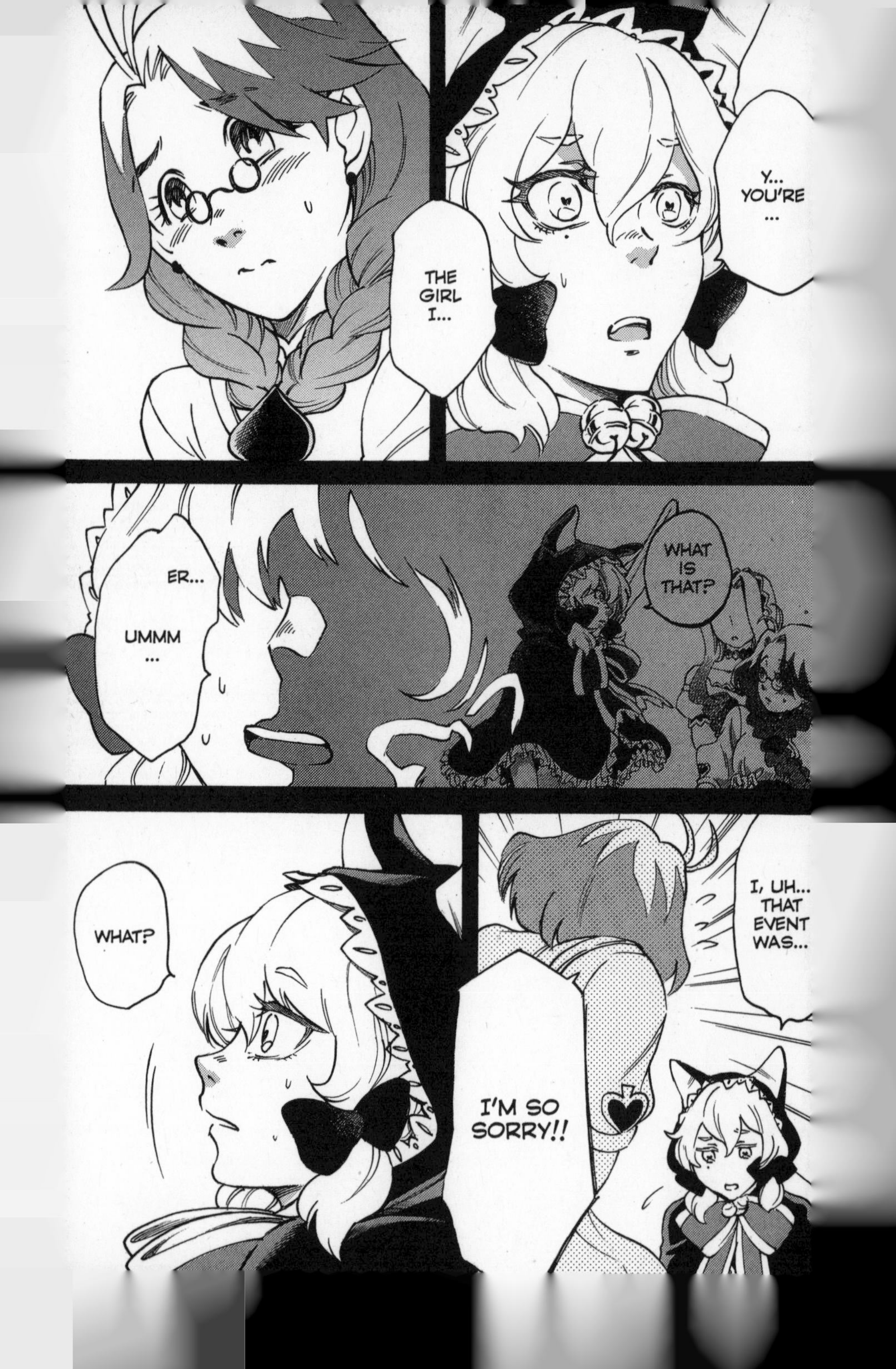
Y... YOU'RE ...
THE GIRL I...
WHAT IS THAT?
ER...
UMMM ...
I, UH... THAT EVENT WAS...
I'M SO SORRY!!
WHAT?

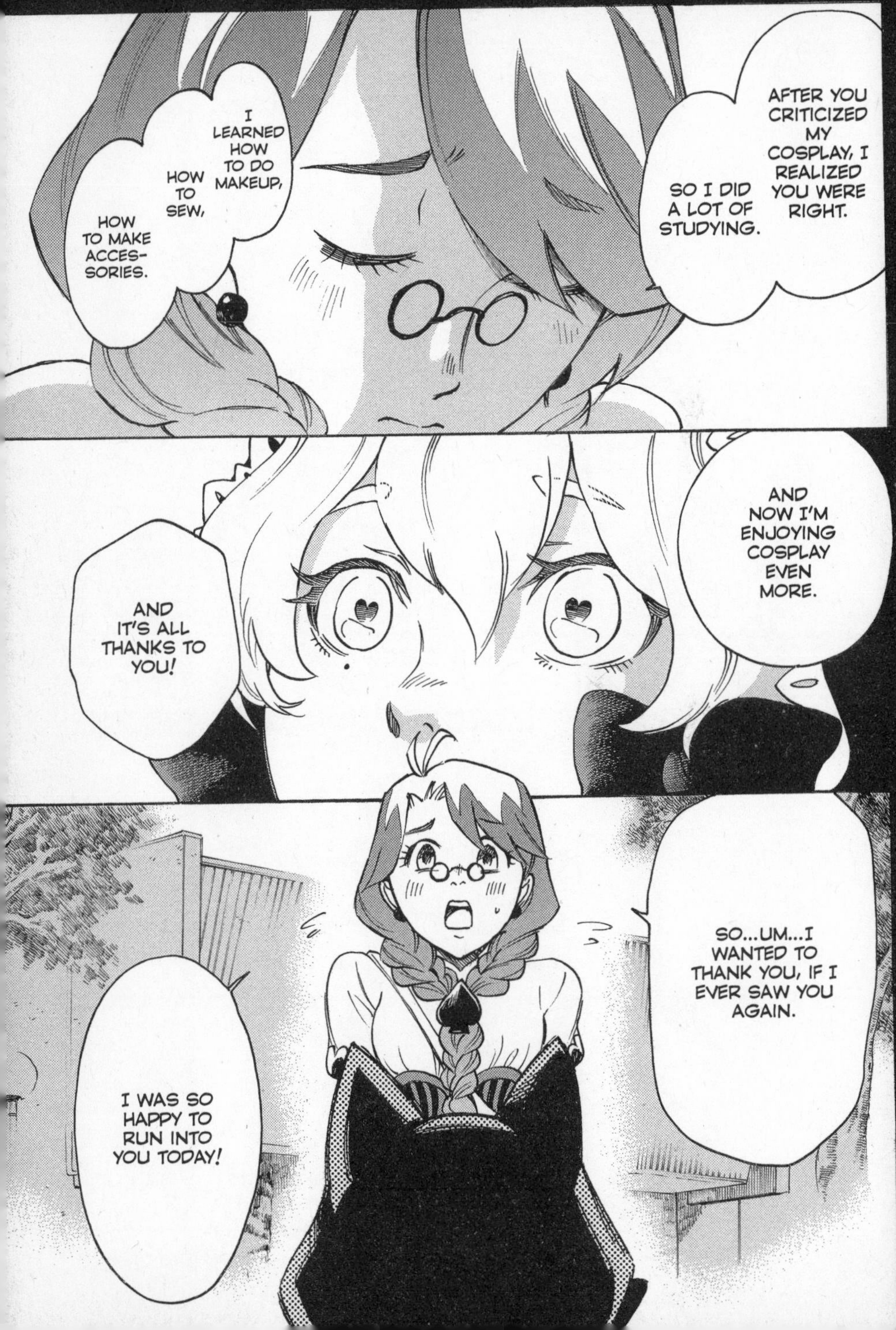
AFTER YOU CRITICIZED MY COSPLAY, I REALIZED YOU WERE RIGHT.
SO I DID A LOT OF STUDYING.
I LEARNED HOW TO DO MAKEUP,
HOW TO SEW,
HOW TO MAKE ACCES-SORIES.
AND NOW I'M ENJOYING COSPLAY EVEN MORE.
AND IT'S ALL THANKS TO YOU!
SO...UM...I WANTED TO THANK YOU, IF I EVER SAW YOU AGAIN.
I WAS SO HAPPY TO RUN INTO YOU TODAY!

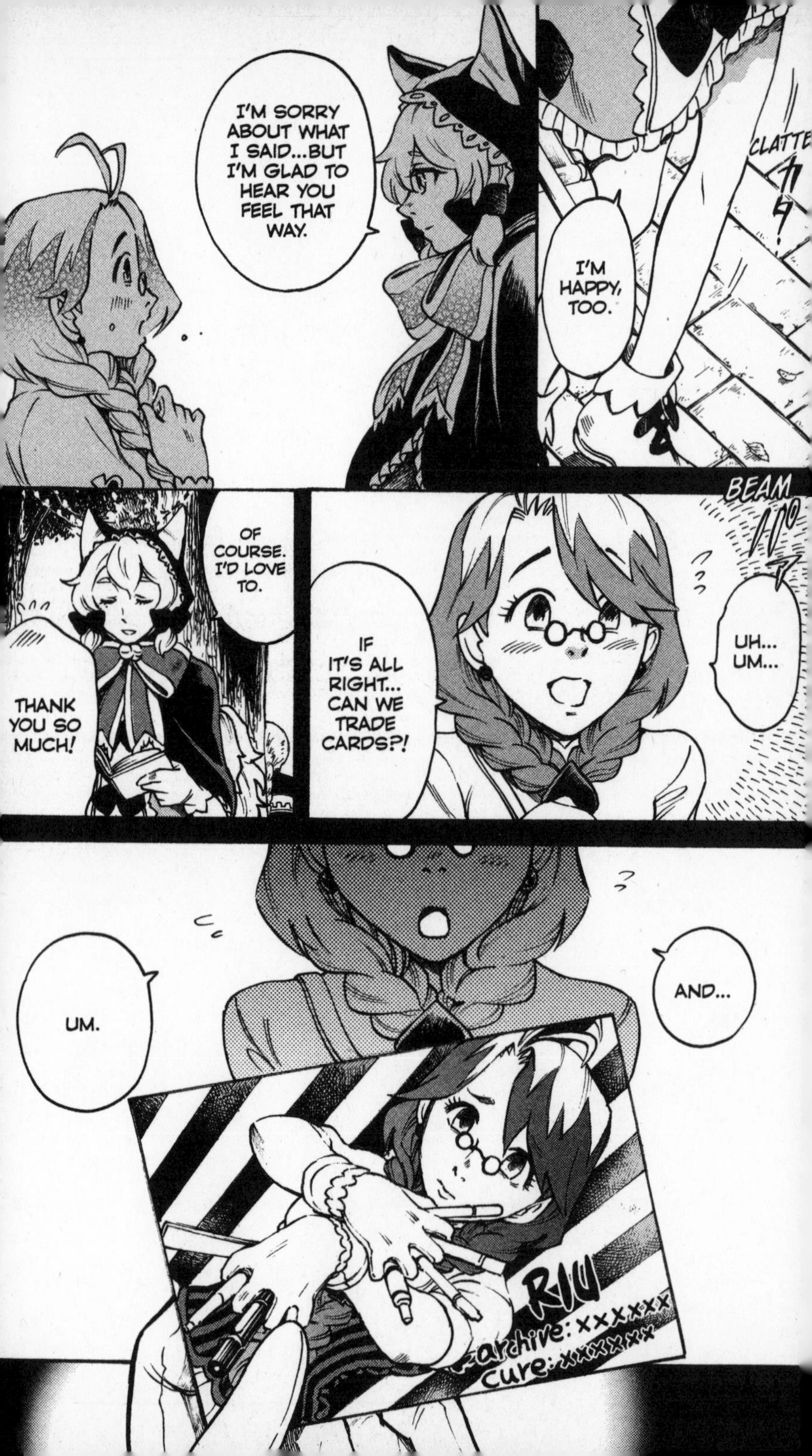
CLATTE
I'M HAPPY, TOO.
I'M SORRY ABOUT WHAT I SAID...BUT I'M GLAD TO HEAR YOU FEEL THAT WAY.
BEAM
UH... UM...
IF IT'S ALL RIGHT... CAN WE TRADE CARDS?!
OF COURSE. I'D LOVE TO.
THANK YOU SO MUCH!
AND...
UM.
RIU
archive: xxxxxx
cure: xxxxxx

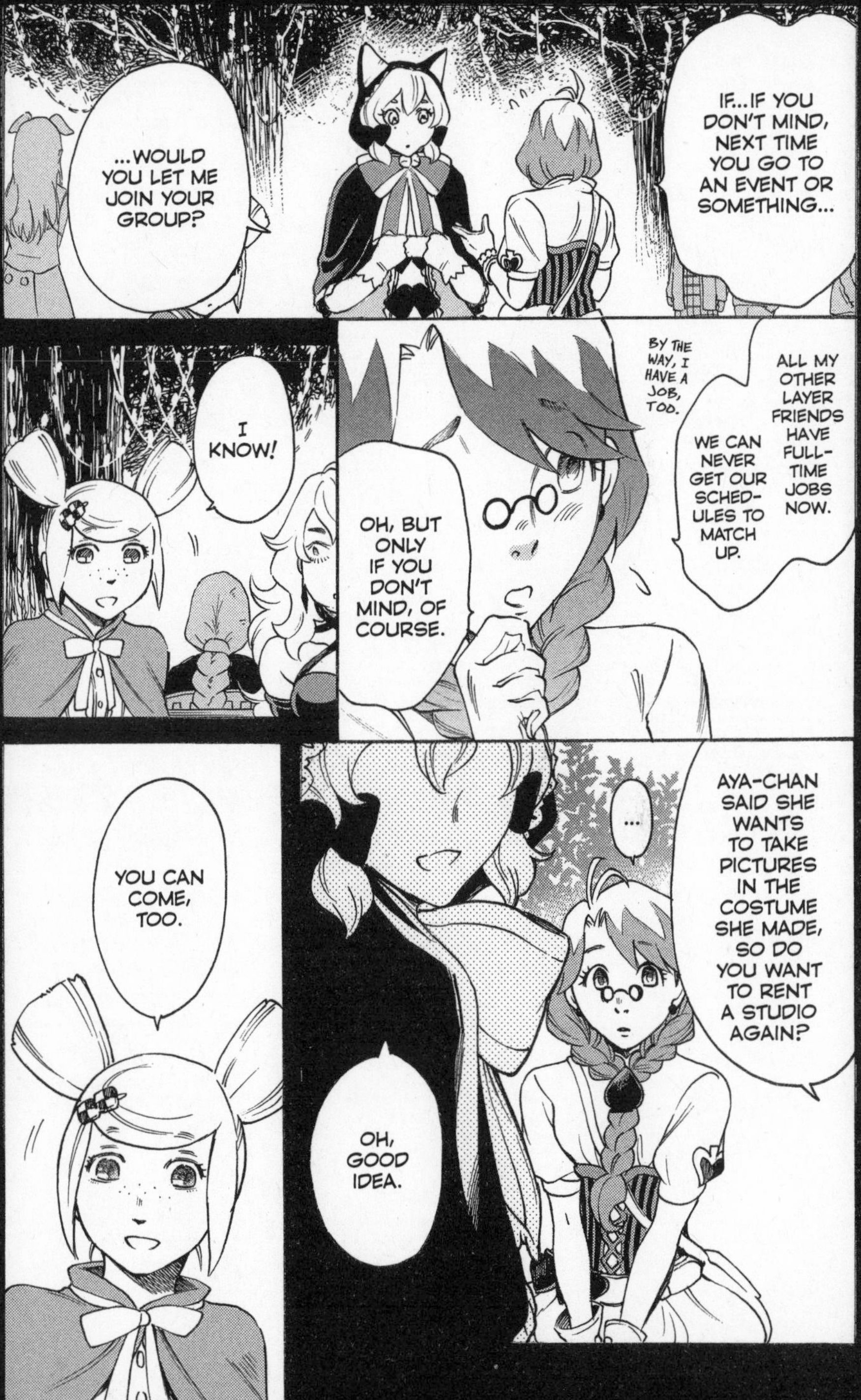
IF...IF YOU DON'T MIND, NEXT TIME YOU GO TO AN EVENT OR SOMETHING...
...WOULD YOU LET ME JOIN YOUR GROUP?
ALL MY OTHER LAYER FRIENDS HAVE FULL-TIME JOBS NOW.
WE CAN NEVER GET OUR SCHEDULES TO MATCH UP.
BY THE WAY, I HAVE A JOB, TOO.
OH, BUT ONLY IF YOU DON'T MIND, OF COURSE.
I KNOW!
AYA-CHAN SAID SHE WANTS TO TAKE PICTURES IN THE COSTUME SHE MADE, SO DO YOU WANT TO RENT A STUDIO AGAIN?
...
OH, GOOD IDEA.
YOU CAN COME, TOO.

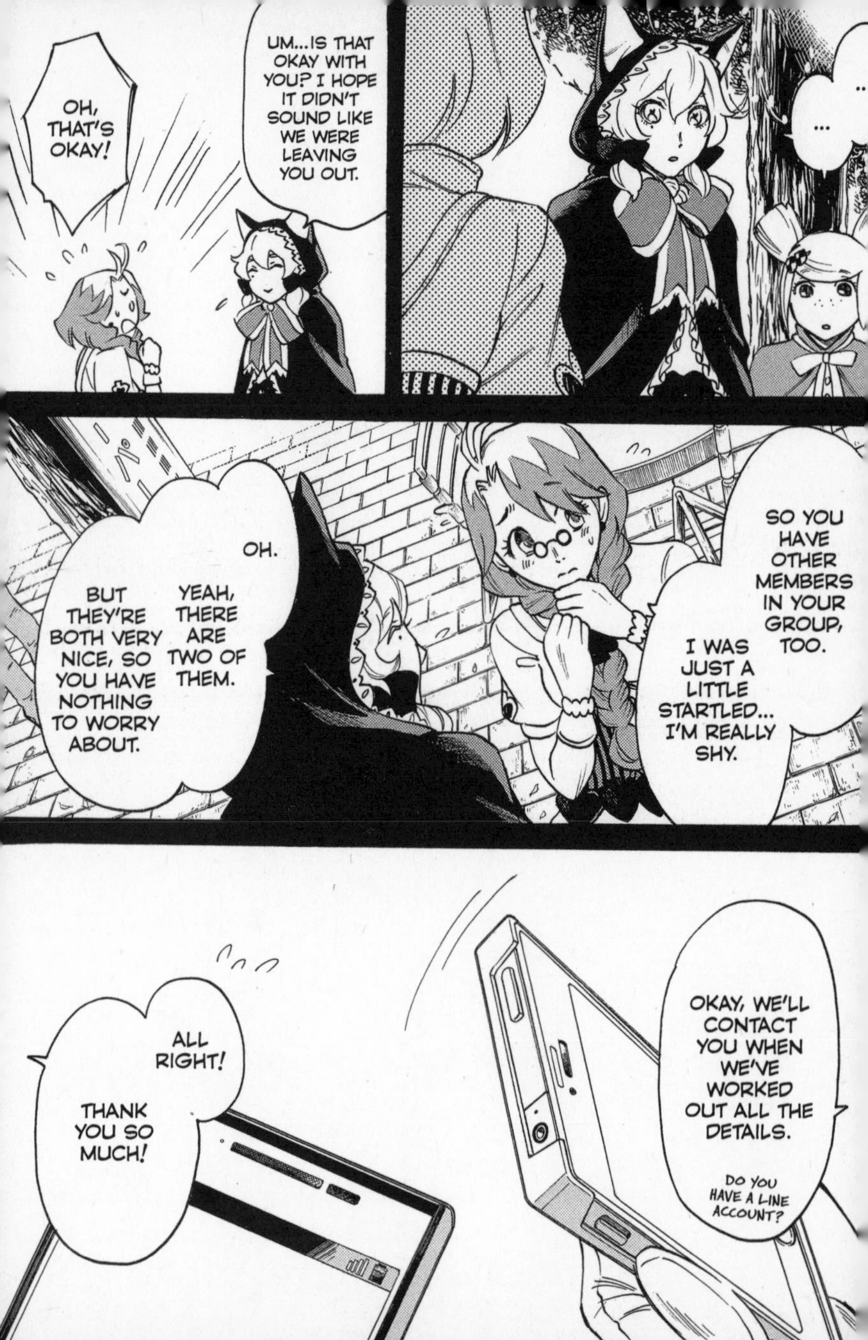
..
...
UM...IS THAT OKAY WITH YOU? I HOPE IT DIDN'T SOUND LIKE WE WERE LEAVING YOU OUT.
OH, THAT'S OKAY!
SO YOU HAVE OTHER MEMBERS IN YOUR GROUP, TOO.
I WAS JUST A LITTLE STARTLED... I'M REALLY SHY.
OH.
YEAH, THERE ARE TWO OF THEM.
BUT THEY'RE BOTH VERY NICE, SO YOU HAVE NOTHING TO WORRY ABOUT.
OKAY, WE'LL CONTACT YOU WHEN WE'VE WORKED OUT ALL THE DETAILS.
DO YOU HAVE A LINE ACCOUNT?
ALL RIGHT!
THANK YOU SO MUCH!

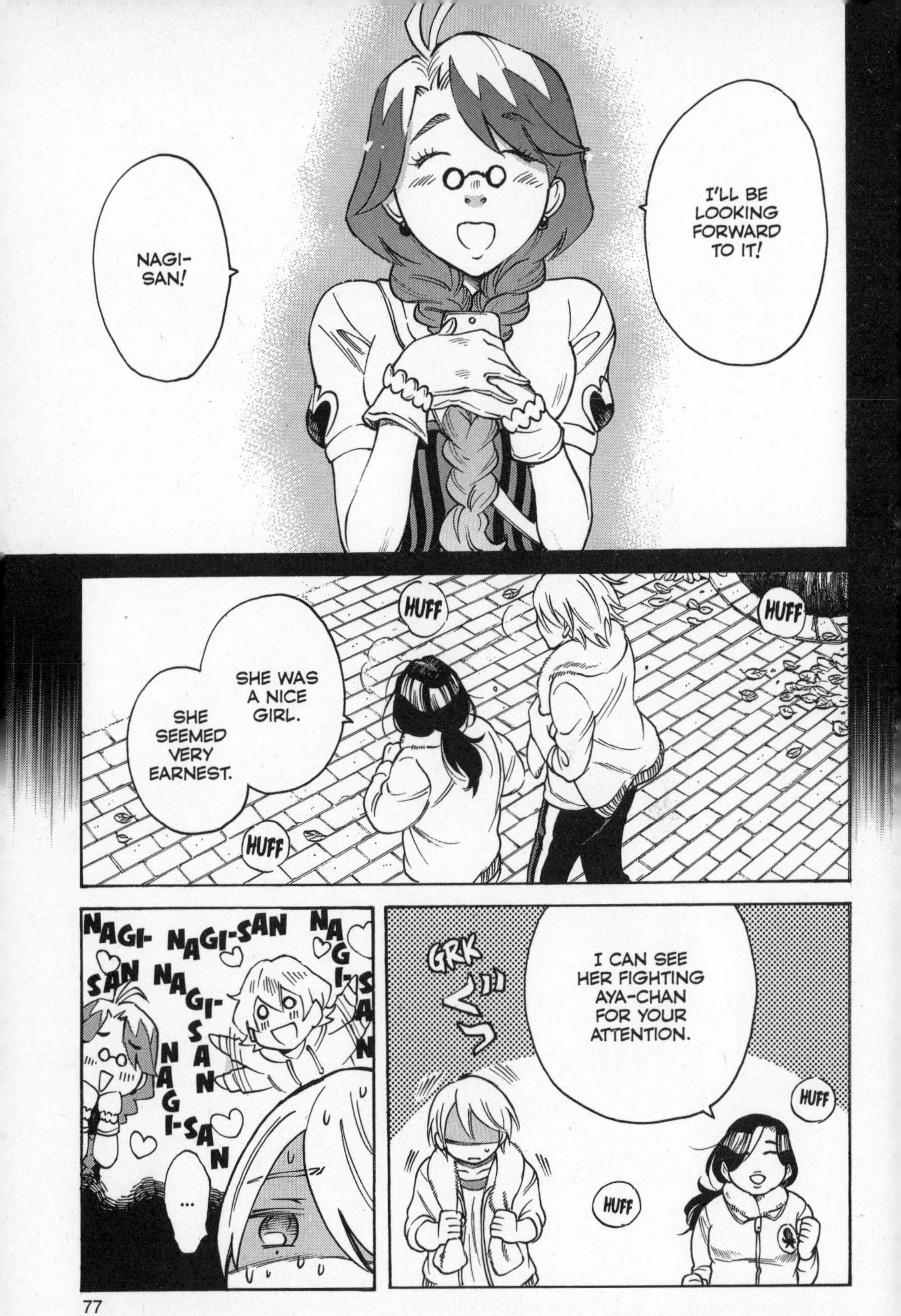

I'LL BE LOOKING FORWARD TO IT!
NAGI-SAN!
HUFF
HUFF
SHE WAS A NICE GIRL.
SHE SEEMED VERY EARNEST.
HUFF
I CAN SEE HER FIGHTING AYA-CHAN FOR YOUR ATTENTION.
GRK
HUFF
HUFF
NAGI-SAN
NAGI-SAN
NAGI-SAN
NAGI-SAN
NAGI-SAN
NAGI-SAN
...

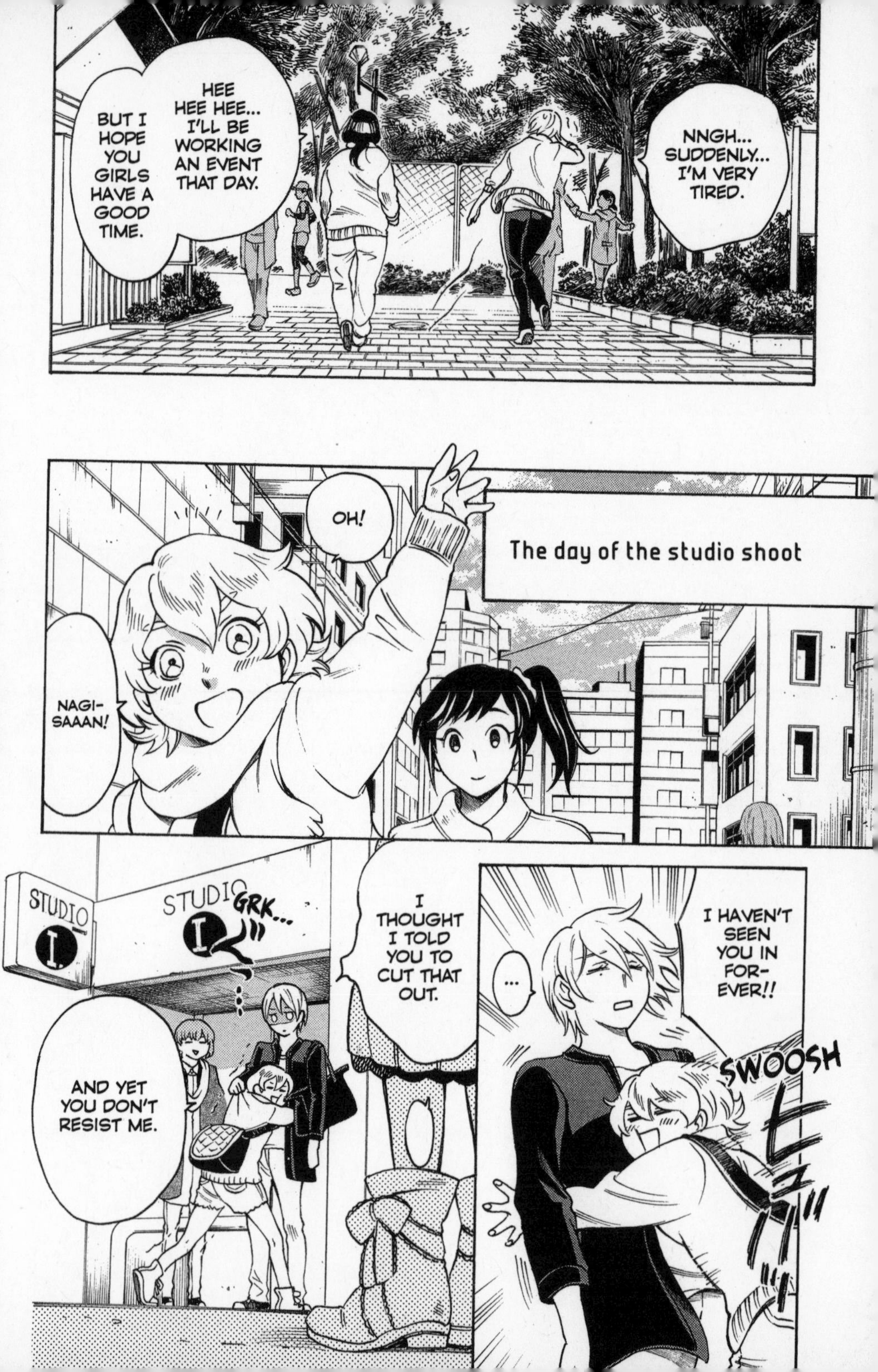
NNGH... SUDDENLY... I'M VERY TIRED.
HEE HEE HEE... I'LL BE WORKING AN EVENT THAT DAY.
BUT I HOPE YOU GIRLS HAVE A GOOD TIME.
The day of the studio shoot
OH!
NAGI-SAAAN!
I HAVEN'T SEEN YOU IN FOR-EVER!!
...
SWOOSH
I THOUGHT I TOLD YOU TO CUT THAT OUT.
STUDIO I
STUDIO I
GRK...
AND YET YOU DON'T RESIST ME.

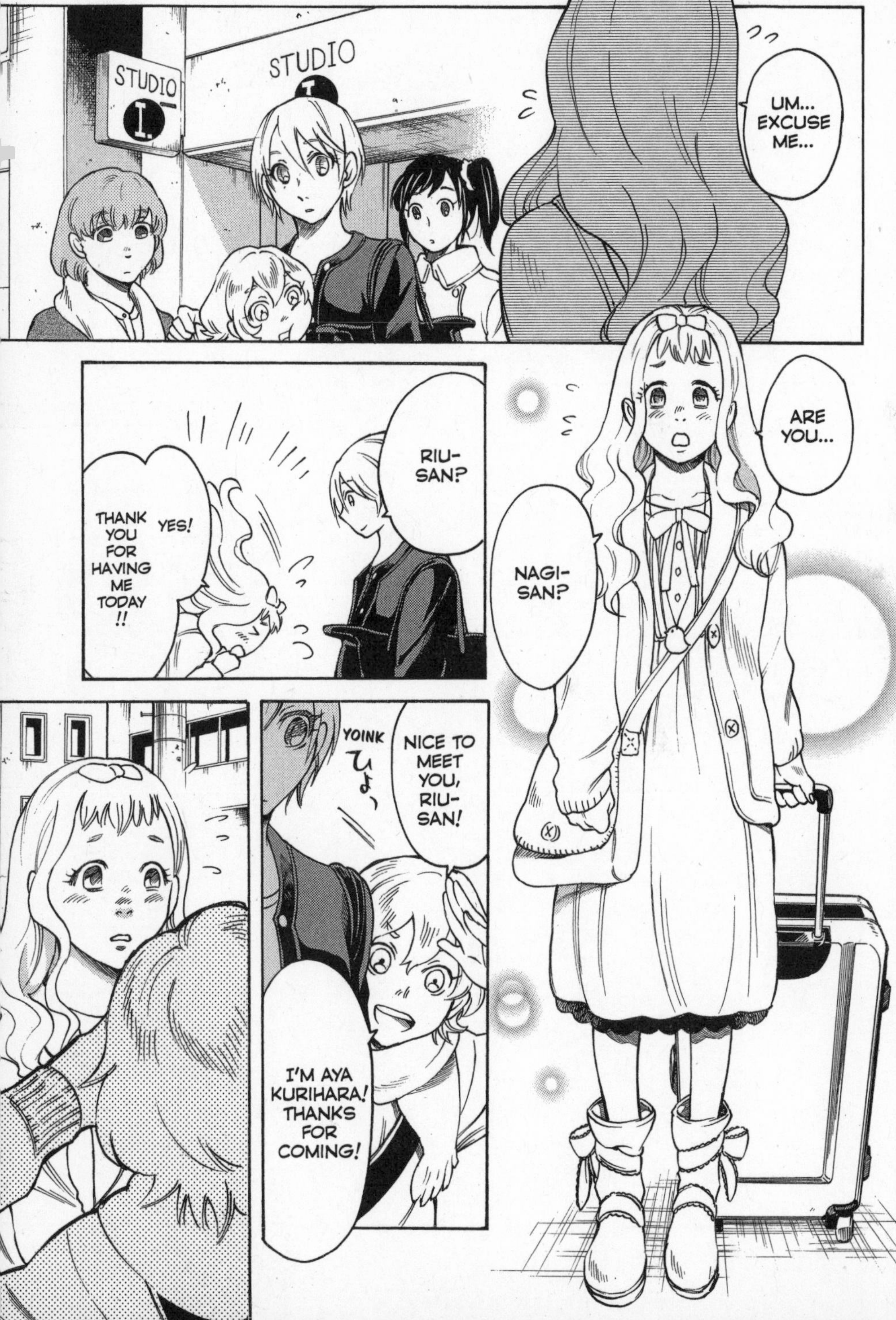
STUDIO
T
STUDIO
I.
UM... EXCUSE ME...
ARE YOU...
NAGI-SAN?
RIU-SAN?
YES!
THANK YOU FOR HAVING ME TODAY!!
NICE TO MEET YOU, RIU-SAN!
YOINK
ひょっ
I'M AYA KURIHARA! THANKS FOR COMING!

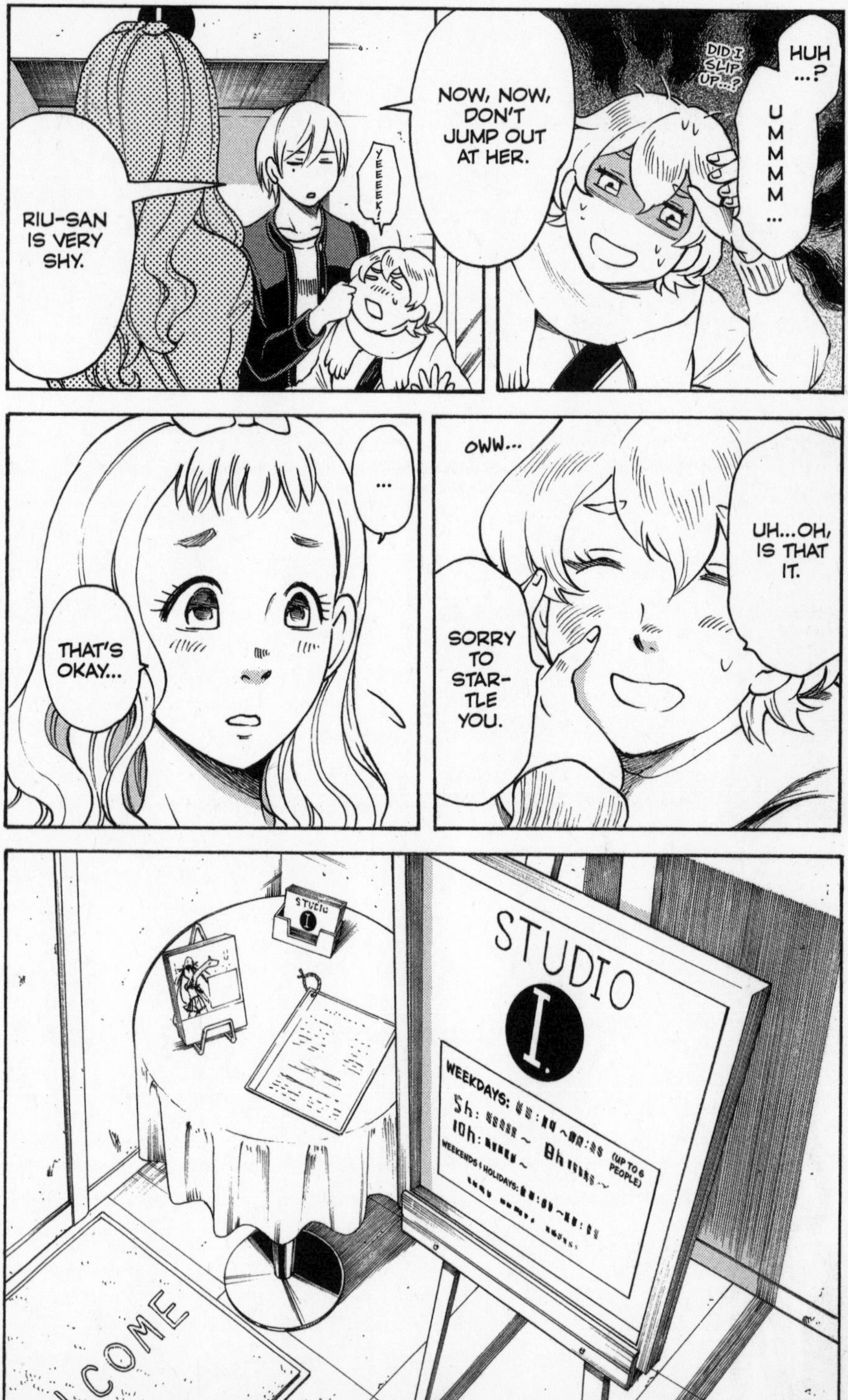
HUH ...?
UMMMM ...
DID I SLIP UP...?
NOW, NOW, DON'T JUMP OUT AT HER.
YEEEEK!
RIU-SAN IS VERY SHY.
OWW...
UH...OH, IS THAT IT.
SORRY TO STAR-TLE YOU.
...
THAT'S OKAY...
STUDIO
I.
WEEKDAYS:
(UP TO 6 PEOPLE)
WEEKENDS & HOLIDAYS:

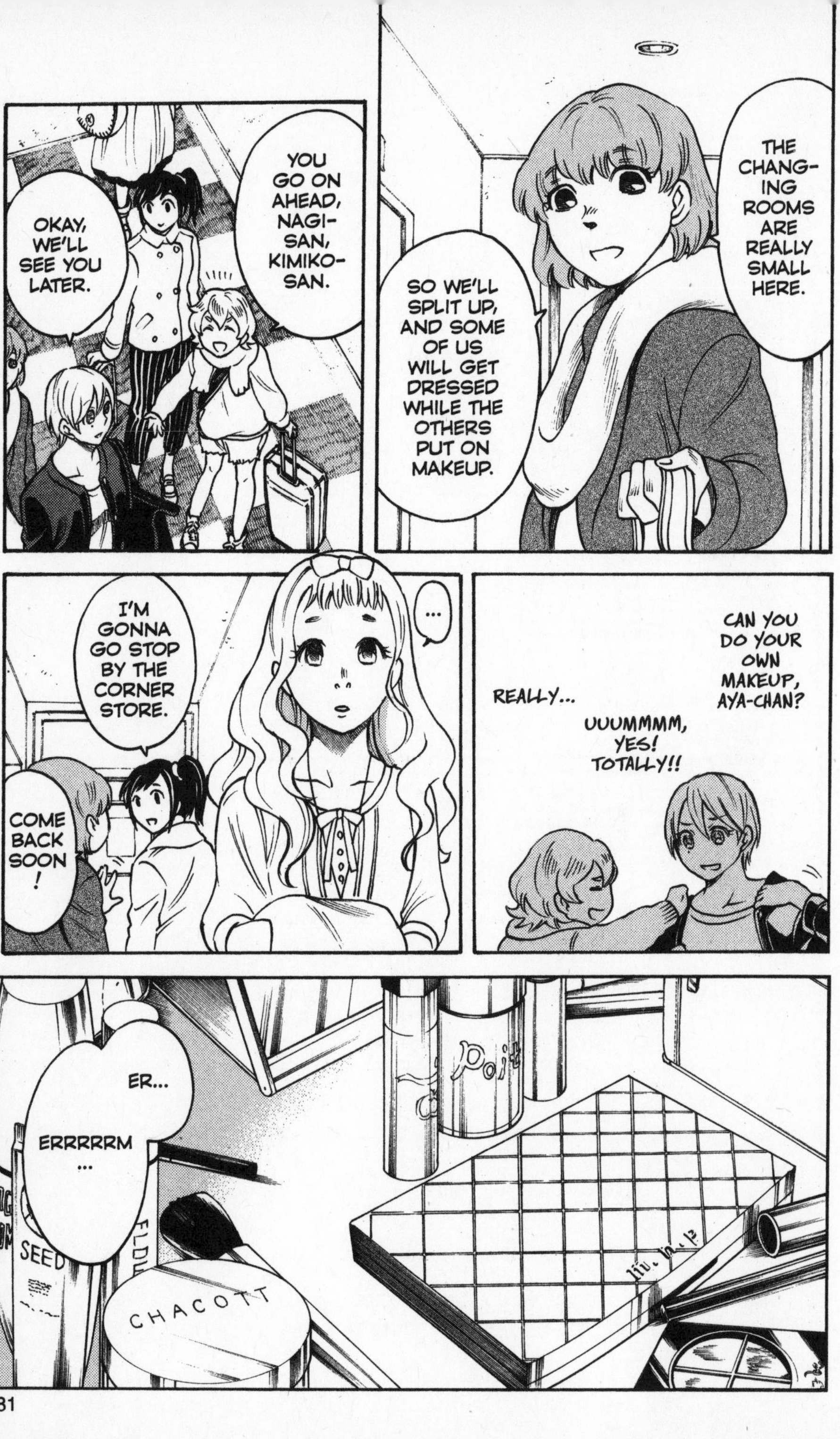
THE CHANGING ROOMS ARE REALLY SMALL HERE.
SO WE'LL SPLIT UP, AND SOME OF US WILL GET DRESSED WHILE THE OTHERS PUT ON MAKEUP.
YOU GO ON AHEAD, NAGI-SAN, KIMIKO-SAN.
OKAY, WE'LL SEE YOU LATER.
CAN YOU DO YOUR OWN MAKEUP, AYA-CHAN?
REALLY...
UUUMMMM, YES! TOTALLY!!
...
I'M GONNA GO STOP BY THE CORNER STORE.
COME BACK SOON!
ER...
ERRRRRM ...
Poit
SEED
CHACOTT

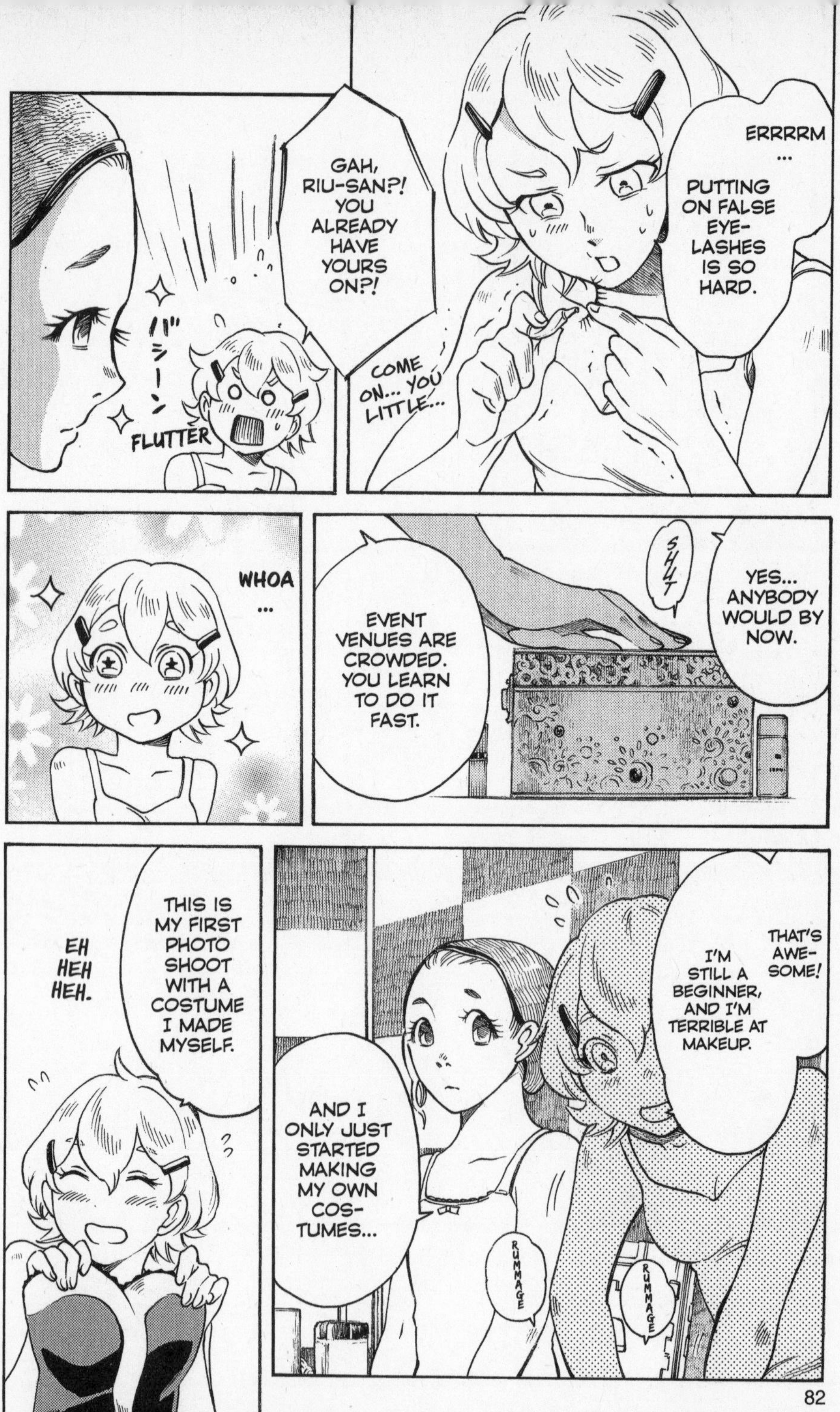
ERRRRM ...
PUTTING ON FALSE EYE-LASHES IS SO HARD.
COME ON... YOU LITTLE...
GAH, RIU-SAN?! YOU ALREADY HAVE YOURS ON?!
バシーン
FLUTTER
YES... ANYBODY WOULD BY NOW.
SHUT
EVENT VENUES ARE CROWDED. YOU LEARN TO DO IT FAST.
WHOA ...
THAT'S AWE-SOME!
I'M STILL A BEGINNER, AND I'M TERRIBLE AT MAKEUP.
AND I ONLY JUST STARTED MAKING MY OWN COS-TUMES...
RUMMAGE
RUMMAGE
THIS IS MY FIRST PHOTO SHOOT WITH A COSTUME I MADE MYSELF.
EH HEH HEH.

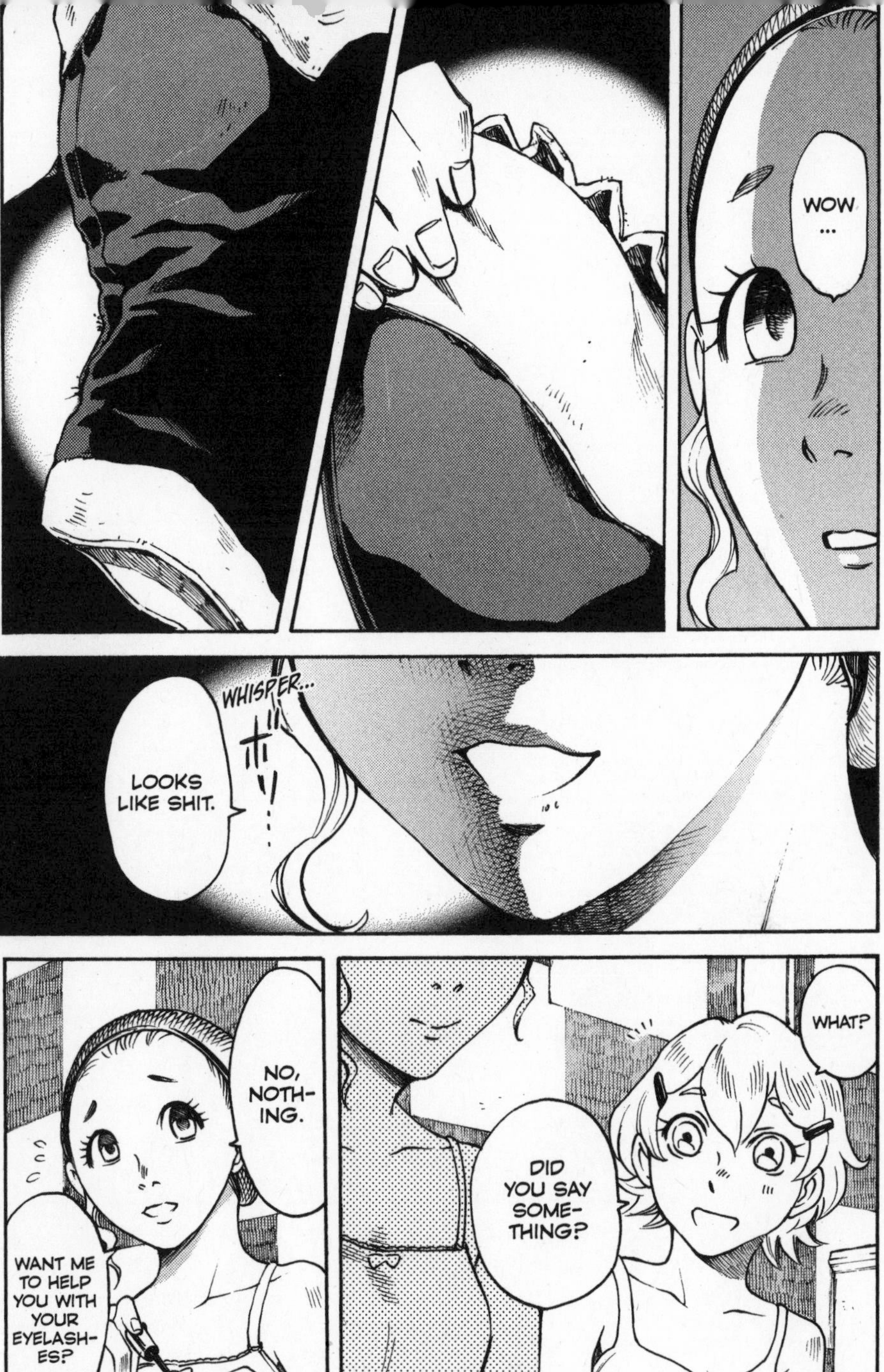
WOW ...
WHISPER...
LOOKS LIKE SHIT.
WHAT?
DID YOU SAY SOME-THING?
NO, NOTH-ING.
WANT ME TO HELP YOU WITH YOUR EYELASH-ES?

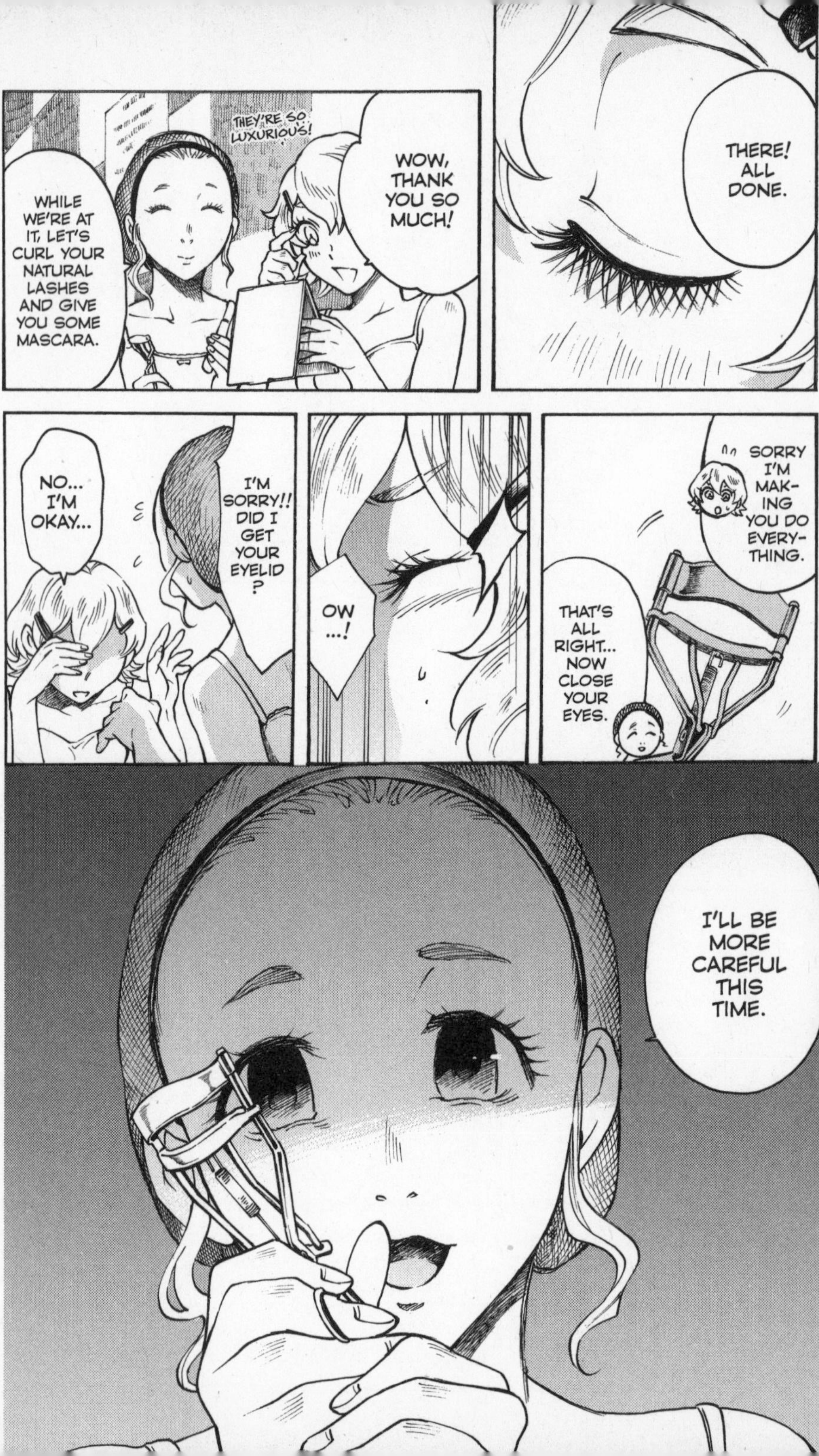
THERE! ALL DONE.
WOW, THANK YOU SO MUCH!
THEY'RE SO LUXURIOUS!
WHILE WE'RE AT IT, LET'S CURL YOUR NATURAL LASHES AND GIVE YOU SOME MASCARA.
SORRY I'M MAKING YOU DO EVERYTHING.
THAT'S ALL RIGHT... NOW CLOSE YOUR EYES.
OW ...!
I'M SORRY!! DID I GET YOUR EYELID ?
NO... I'M OKAY...
I'LL BE MORE CAREFUL THIS TIME.

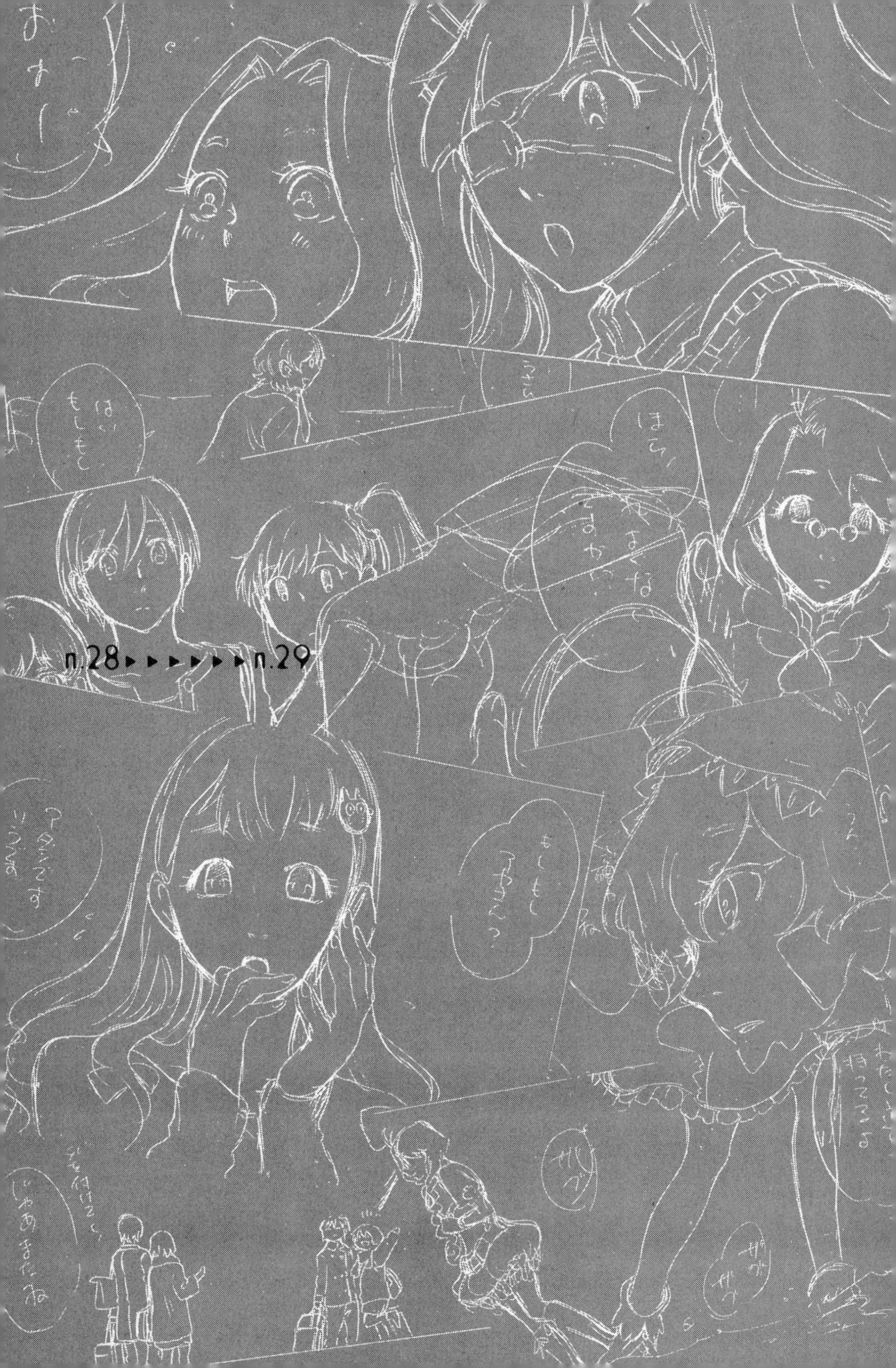
n.28▸▸▸▸▸▸n.29

COSPLAY CARD

COLLECTION

3

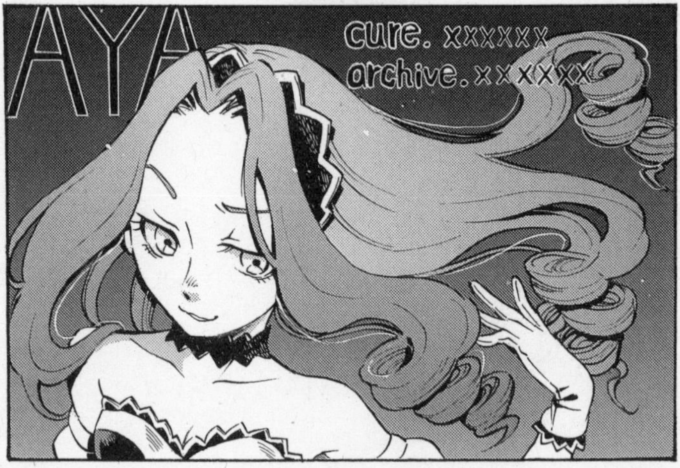
AYA
cure. xxxxxx
archive. xxxxxx

AYA AS LILY

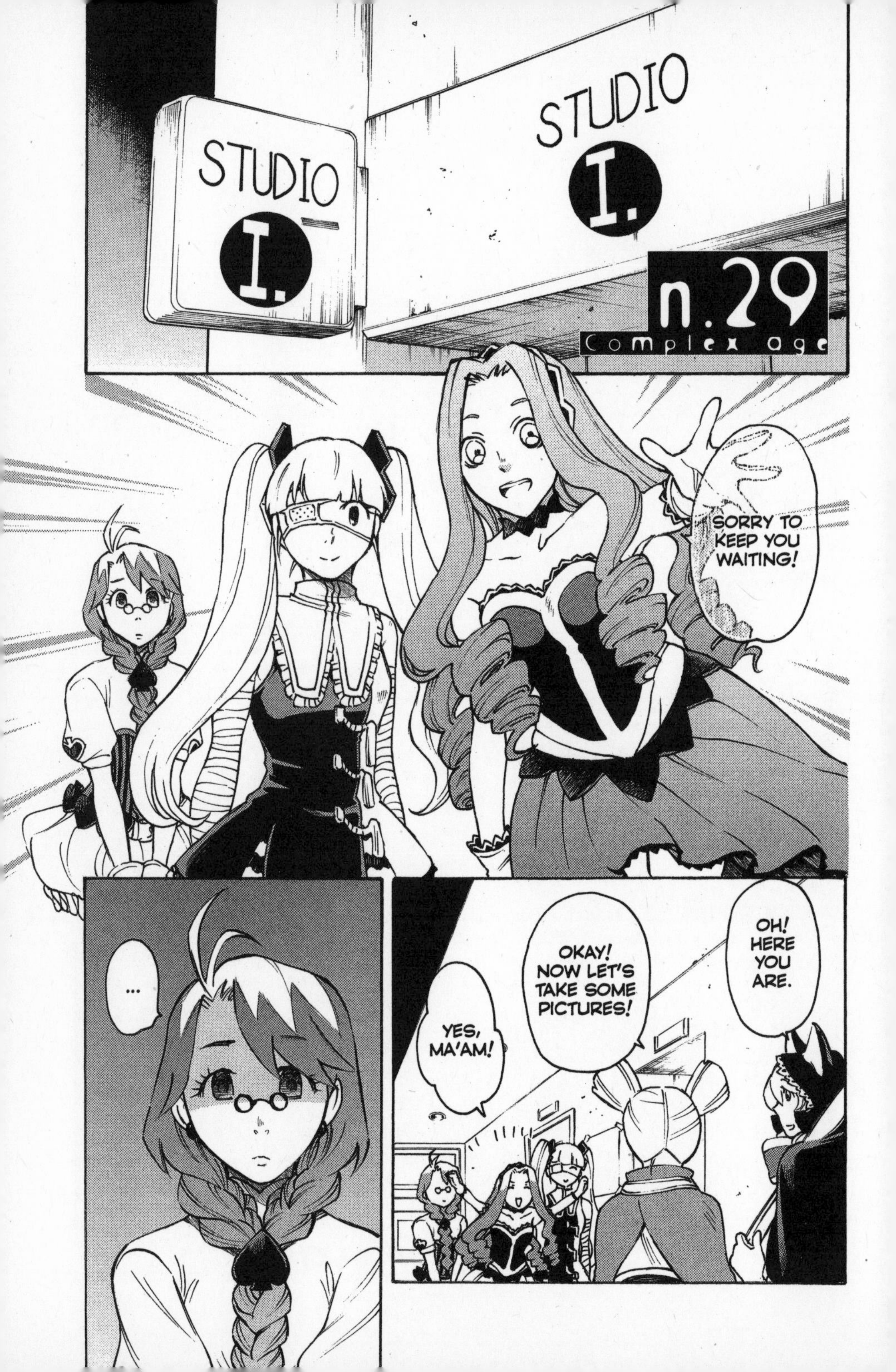
STUDIO I.
STUDIO I.
n.29
Complex age
SORRY TO KEEP YOU WAITING!
OH! HERE YOU ARE.
OKAY! NOW LET'S TAKE SOME PICTURES!
YES, MA'AM!
...

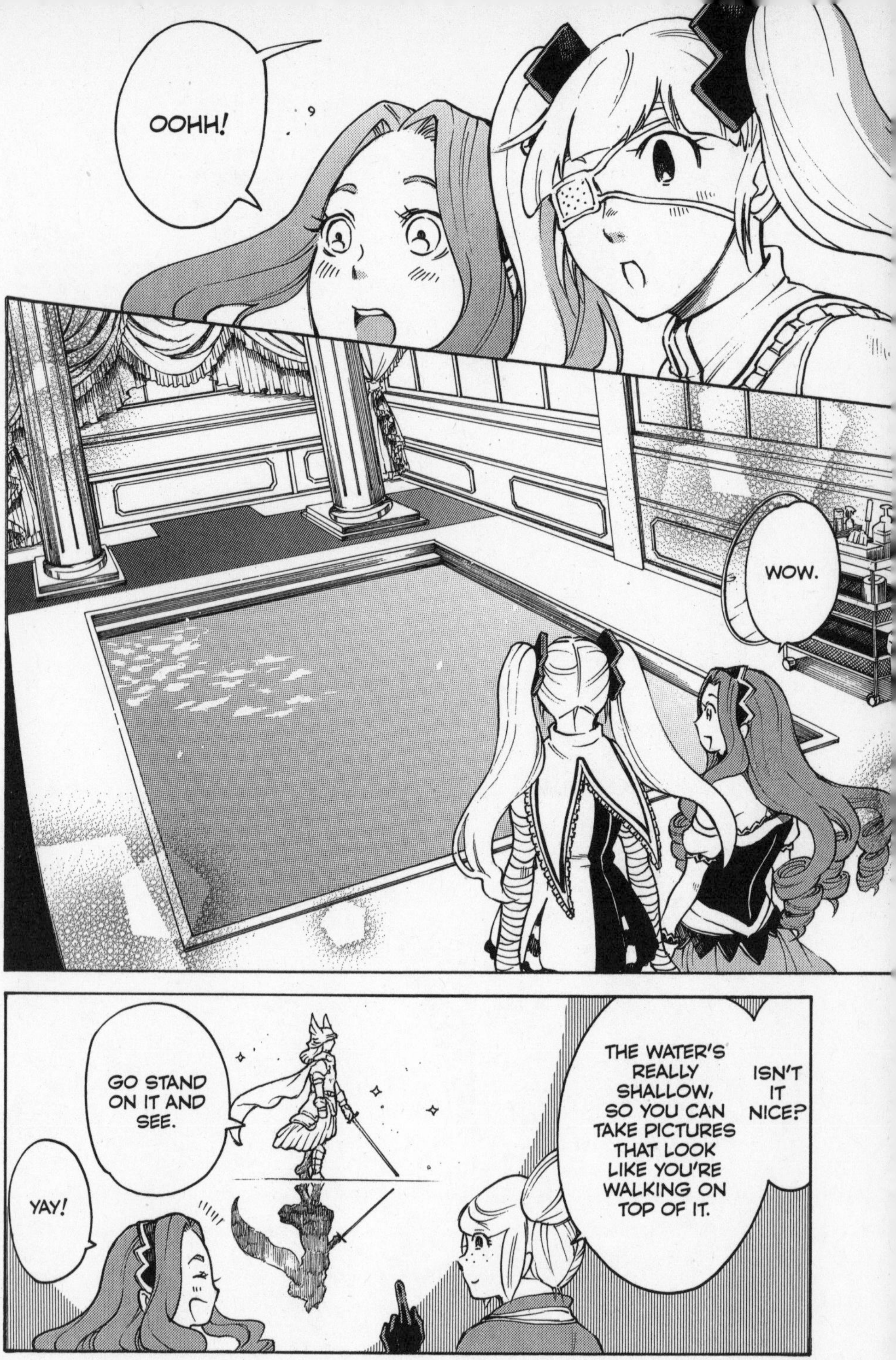
OOHH!
WOW.
ISN'T IT NICE?
THE WATER'S REALLY SHALLOW, SO YOU CAN TAKE PICTURES THAT LOOK LIKE YOU'RE WALKING ON TOP OF IT.
GO STAND ON IT AND SEE.
YAY!

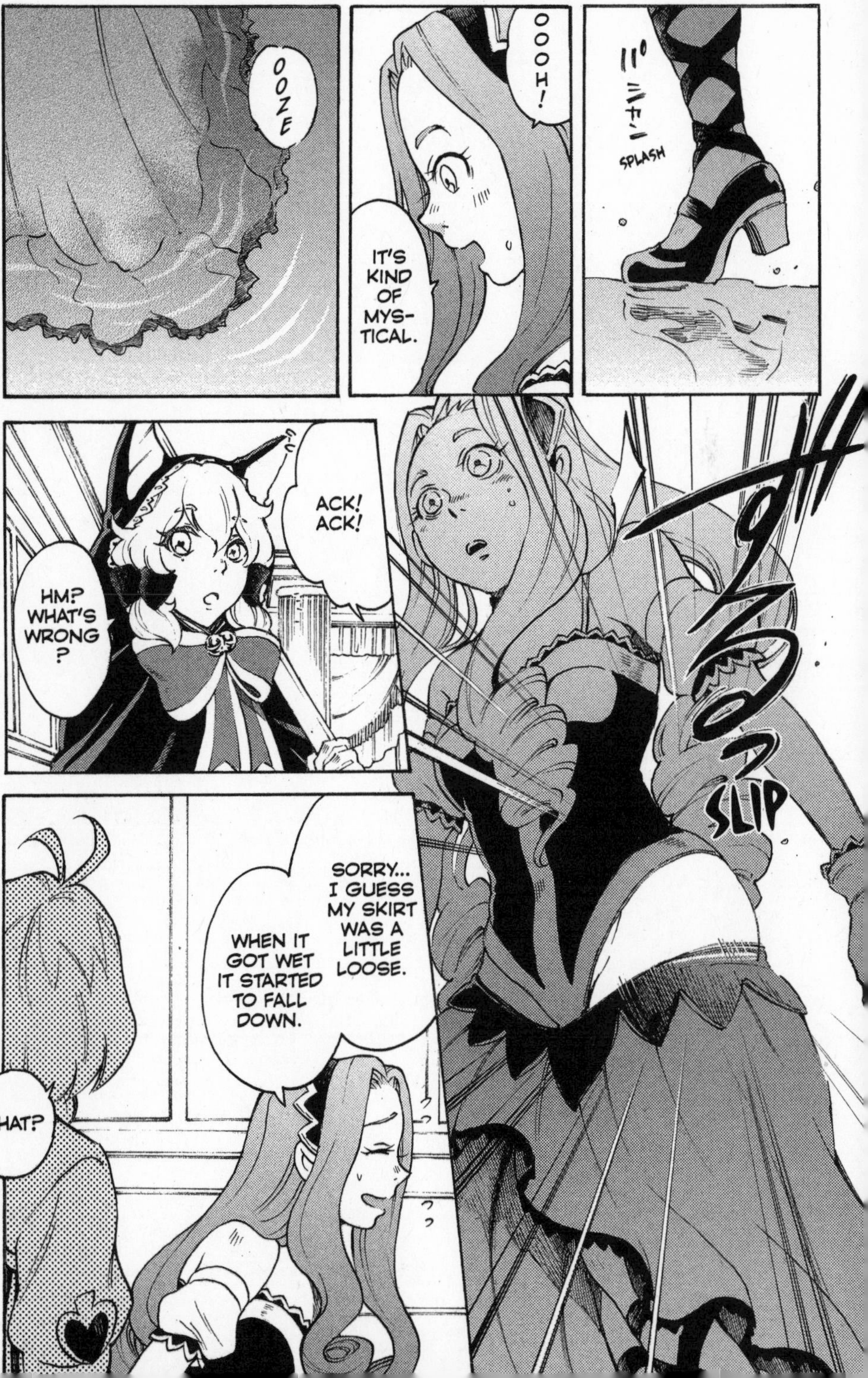
SPLASH
OOOOH!
IT'S KIND OF MYSTICAL.
OOZE
SLIP
ACK! ACK!
HM? WHAT'S WRONG?
SORRY... I GUESS MY SKIRT WAS A LITTLE LOOSE.
WHEN IT GOT WET IT STARTED TO FALL DOWN.
WHAT?

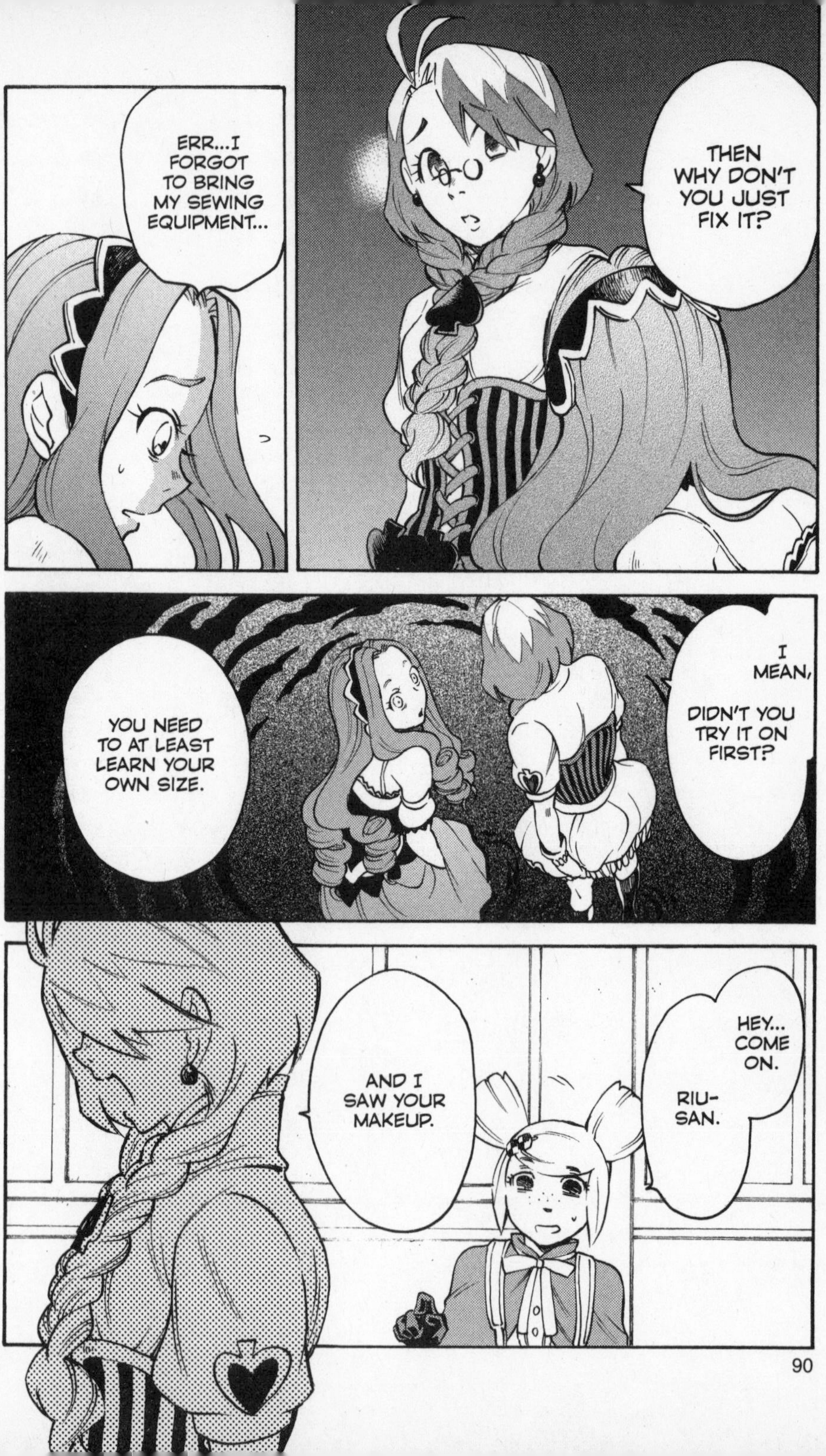
THEN WHY DON'T YOU JUST FIX IT?
ERR...I FORGOT TO BRING MY SEWING EQUIPMENT...
I MEAN,
DIDN'T YOU TRY IT ON FIRST?
YOU NEED TO AT LEAST LEARN YOUR OWN SIZE.
HEY... COME ON.
RIU-SAN.
AND I SAW YOUR MAKEUP.

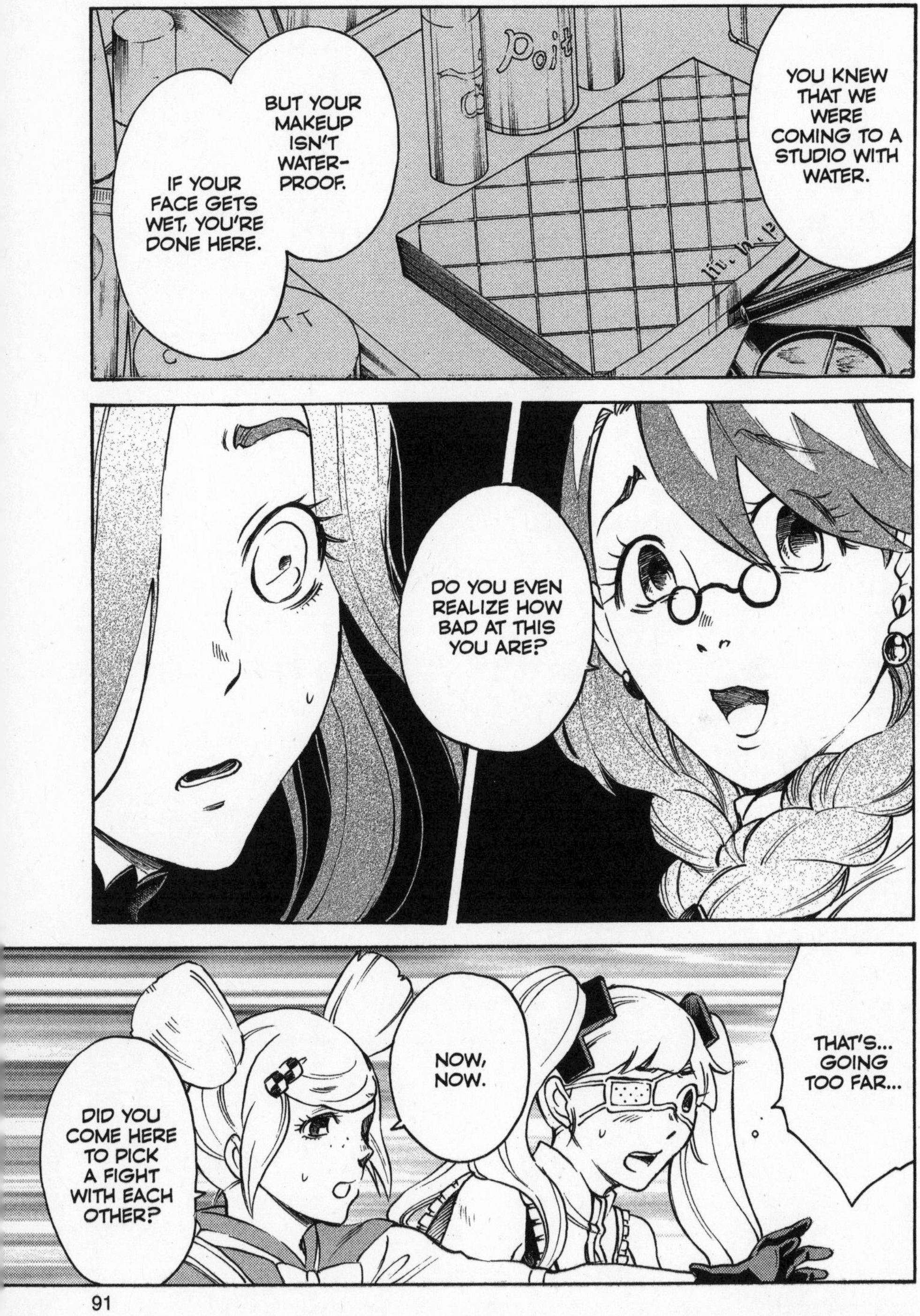
YOU KNEW THAT WE WERE COMING TO A STUDIO WITH WATER.
BUT YOUR MAKEUP ISN'T WATER-PROOF.
IF YOUR FACE GETS WET, YOU'RE DONE HERE.
DO YOU EVEN REALIZE HOW BAD AT THIS YOU ARE?
THAT'S... GOING TOO FAR...
NOW, NOW.
DID YOU COME HERE TO PICK A FIGHT WITH EACH OTHER?

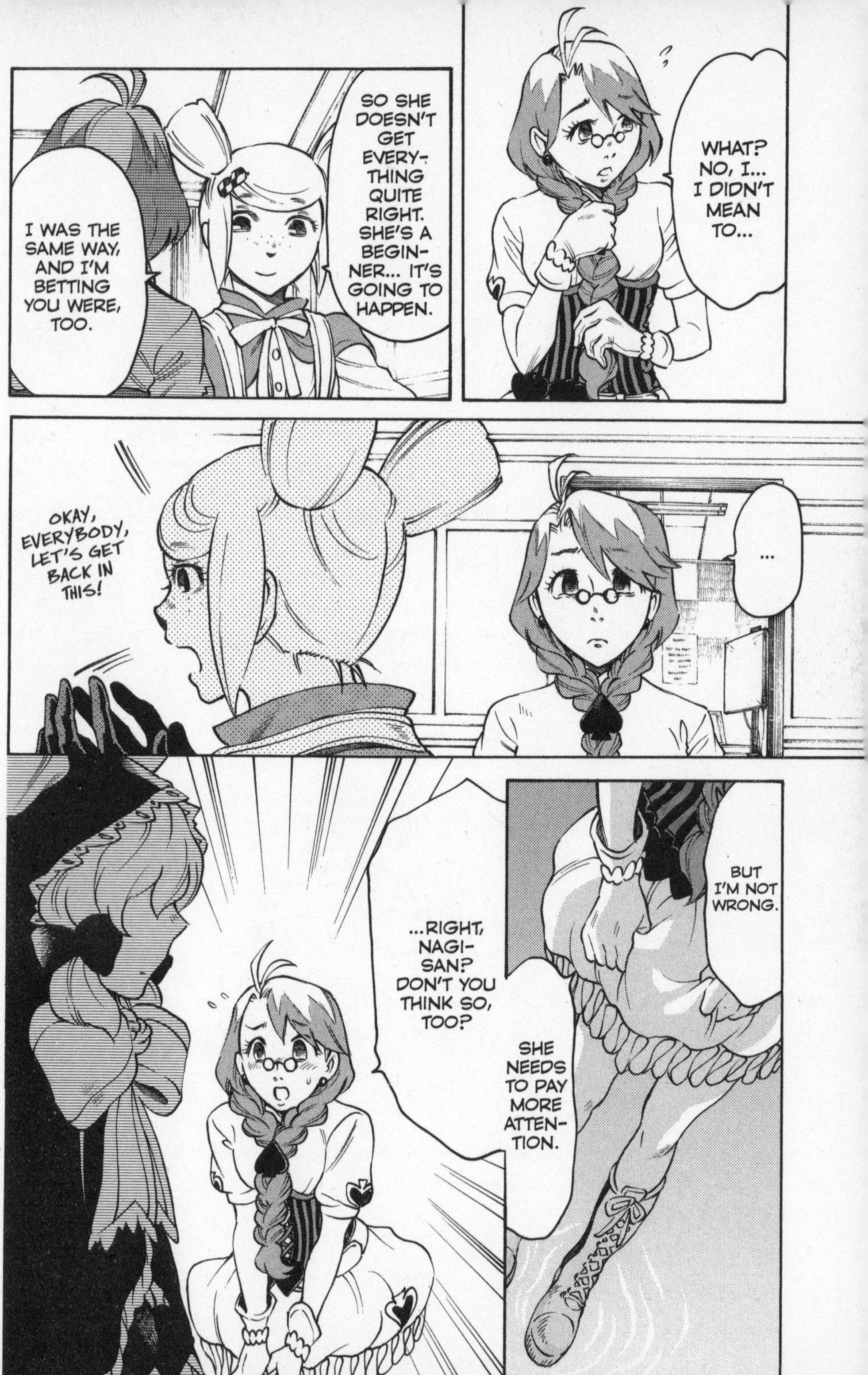
WHAT? NO, I... I DIDN'T MEAN TO...
SO SHE DOESN'T GET EVERY-THING QUITE RIGHT. SHE'S A BEGIN-NER... IT'S GOING TO HAPPEN.
I WAS THE SAME WAY, AND I'M BETTING YOU WERE, TOO.
...
OKAY, EVERYBODY, LET'S GET BACK IN THIS!
BUT I'M NOT WRONG.
SHE NEEDS TO PAY MORE ATTEN-TION.
...RIGHT, NAGI-SAN? DON'T YOU THINK SO, TOO?

SEE?

SO...

YOU MAY BE RIGHT.

YEAH.

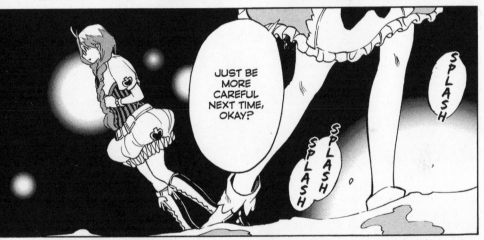

JUST BE MORE CAREFUL NEXT TIME, OKAY?

SPLASH

SPLASH

SPLASH

WHY ...?

I-I'M SORRY.

I BROUGHT MY SEWING STUFF. LET ME SEE IT.

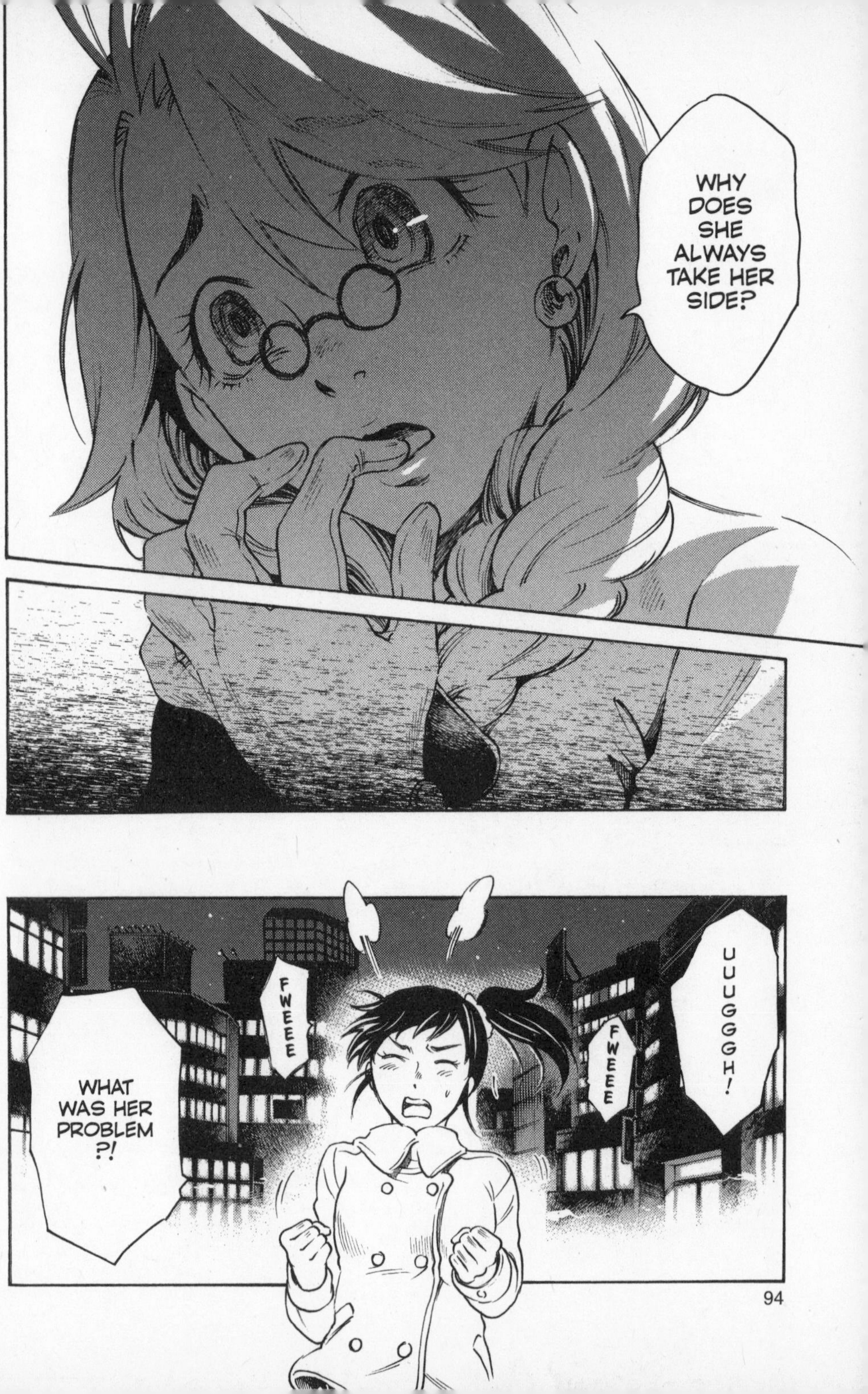
WHY DOES SHE ALWAYS TAKE HER SIDE?
UUUGGGH!
FWEEE
FWEEE
WHAT WAS HER PROBLEM?!

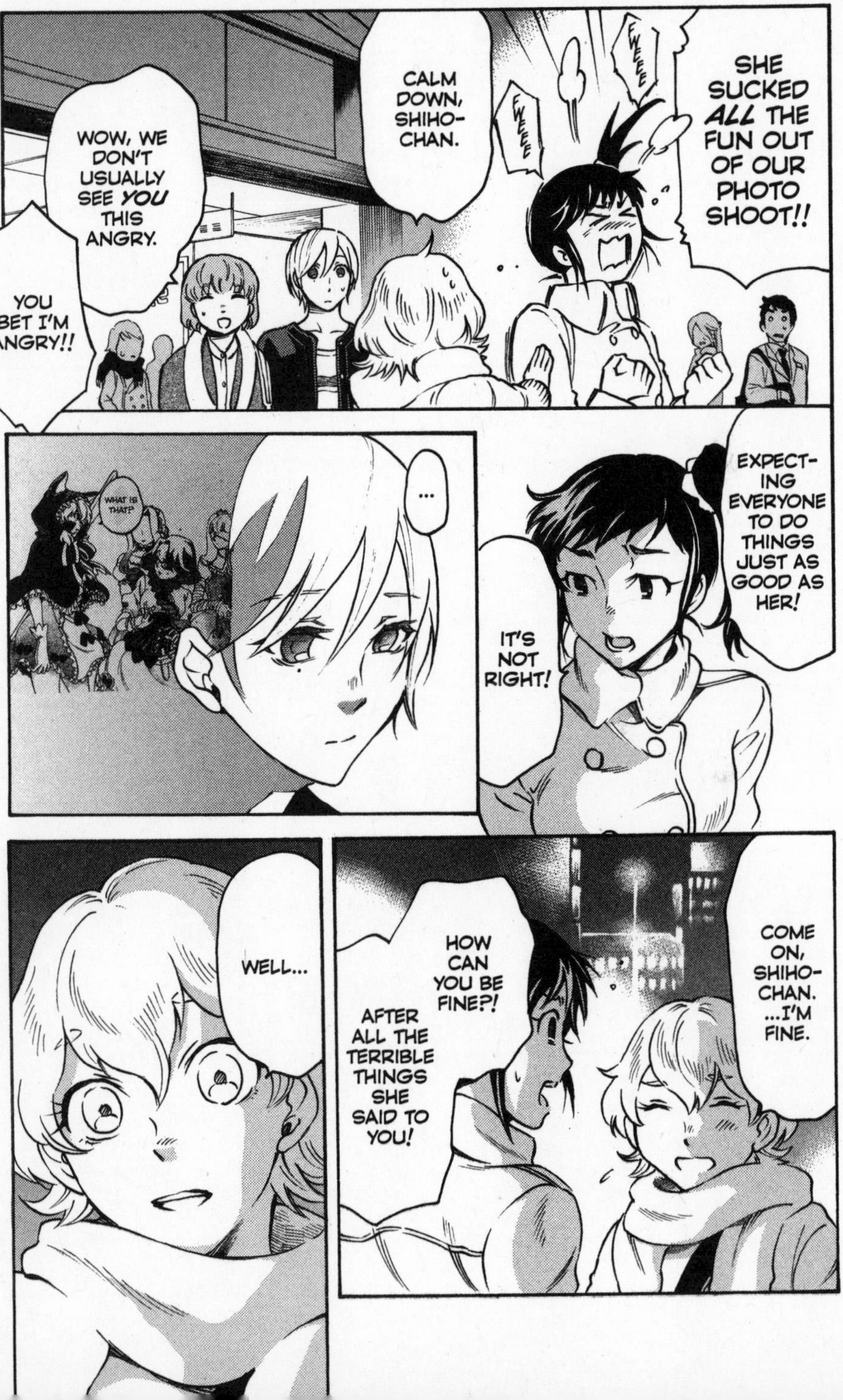
SHE SUCKED ALL THE FUN OUT OF OUR PHOTO SHOOT!!
FWEEE
FWEEE
CALM DOWN, SHIHO-CHAN.
WOW, WE DON'T USUALLY SEE YOU THIS ANGRY.
YOU BET I'M ANGRY!!
EXPECTING EVERYONE TO DO THINGS JUST AS GOOD AS HER!
IT'S NOT RIGHT!
...
WHAT IS THAT?
COME ON, SHIHO-CHAN. ...I'M FINE.
HOW CAN YOU BE FINE?!
AFTER ALL THE TERRIBLE THINGS SHE SAID TO YOU!
WELL...

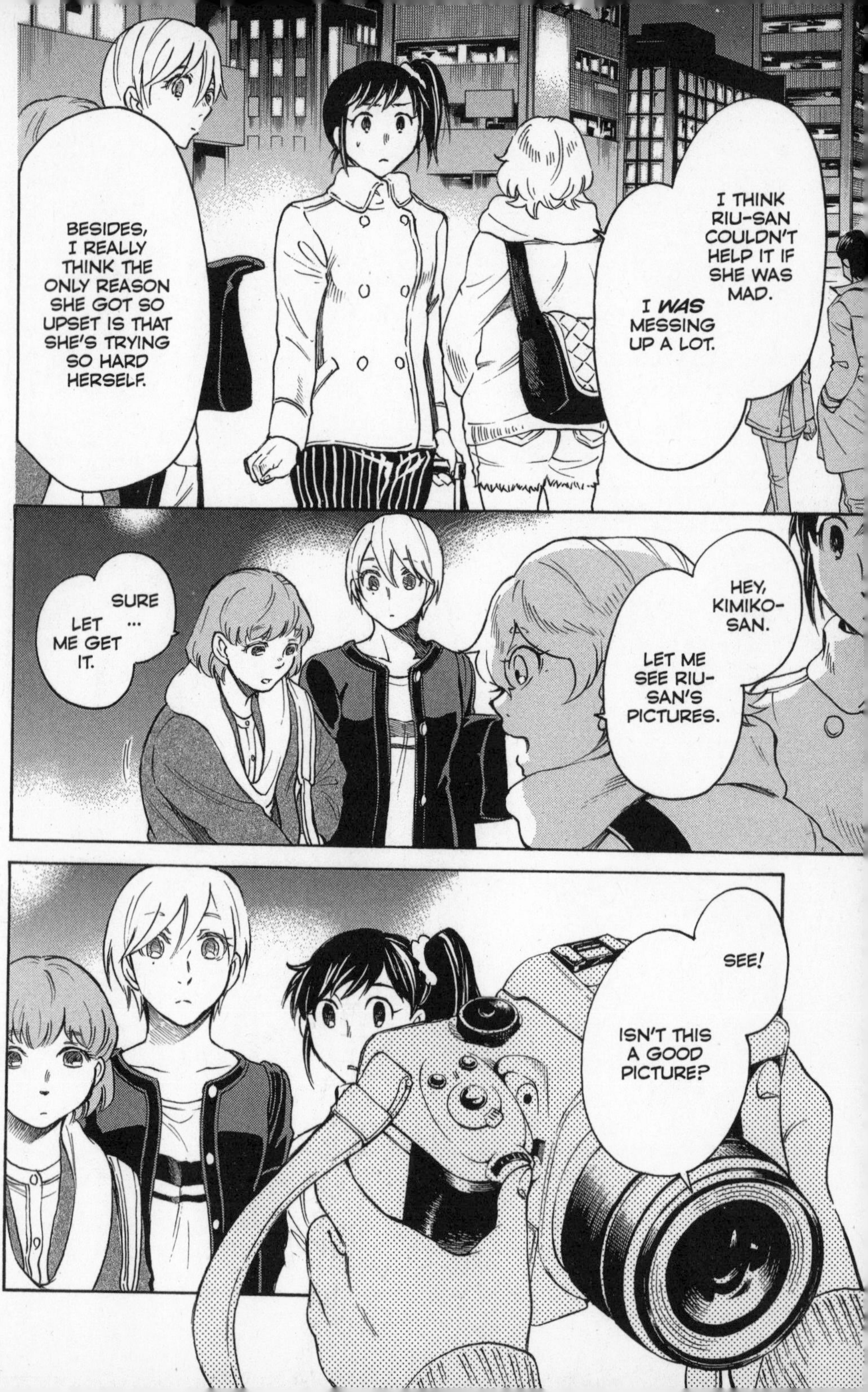
I THINK RIU-SAN COULDN'T HELP IT IF SHE WAS MAD.
I *WAS* MESSING UP A LOT.
BESIDES, I REALLY THINK THE ONLY REASON SHE GOT SO UPSET IS THAT SHE'S TRYING SO HARD HERSELF.
HEY, KIMIKO-SAN.
LET ME SEE RIU-SAN'S PICTURES.
SURE ... LET ME GET IT.
SEE!
ISN'T THIS A GOOD PICTURE?

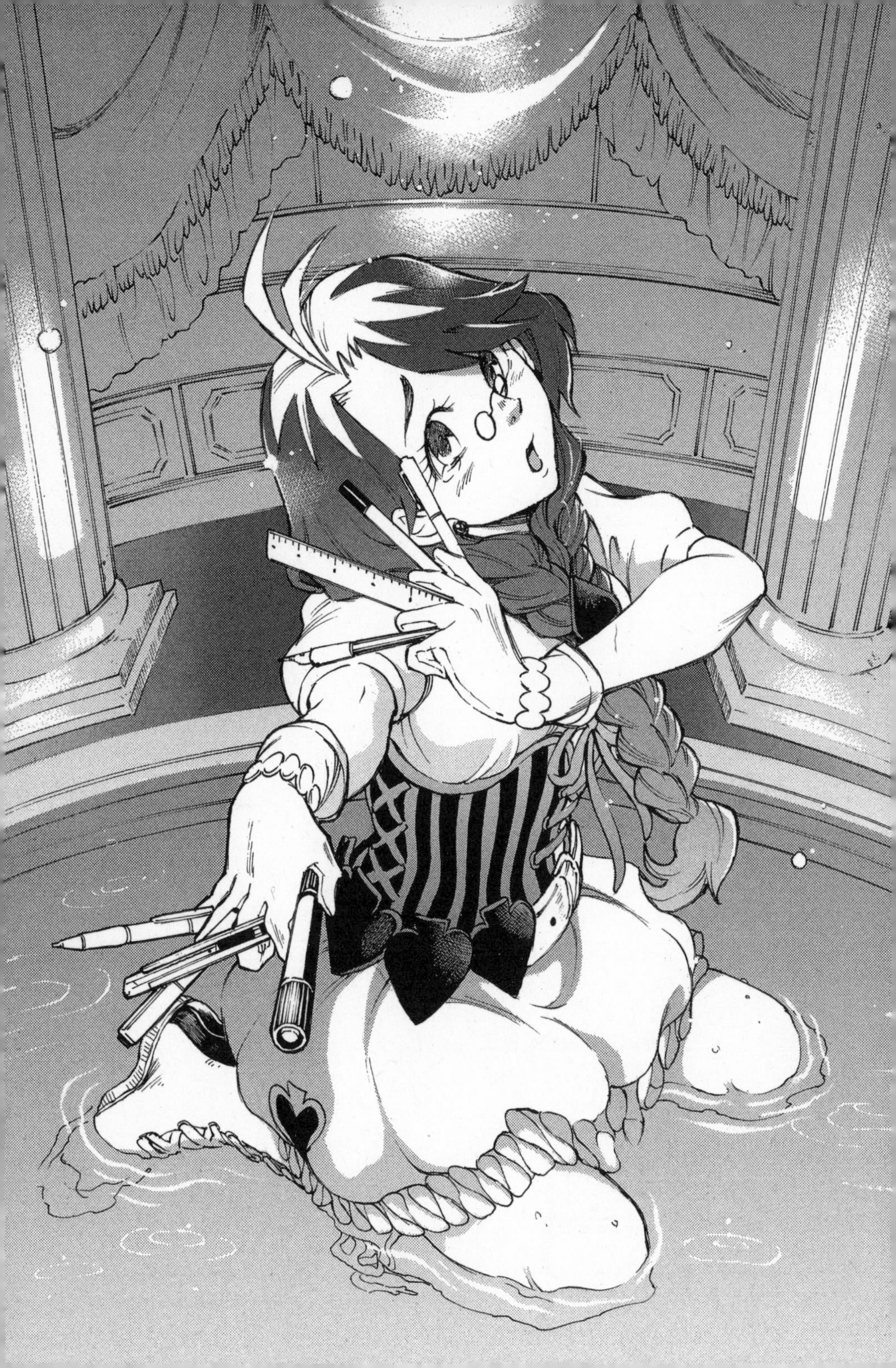

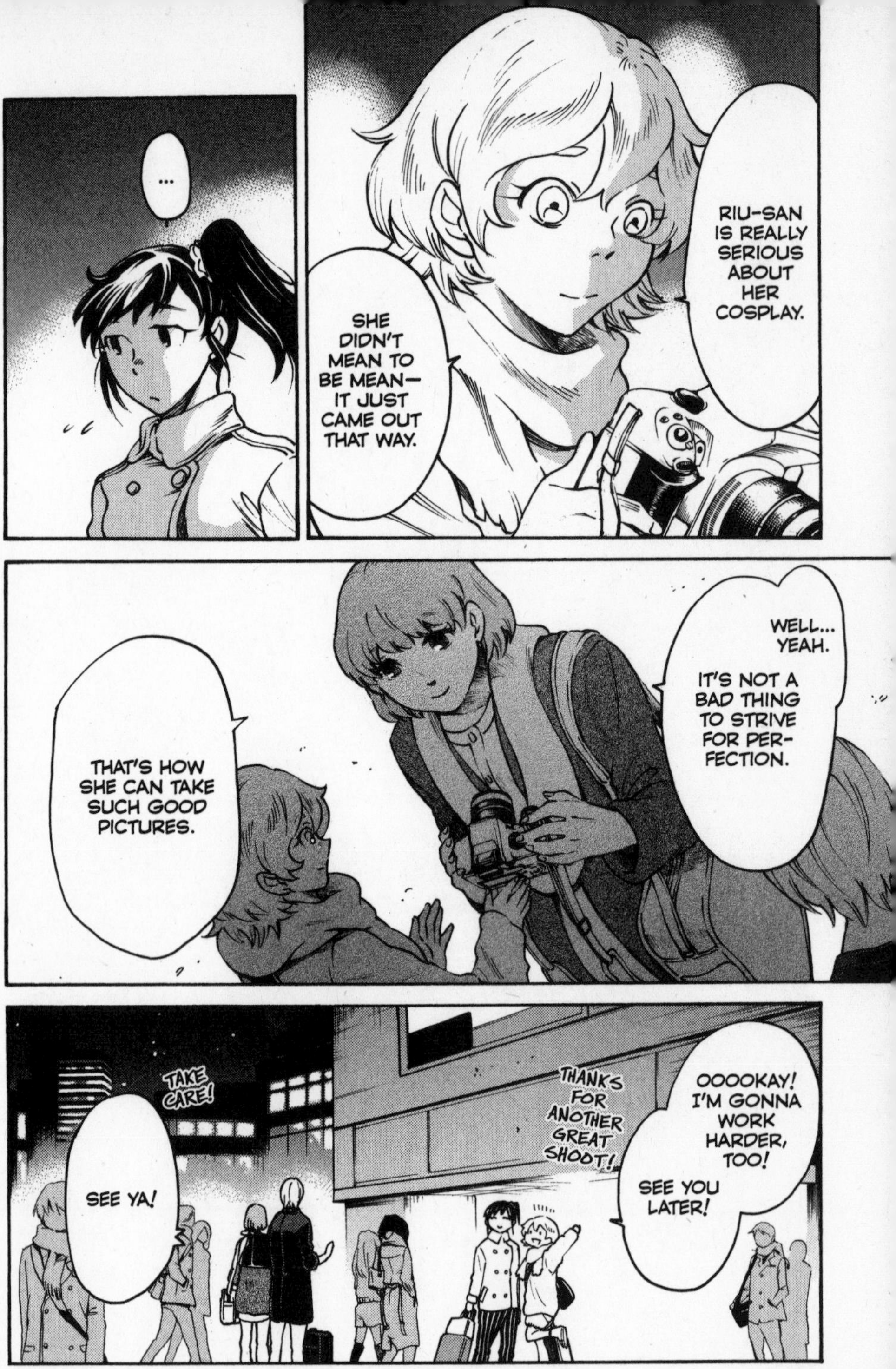
RIU-SAN IS REALLY SERIOUS ABOUT HER COSPLAY.
SHE DIDN'T MEAN TO BE MEAN— IT JUST CAME OUT THAT WAY.
...
WELL... YEAH.
IT'S NOT A BAD THING TO STRIVE FOR PER-FECTION.
THAT'S HOW SHE CAN TAKE SUCH GOOD PICTURES.
OOOOKAY! I'M GONNA WORK HARDER, TOO!
SEE YOU LATER!
THANKS FOR ANOTHER GREAT SHOOT!
TAKE CARE!
SEE YA!

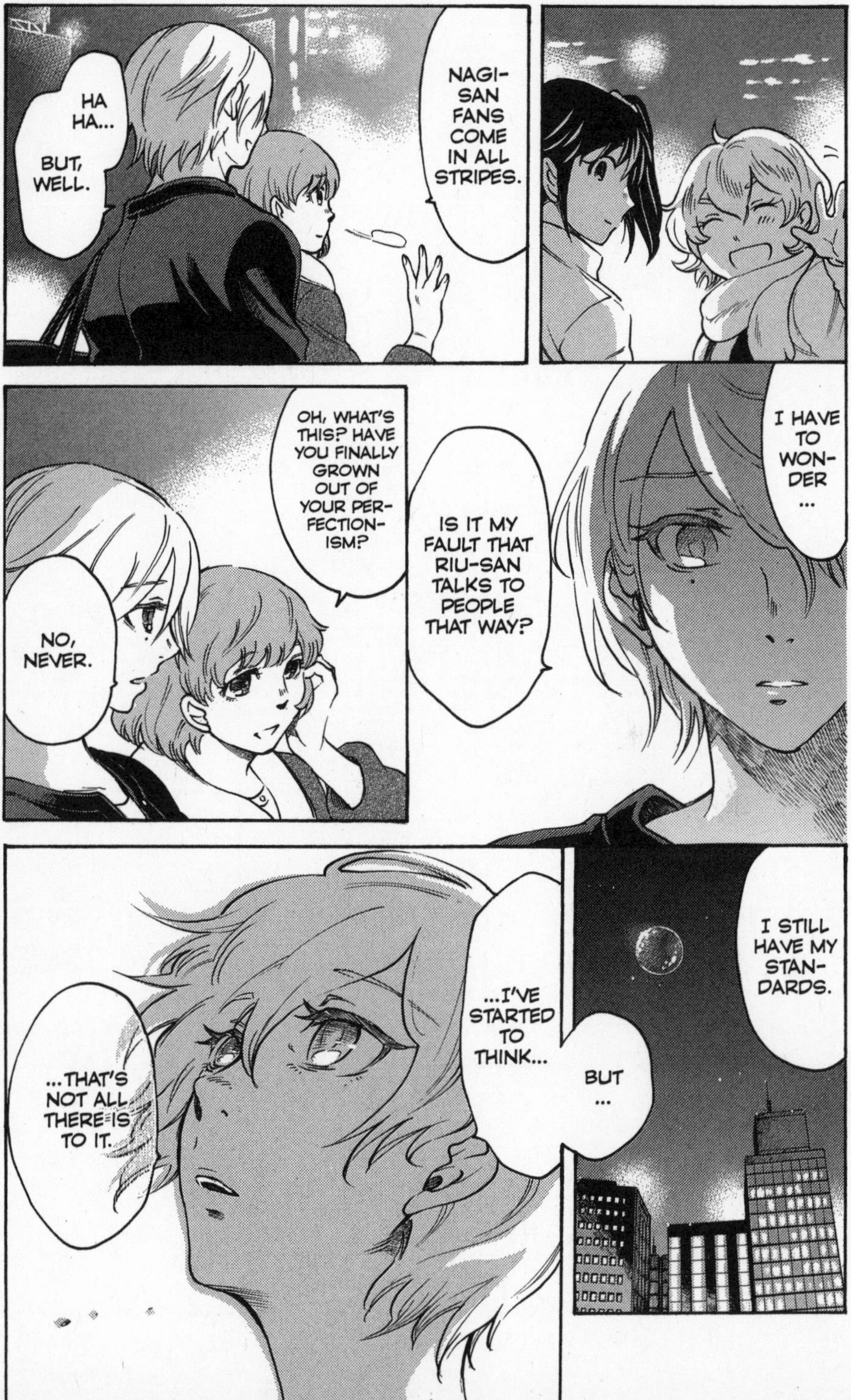
NAGI-SAN FANS COME IN ALL STRIPES.
HA HA... BUT, WELL.
I HAVE TO WONDER...
IS IT MY FAULT THAT RIU-SAN TALKS TO PEOPLE THAT WAY?
OH, WHAT'S THIS? HAVE YOU FINALLY GROWN OUT OF YOUR PERFECTIONISM?
NO, NEVER.
I STILL HAVE MY STANDARDS.
BUT...
...I'VE STARTED TO THINK...
...THAT'S NOT ALL THERE IS TO IT.

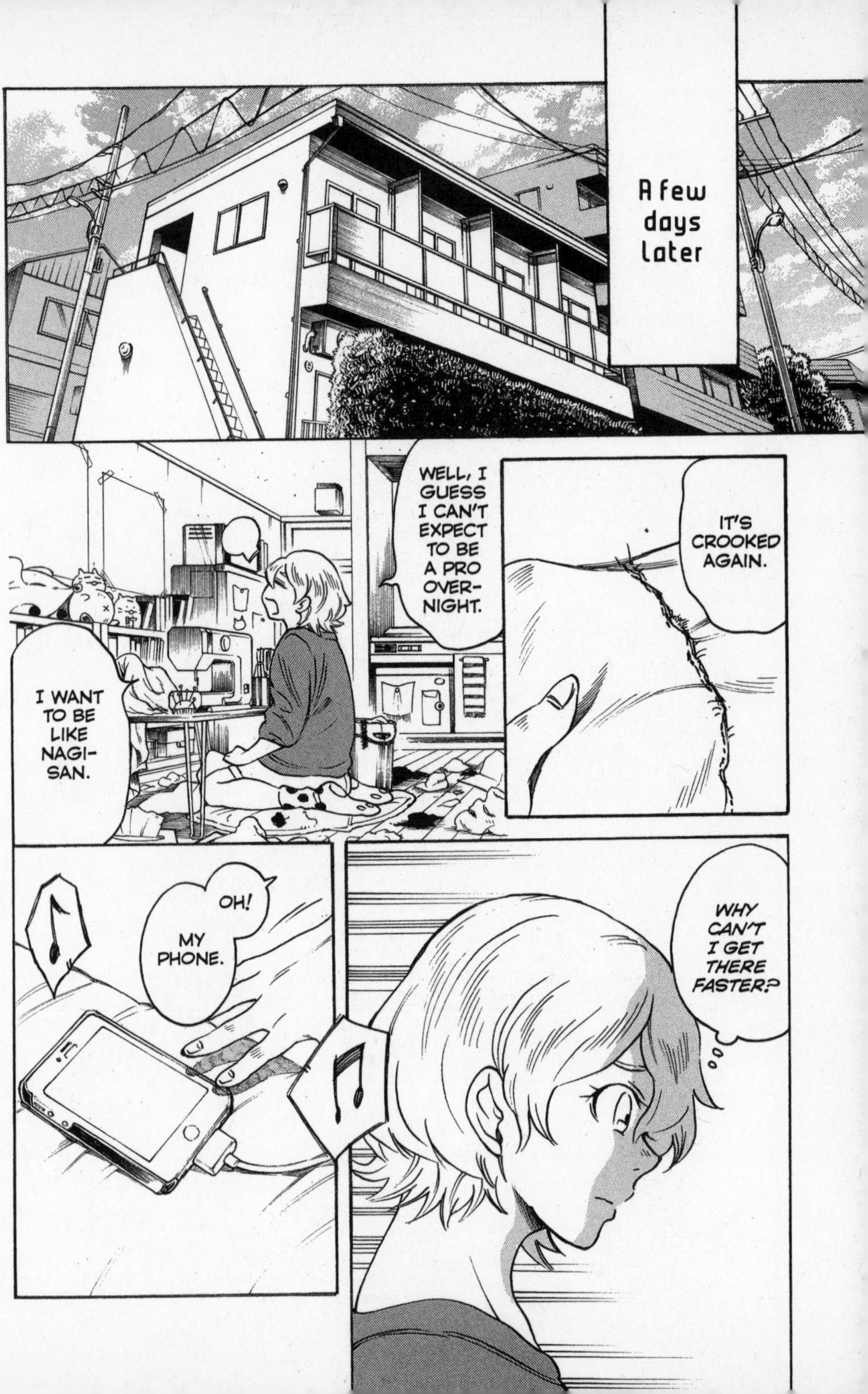
A few days later
IT'S CROOKED AGAIN.
WELL, I GUESS I CAN'T EXPECT TO BE A PRO OVER-NIGHT.
I WANT TO BE LIKE NAGI-SAN.
WHY CAN'T I GET THERE FASTER?
OH!
MY PHONE.

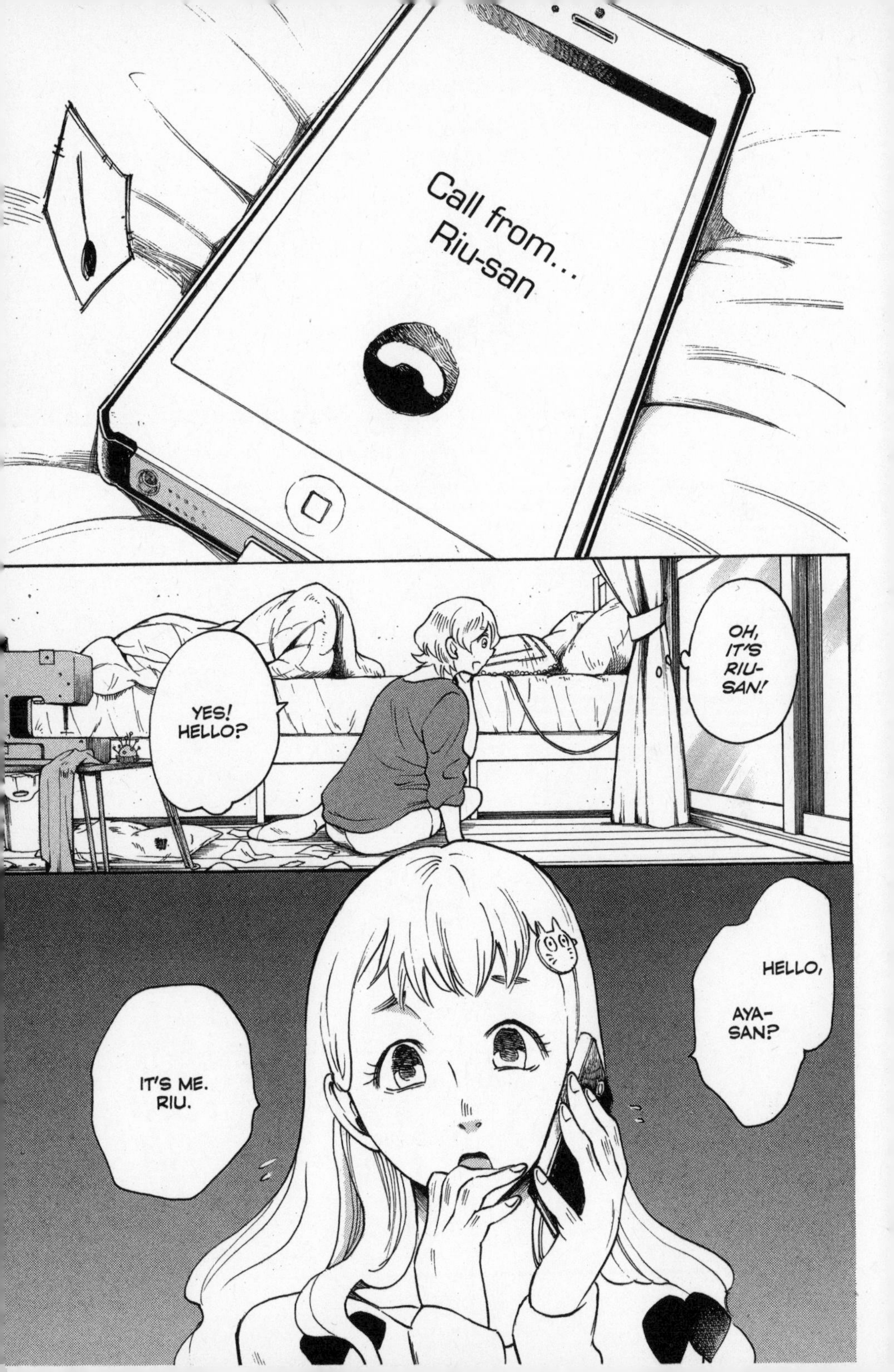
Call from... Riu-san
OH, IT'S RIU-SAN!
YES! HELLO?
HELLO, AYA-SAN?
IT'S ME. RIU.

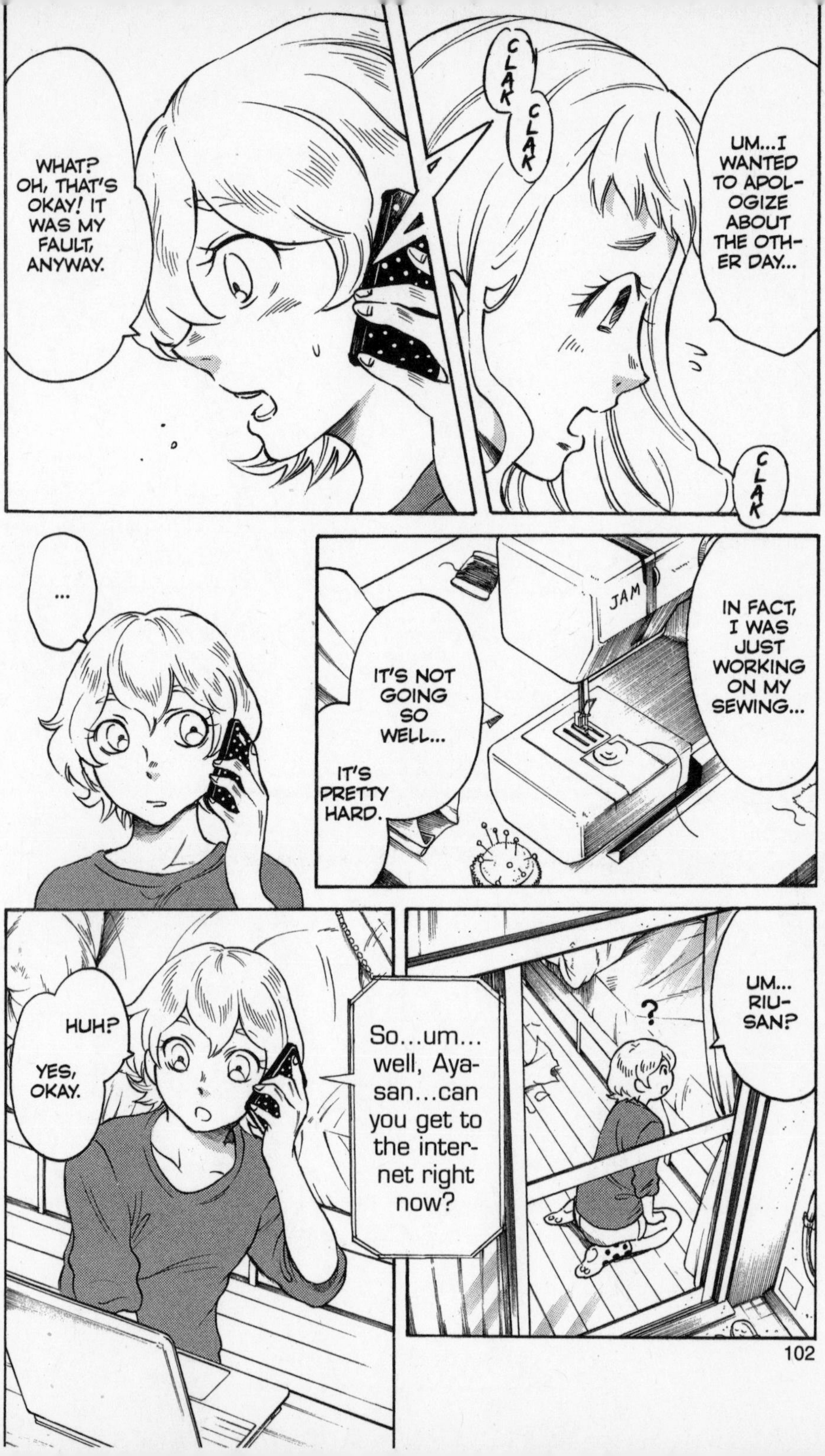
CLAK CLAK
UM...I WANTED TO APOLOGIZE ABOUT THE OTHER DAY...
CLAK
WHAT? OH, THAT'S OKAY! IT WAS MY FAULT, ANYWAY.
IN FACT, I WAS JUST WORKING ON MY SEWING...
JAM
IT'S NOT GOING SO WELL...
IT'S PRETTY HARD.
...
UM... RIU-SAN?
?
So...um... well, Aya-san...can you get to the internet right now?
HUH?
YES, OKAY.

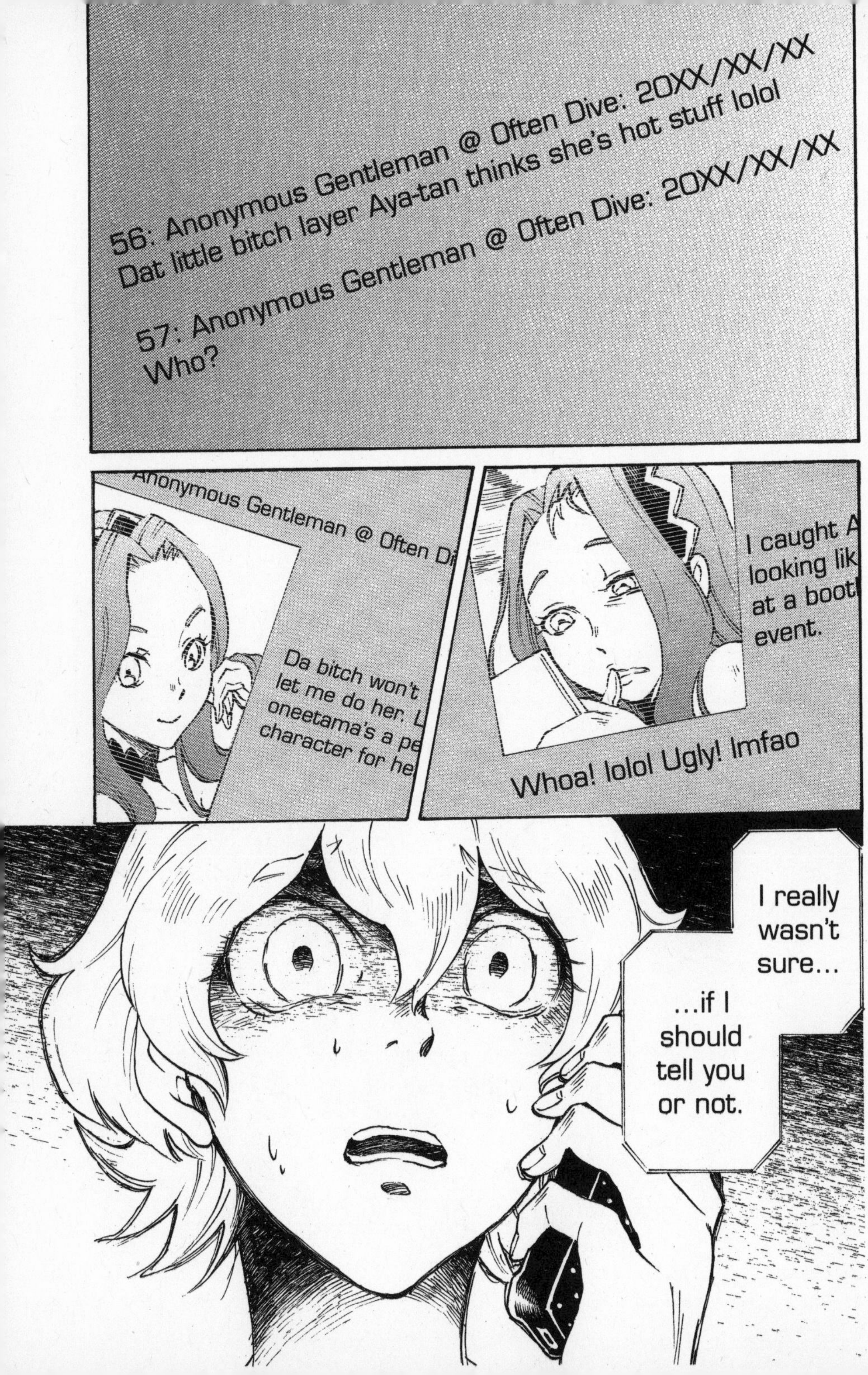
56: Anonymous Gentleman @ Often Dive: 20XX/XX/XX
Dat little bitch layer Aya-tan thinks she's hot stuff lolol
57: Anonymous Gentleman @ Often Dive: 20XX/XX/XX
Who?
I caught A
looking lik
at a boot
event.
Whoa! lolol Ugly! lmfao
Anonymous Gentleman @ Often Di
Da bitch won't
let me do her. L
oneetama's a pe
character for he
I really wasn't sure...
...if I should tell you or not.

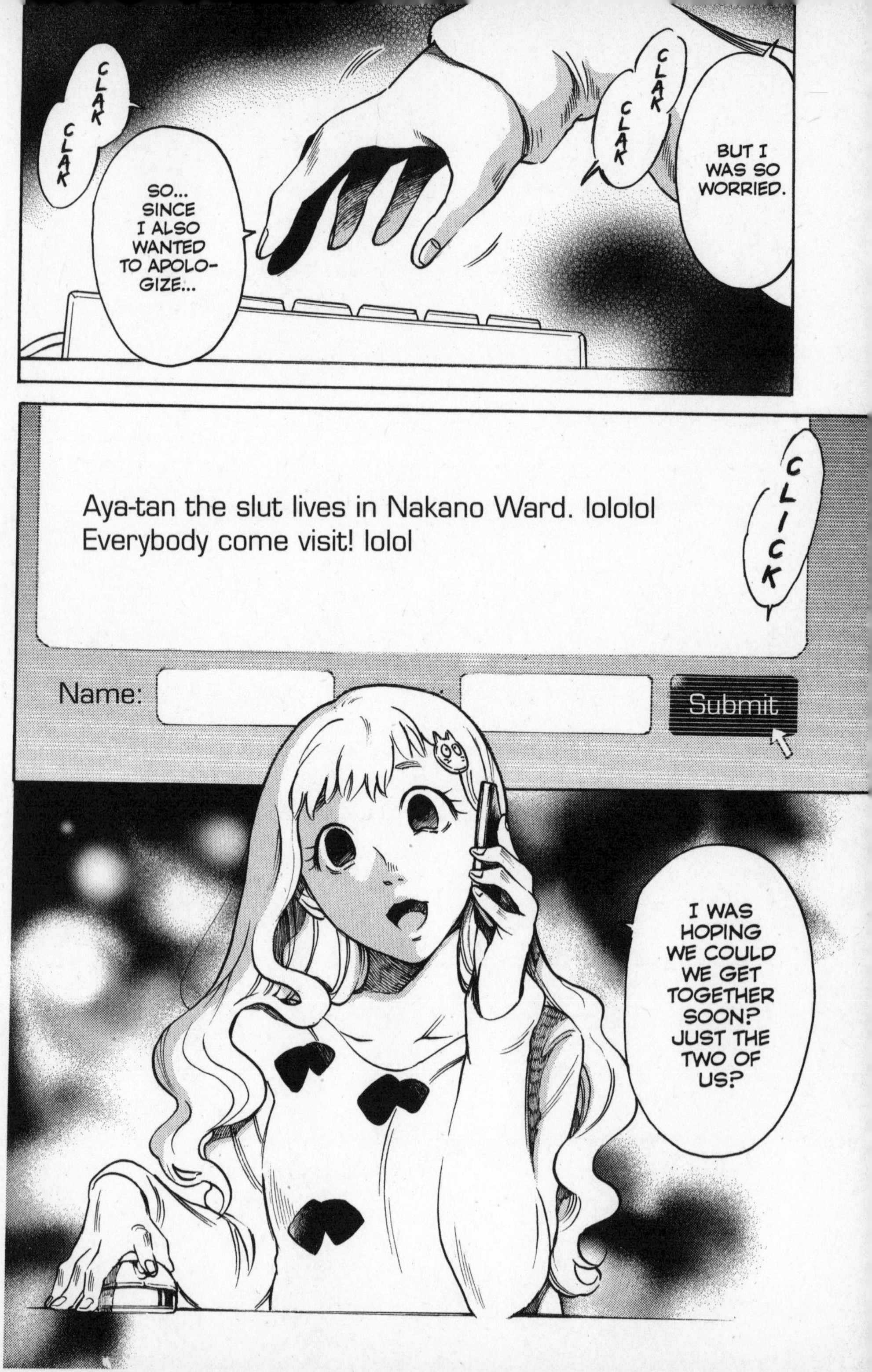
CLAK CLAK
BUT I WAS SO WORRIED.
CLAK CLAK
SO... SINCE I ALSO WANTED TO APOLOGIZE...
CLICK
Aya-tan the slut lives in Nakano Ward. lololol
Everybody come visit! lolol
Name:
Submit
I WAS HOPING WE COULD WE GET TOGETHER SOON? JUST THE TWO OF US?

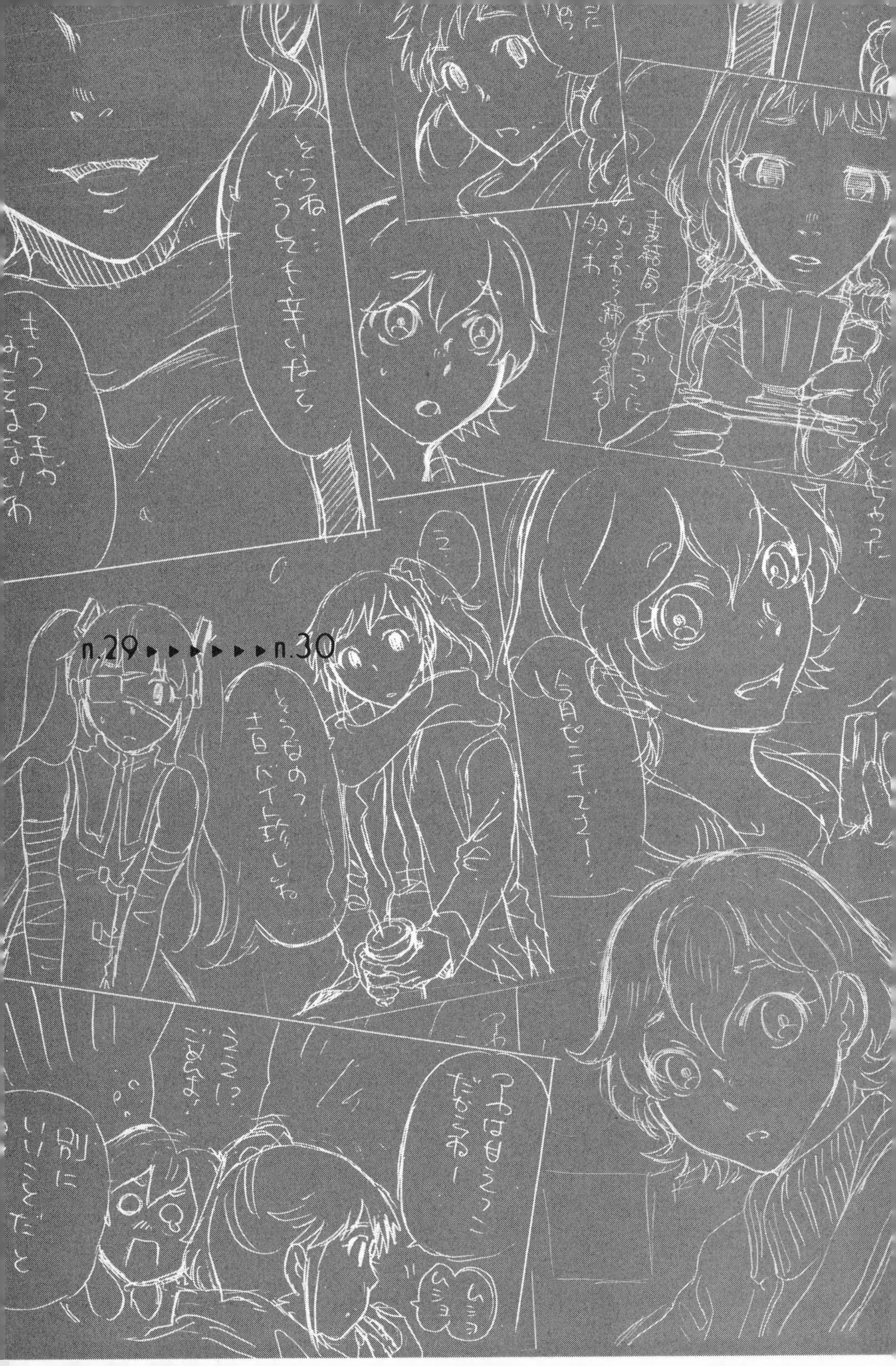
n.29 ▶▶▶▶▶▶ n.30

COSPLAY CARD

COLLECTION

4

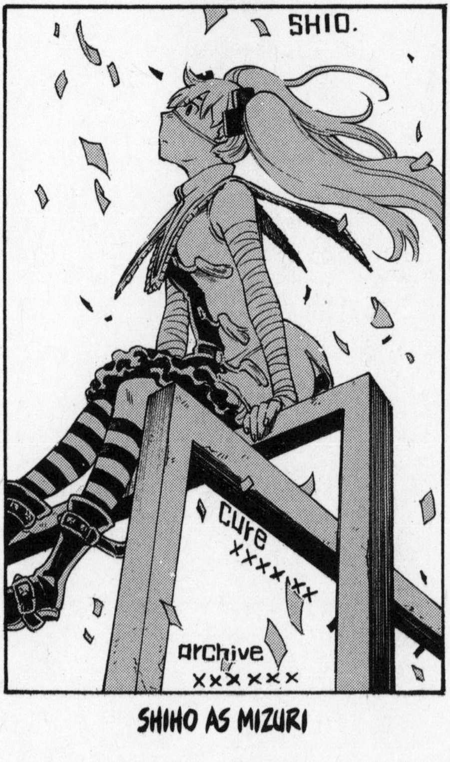
SHIO.
cure
xxxx xx
archive
xxxxxx

SHIHO AS MIZURI

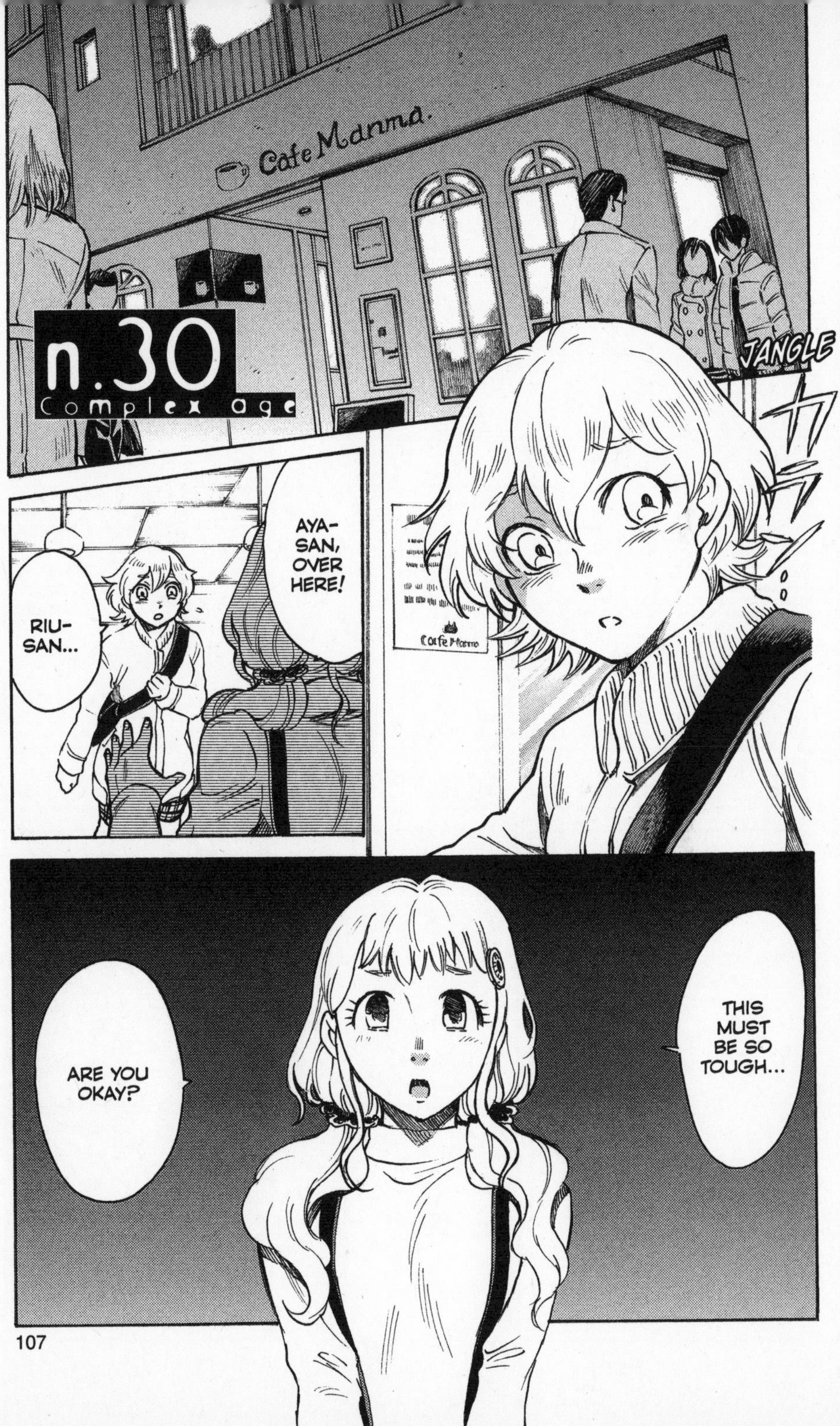
Cafe Manma.
n.30
Complex age
JANGLE
AYA-SAN, OVER HERE!
RIU-SAN...
THIS MUST BE SO TOUGH...
ARE YOU OKAY?

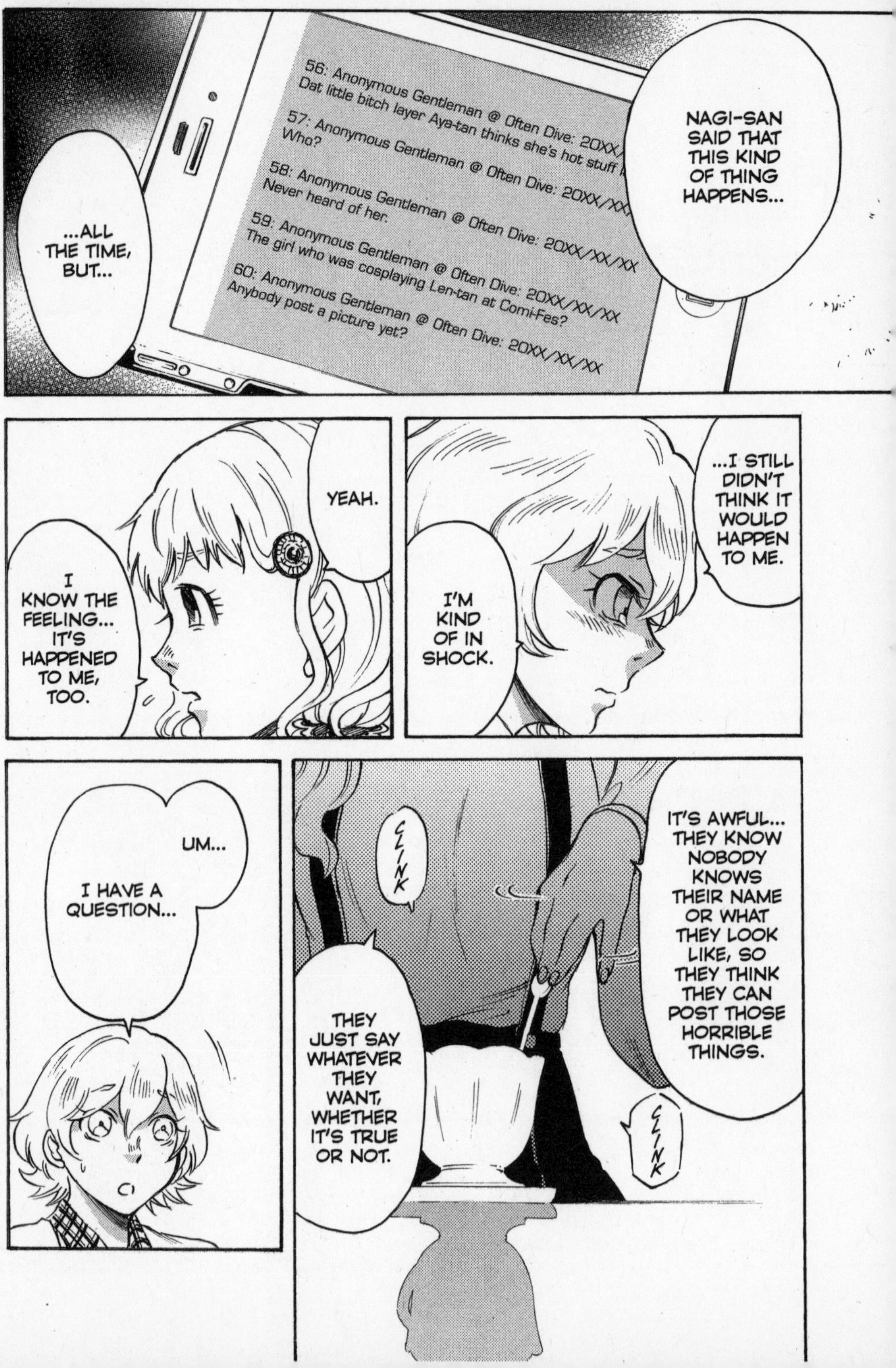
NAGI-SAN SAID THAT THIS KIND OF THING HAPPENS...
56: Anonymous Gentleman @ Often Dive: 20XX/
Dat little bitch layer Aya-tan thinks she's hot stuff
57: Anonymous Gentleman @ Often Dive: 20XX/XX/
Who?
58: Anonymous Gentleman @ Often Dive: 20XX/XX/
Never heard of her.
59: Anonymous Gentleman @ Often Dive: 20XX/XX/XX
The girl who was cosplaying Len-tan at Comi-Fes?
60: Anonymous Gentleman @ Often Dive: 20XX/XX/XX
Anybody post a picture yet?
...ALL THE TIME, BUT...
...I STILL DIDN'T THINK IT WOULD HAPPEN TO ME.
I'M KIND OF IN SHOCK.
YEAH.
I KNOW THE FEELING... IT'S HAPPENED TO ME, TOO.
IT'S AWFUL... THEY KNOW NOBODY KNOWS THEIR NAME OR WHAT THEY LOOK LIKE, SO THEY THINK THEY CAN POST THOSE HORRIBLE THINGS.
CLINK
THEY JUST SAY WHATEVER THEY WANT, WHETHER IT'S TRUE OR NOT.
CLINK
UM...
I HAVE A QUESTION...

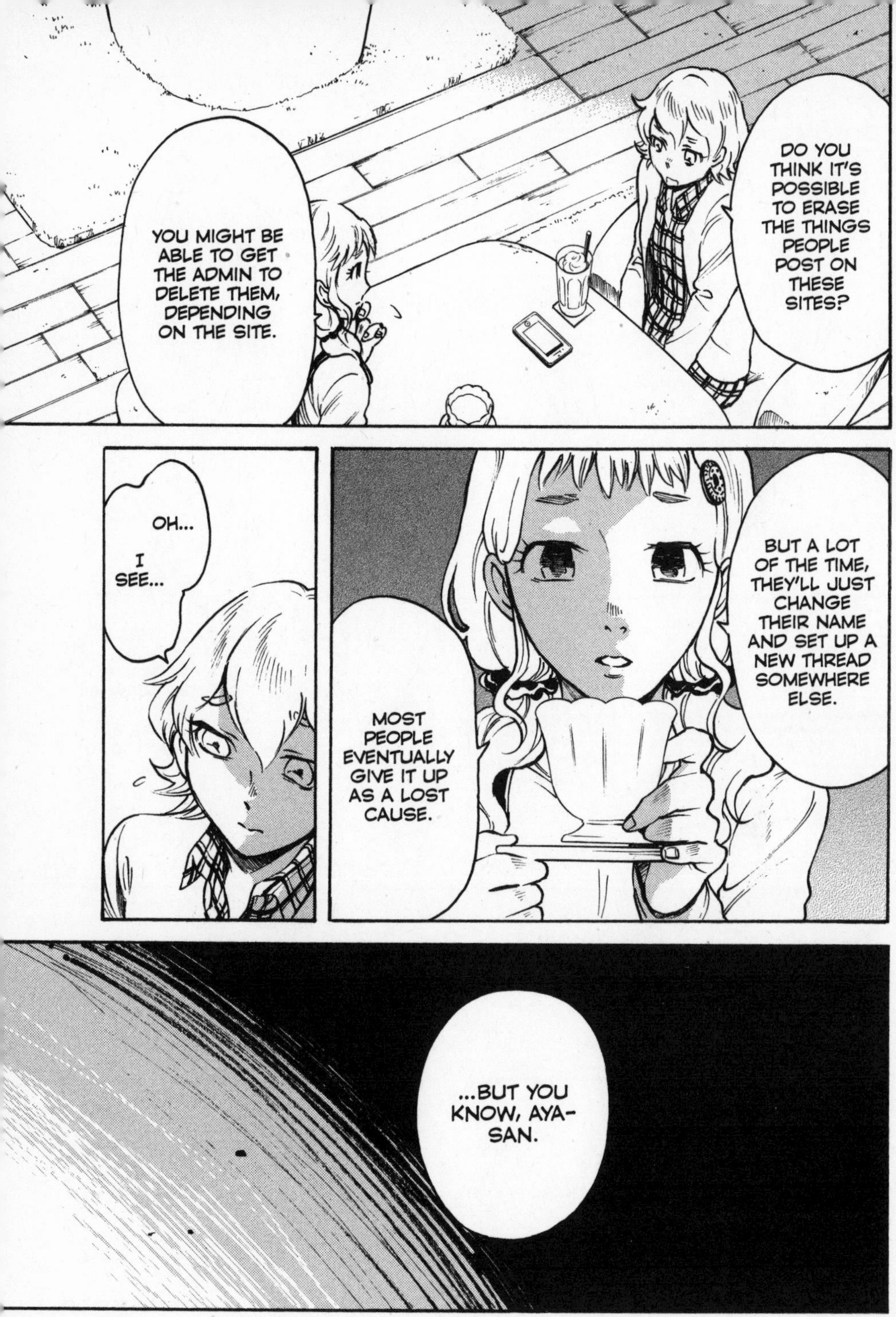
DO YOU THINK IT'S POSSIBLE TO ERASE THE THINGS PEOPLE POST ON THESE SITES?
YOU MIGHT BE ABLE TO GET THE ADMIN TO DELETE THEM, DEPENDING ON THE SITE.
BUT A LOT OF THE TIME, THEY'LL JUST CHANGE THEIR NAME AND SET UP A NEW THREAD SOMEWHERE ELSE.
MOST PEOPLE EVENTUALLY GIVE IT UP AS A LOST CAUSE.
OH...
I SEE...
...BUT YOU KNOW, AYA-SAN.

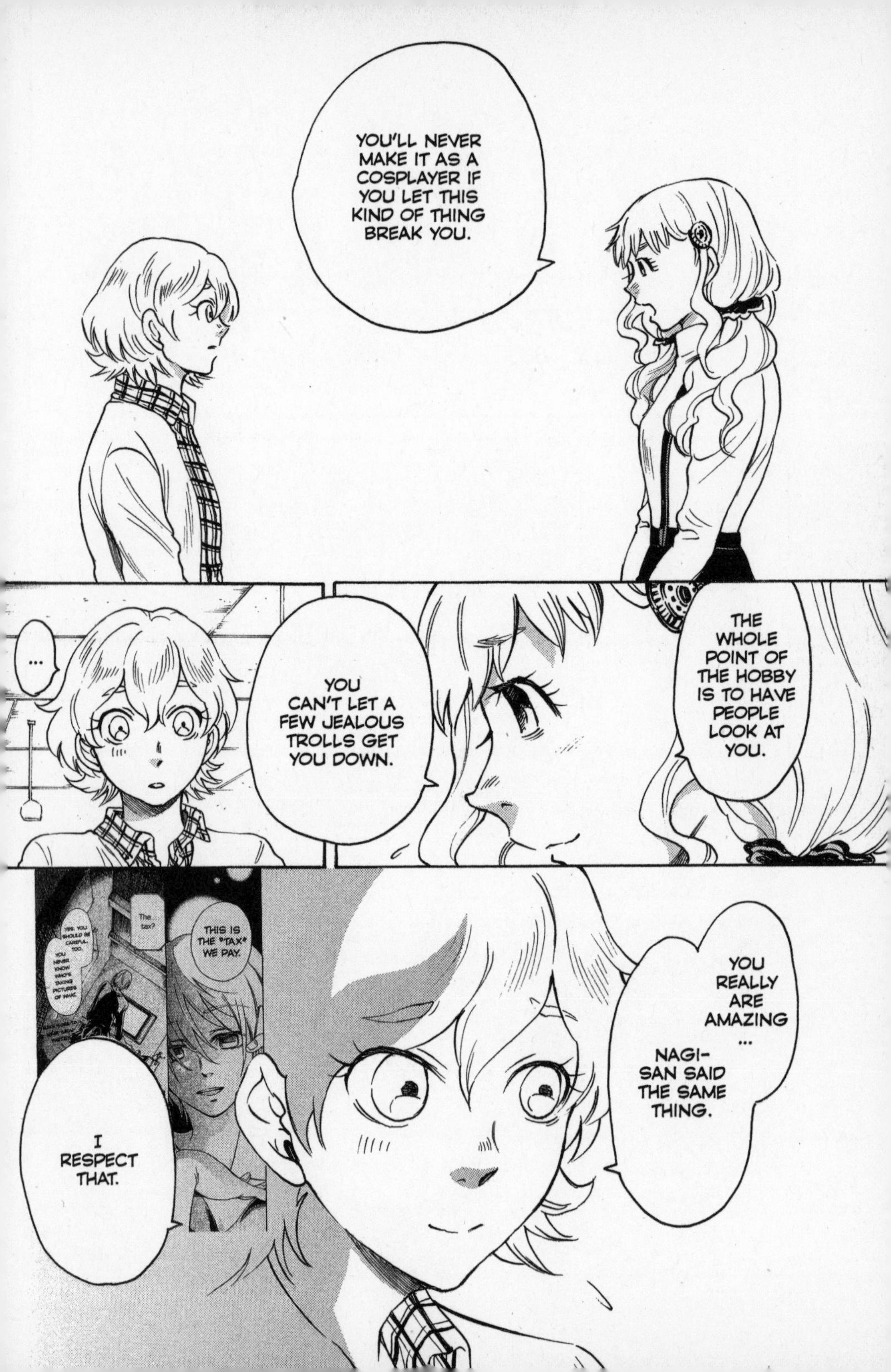
YOU'LL NEVER MAKE IT AS A COSPLAYER IF YOU LET THIS KIND OF THING BREAK YOU.
THE WHOLE POINT OF THE HOBBY IS TO HAVE PEOPLE LOOK AT YOU.
YOU CAN'T LET A FEW JEALOUS TROLLS GET YOU DOWN.
...
YOU REALLY ARE AMAZING...
NAGI-SAN SAID THE SAME THING.
THIS IS THE "TAX" WE PAY.
The... tax?
YES. YOU SHOULD BE CAREFUL, TOO.
YOU NEVER KNOW WHO'S TAKING PICTURES OF WHAT.
I RESPECT THAT.

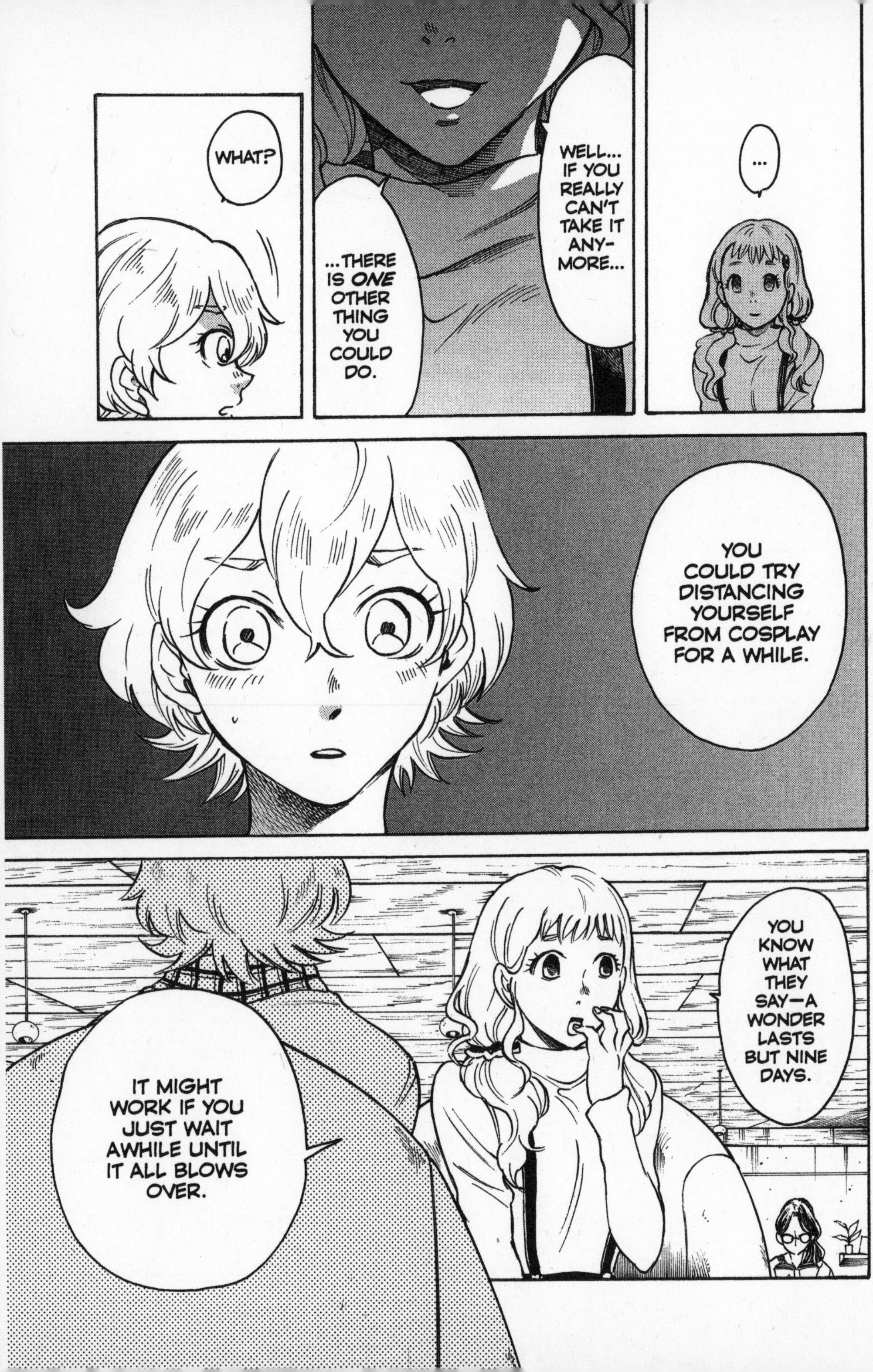
...
WELL... IF YOU REALLY CAN'T TAKE IT ANY-MORE...
...THERE IS *ONE* OTHER THING YOU COULD DO.
WHAT?
YOU COULD TRY DISTANCING YOURSELF FROM COSPLAY FOR A WHILE.
YOU KNOW WHAT THEY SAY—A WONDER LASTS BUT NINE DAYS.
IT MIGHT WORK IF YOU JUST WAIT AWHILE UNTIL IT ALL BLOWS OVER.

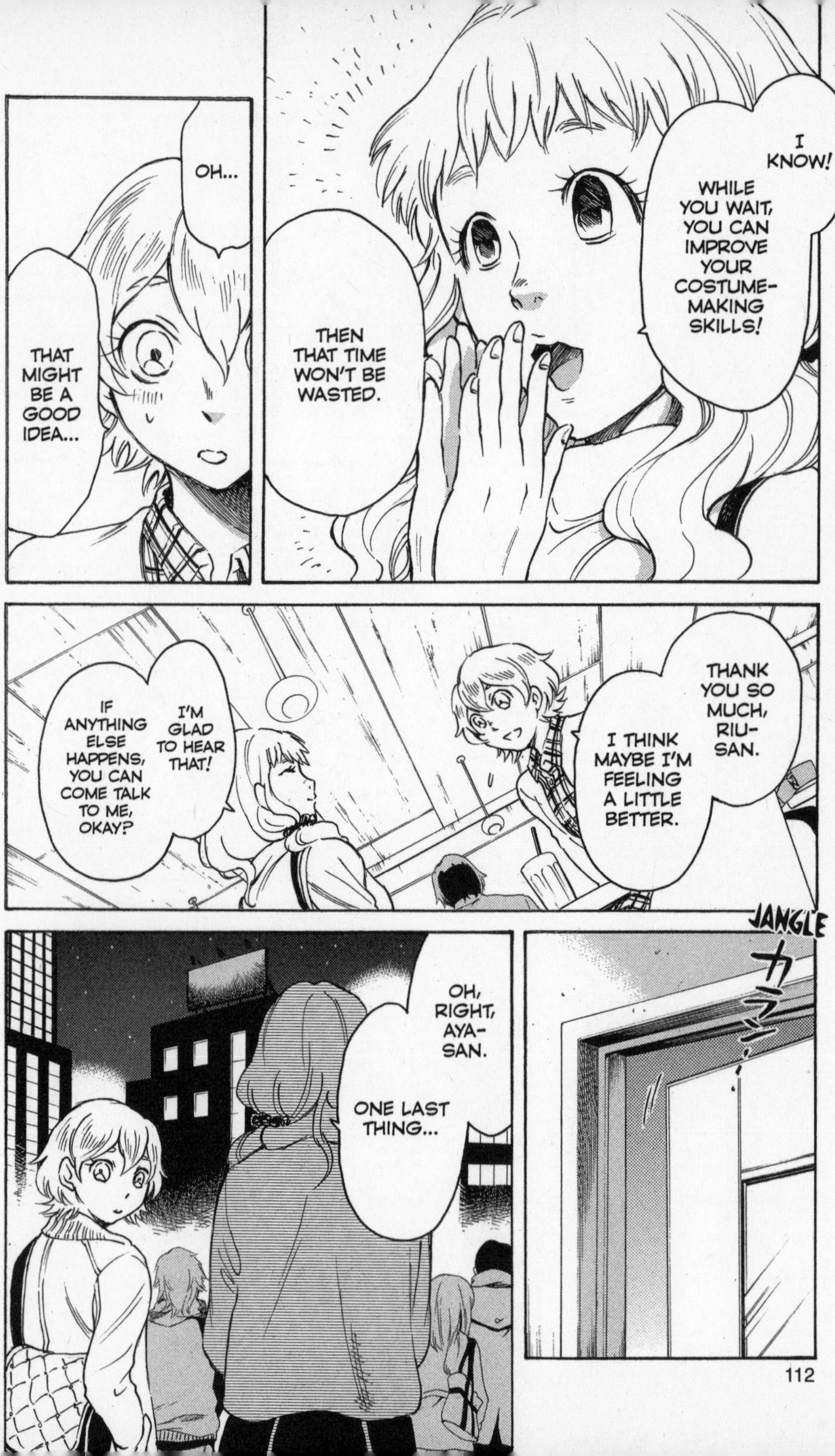
I KNOW!
WHILE YOU WAIT, YOU CAN IMPROVE YOUR COSTUME-MAKING SKILLS!
THEN THAT TIME WON'T BE WASTED.
OH...
THAT MIGHT BE A GOOD IDEA...
THANK YOU SO MUCH, RIU-SAN.
I THINK MAYBE I'M FEELING A LITTLE BETTER.
I'M GLAD TO HEAR THAT!
IF ANYTHING ELSE HAPPENS, YOU CAN COME TALK TO ME, OKAY?
JANGLE
OH, RIGHT, AYA-SAN.
ONE LAST THING...

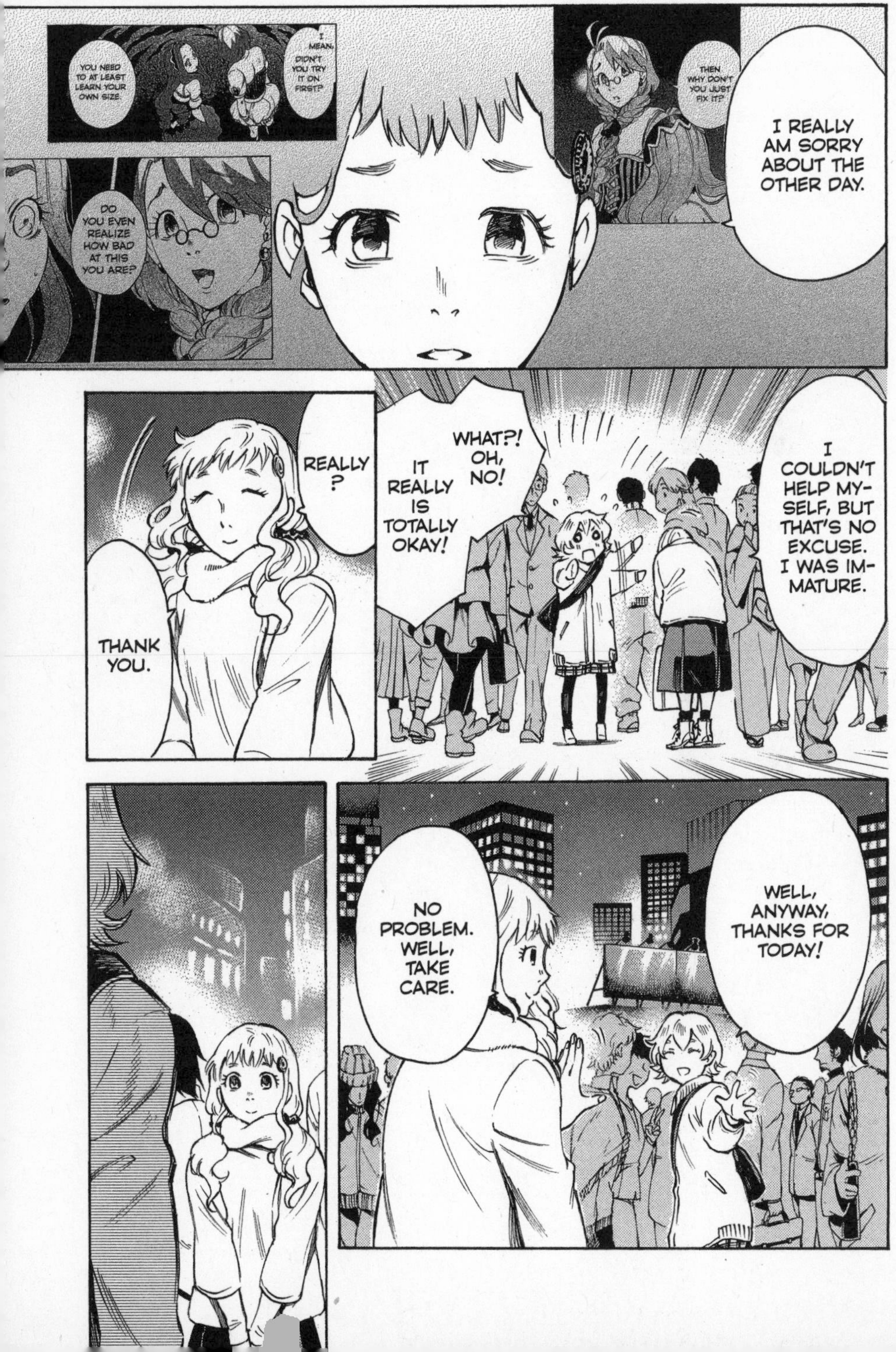
I REALLY AM SORRY ABOUT THE OTHER DAY.
THEN WHY DON'T YOU JUST FIX IT?
I MEAN, DIDN'T YOU TRY IT ON FIRST?
YOU NEED TO AT LEAST LEARN YOUR OWN SIZE.
DO YOU EVEN REALIZE HOW BAD AT THIS YOU ARE?
I COULDN'T HELP MY-SELF, BUT THAT'S NO EXCUSE. I WAS IM-MATURE.
WHAT?! OH, NO!
IT REALLY IS TOTALLY OKAY!
REALLY?
THANK YOU.
WELL, ANYWAY, THANKS FOR TODAY!
NO PROBLEM. WELL, TAKE CARE.

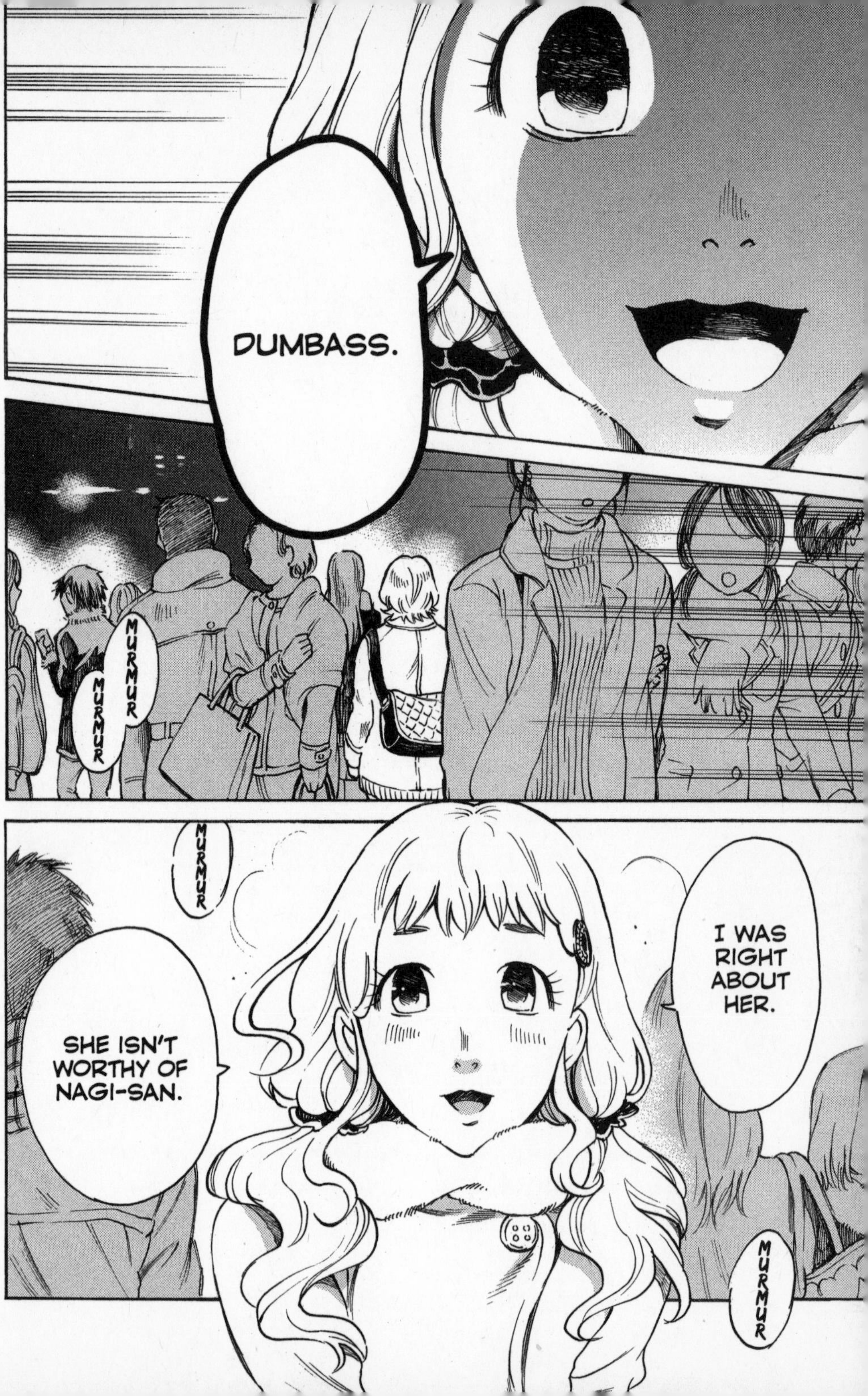
DUMBASS.
MURMUR
MURMUR
I WAS RIGHT ABOUT HER.
MURMUR
SHE ISN'T WORTHY OF NAGI-SAN.
MURMUR

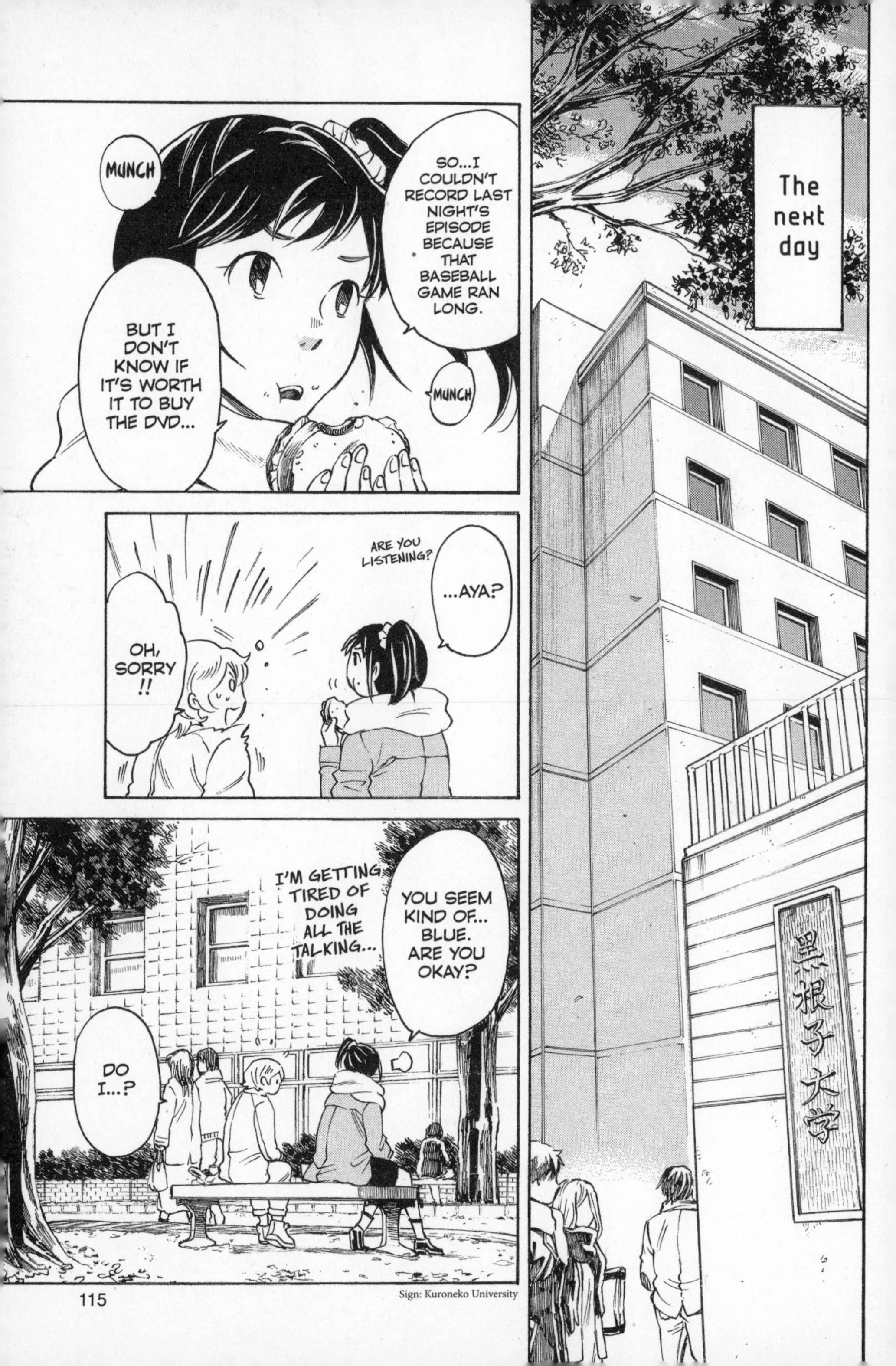
The next day
黒根子大学
SO...I COULDN'T RECORD LAST NIGHT'S EPISODE BECAUSE THAT BASEBALL GAME RAN LONG.
MUNCH
MUNCH
BUT I DON'T KNOW IF IT'S WORTH IT TO BUY THE DVD...
ARE YOU LISTENING?
...AYA?
OH, SORRY!!
YOU SEEM KIND OF... BLUE. ARE YOU OKAY?
I'M GETTING TIRED OF DOING ALL THE TALKING...
DO I...?

Sign: Kuroneko University

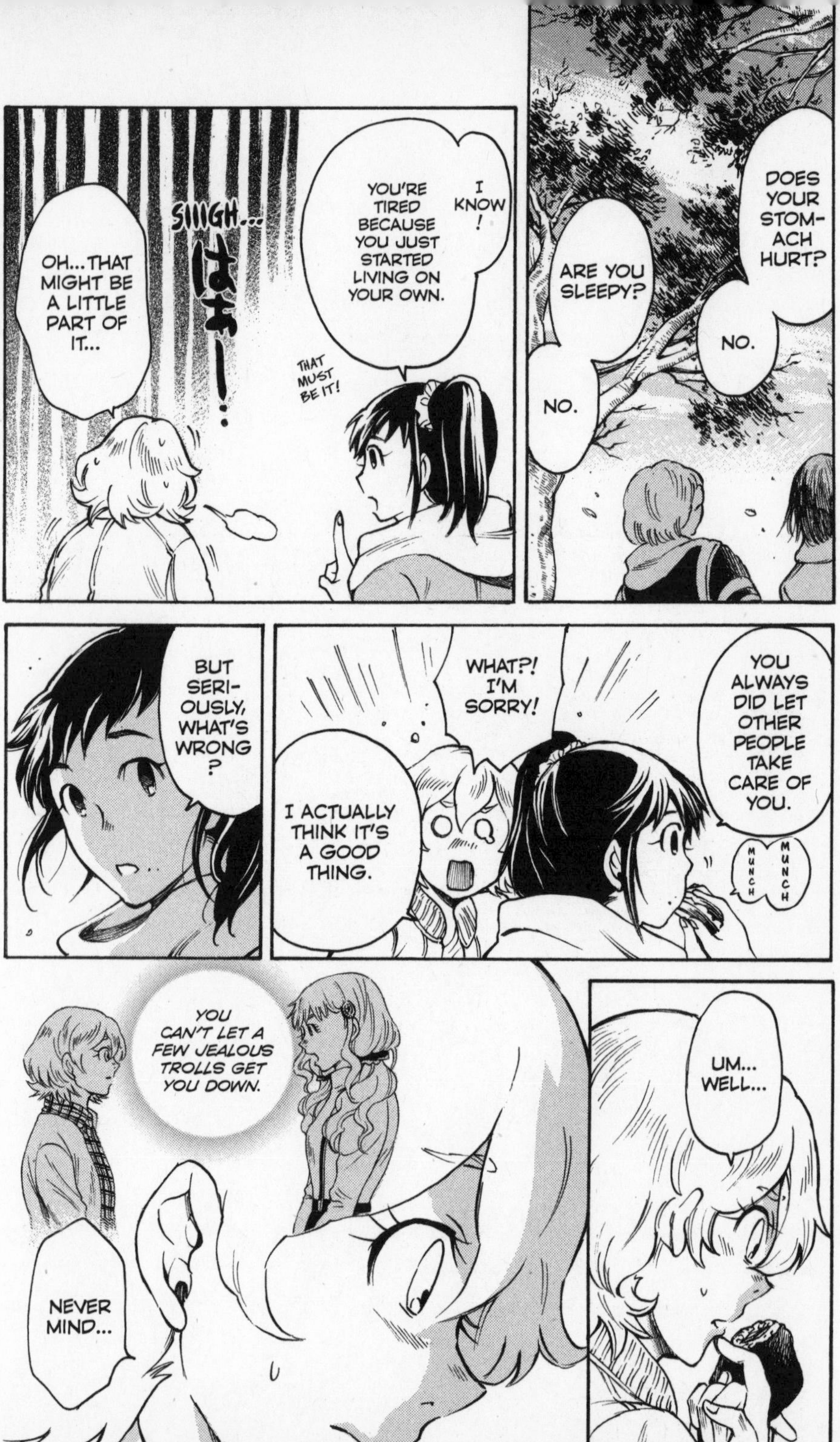
DOES YOUR STOM-ACH HURT?
NO.
ARE YOU SLEEPY?
NO.
I KNOW!
YOU'RE TIRED BECAUSE YOU JUST STARTED LIVING ON YOUR OWN.
THAT MUST BE IT!
SIIIGH... はぁー!
OH...THAT MIGHT BE A LITTLE PART OF IT...
YOU ALWAYS DID LET OTHER PEOPLE TAKE CARE OF YOU.
MUNCH
MUNCH
WHAT?! I'M SORRY!
I ACTUALLY THINK IT'S A GOOD THING.
BUT SERI-OUSLY, WHAT'S WRONG?
UM... WELL...
YOU CAN'T LET A FEW JEALOUS TROLLS GET YOU DOWN.
NEVER MIND...

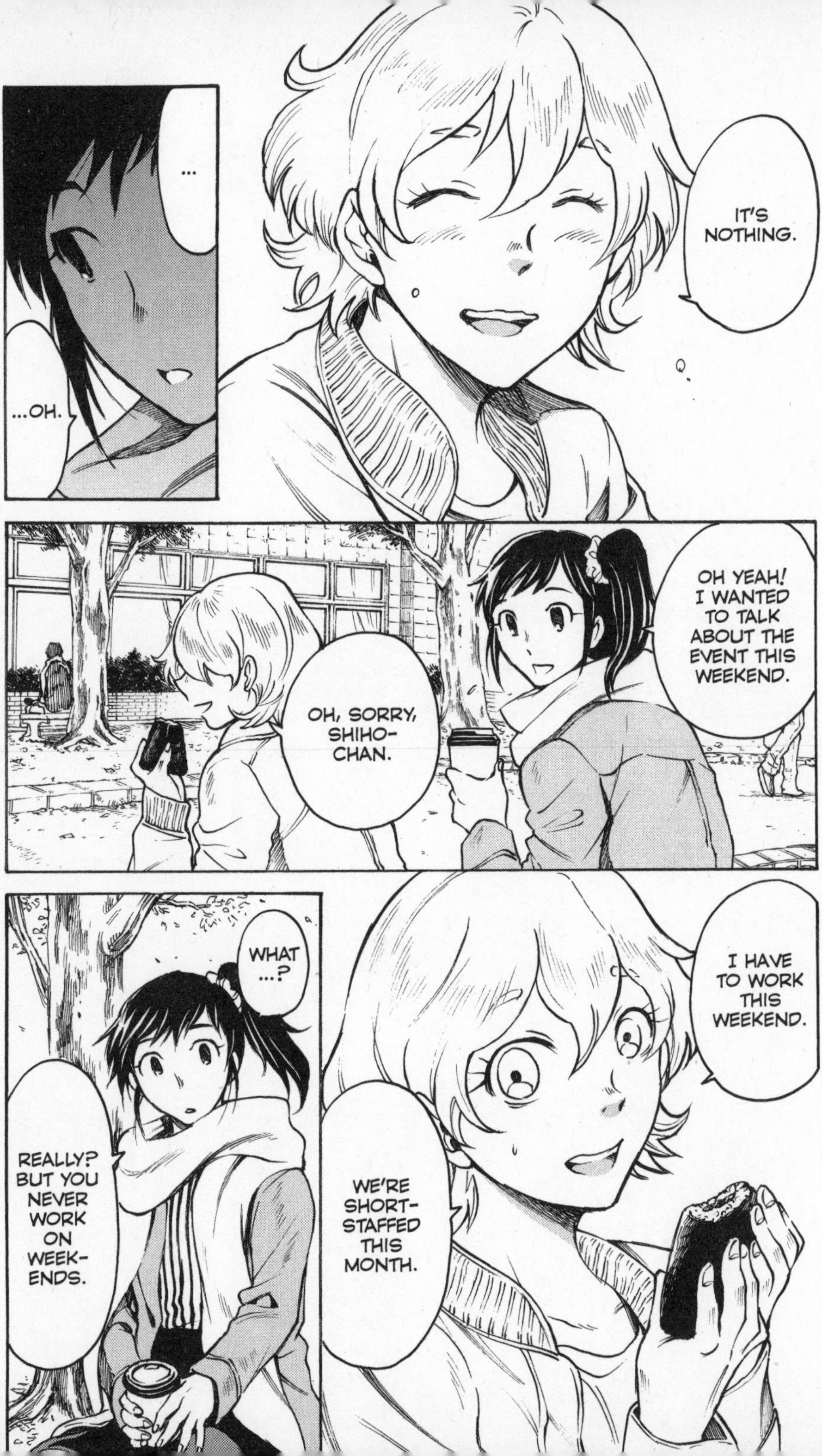
IT'S NOTHING.
...
...OH.
OH YEAH! I WANTED TO TALK ABOUT THE EVENT THIS WEEKEND.
OH, SORRY, SHIHO-CHAN.
I HAVE TO WORK THIS WEEKEND.
WE'RE SHORT-STAFFED THIS MONTH.
WHAT ...?
REALLY? BUT YOU NEVER WORK ON WEEK-ENDS.

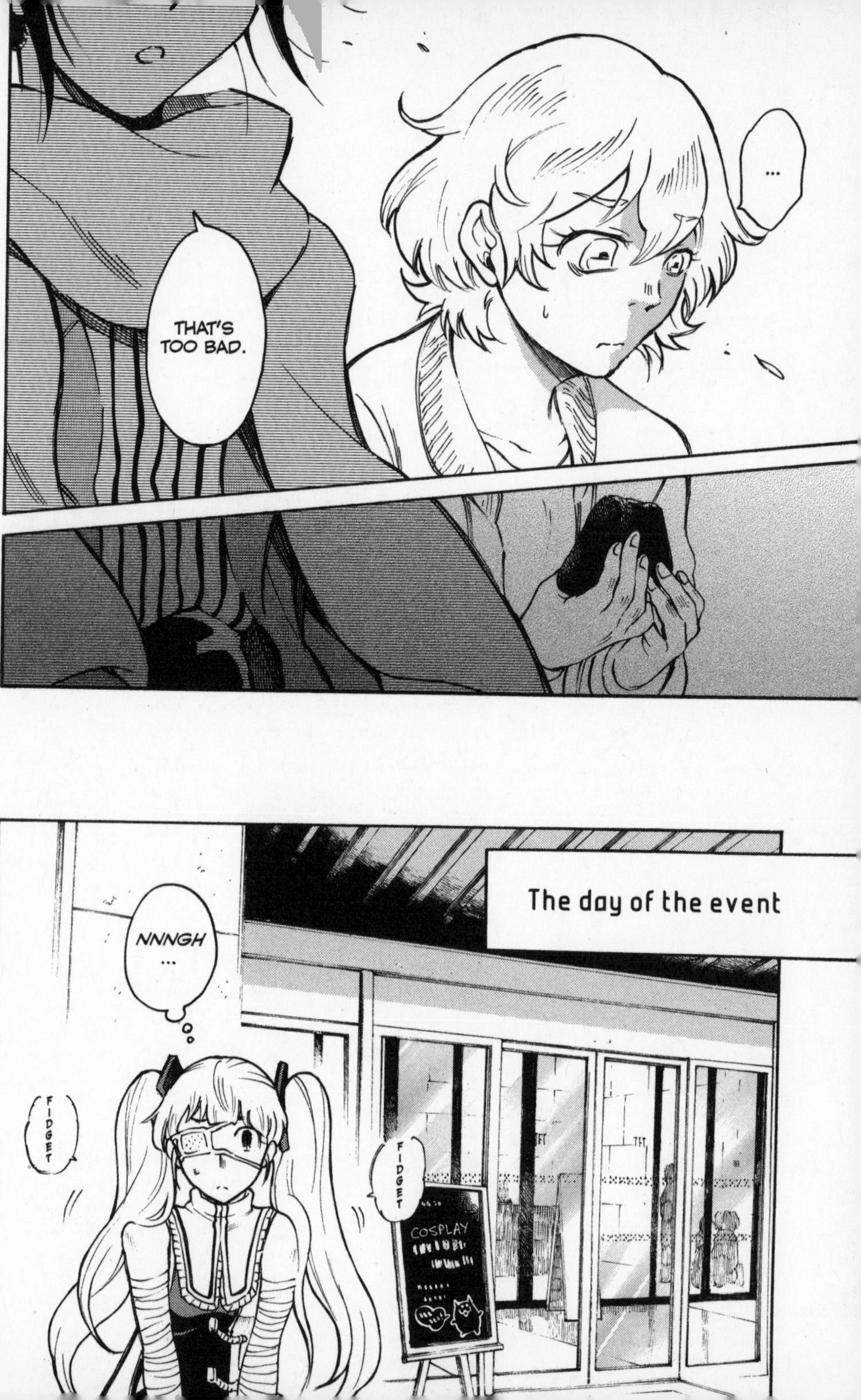
...
THAT'S TOO BAD.
The day of the event
NNNGH ...
FIDGET
FIDGET

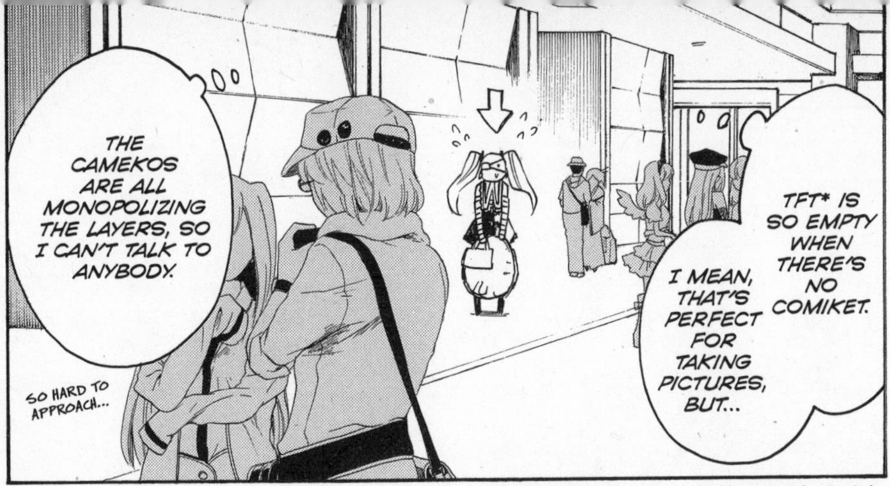
TFT* IS SO EMPTY WHEN THERE'S NO COMIKET.
I MEAN, THAT'S PERFECT FOR TAKING PICTURES, BUT...
THE CAMEKOS ARE ALL MONOPOLIZING THE LAYERS, SO I CAN'T TALK TO ANYBODY.
SO HARD TO APPROACH...

*Short for Tokyo Fashion Town, a building near Tokyo Big Sight.

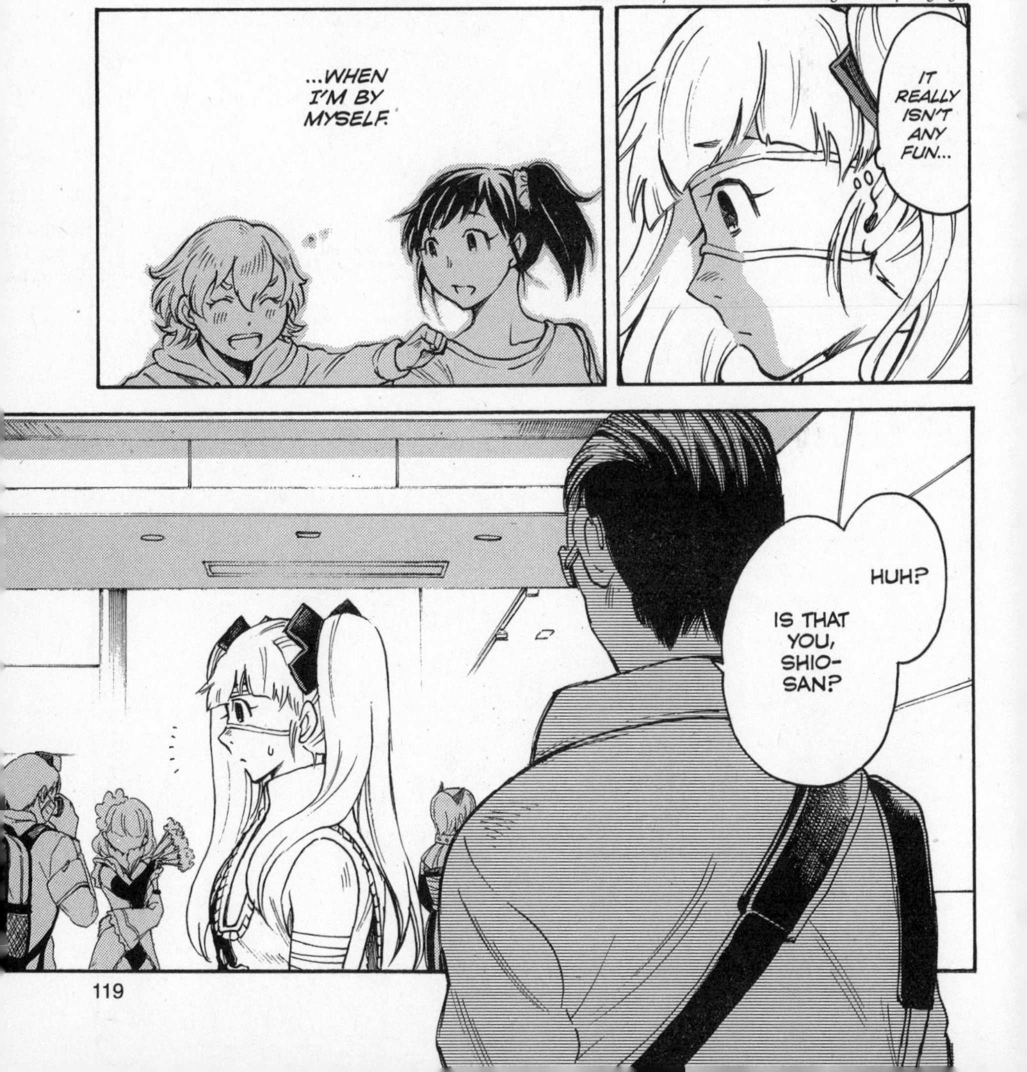
IT REALLY ISN'T ANY FUN...
...WHEN I'M BY MYSELF.
HUH?
IS THAT YOU, SHIO-SAN?

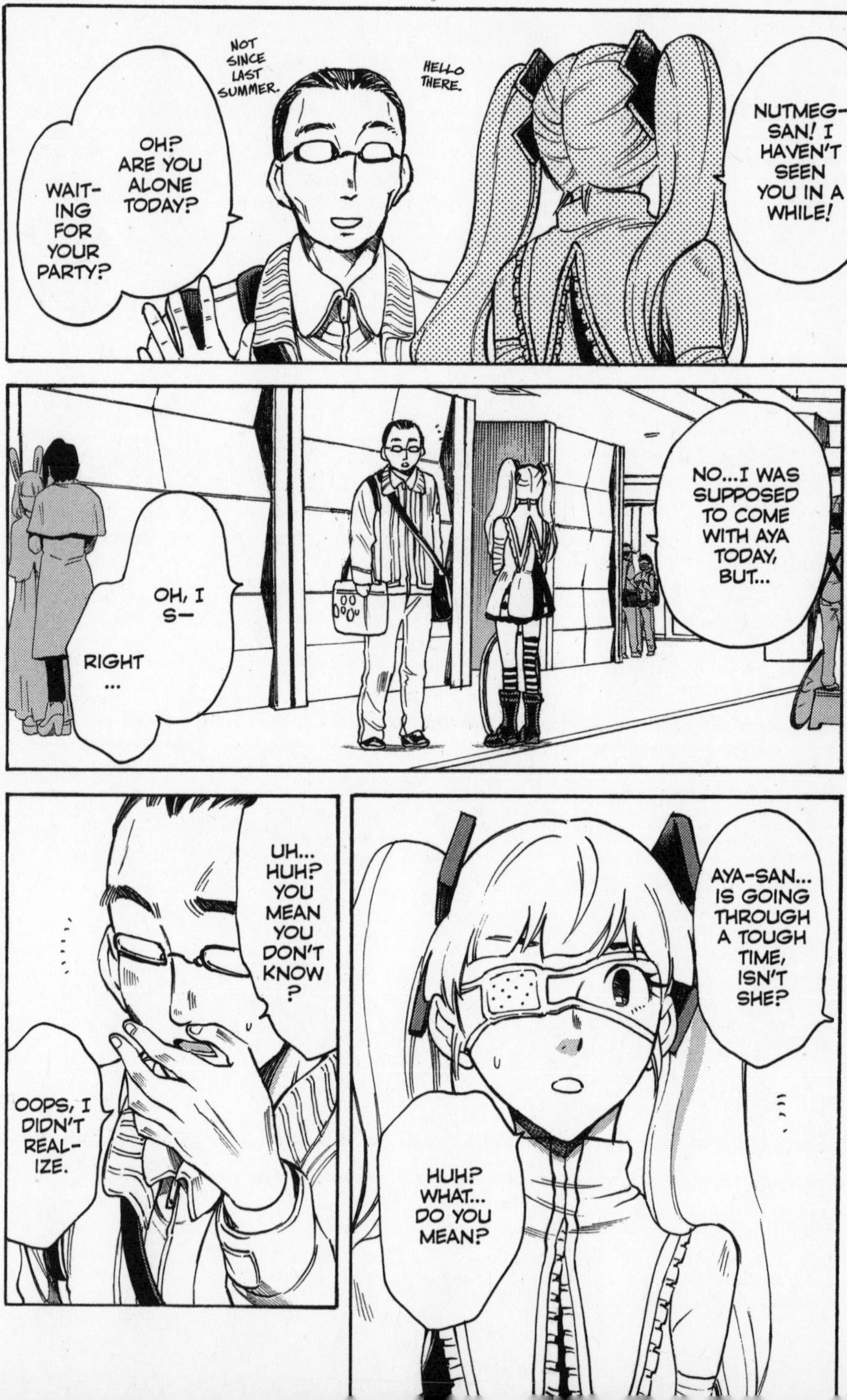
NUTMEG-SAN! I HAVEN'T SEEN YOU IN A WHILE!
HELLO THERE.
NOT SINCE LAST SUMMER.
OH? ARE YOU ALONE TODAY?
WAITING FOR YOUR PARTY?
NO...I WAS SUPPOSED TO COME WITH AYA TODAY, BUT...
OH, I S—
RIGHT ...
AYA-SAN... IS GOING THROUGH A TOUGH TIME, ISN'T SHE?
...
HUH? WHAT... DO YOU MEAN?
UH... HUH? YOU MEAN YOU DON'T KNOW?
...
OOPS, I DIDN'T REALIZE.

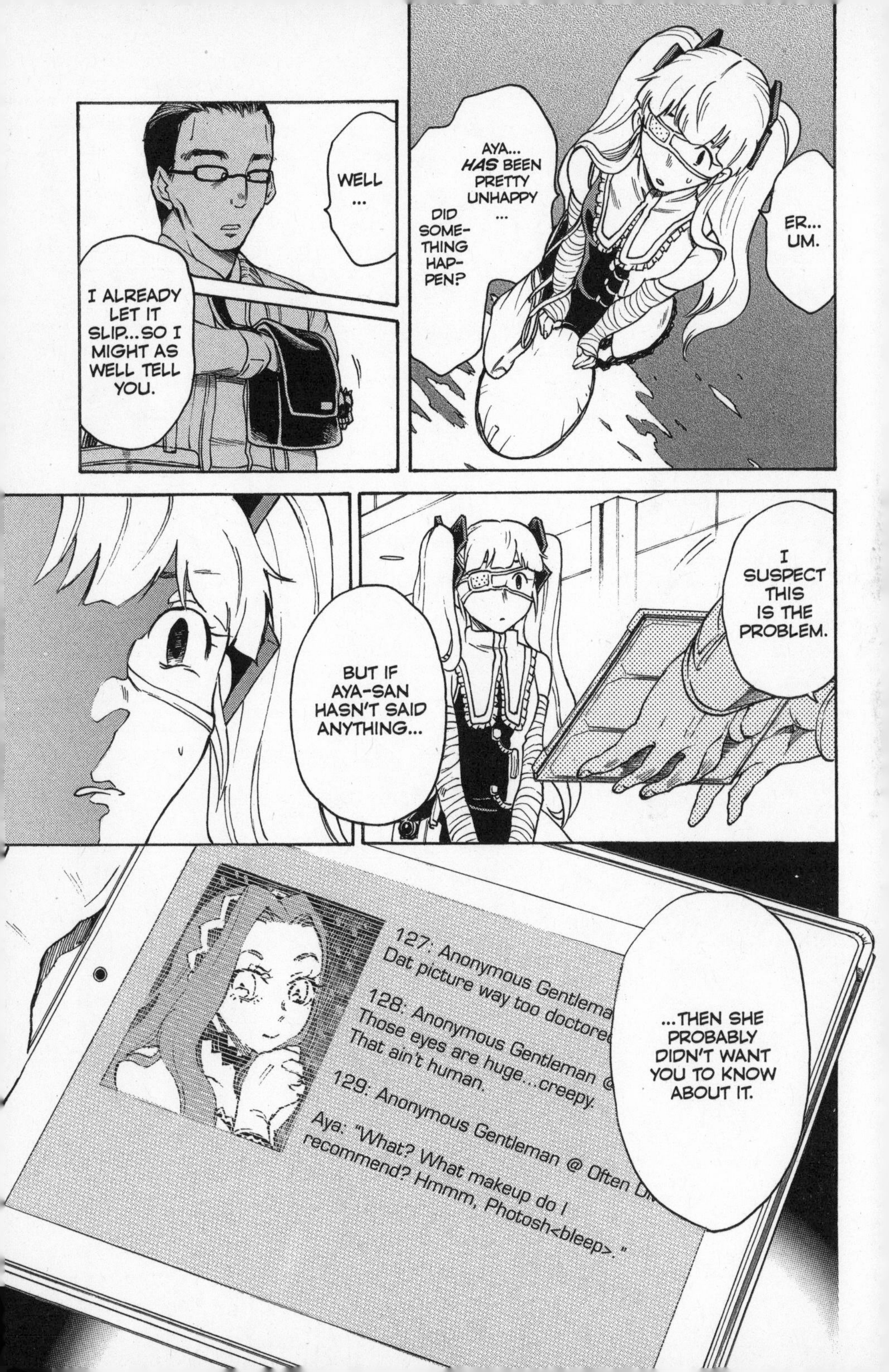
ER... UM.
AYA... HAS BEEN PRETTY UNHAPPY ...
DID SOMETHING HAPPEN?
WELL ...
I ALREADY LET IT SLIP...SO I MIGHT AS WELL TELL YOU.
I SUSPECT THIS IS THE PROBLEM.
BUT IF AYA-SAN HASN'T SAID ANYTHING...
...THEN SHE PROBABLY DIDN'T WANT YOU TO KNOW ABOUT IT.
127: Anonymous Gentlema
Dat picture way too doctore
128: Anonymous Gentleman @
Those eyes are huge...creepy.
That ain't human.
129: Anonymous Gentleman @ Often D
Aya: "What? What makeup do I recommend? Hmmm, Photosh<bleep>."

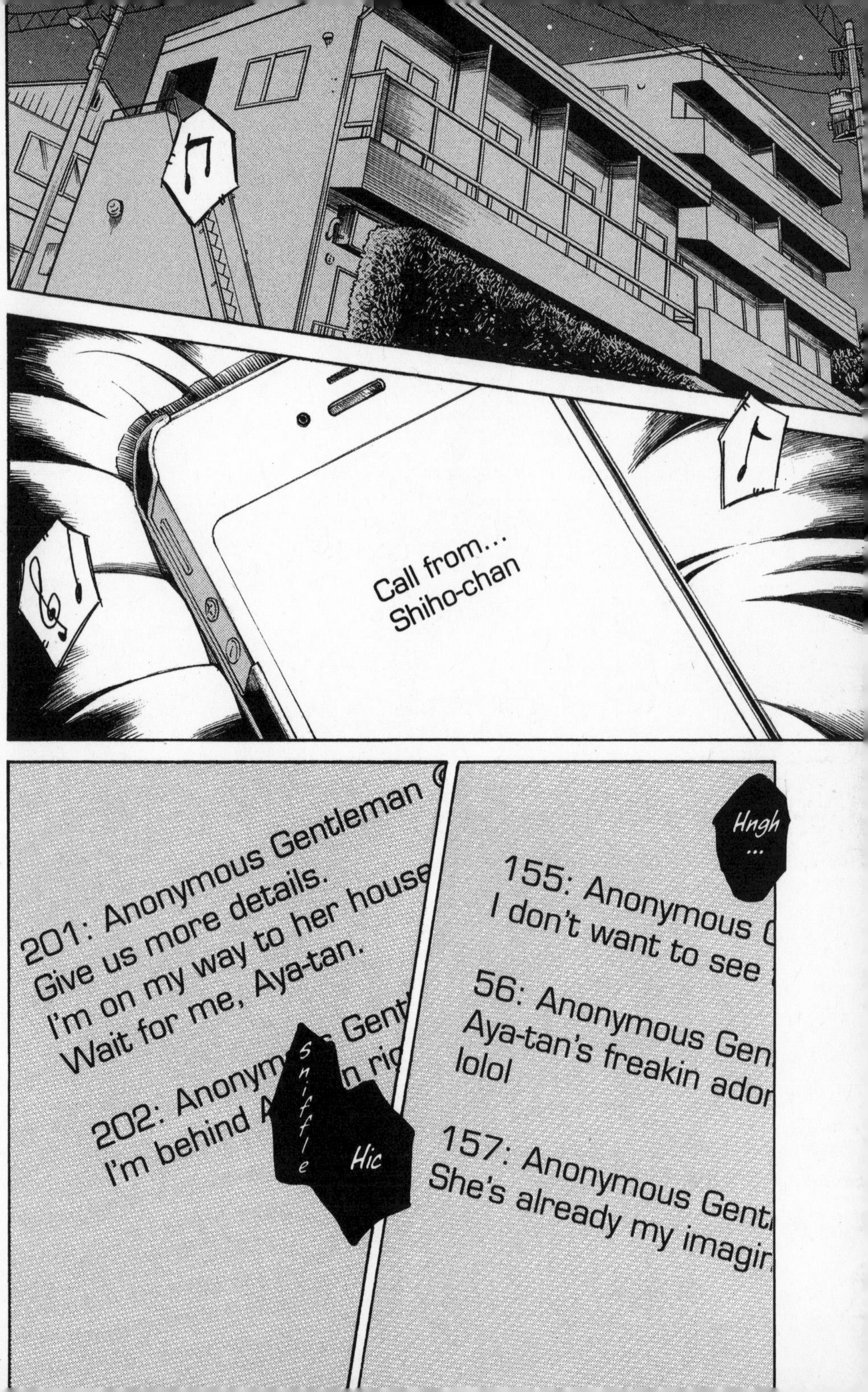
Call from...
Shiho-chan
Hngh...
155: Anonymous
I don't want to see
56: Anonymous Gen
Aya-tan's freakin ador
lolol
157: Anonymous Gent
She's already my imagi
201: Anonymous Gentleman
Give us more details.
I'm on my way to her house
Wait for me, Aya-tan.
202: Anonym
I'm behind A
Sniffle
Hic

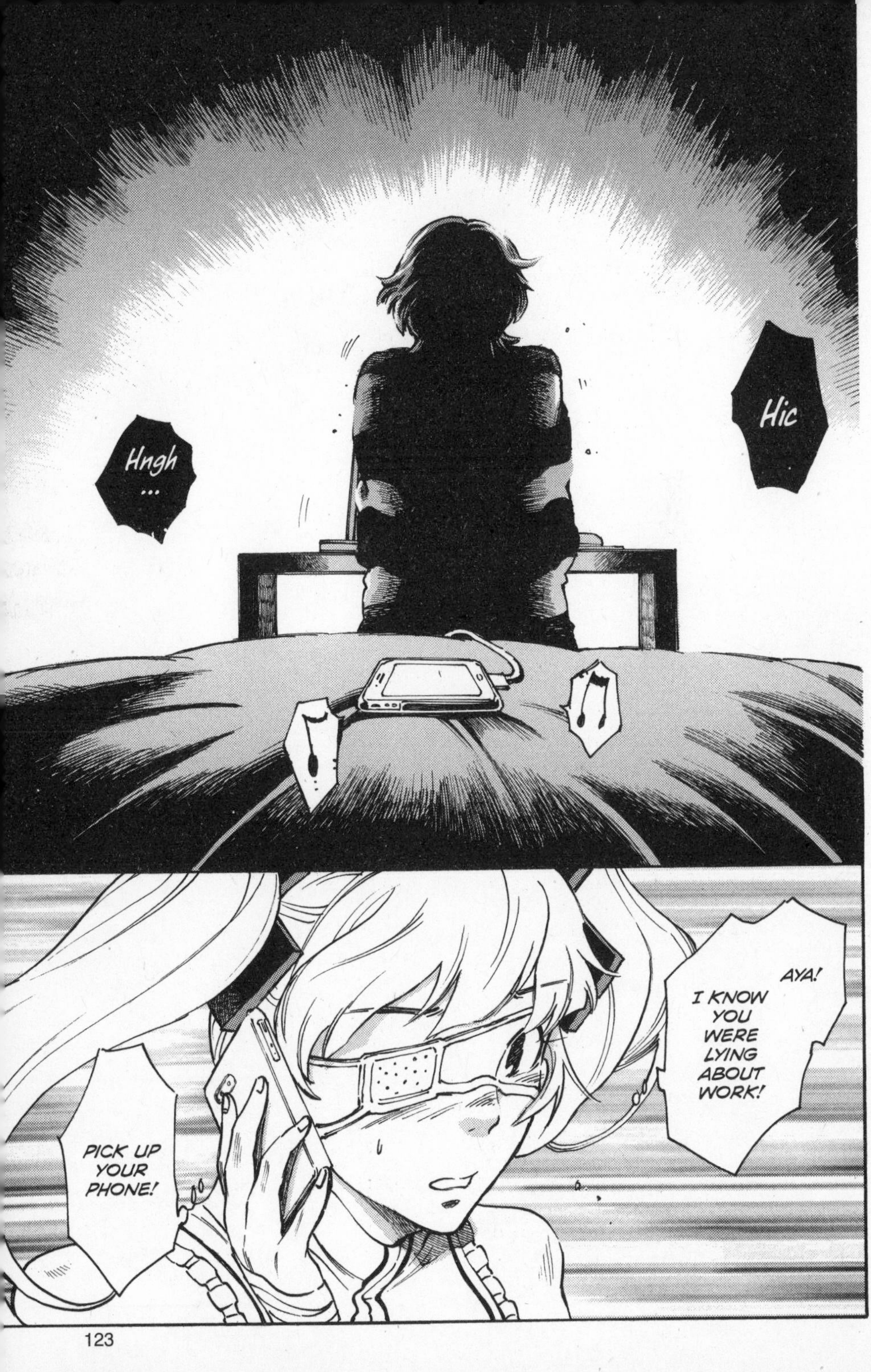
Hic
Hngh ...
AYA! I KNOW YOU WERE LYING ABOUT WORK!
PICK UP YOUR PHONE!

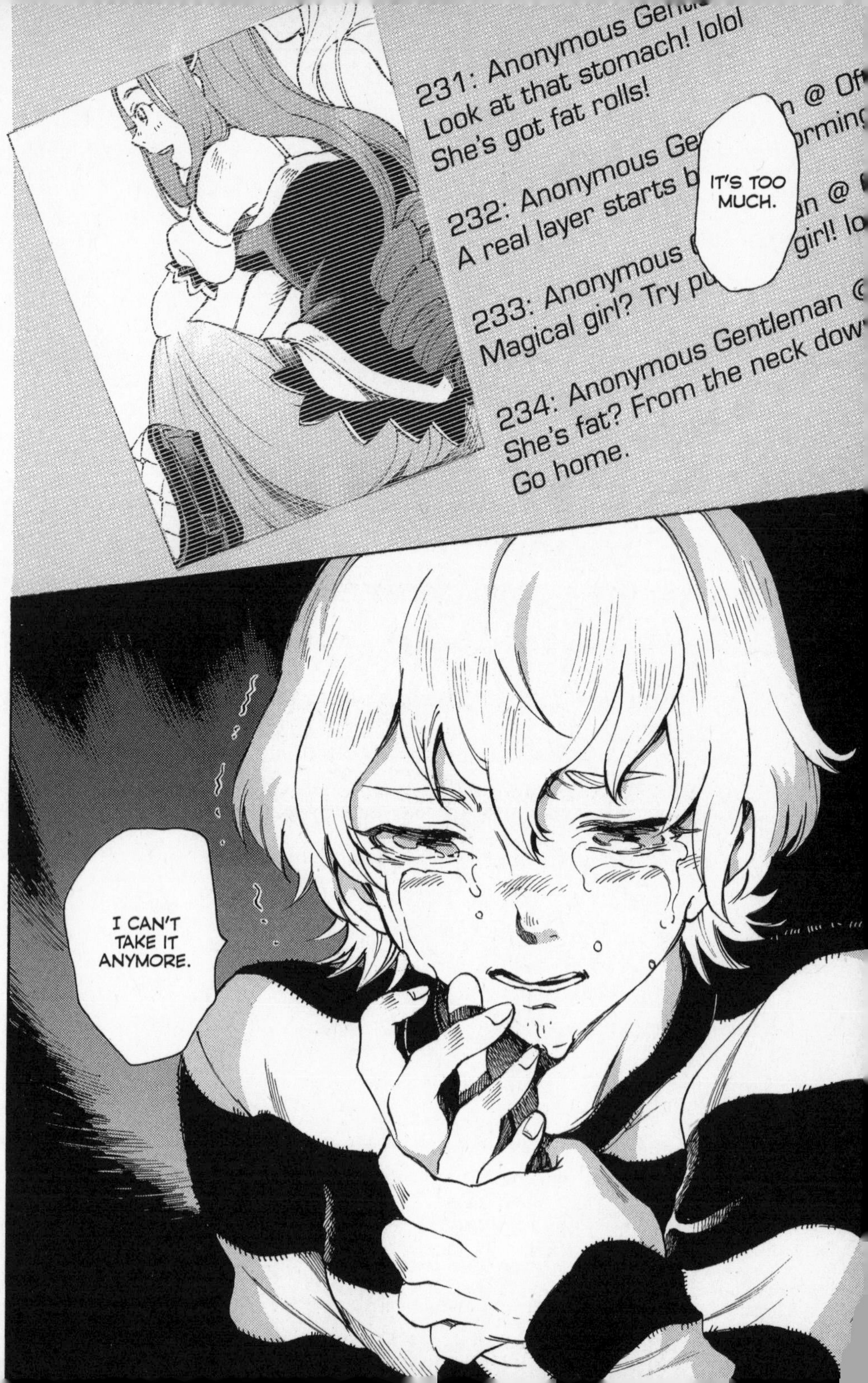
231: Anonymous
Look at that stomach! lolol
She's got fat rolls!
232: Anonymous
A real layer starts
233: Anonymous
Magical girl? Try
girl! lo
234: Anonymous Gentleman
She's fat? From the neck
Go home.
IT'S TOO MUCH.
I CAN'T TAKE IT ANYMORE.

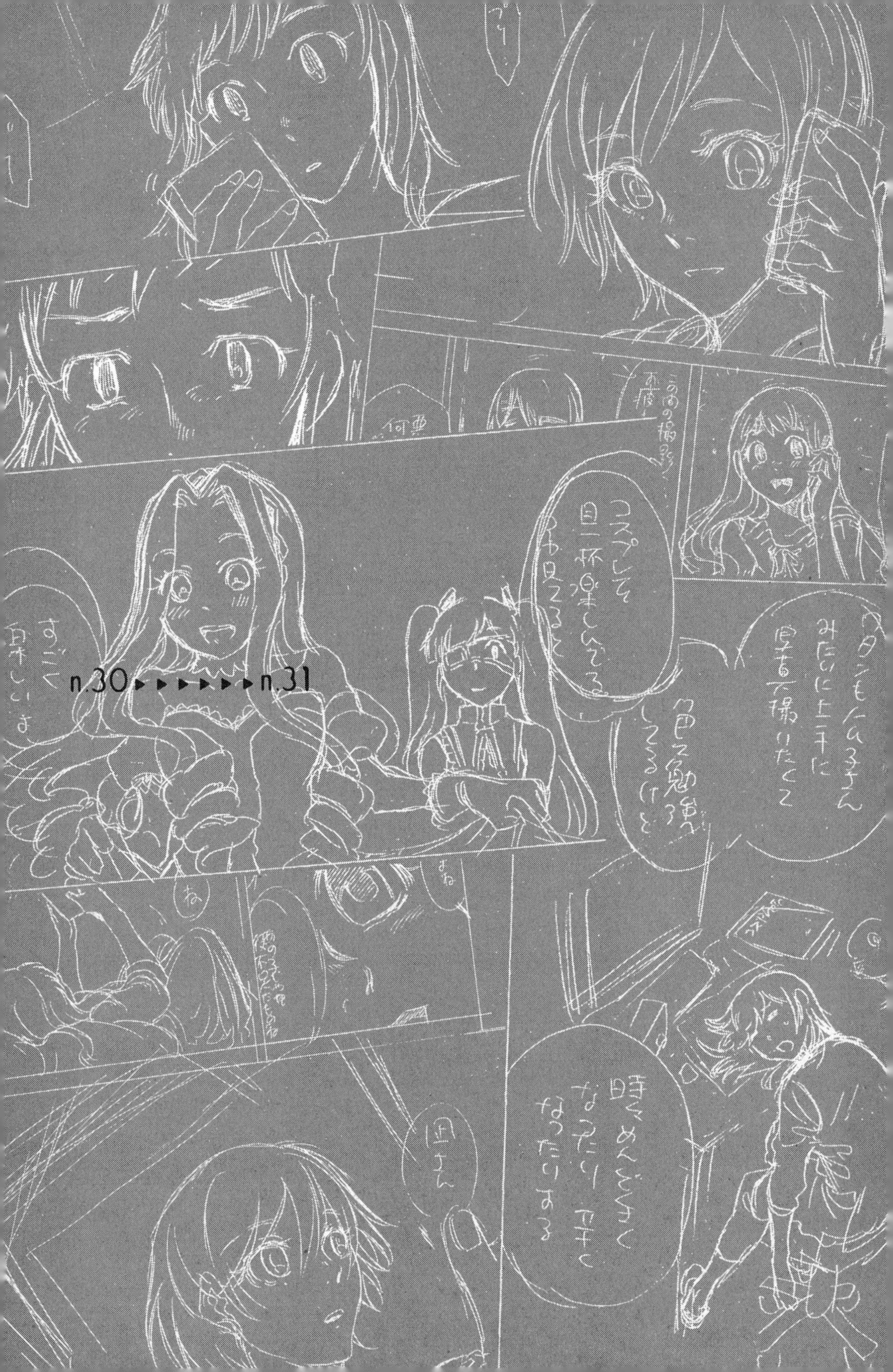
ワタシもムム子さんみたいに上手に写真撮りたくて色々勉強してるけど
コスプレして目一杯楽しんでるのが見えると
すごく嬉しいです
時々めんどくさくなったり辛くなったりする

n.30 ▸▸▸▸▸▸ n.31

COSPLAY CARD

COLLECTION

5

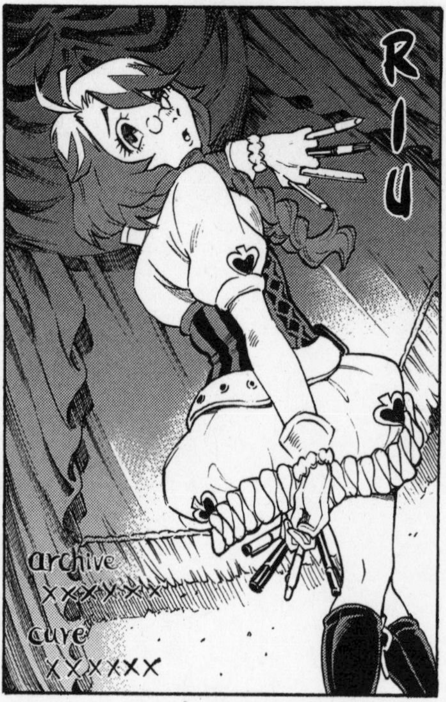
R-I-U
archive
XXXXXXX
cure
XXXXXX

RIU AS KUSU KUSU

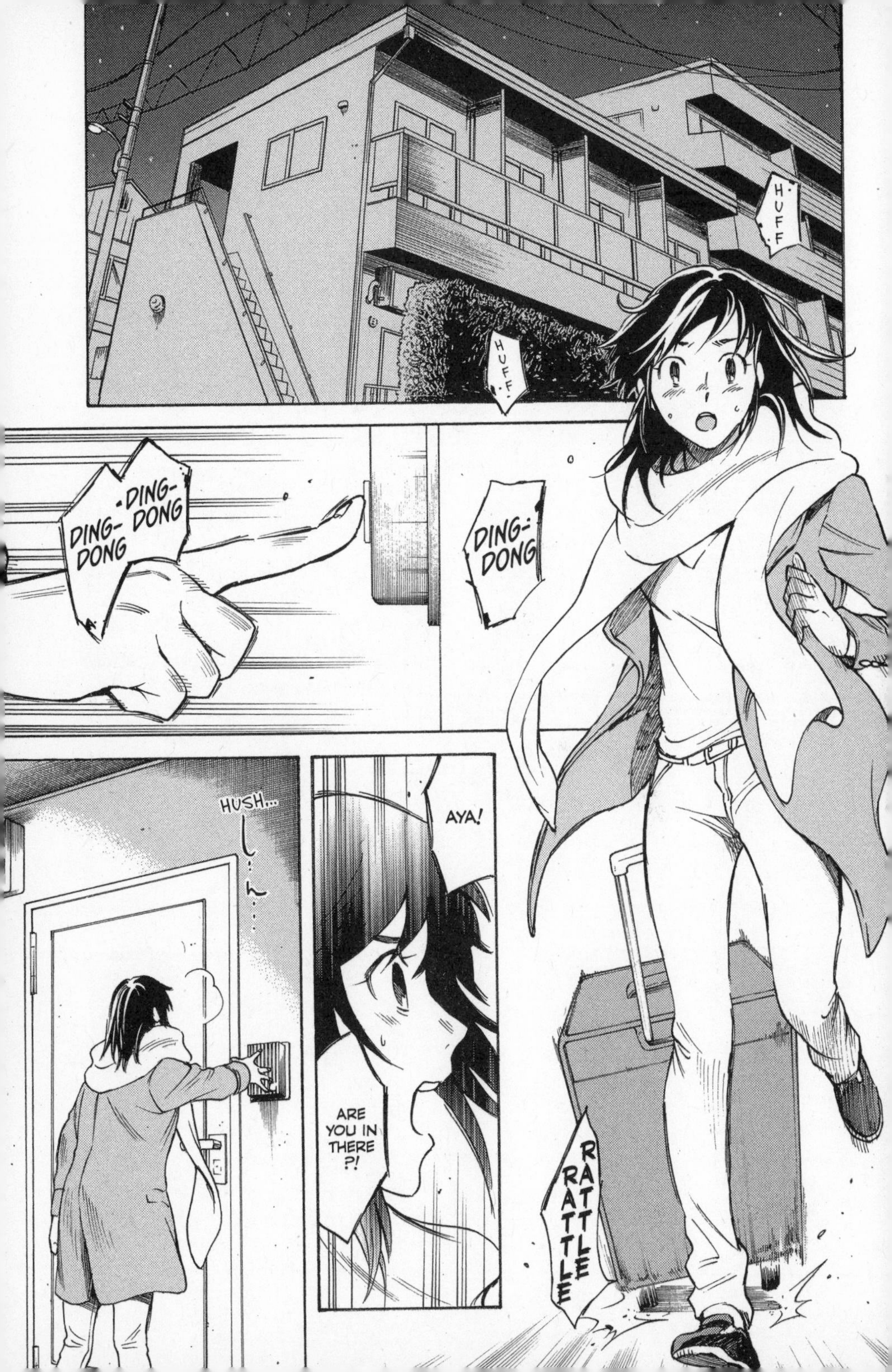

HUFF
HUFF
RATTLE RATTLE
DING-DONG
DING-DONG DING-DONG
AYA!
ARE YOU IN THERE?!
HUSH...
しーん…

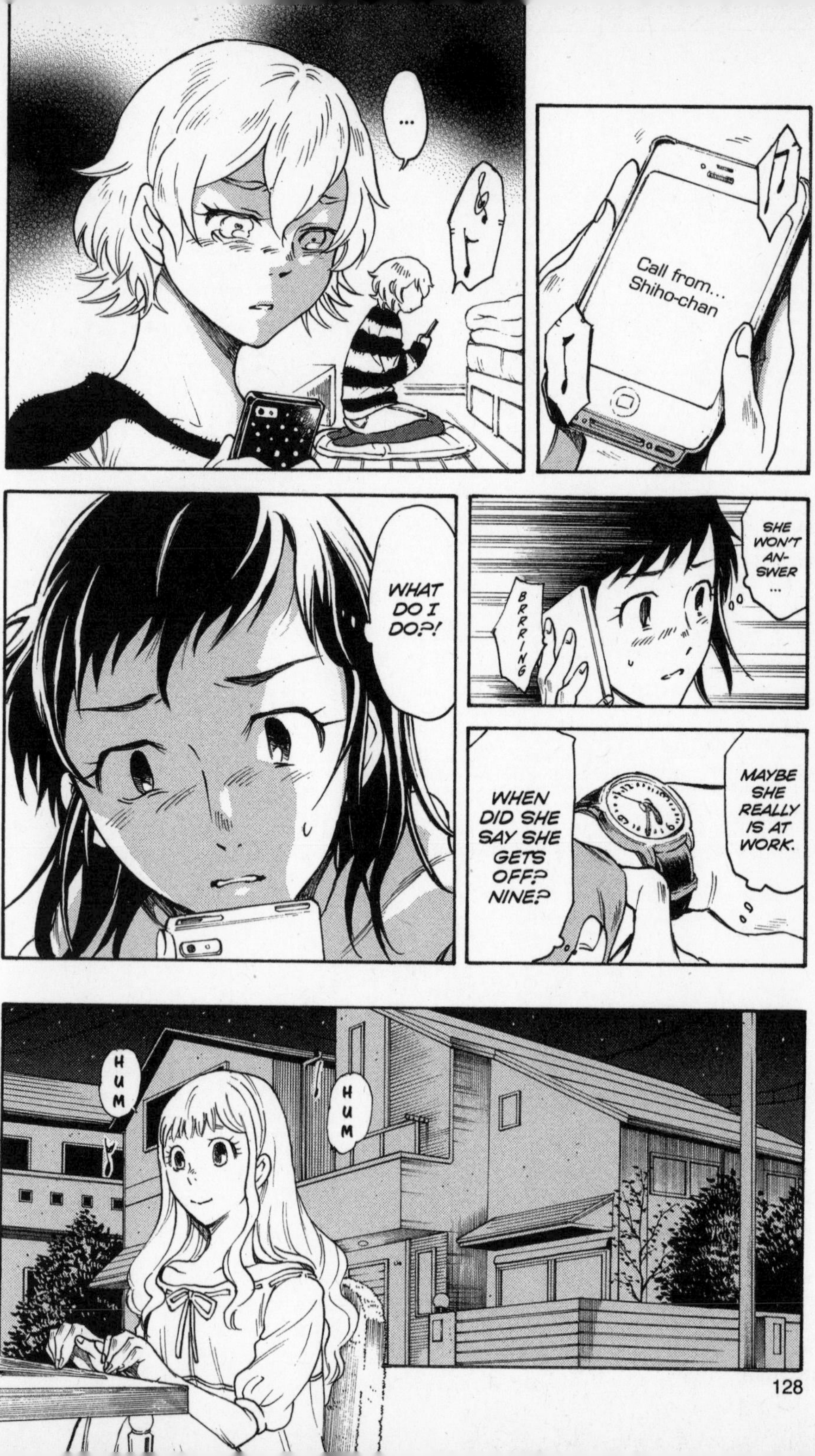
Call from...
Shiho-chan
...
SHE WON'T AN-SWER...
BRRRING
MAYBE SHE REALLY IS AT WORK.
WHEN DID SHE SAY SHE GETS OFF? NINE?
WHAT DO I DO?!
HUM
HUM

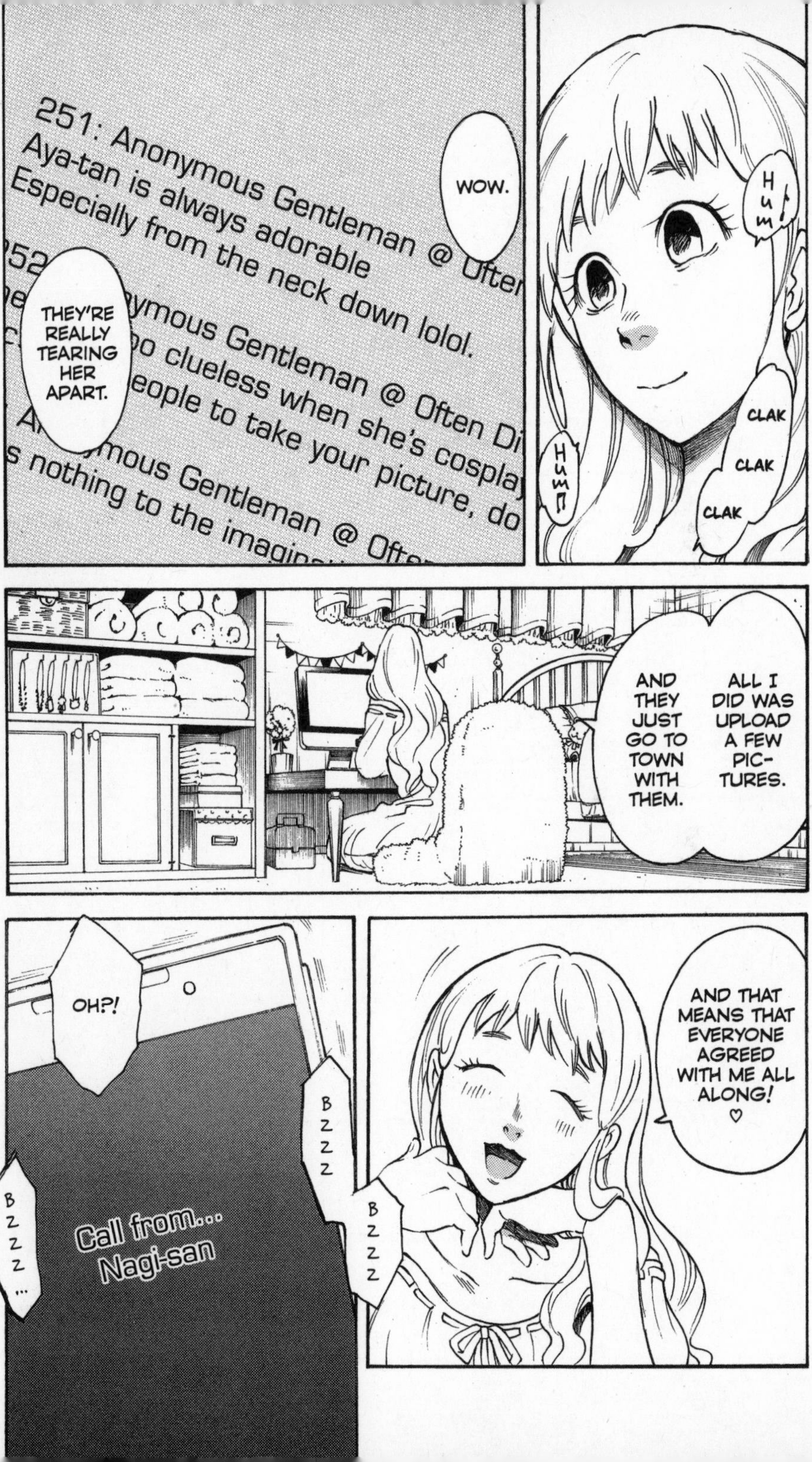
Hum♪
CLAK
CLAK
CLAK
Hum♪
WOW.
251: Anonymous Gentleman @ Ofter
Aya-tan is always adorable
Especially from the neck down lolol.
THEY'RE REALLY TEARING HER APART.
ALL I DID WAS UPLOAD A FEW PICTURES.
AND THEY JUST GO TO TOWN WITH THEM.
AND THAT MEANS THAT EVERYONE AGREED WITH ME ALL ALONG! ♡
BZZZ
BZZZ
OH?!
BZZZ
BZZZ...
Call from... Nagi-san

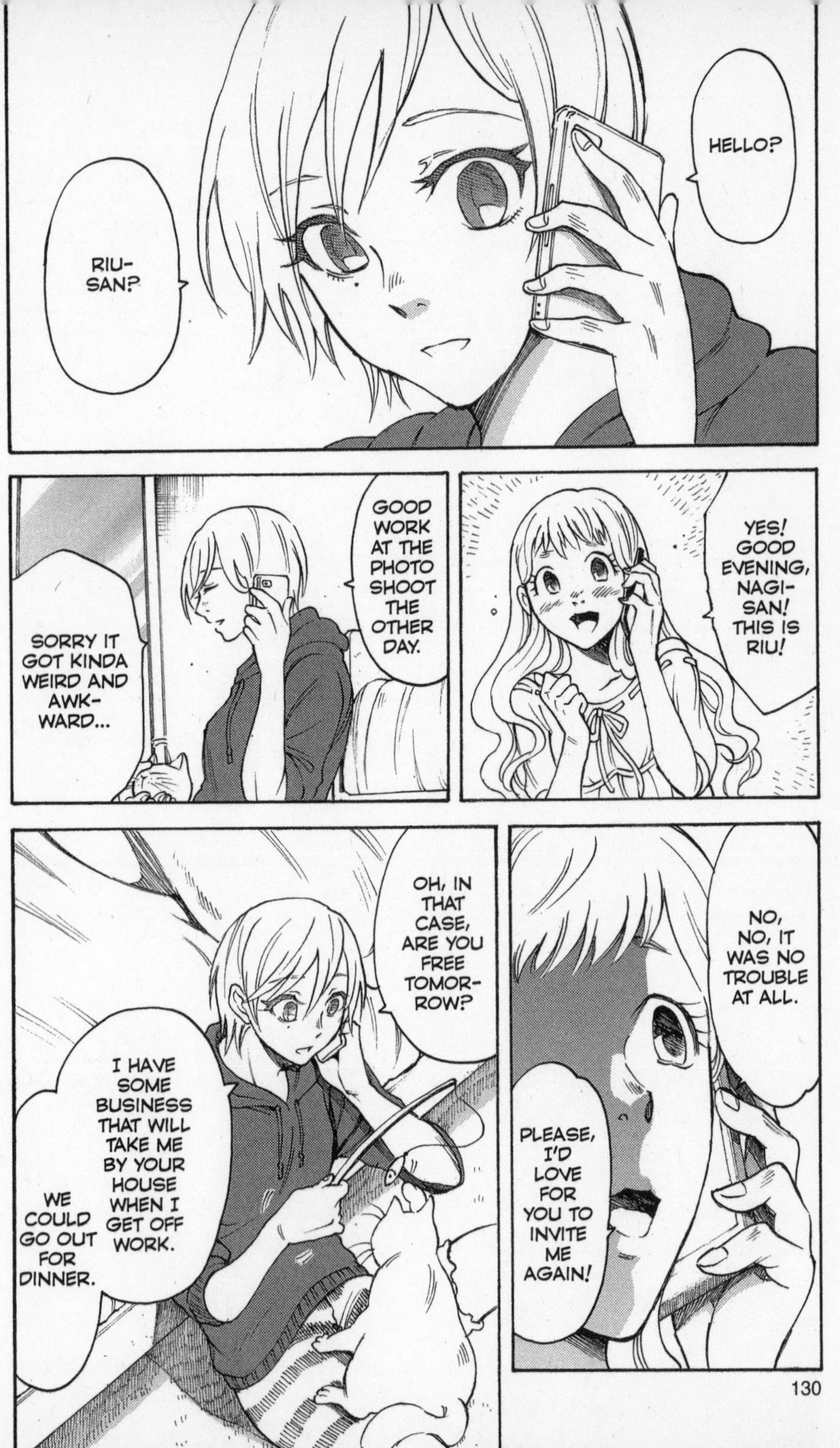
HELLO?
RIU-SAN?
YES! GOOD EVENING, NAGI-SAN! THIS IS RIU!
GOOD WORK AT THE PHOTO SHOOT THE OTHER DAY.
SORRY IT GOT KINDA WEIRD AND AWK-WARD...
NO, NO, IT WAS NO TROUBLE AT ALL.
PLEASE, I'D LOVE FOR YOU TO INVITE ME AGAIN!
OH, IN THAT CASE, ARE YOU FREE TOMOR-ROW?
I HAVE SOME BUSINESS THAT WILL TAKE ME BY YOUR HOUSE WHEN I GET OFF WORK.
WE COULD GO OUT FOR DINNER.

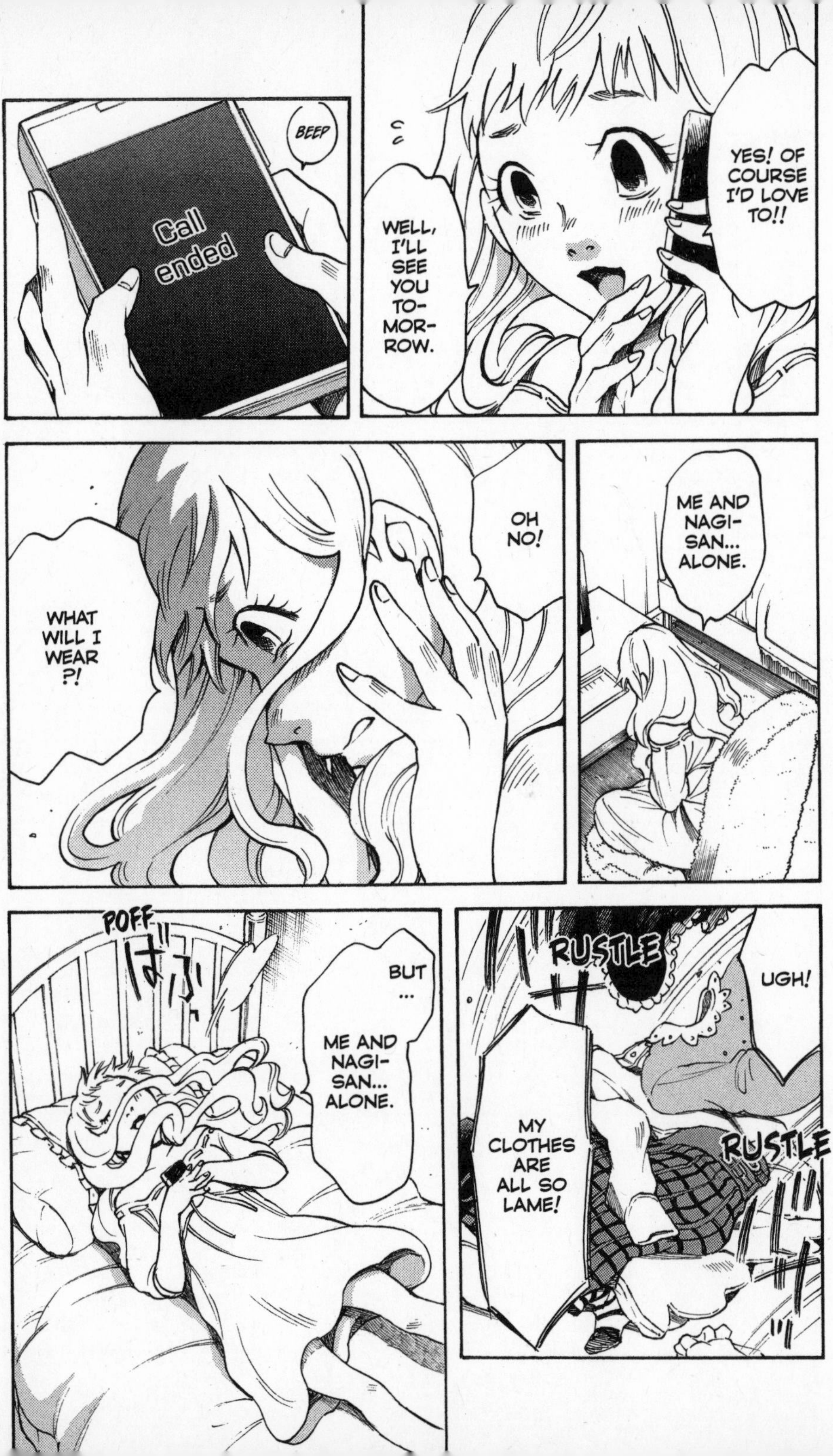
YES! OF COURSE I'D LOVE TO!!
WELL, I'LL SEE YOU TO-MOR-ROW.
BEEP
Call ended
ME AND NAGI-SAN... ALONE.
OH NO!
WHAT WILL I WEAR ?!
UGH!
RUSTLE
MY CLOTHES ARE ALL SO LAME!
RUSTLE
BUT ...
ME AND NAGI-SAN... ALONE.
POFF
ばふ

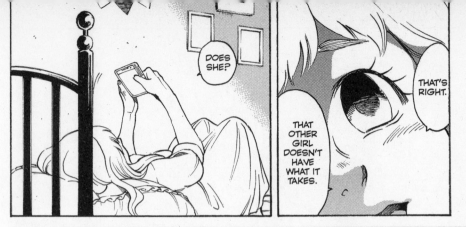

DOES SHE?

THAT'S RIGHT.

THAT OTHER GIRL DOESN'T HAVE WHAT IT TAKES.

NAGI-SAN.

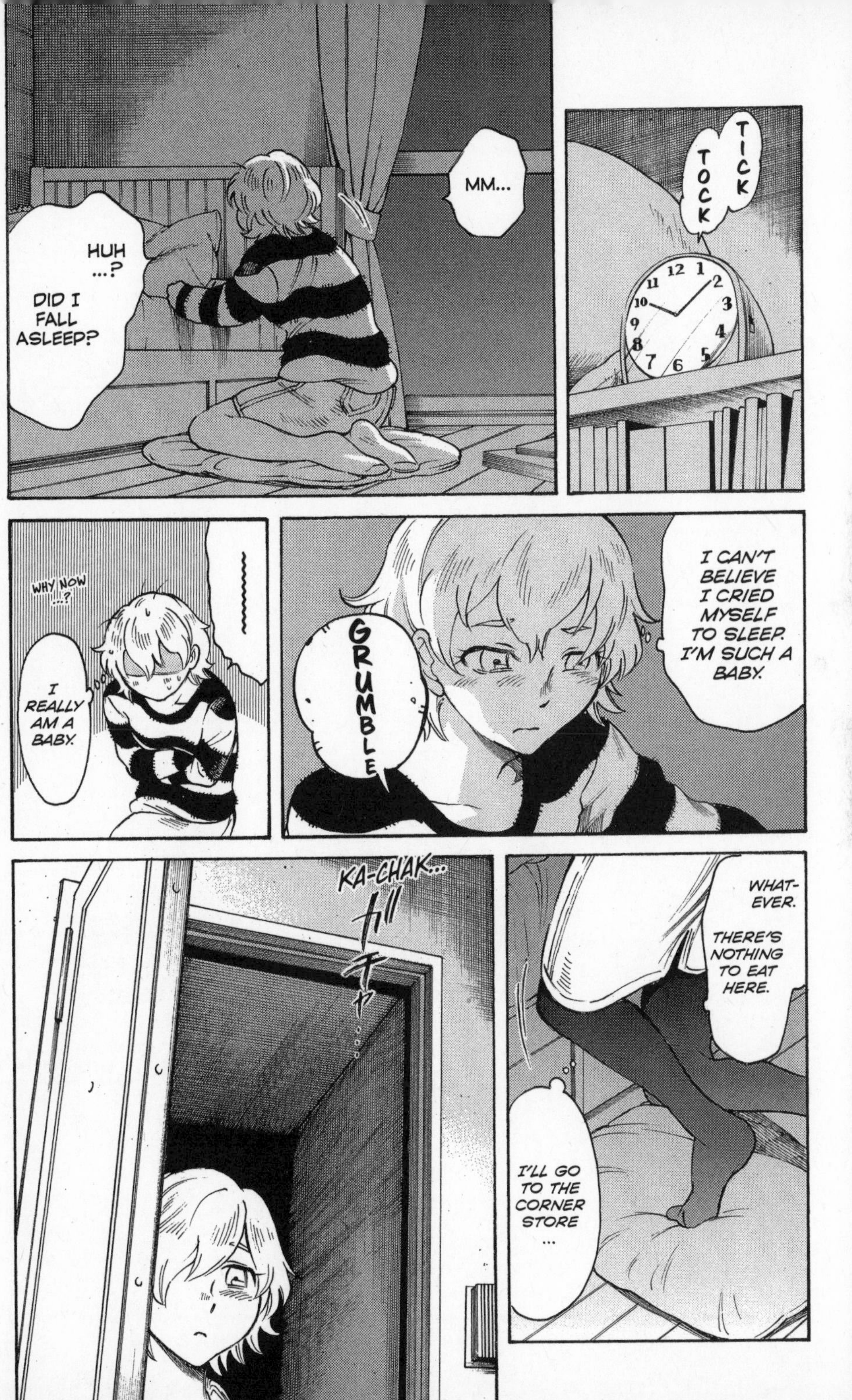
TICK TOCK
MM...
HUH ...? DID I FALL ASLEEP?
I CAN'T BELIEVE I CRIED MYSELF TO SLEEP. I'M SUCH A BABY.
GRUMBLE
~~~~~
WHY NOW ...?
I REALLY AM A BABY.
WHAT-EVER.
THERE'S NOTHING TO EAT HERE.
I'LL GO TO THE CORNER STORE ...
KA-CHAK...
ガチャ
~~~~~

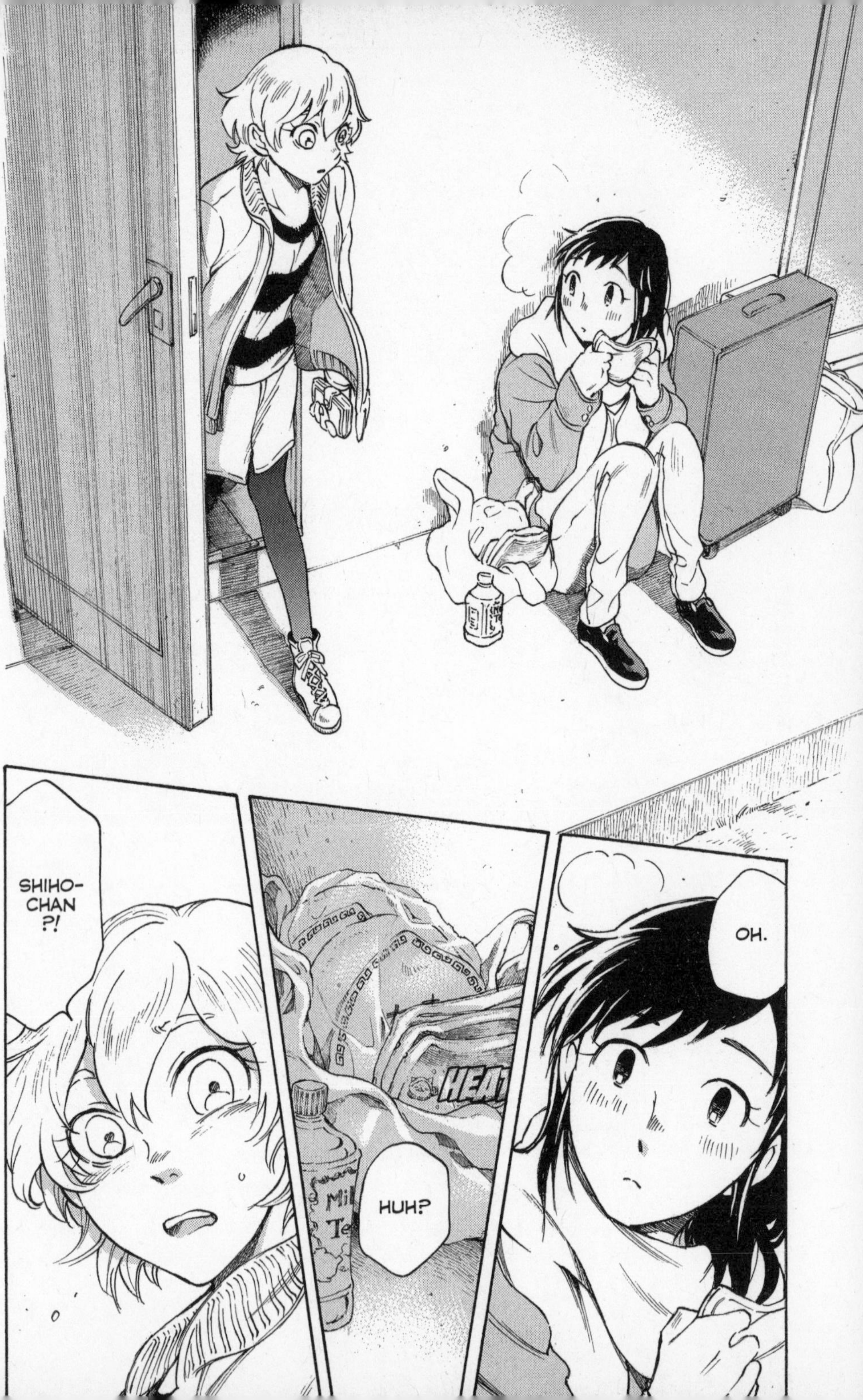
OH.
HUH?
SHIHO-CHAN?!

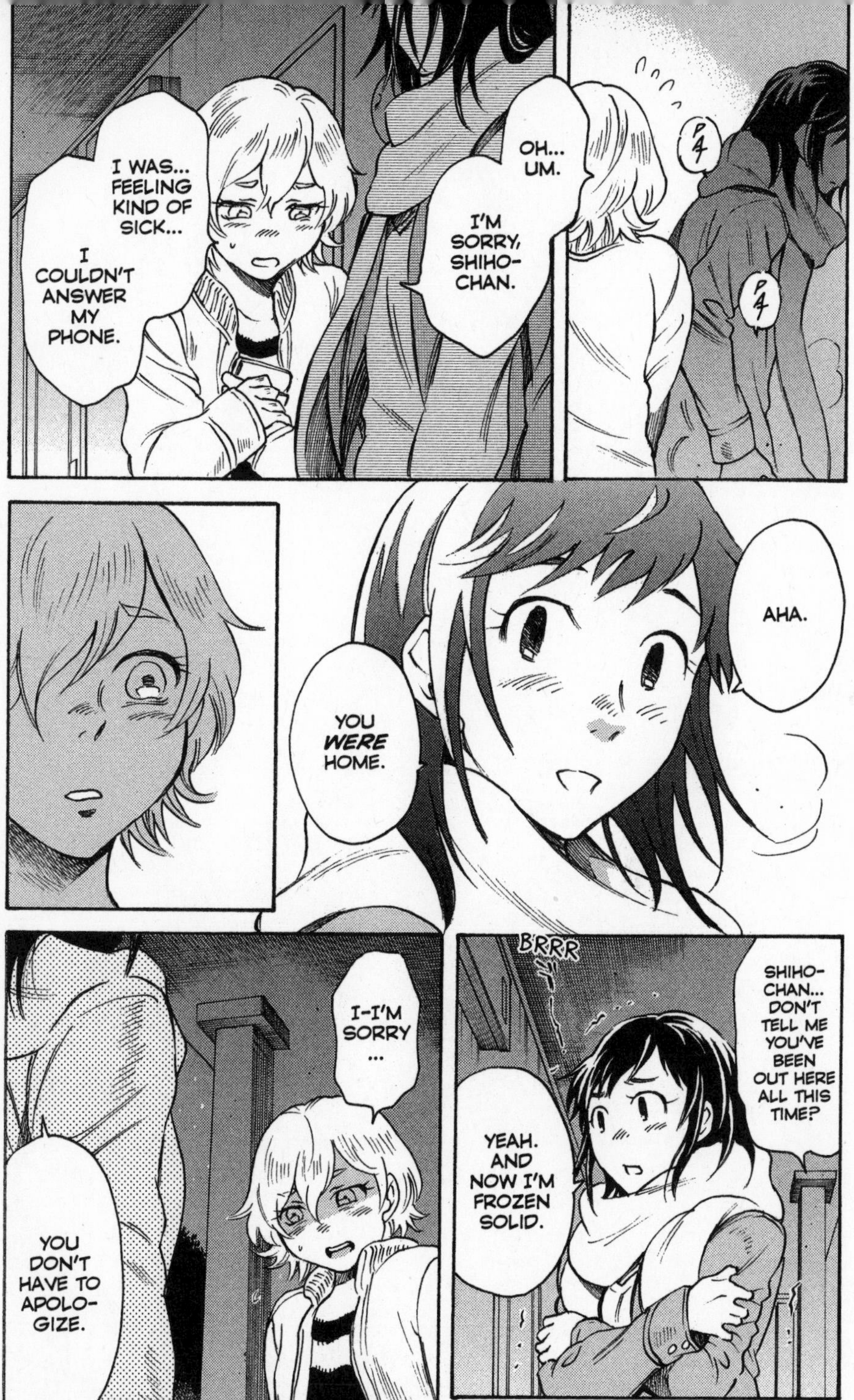
OH... UM.
I'M SORRY, SHIHO-CHAN.
I WAS... FEELING KIND OF SICK...
I COULDN'T ANSWER MY PHONE.
AHA.
YOU *WERE* HOME.
BRRR
SHIHO-CHAN... DON'T TELL ME YOU'VE BEEN OUT HERE ALL THIS TIME?
YEAH. AND NOW I'M FROZEN SOLID.
I-I'M SORRY ...
YOU DON'T HAVE TO APOLO-GIZE.

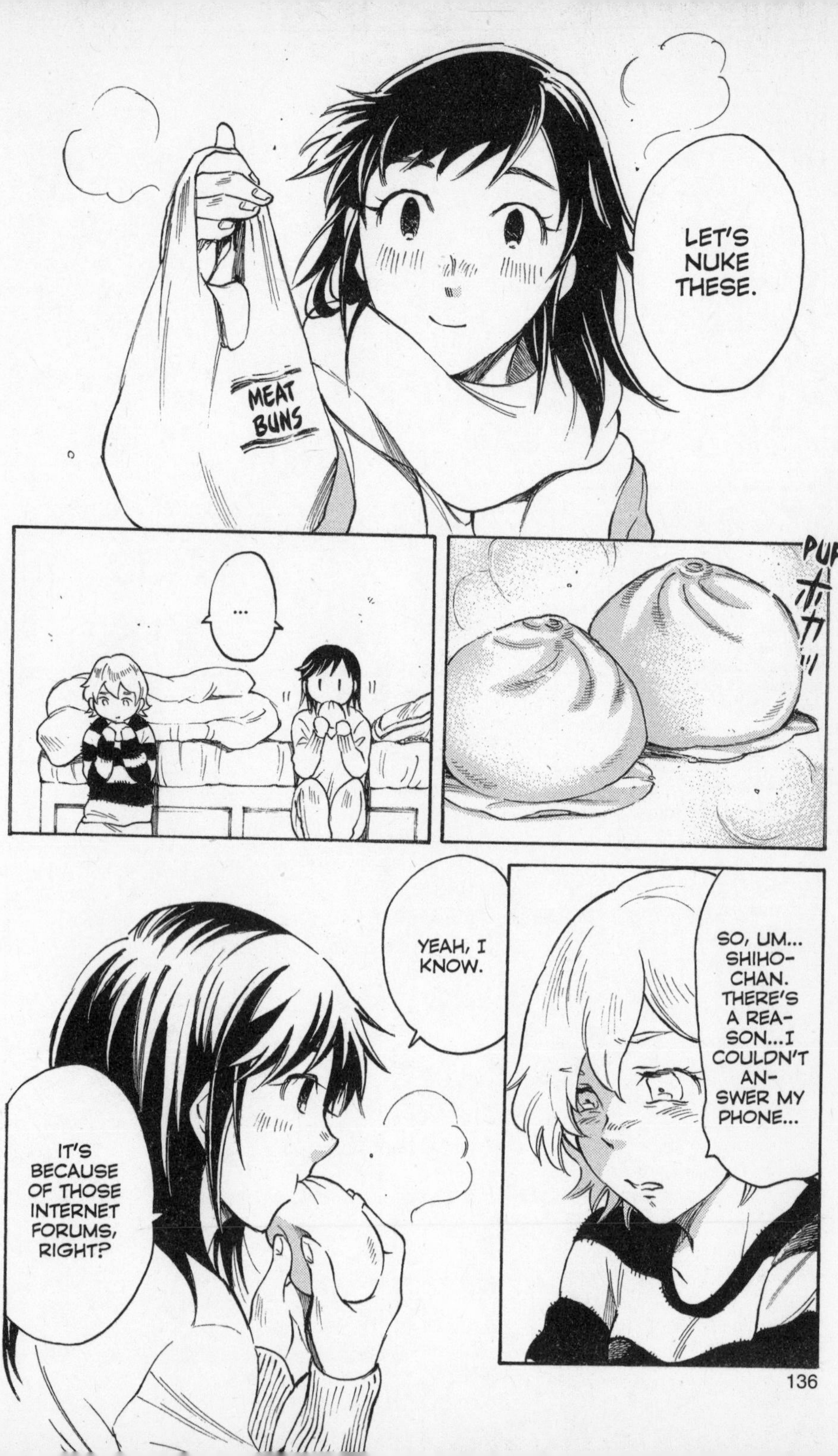
LET'S NUKE THESE.
MEAT BUNS
PUFF
...
SO, UM... SHIHO-CHAN. THERE'S A REA-SON...I COULDN'T AN-SWER MY PHONE...
YEAH, I KNOW.
IT'S BECAUSE OF THOSE INTERNET FORUMS, RIGHT?

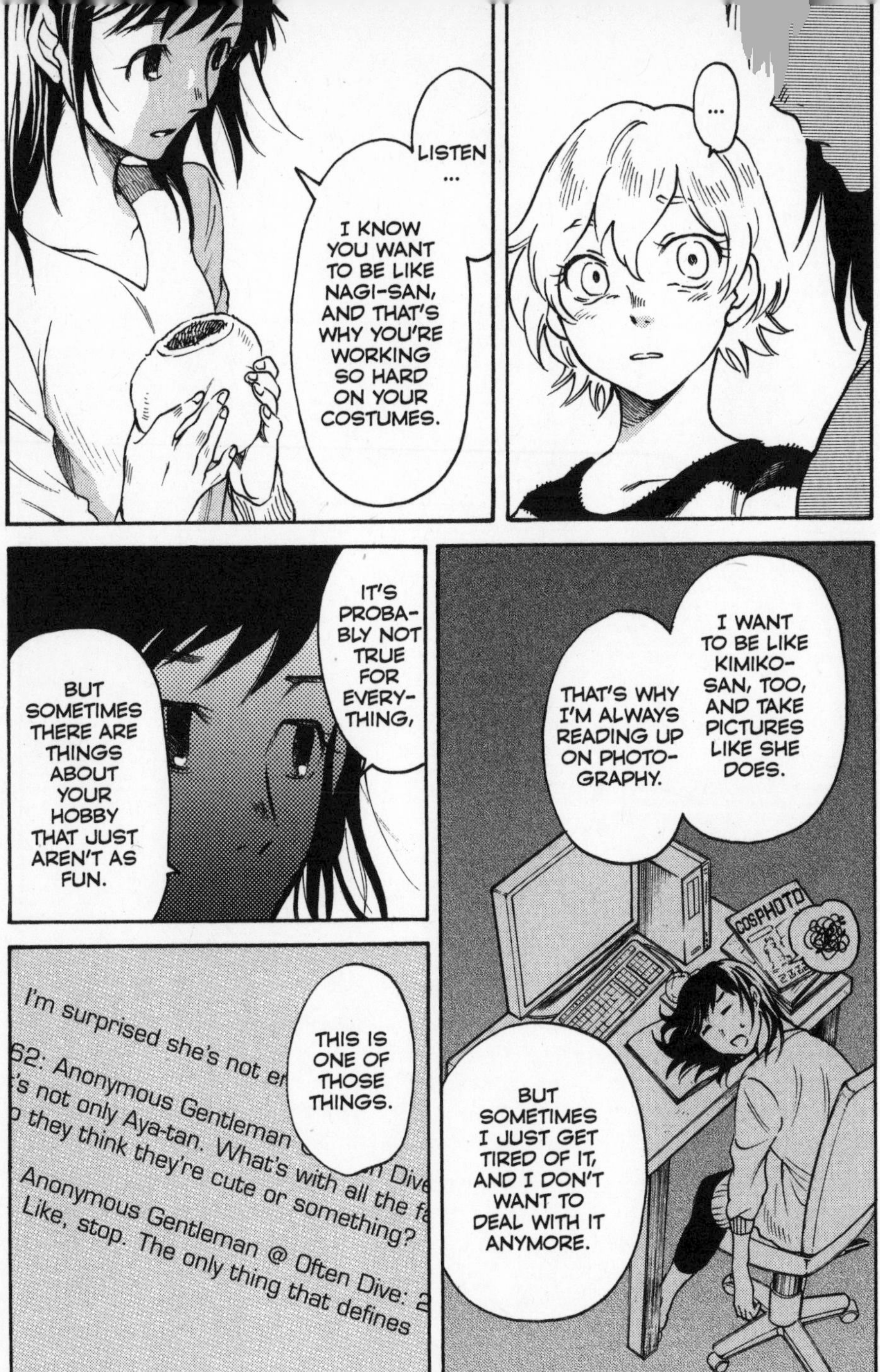
...
LISTEN ...
I KNOW YOU WANT TO BE LIKE NAGI-SAN, AND THAT'S WHY YOU'RE WORKING SO HARD ON YOUR COSTUMES.
I WANT TO BE LIKE KIMIKO-SAN, TOO, AND TAKE PICTURES LIKE SHE DOES.
THAT'S WHY I'M ALWAYS READING UP ON PHOTOGRAPHY.
COSPHOTO
BUT SOMETIMES I JUST GET TIRED OF IT, AND I DON'T WANT TO DEAL WITH IT ANYMORE.
IT'S PROBABLY NOT TRUE FOR EVERYTHING,
BUT SOMETIMES THERE ARE THINGS ABOUT YOUR HOBBY THAT JUST AREN'T AS FUN.
I'm surprised she's not e
62: Anonymous Gentleman
's not only Aya-tan. What's with all the f
they think they're cute or something?
Anonymous Gentleman @ Often Dive:
Like, stop. The only thing that defines
THIS IS ONE OF THOSE THINGS.

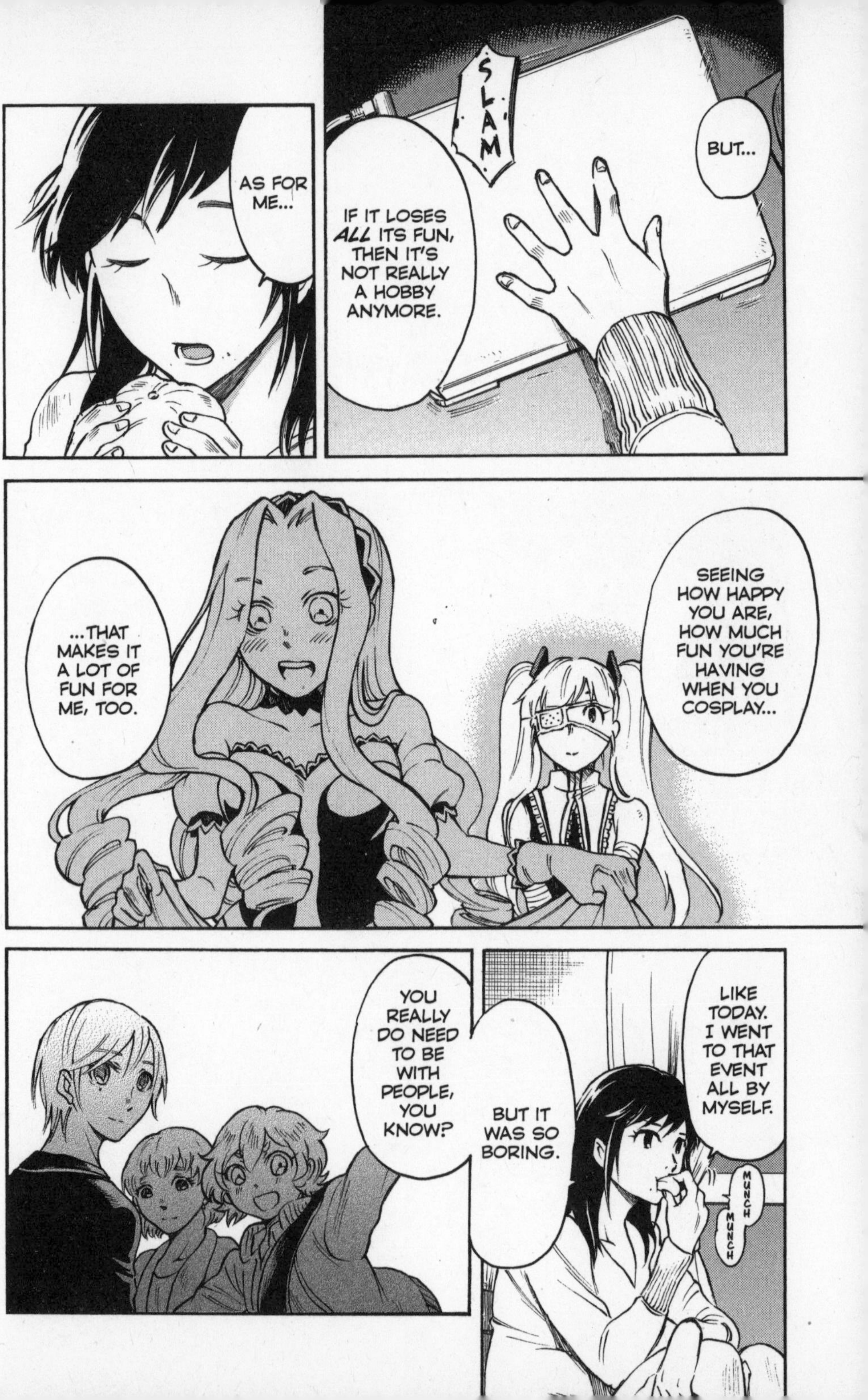
BUT...
SLAM
IF IT LOSES ALL ITS FUN, THEN IT'S NOT REALLY A HOBBY ANYMORE.
AS FOR ME...
SEEING HOW HAPPY YOU ARE, HOW MUCH FUN YOU'RE HAVING WHEN YOU COSPLAY...
...THAT MAKES IT A LOT OF FUN FOR ME, TOO.
LIKE TODAY. I WENT TO THAT EVENT ALL BY MYSELF.
MUNCH MUNCH
BUT IT WAS SO BORING.
YOU REALLY DO NEED TO BE WITH PEOPLE, YOU KNOW?

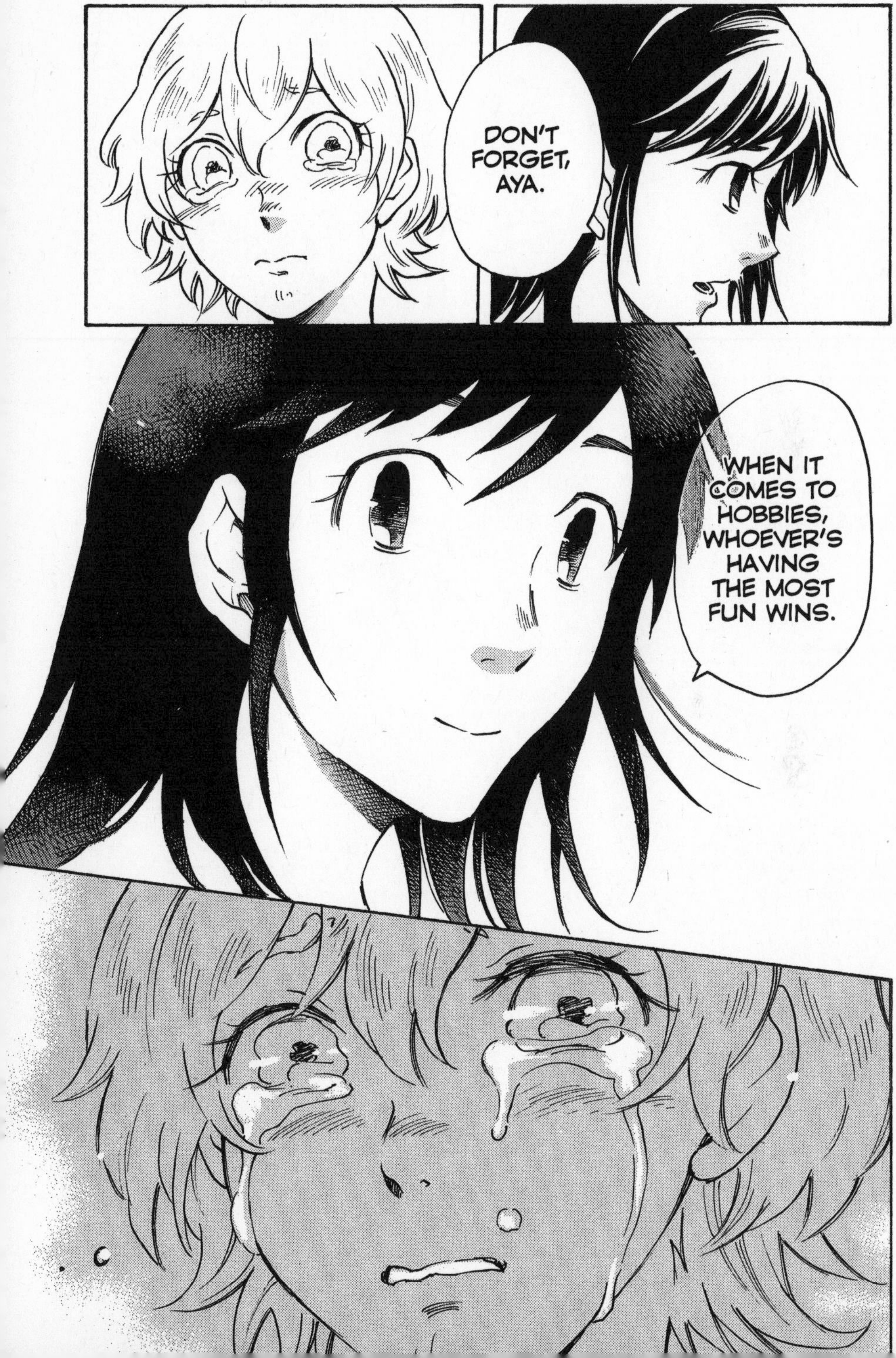
DON'T FORGET, AYA.
WHEN IT COMES TO HOBBIES, WHOEVER'S HAVING THE MOST FUN WINS.

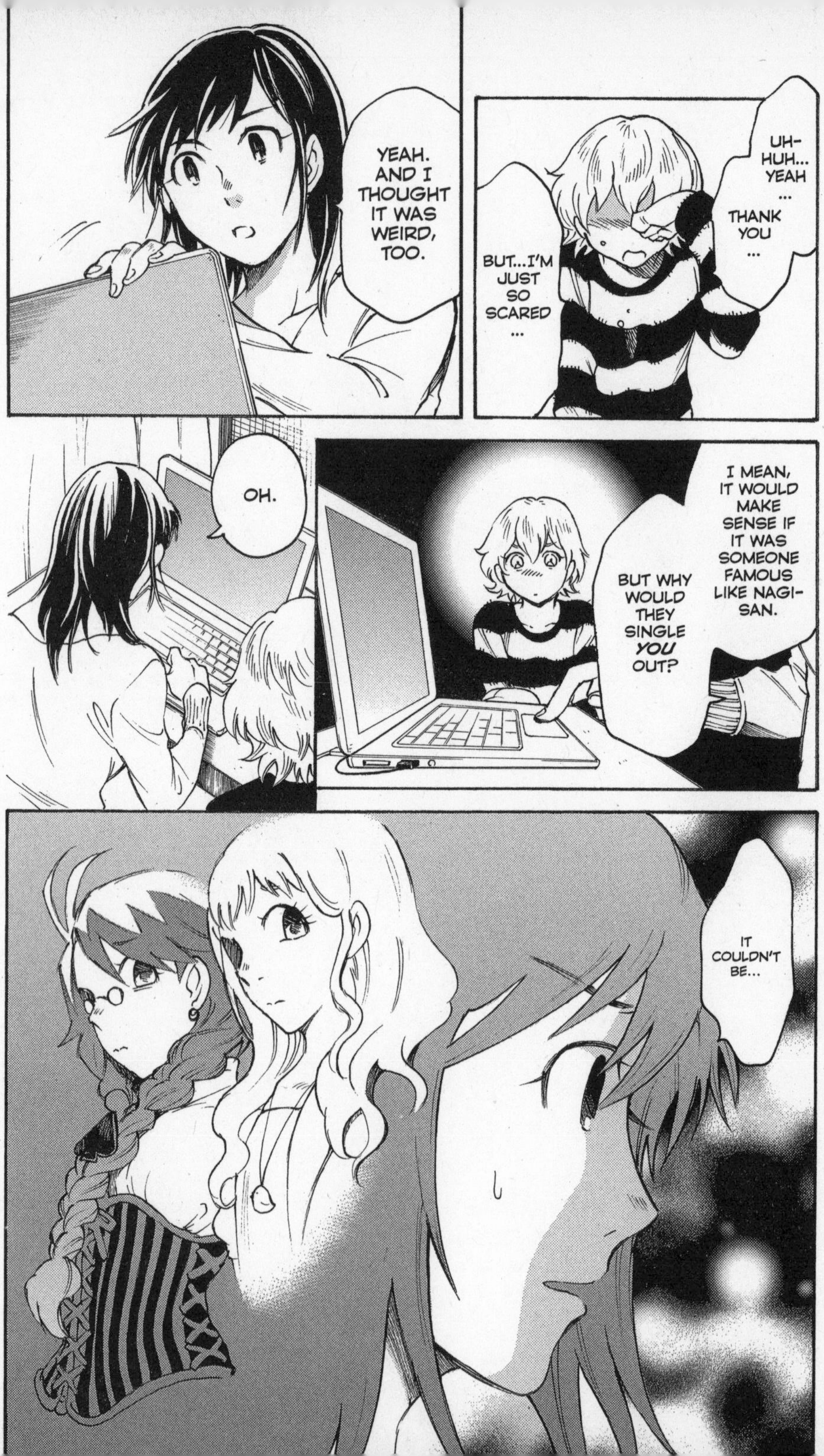
UH-HUH... YEAH ... THANK YOU ...
BUT...I'M JUST SO SCARED ...
YEAH. AND I THOUGHT IT WAS WEIRD, TOO.
I MEAN, IT WOULD MAKE SENSE IF IT WAS SOMEONE FAMOUS LIKE NAGI-SAN.
BUT WHY WOULD THEY SINGLE *YOU* OUT?
OH.
IT COULDN'T BE...

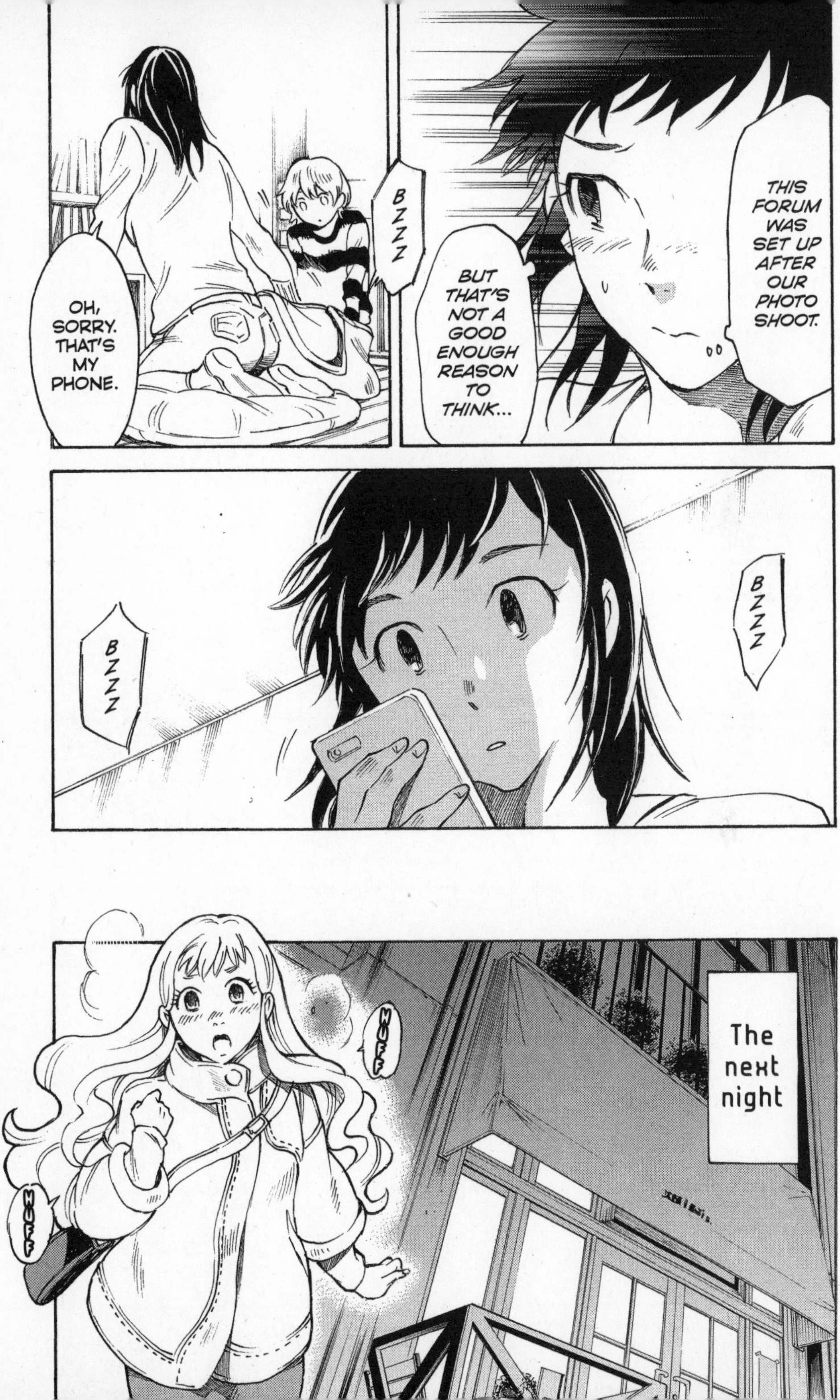
THIS FORUM WAS SET UP AFTER OUR PHOTO SHOOT.
BUT THAT'S NOT A GOOD ENOUGH REASON TO THINK...
BZZZ
OH, SORRY. THAT'S MY PHONE.
BZZZ
BZZZ
The next night
HUFF
HUFF

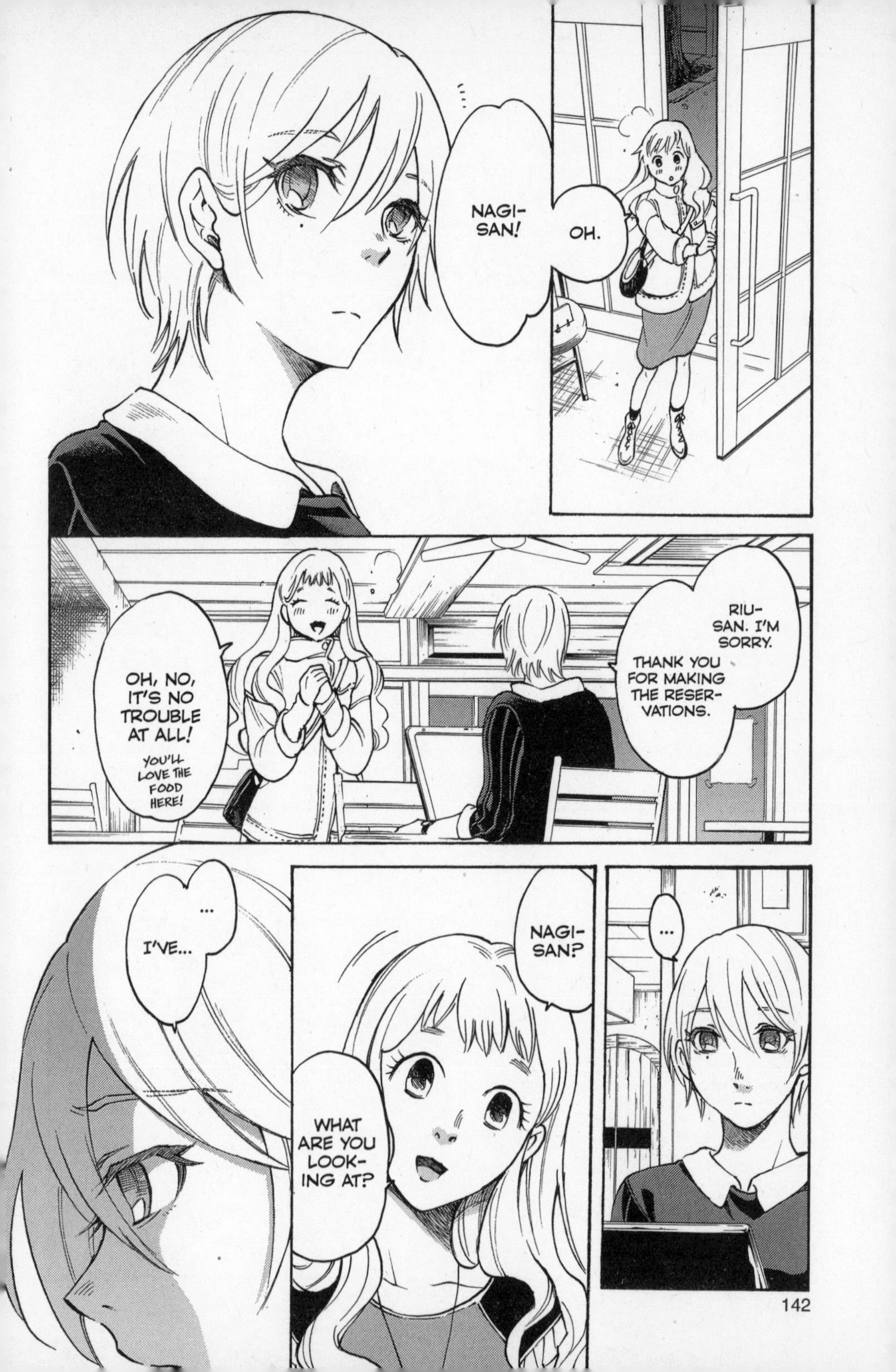
OH.
NAGI-SAN!
RIU-SAN. I'M SORRY.
THANK YOU FOR MAKING THE RESERVATIONS.
OH, NO, IT'S NO TROUBLE AT ALL!
YOU'LL LOVE THE FOOD HERE!
...
NAGI-SAN?
WHAT ARE YOU LOOKING AT?
...
I'VE...

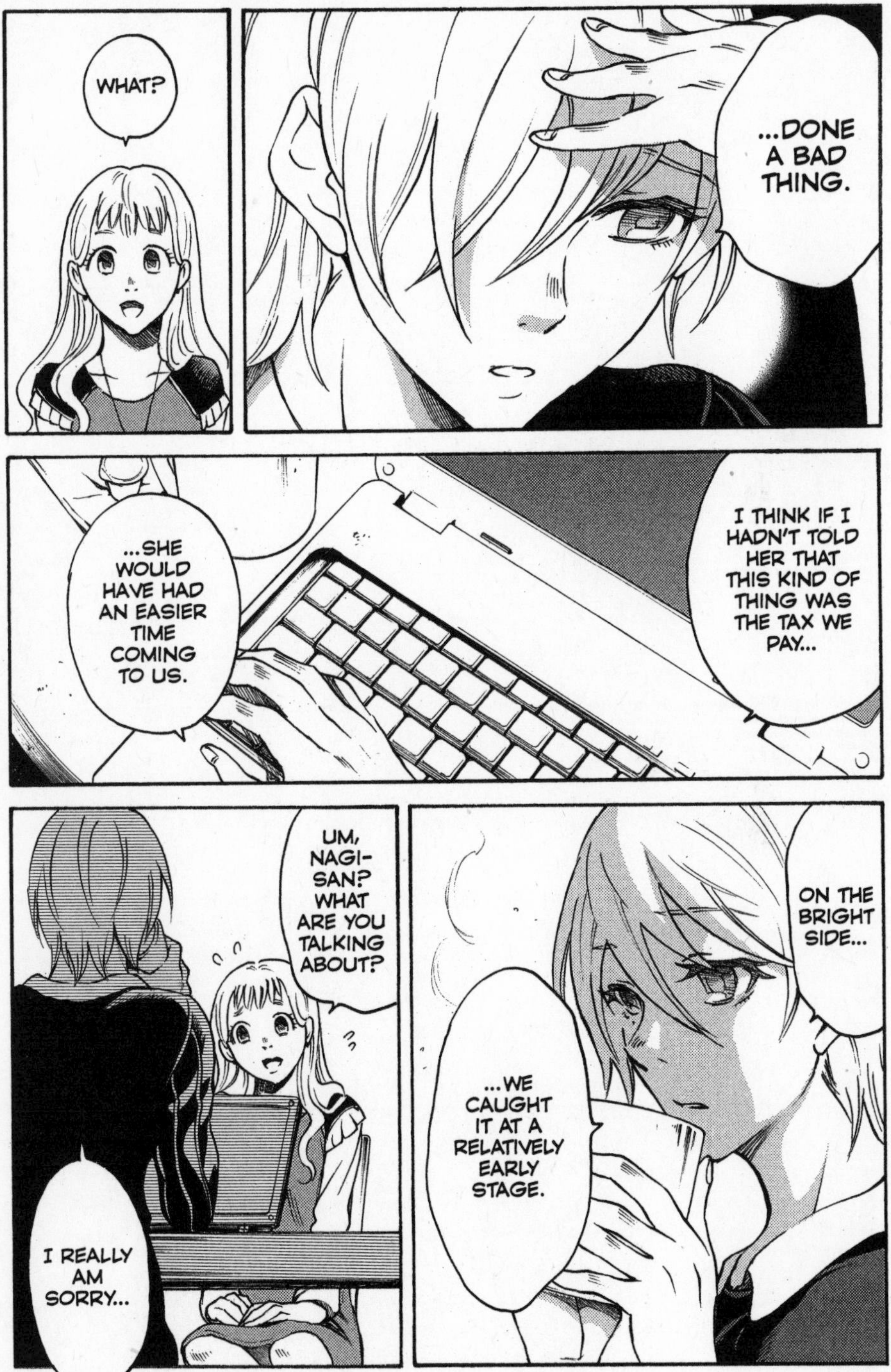
...DONE A BAD THING.
WHAT?
I THINK IF I HADN'T TOLD HER THAT THIS KIND OF THING WAS THE TAX WE PAY...
...SHE WOULD HAVE HAD AN EASIER TIME COMING TO US.
ON THE BRIGHT SIDE...
...WE CAUGHT IT AT A RELATIVELY EARLY STAGE.
UM, NAGI-SAN? WHAT ARE YOU TALKING ABOUT?
I REALLY AM SORRY...

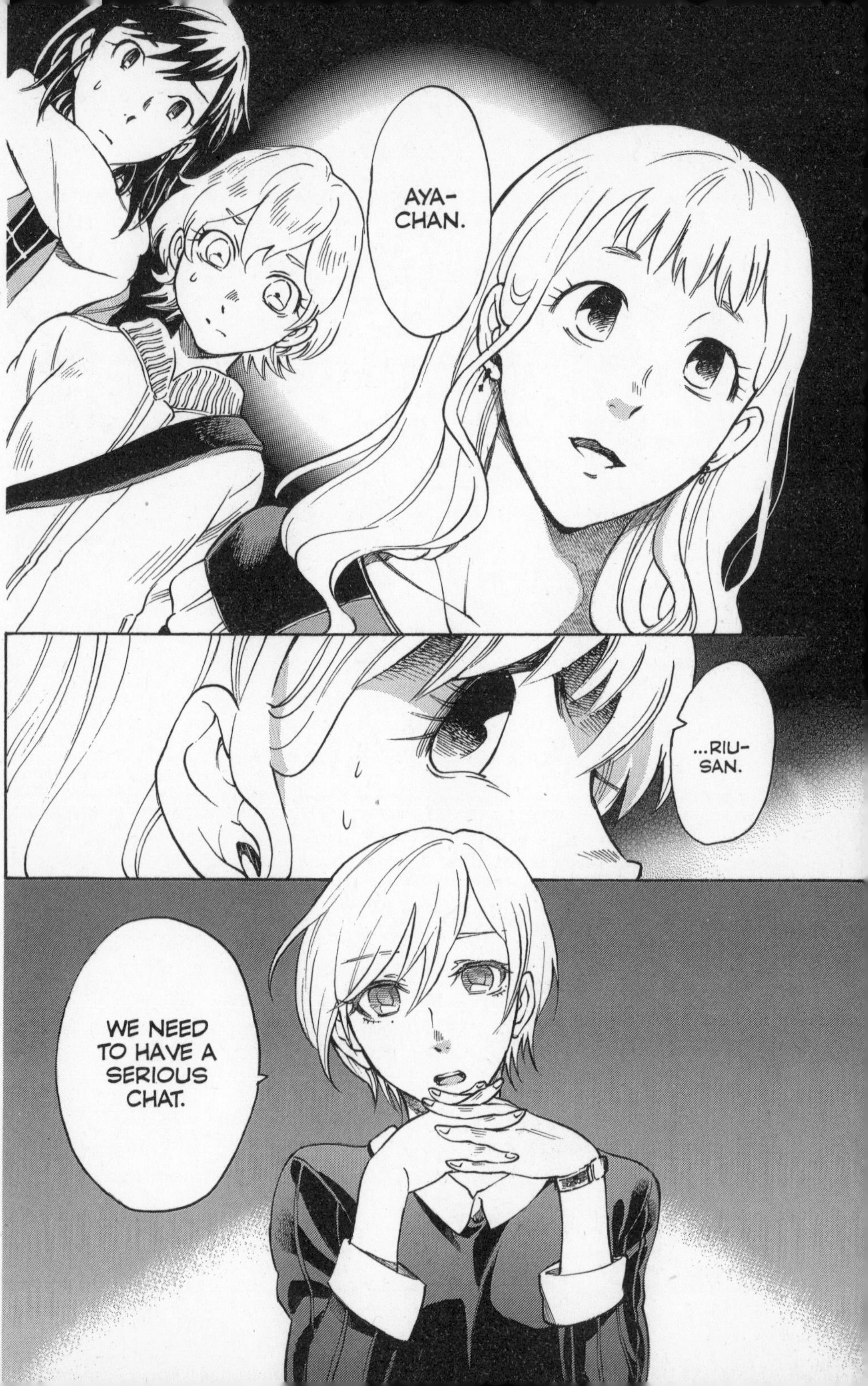
AYA-CHAN.
...RIU-SAN.
WE NEED TO HAVE A SERIOUS CHAT.

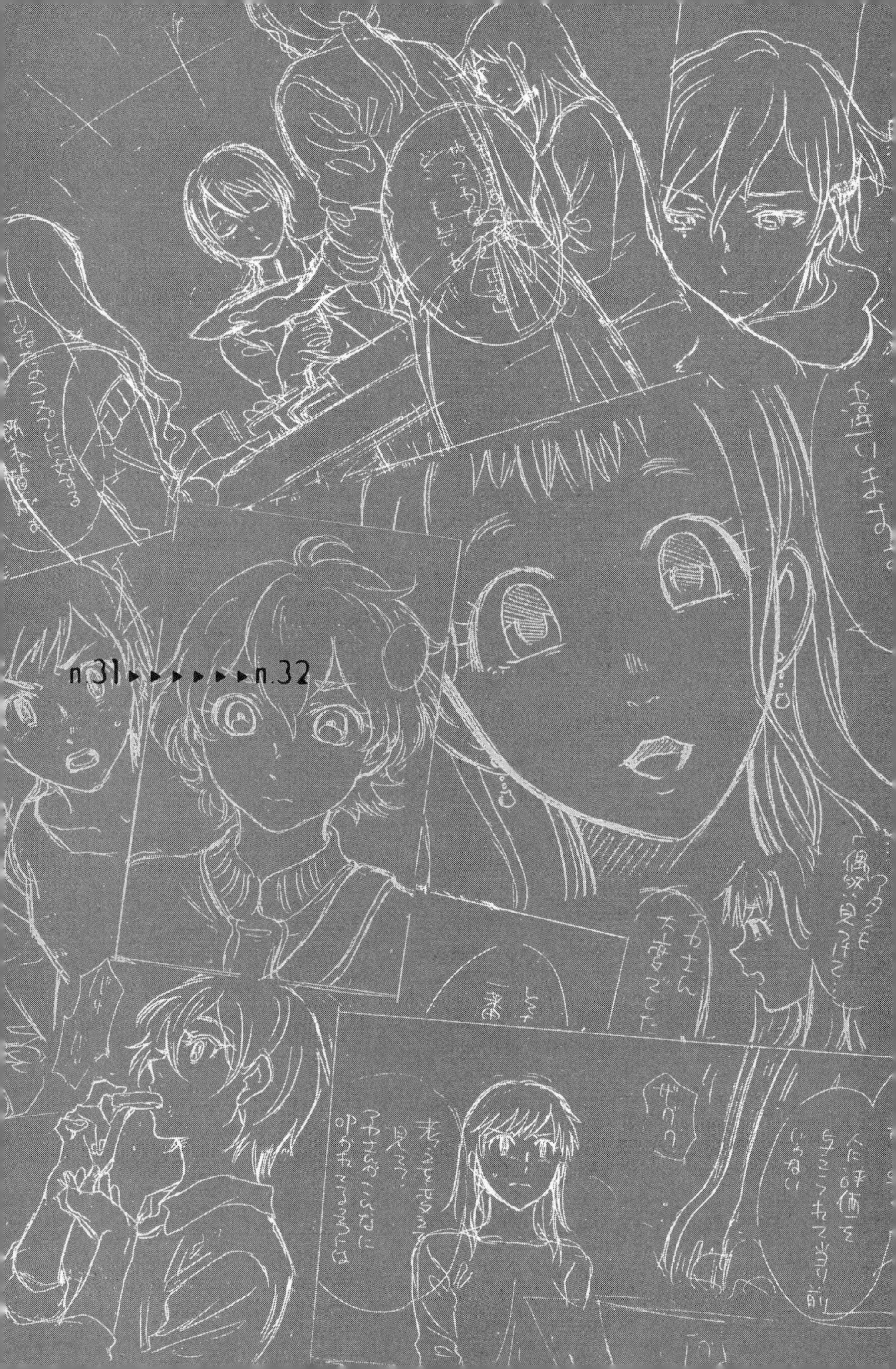
n.31▶▶▶▶▶▶▶n.32

COSPLAY CARD
COLLECTION
6

葉子
-YOUKO-

archive：xxxx Cure：xxxx

HAYAMA AS RURUU

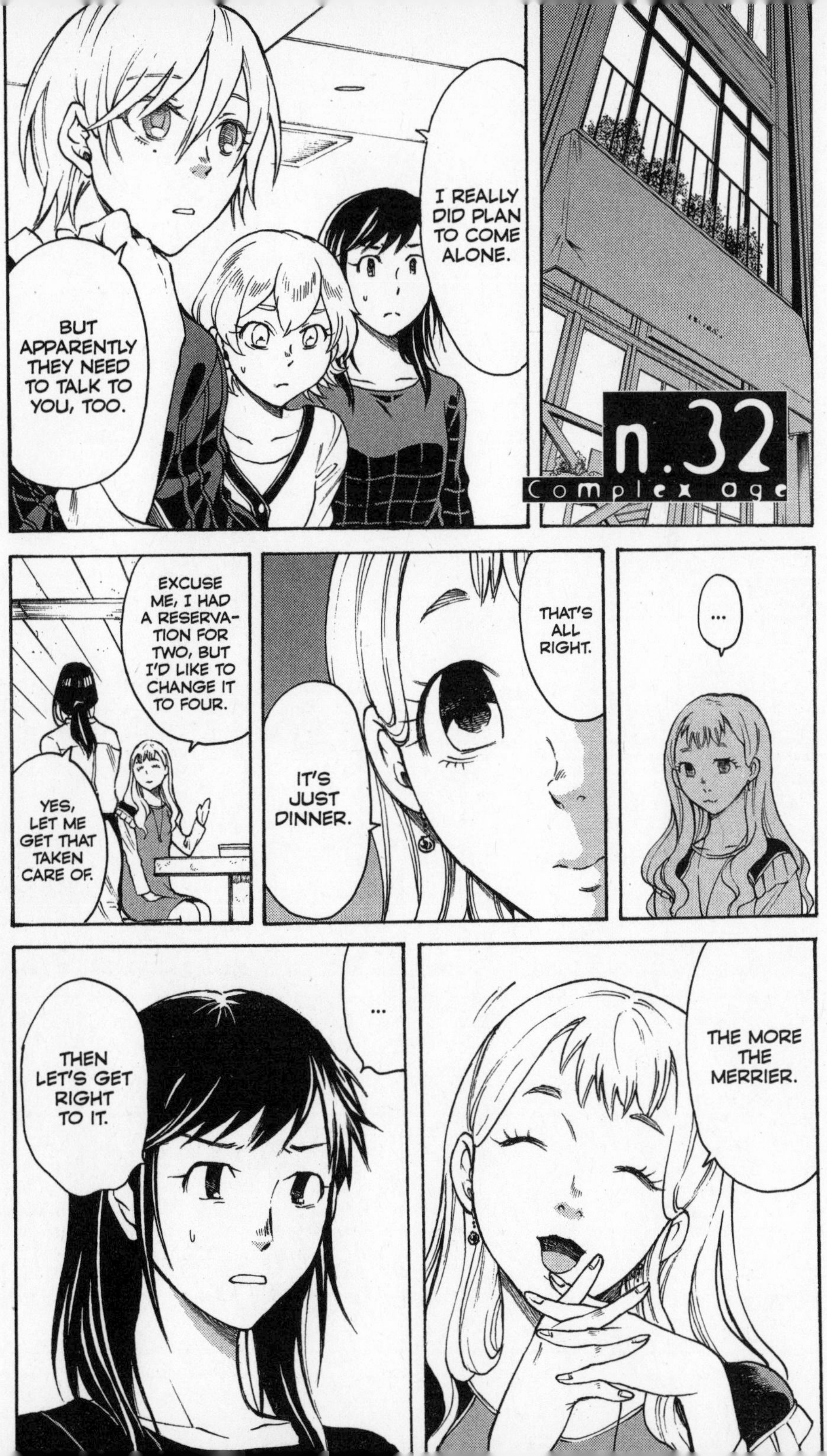
n.32
Complex age
I REALLY DID PLAN TO COME ALONE.
BUT APPARENTLY THEY NEED TO TALK TO YOU, TOO.
...
THAT'S ALL RIGHT.
IT'S JUST DINNER.
EXCUSE ME, I HAD A RESERVATION FOR TWO, BUT I'D LIKE TO CHANGE IT TO FOUR.
YES, LET ME GET THAT TAKEN CARE OF.
THE MORE THE MERRIER.
...
THEN LET'S GET RIGHT TO IT.

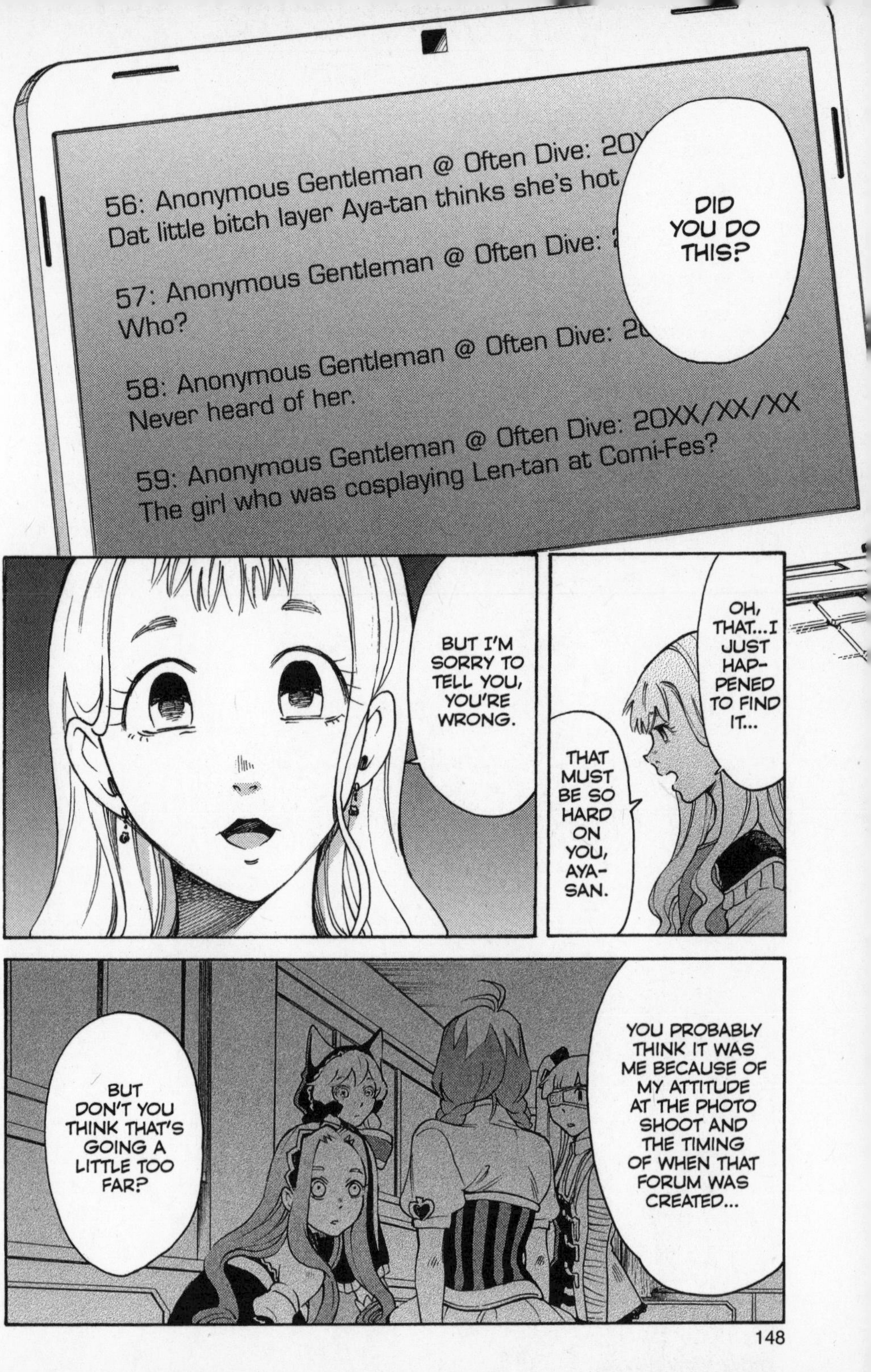
DID YOU DO THIS?
56: Anonymous Gentleman @ Often Dive: 20X
Dat little bitch layer Aya-tan thinks she's hot
57: Anonymous Gentleman @ Often Dive: 2
Who?
58: Anonymous Gentleman @ Often Dive: 20
Never heard of her.
59: Anonymous Gentleman @ Often Dive: 20XX/XX/XX
The girl who was cosplaying Len-tan at Comi-Fes?
OH, THAT...I JUST HAP-PENED TO FIND IT...
THAT MUST BE SO HARD ON YOU, AYA-SAN.
BUT I'M SORRY TO TELL YOU, YOU'RE WRONG.
YOU PROBABLY THINK IT WAS ME BECAUSE OF MY ATTITUDE AT THE PHOTO SHOOT AND THE TIMING OF WHEN THAT FORUM WAS CREATED...
BUT DON'T YOU THINK THAT'S GOING A LITTLE TOO FAR?

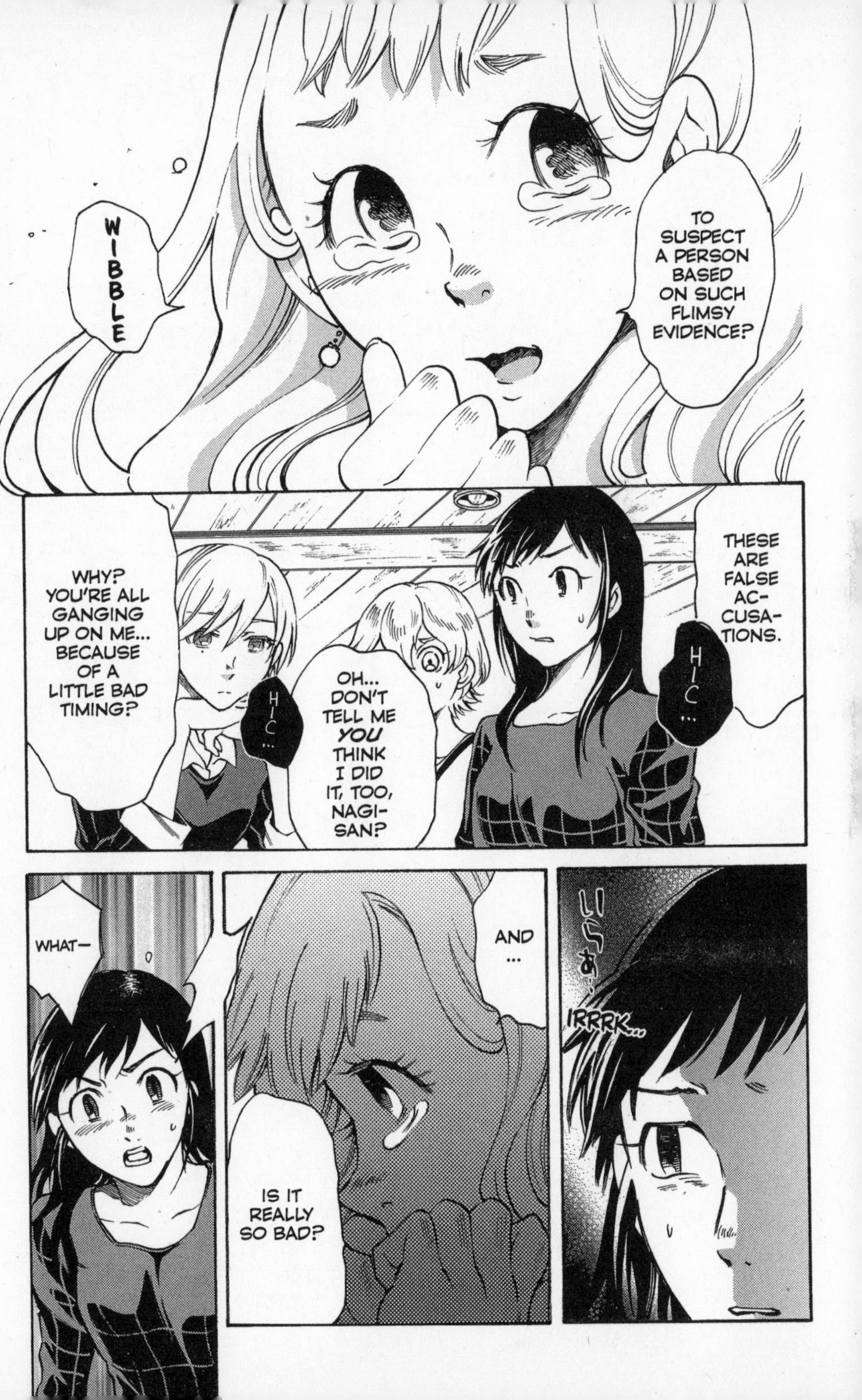
TO SUSPECT A PERSON BASED ON SUCH FLIMSY EVIDENCE?
WIBBLE
THESE ARE FALSE AC-CUSA-TIONS.
HIC...
OH... DON'T TELL ME *YOU* THINK I DID IT, TOO, NAGI-SAN?
HIC...
WHY? YOU'RE ALL GANGING UP ON ME... BECAUSE OF A LITTLE BAD TIMING?
いらぁ
IRRRK...
AND...
IS IT REALLY SO BAD?
WHAT—

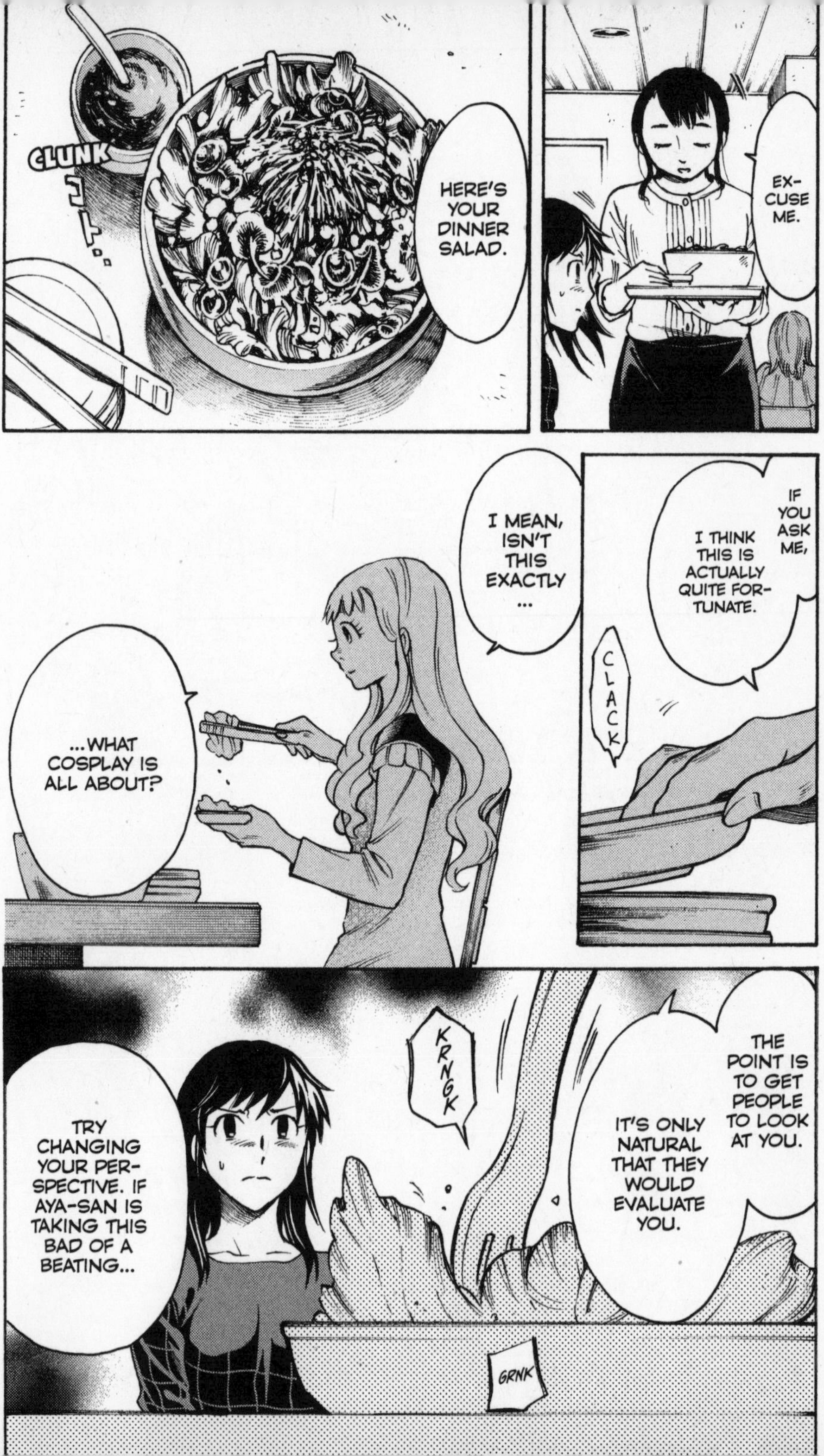
EX-CUSE ME.
HERE'S YOUR DINNER SALAD.
CLUNK
コト
IF YOU ASK ME,
I THINK THIS IS ACTUALLY QUITE FOR-TUNATE.
CLACK
I MEAN, ISN'T THIS EXACTLY ...
...WHAT COSPLAY IS ALL ABOUT?
THE POINT IS TO GET PEOPLE TO LOOK AT YOU.
IT'S ONLY NATURAL THAT THEY WOULD EVALUATE YOU.
KRNGK
GRNK
TRY CHANGING YOUR PER-SPECTIVE. IF AYA-SAN IS TAKING THIS BAD OF A BEATING...

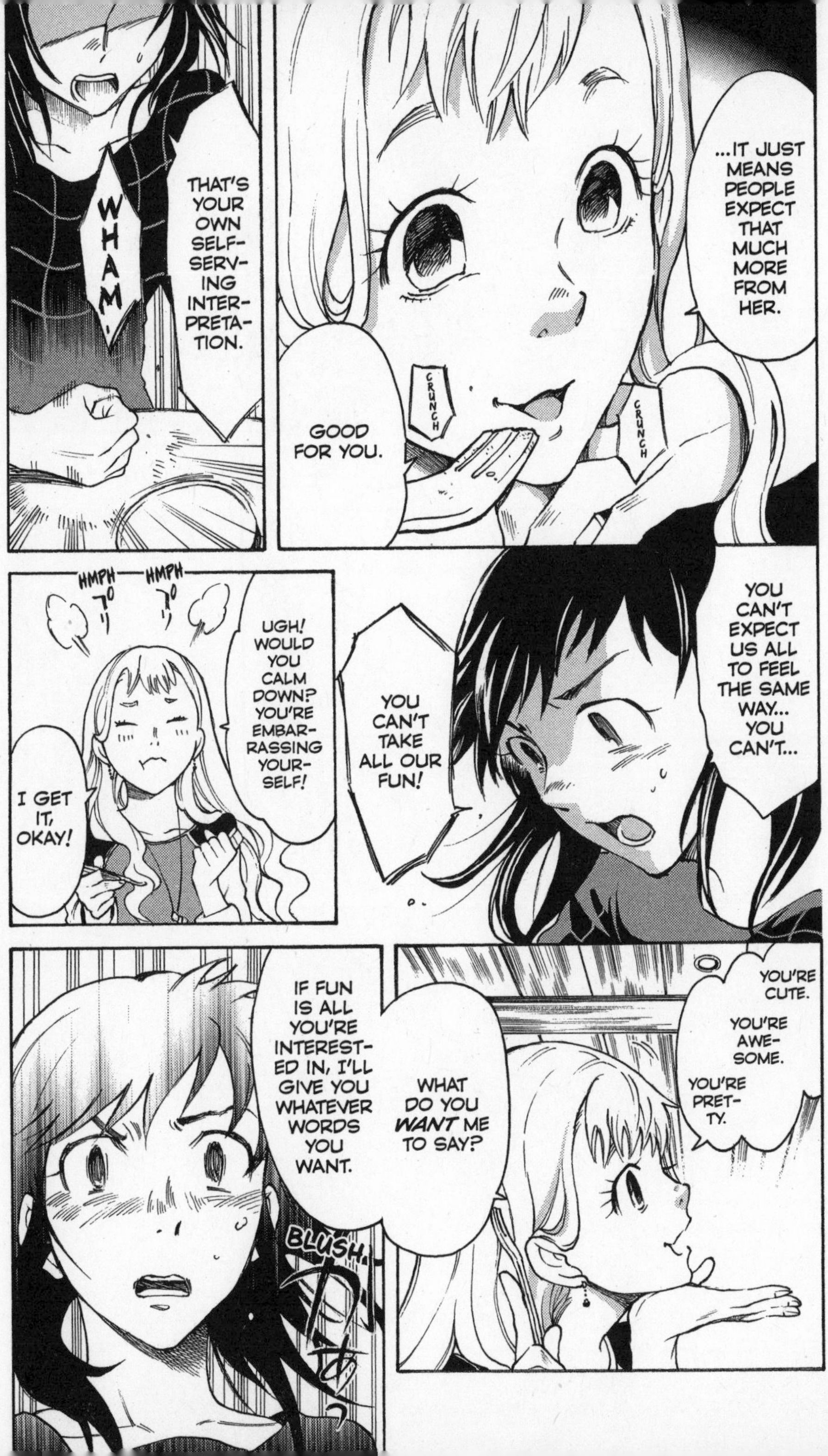
...IT JUST MEANS PEOPLE EXPECT THAT MUCH MORE FROM HER.
CRUNCH
CRUNCH
GOOD FOR YOU.
WHAM
THAT'S YOUR OWN SELF-SERVING INTERPRETATION.
YOU CAN'T EXPECT US ALL TO FEEL THE SAME WAY... YOU CAN'T...
YOU CAN'T TAKE ALL OUR FUN!
HMPH
HMPH
UGH! WOULD YOU CALM DOWN? YOU'RE EMBARRASSING YOURSELF!
I GET IT, OKAY!
YOU'RE CUTE.
YOU'RE AWESOME.
YOU'RE PRETTY.
WHAT DO YOU *WANT* ME TO SAY?
IF FUN IS ALL YOU'RE INTERESTED IN, I'LL GIVE YOU WHATEVER WORDS YOU WANT.
BLUSH

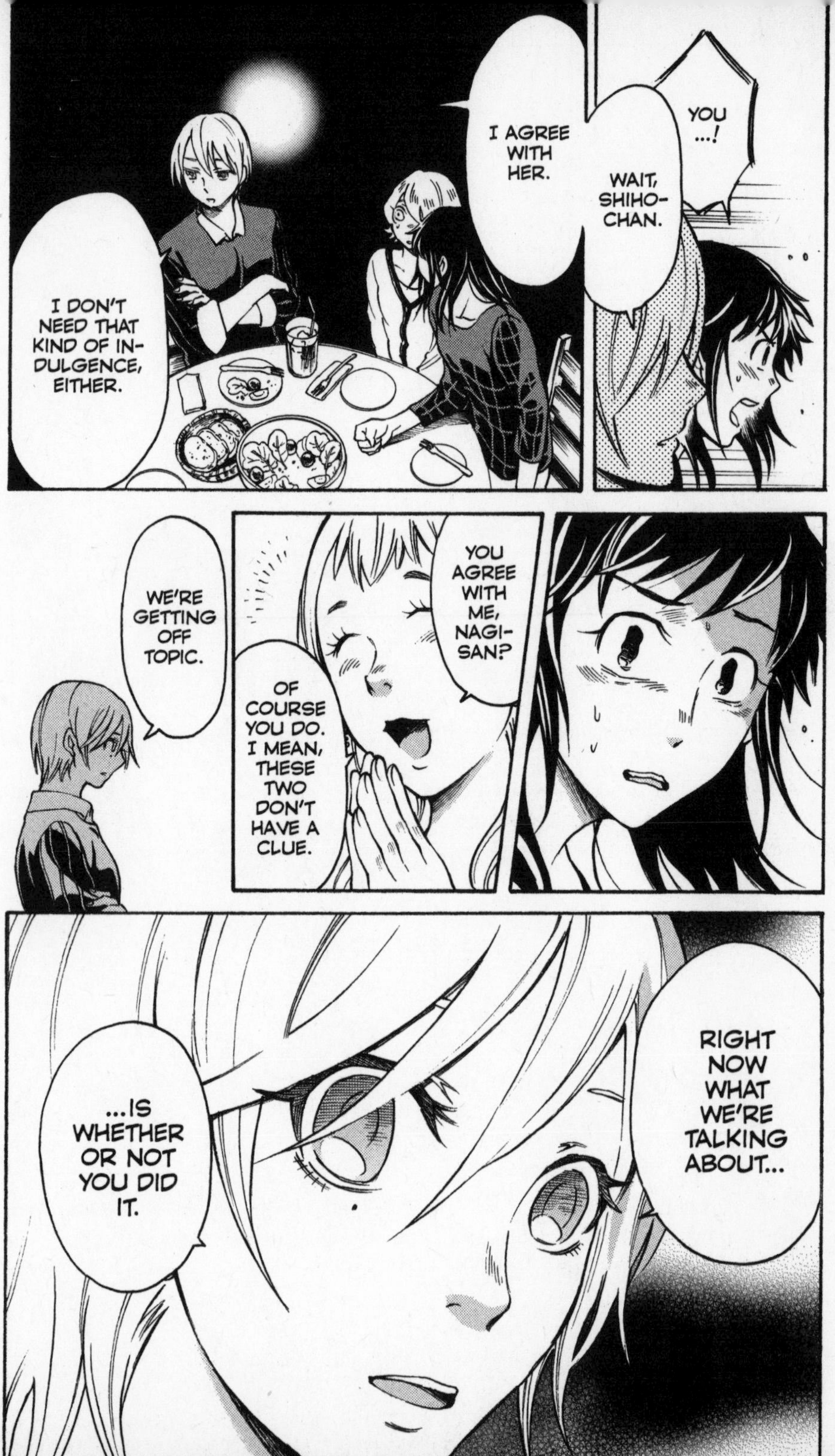
YOU ...!
WAIT, SHIHO-CHAN.
I AGREE WITH HER.
I DON'T NEED THAT KIND OF IN-DULGENCE, EITHER.
YOU AGREE WITH ME, NAGI-SAN?
OF COURSE YOU DO. I MEAN, THESE TWO DON'T HAVE A CLUE.
WE'RE GETTING OFF TOPIC.
RIGHT NOW WHAT WE'RE TALKING ABOUT...
...IS WHETHER OR NOT YOU DID IT.

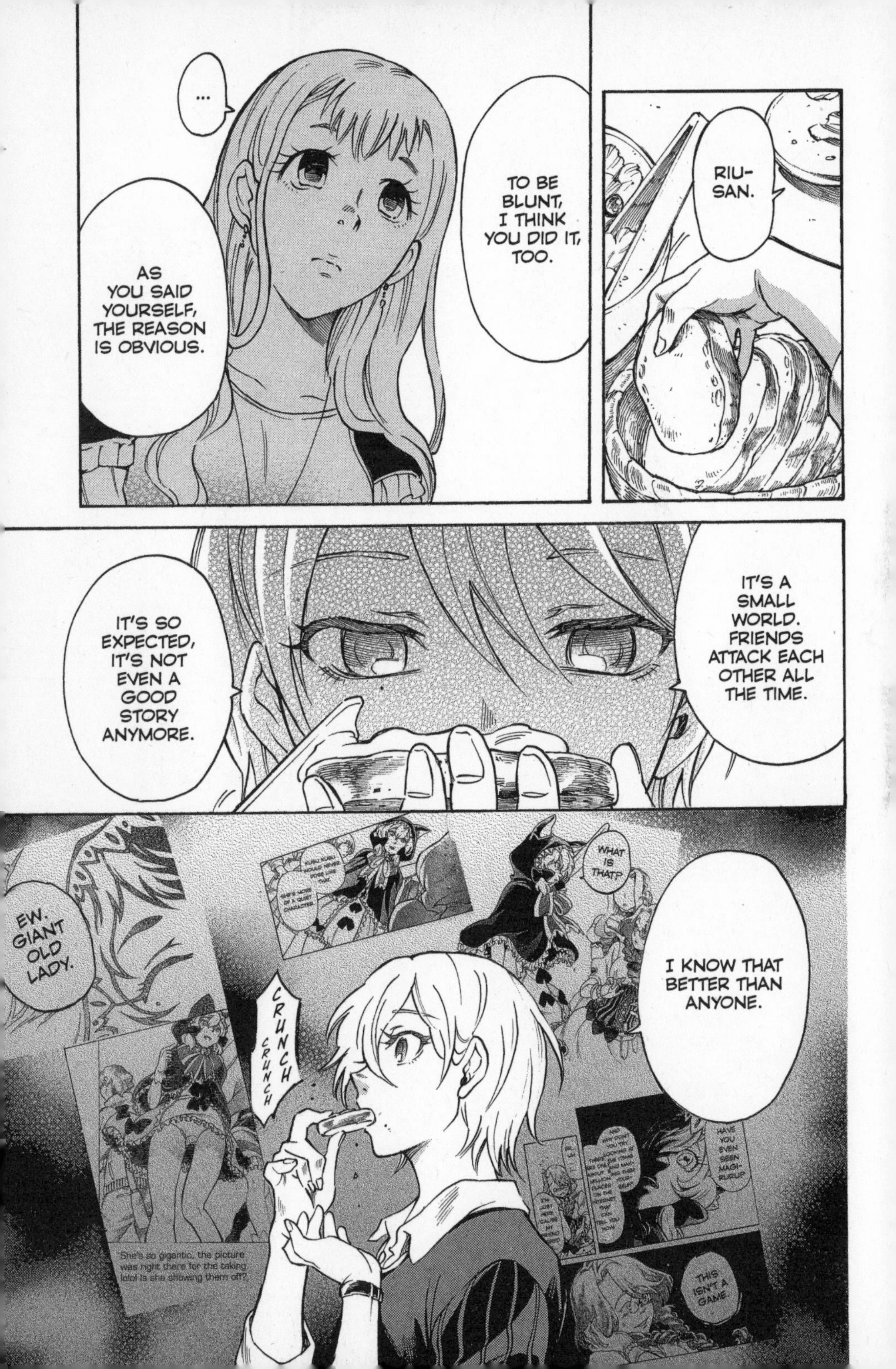
RIU-SAN.
TO BE BLUNT, I THINK YOU DID IT, TOO.
...
AS YOU SAID YOURSELF, THE REASON IS OBVIOUS.
IT'S A SMALL WORLD. FRIENDS ATTACK EACH OTHER ALL THE TIME.
IT'S SO EXPECTED, IT'S NOT EVEN A GOOD STORY ANYMORE.
I KNOW THAT BETTER THAN ANYONE.
WHAT IS THAT?
KUSU KUSU WOULD NEVER POSE LIKE THAT
SHE'S MORE OF A QUIET CHARACTER
EW. GIANT OLD LADY.
CRUNCH CRUNCH
HAVE YOU EVEN SEEN MAGI-RURU?
THIS ISN'T A GAME.
She's so gigantic, the picture was right there for the taking. lolol Is she showing them off?

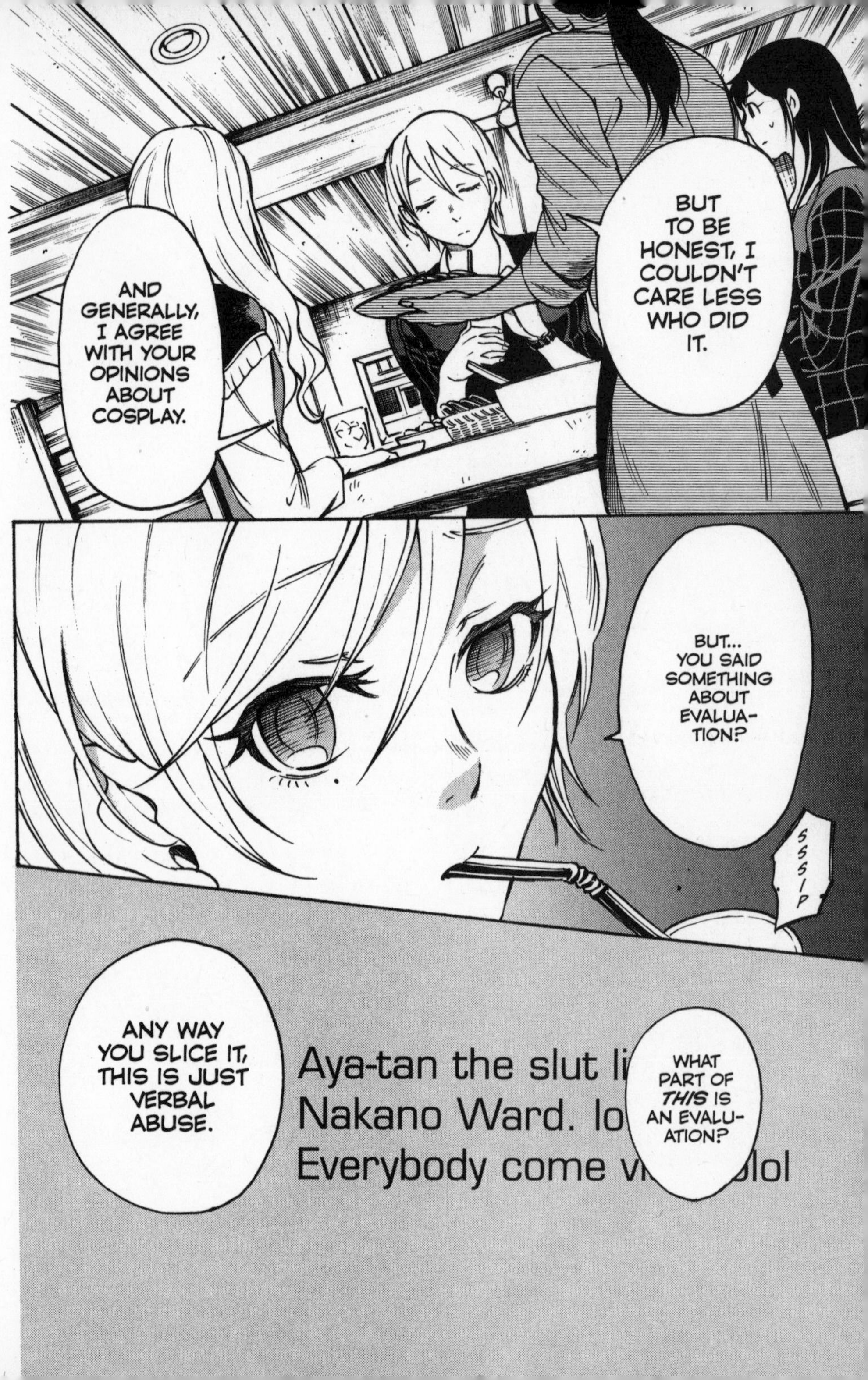
BUT TO BE HONEST, I COULDN'T CARE LESS WHO DID IT.
AND GENERALLY, I AGREE WITH YOUR OPINIONS ABOUT COSPLAY.
BUT... YOU SAID SOMETHING ABOUT EVALUATION?
SSSIP
Aya-tan the slut li
Nakano Ward. lo
Everybody come vi lol
WHAT PART OF *THIS* IS AN EVALUATION?
ANY WAY YOU SLICE IT, THIS IS JUST VERBAL ABUSE.

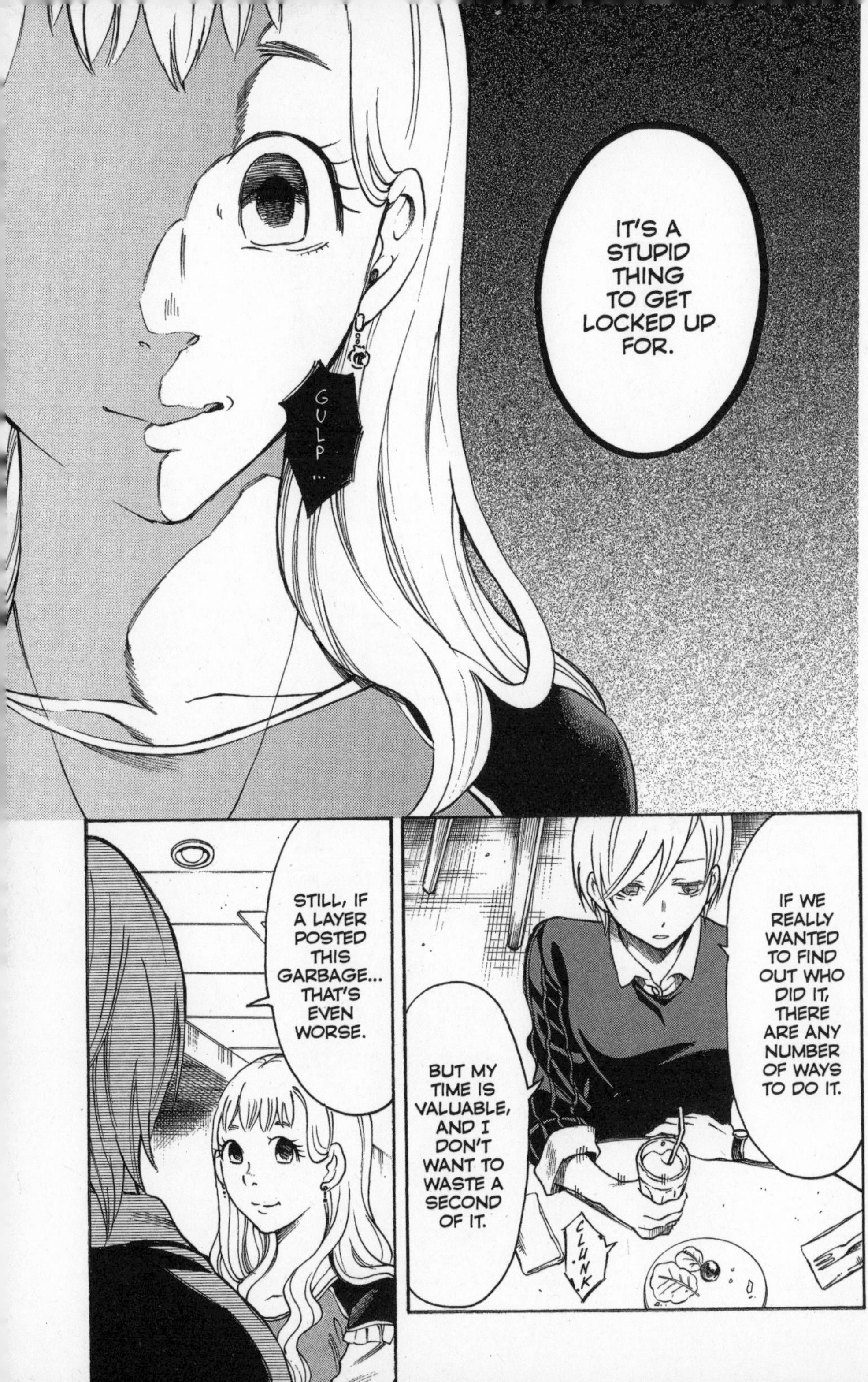
IT'S A STUPID THING TO GET LOCKED UP FOR.
GULP...
IF WE REALLY WANTED TO FIND OUT WHO DID IT, THERE ARE ANY NUMBER OF WAYS TO DO IT.
BUT MY TIME IS VALUABLE, AND I DON'T WANT TO WASTE A SECOND OF IT.
CLUNK
STILL, IF A LAYER POSTED THIS GARBAGE... THAT'S EVEN WORSE.

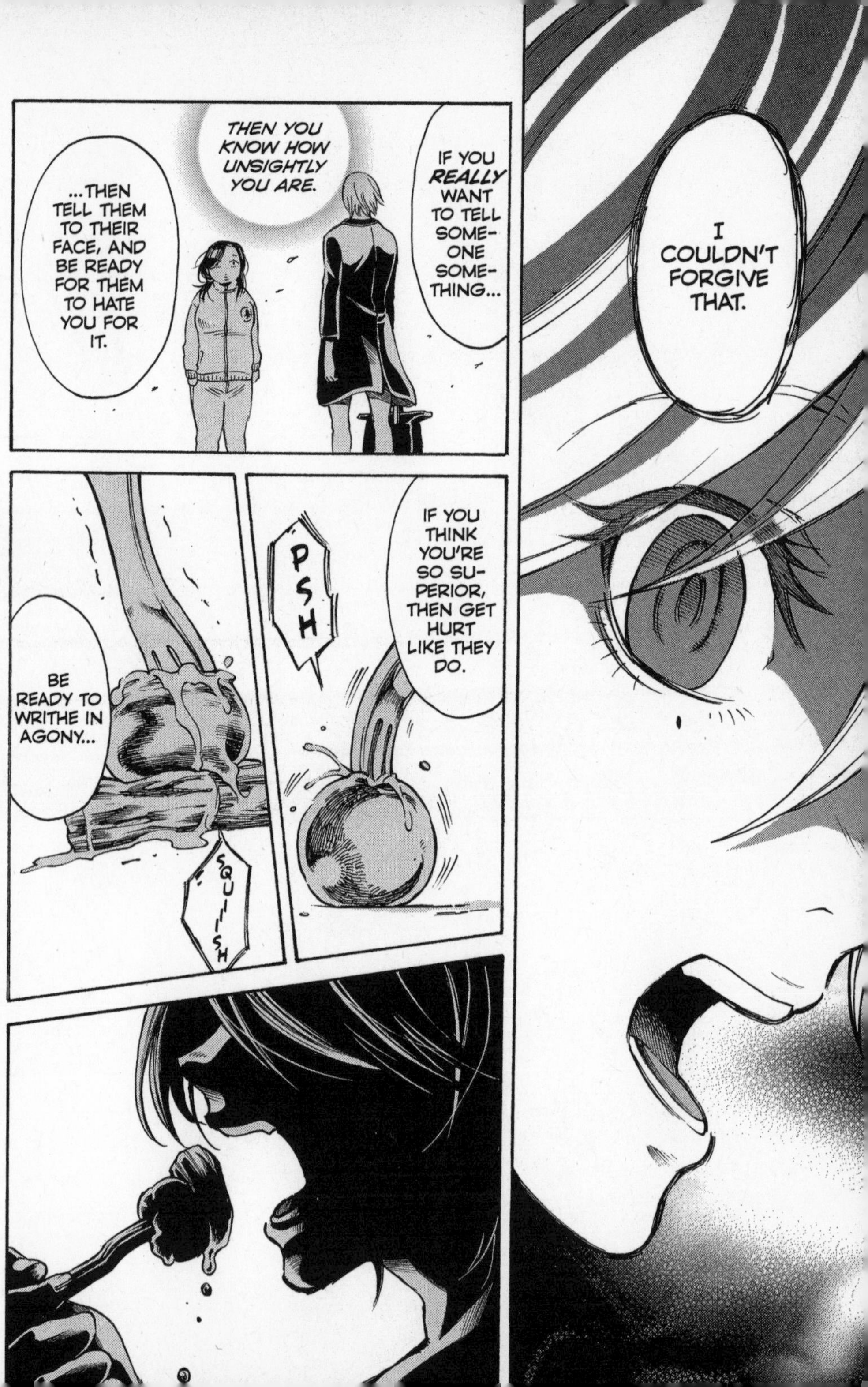
I COULDN'T FORGIVE THAT.
IF YOU REALLY WANT TO TELL SOME-ONE SOME-THING...
THEN YOU KNOW HOW UNSIGHTLY YOU ARE.
...THEN TELL THEM TO THEIR FACE, AND BE READY FOR THEM TO HATE YOU FOR IT.
IF YOU THINK YOU'RE SO SU-PERIOR, THEN GET HURT LIKE THEY DO.
PSH
BE READY TO WRITHE IN AGONY...
SQUIISH

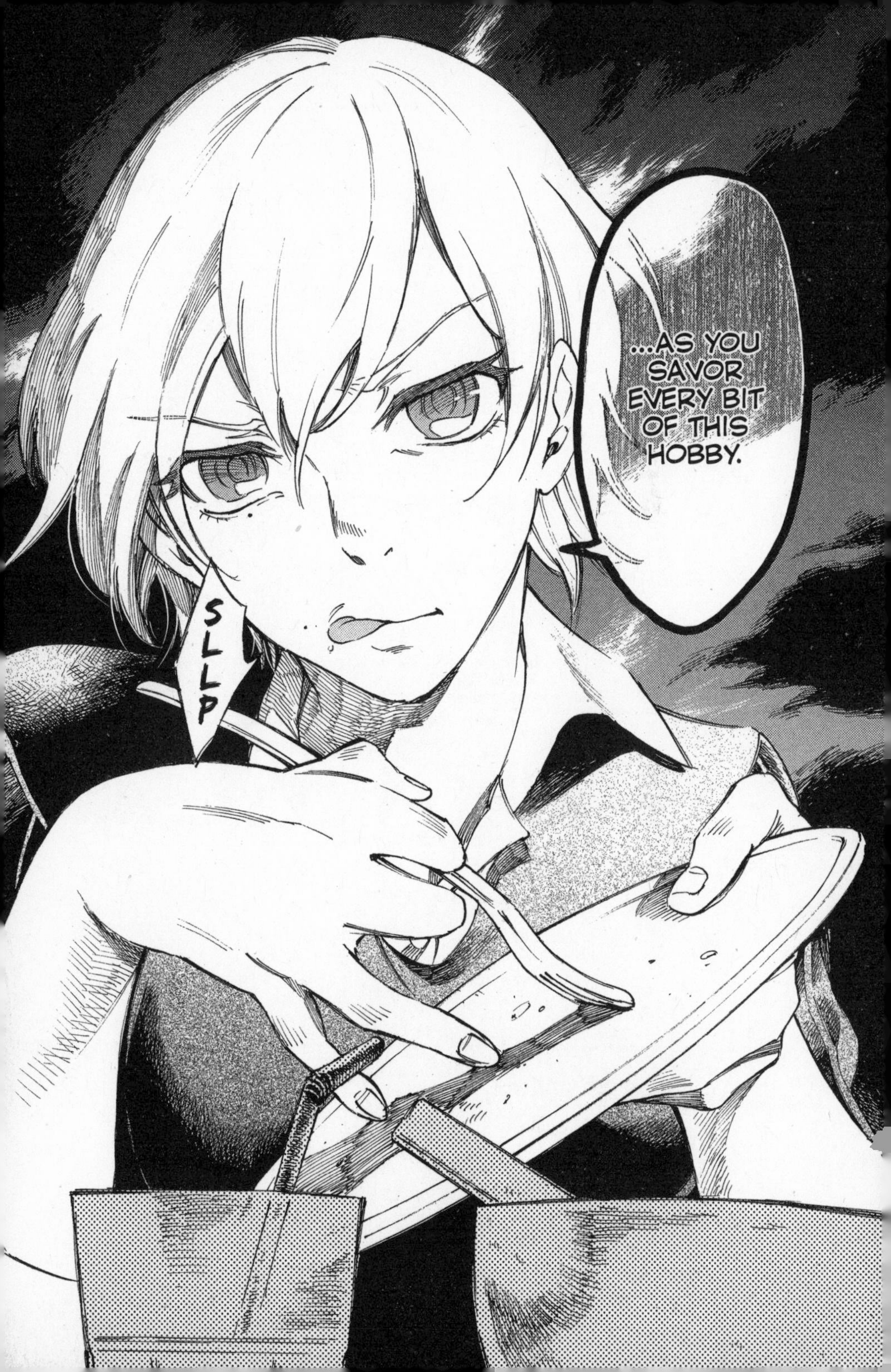
...AS YOU SAVOR EVERY BIT OF THIS HOBBY.
SLLP

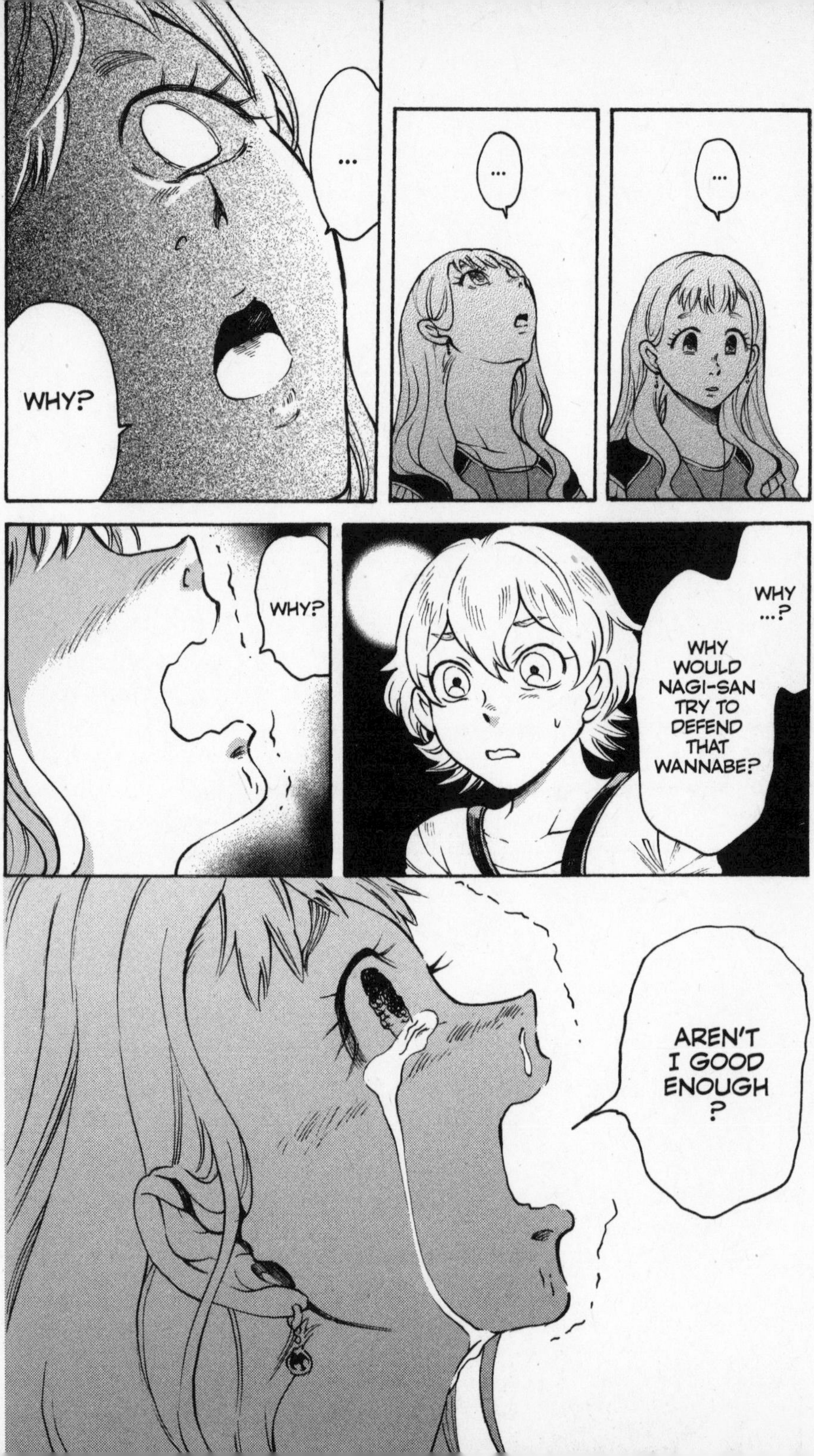
...
...
...
WHY?
WHY ...?
WHY WOULD NAGI-SAN TRY TO DEFEND THAT WANNABE?
WHY?
AREN'T I GOOD ENOUGH ?

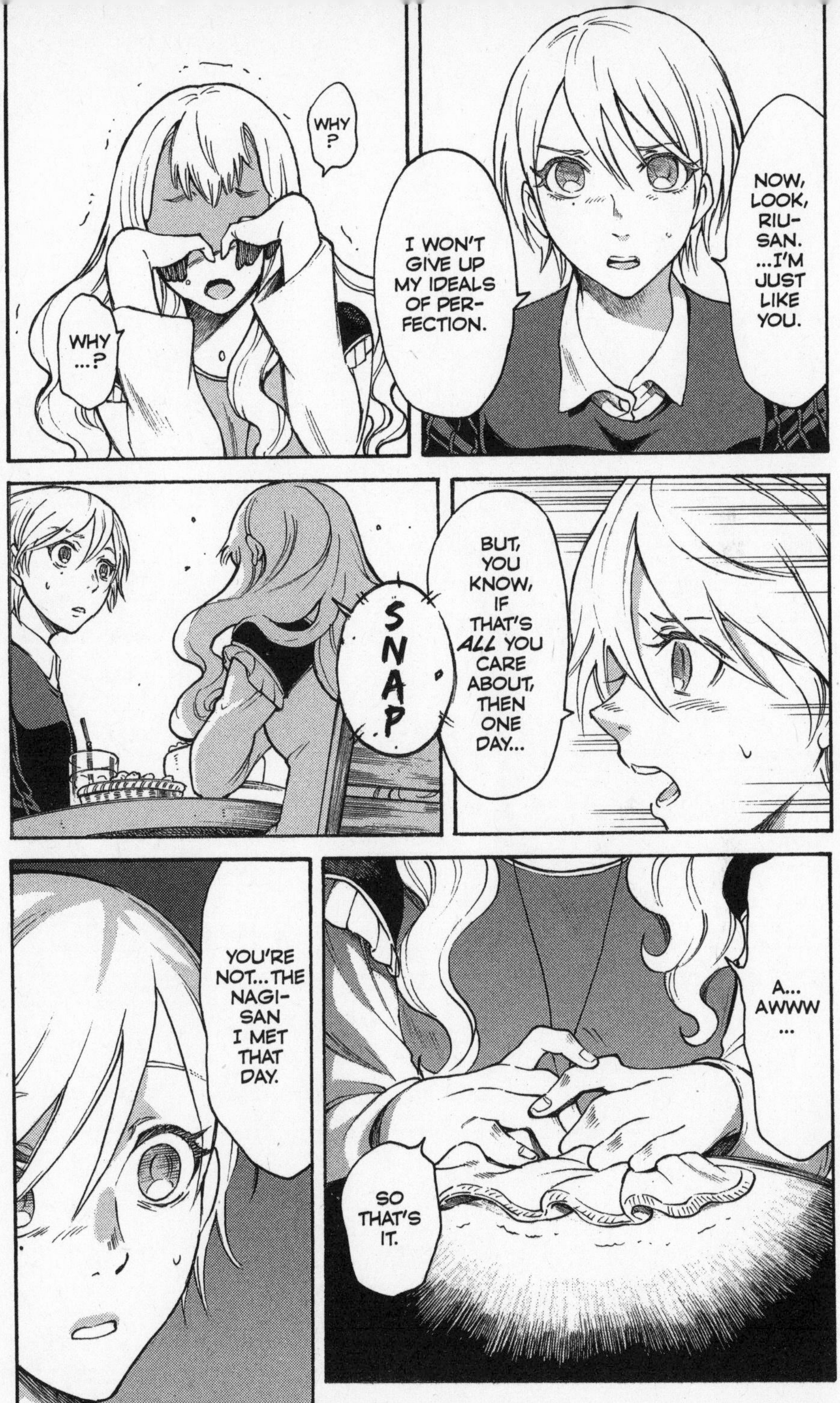
NOW, LOOK, RIU-SAN. ...I'M JUST LIKE YOU.
I WON'T GIVE UP MY IDEALS OF PER-FECTION.
WHY ?
WHY ...?
BUT, YOU KNOW, IF THAT'S *ALL* YOU CARE ABOUT, THEN ONE DAY...
SNAP
A... AWWW ...
SO THAT'S IT.
YOU'RE NOT...THE NAGI-SAN I MET THAT DAY.

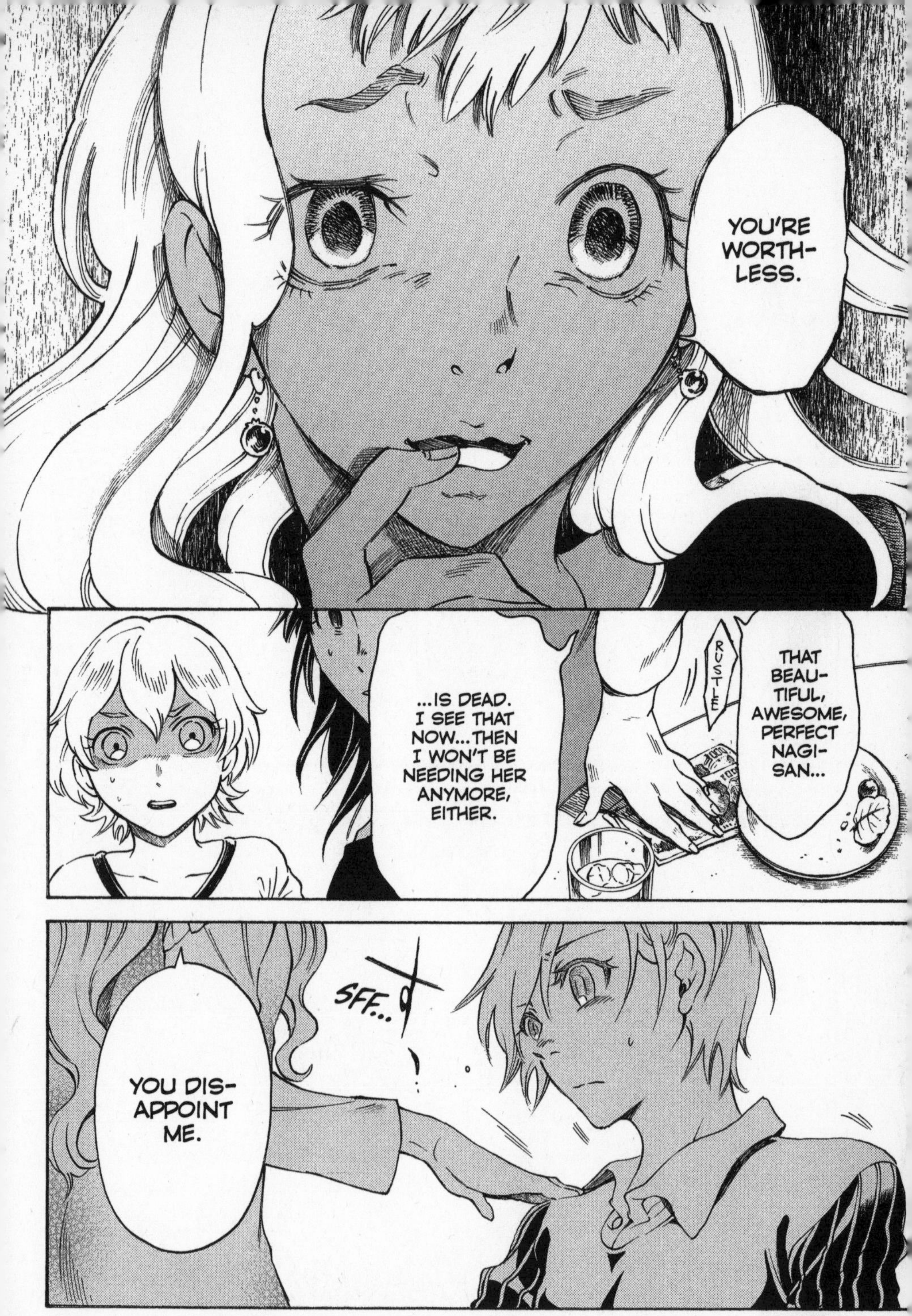
YOU'RE WORTH-LESS.
RUSTLE
THAT BEAU-TIFUL, AWESOME, PERFECT NAGI-SAN...
...IS DEAD. I SEE THAT NOW...THEN I WON'T BE NEEDING HER ANYMORE, EITHER.
SFF...
YOU DIS-APPOINT ME.

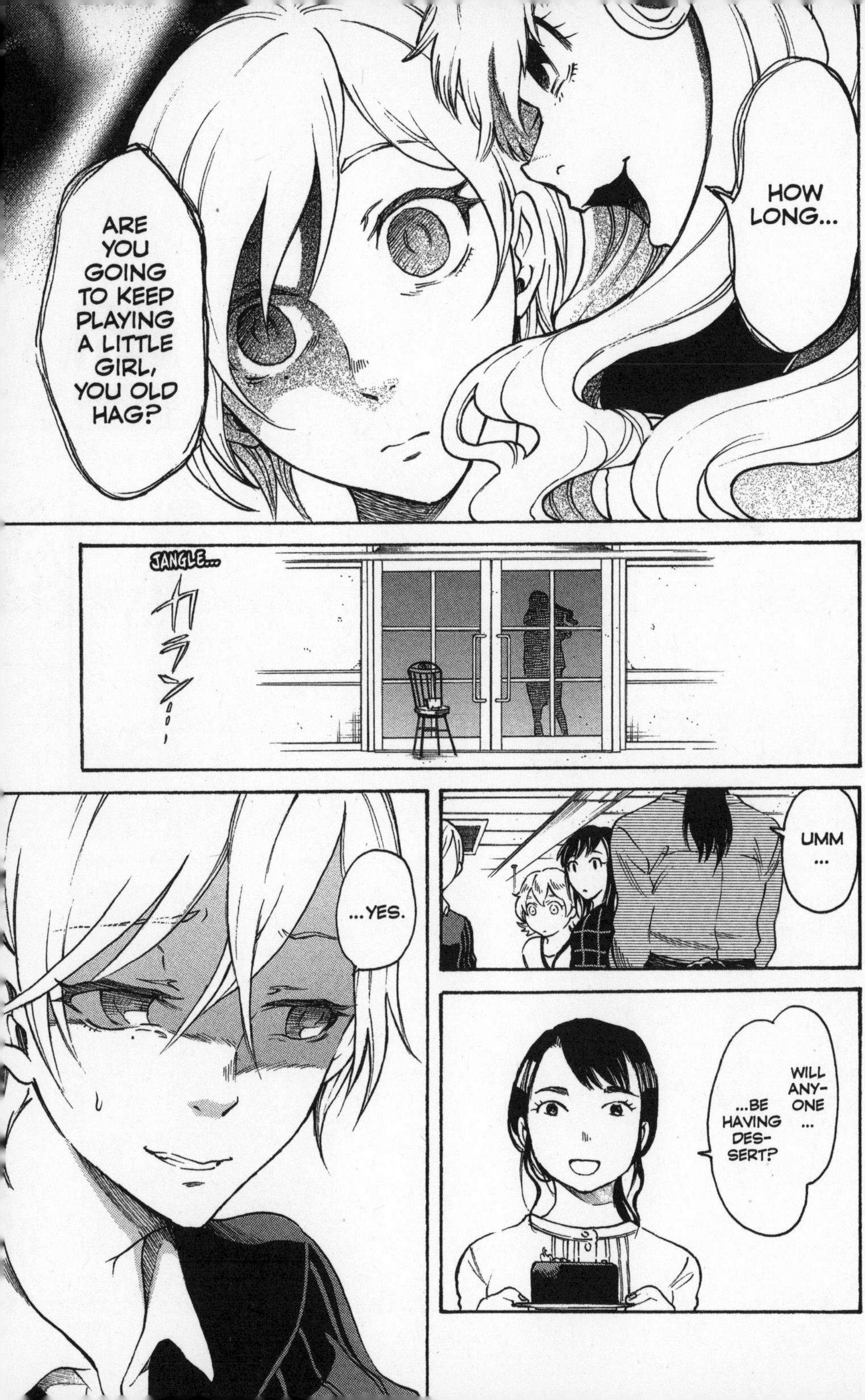
HOW LONG...
ARE YOU GOING TO KEEP PLAYING A LITTLE GIRL, YOU OLD HAG?
JANGLE...
カラン...
UMM ...
WILL ANY-ONE ... ...BE HAVING DES-SERT?
...YES.

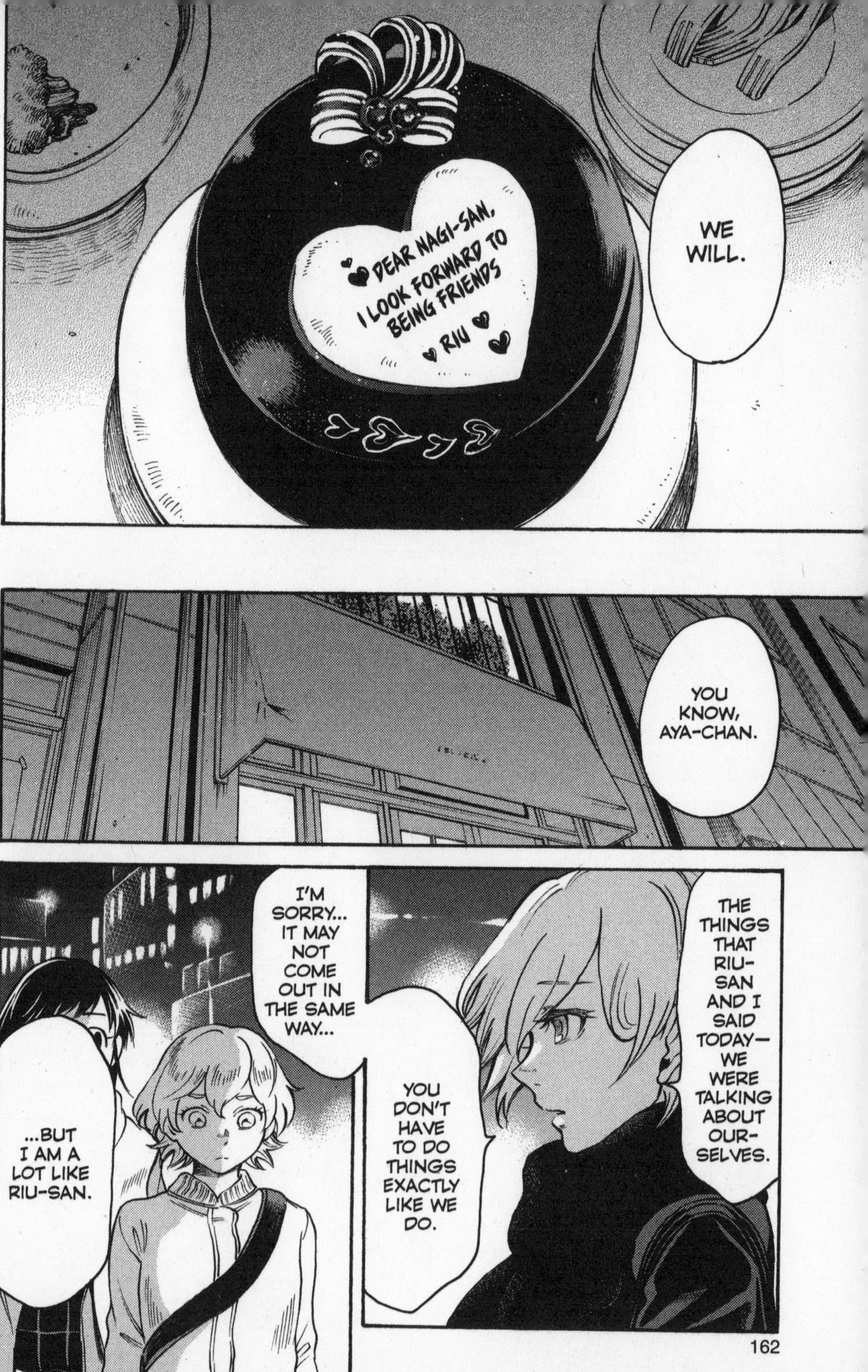
WE WILL.
DEAR NAGI-SAN, I LOOK FORWARD TO BEING FRIENDS
RIU
YOU KNOW, AYA-CHAN.
THE THINGS THAT RIU-SAN AND I SAID TODAY—WE WERE TALKING ABOUT OUR-SELVES.
YOU DON'T HAVE TO DO THINGS EXACTLY LIKE WE DO.
I'M SORRY... IT MAY NOT COME OUT IN THE SAME WAY...
...BUT I AM A LOT LIKE RIU-SAN.

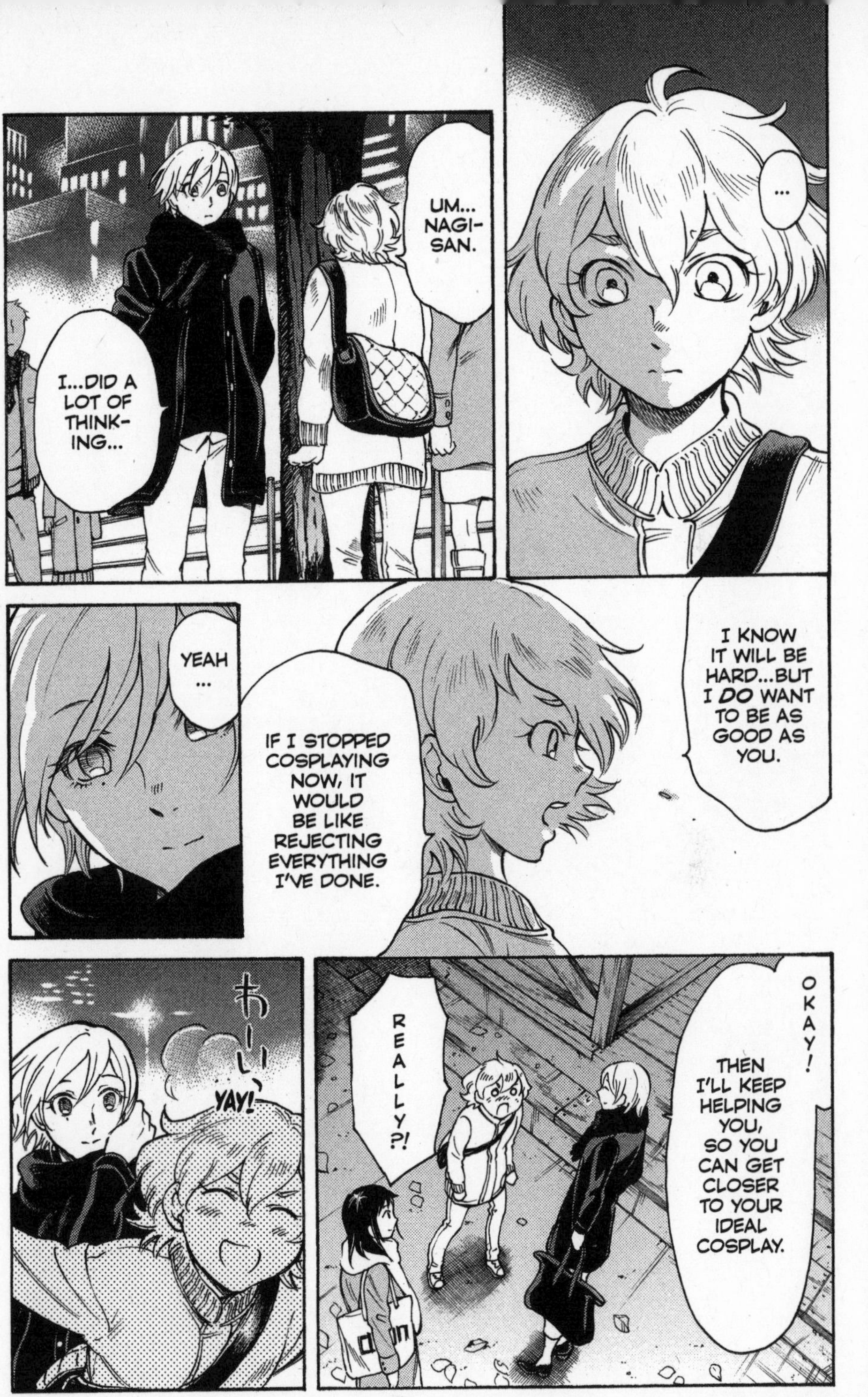
...
UM... NAGI-SAN.
I...DID A LOT OF THINKING...
I KNOW IT WILL BE HARD...BUT I *DO* WANT TO BE AS GOOD AS YOU.
IF I STOPPED COSPLAYING NOW, IT WOULD BE LIKE REJECTING EVERYTHING I'VE DONE.
YEAH ...
OKAY!
THEN I'LL KEEP HELPING YOU, SO YOU CAN GET CLOSER TO YOUR IDEAL COSPLAY.
REALLY?!
わーい
YAY!

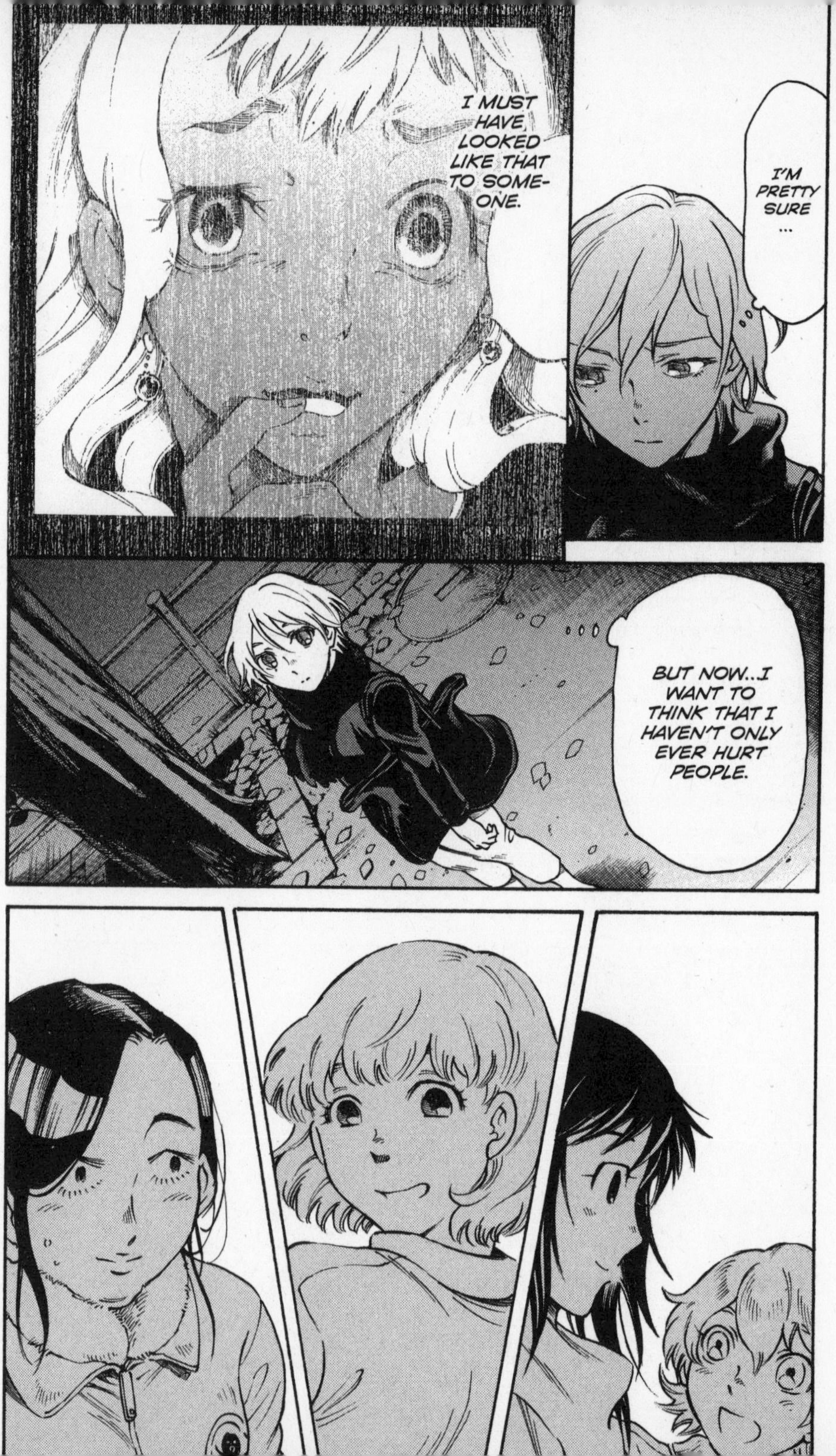
I'M PRETTY SURE ...
I MUST HAVE LOOKED LIKE THAT TO SOME-ONE.
BUT NOW...I WANT TO THINK THAT I HAVEN'T ONLY EVER HURT PEOPLE.

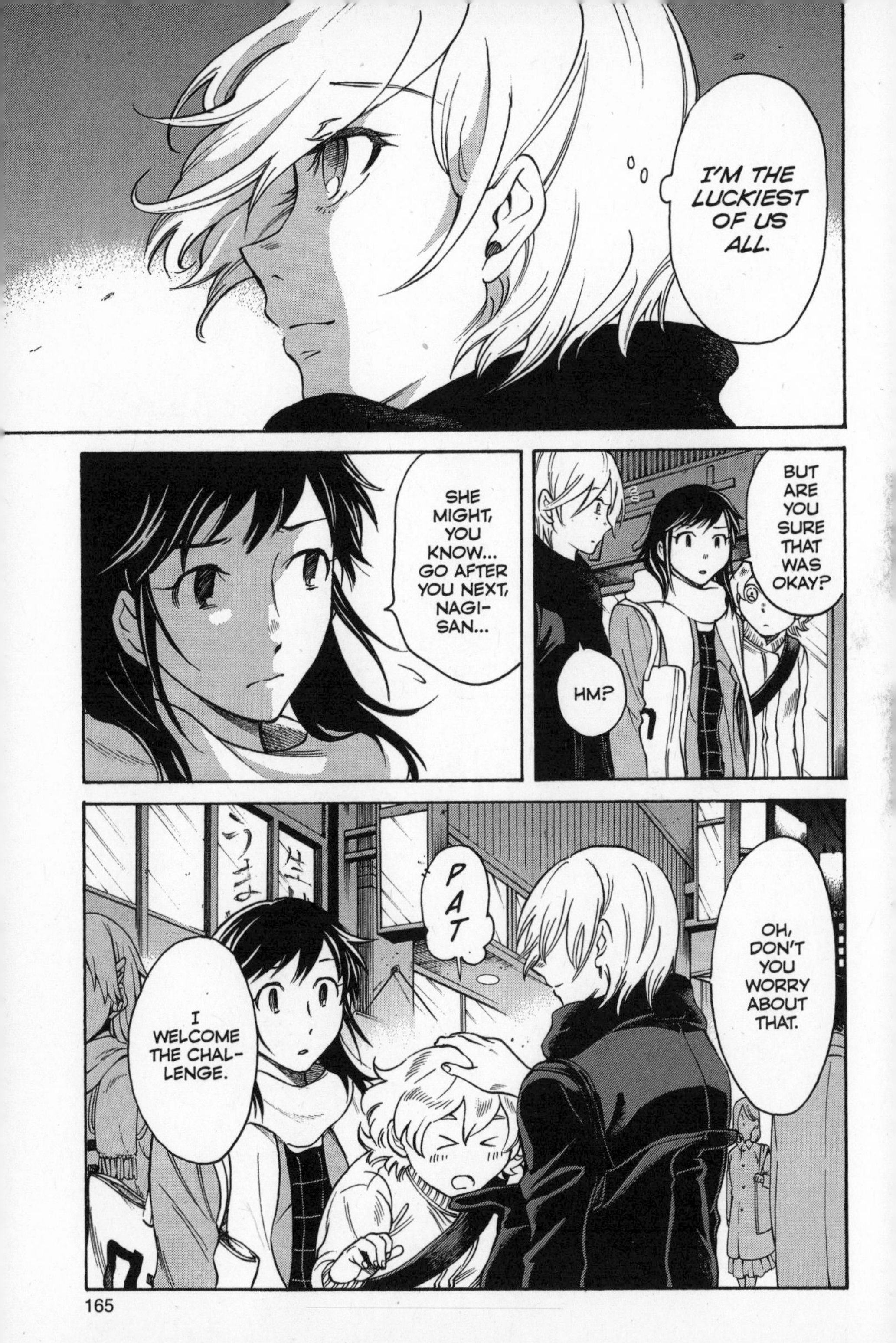
I'M THE LUCKIEST OF US ALL.
BUT ARE YOU SURE THAT WAS OKAY?
HM?
SHE MIGHT, YOU KNOW... GO AFTER YOU NEXT, NAGI-SAN...
OH, DON'T YOU WORRY ABOUT THAT.
PAT
I WELCOME THE CHAL-LENGE.

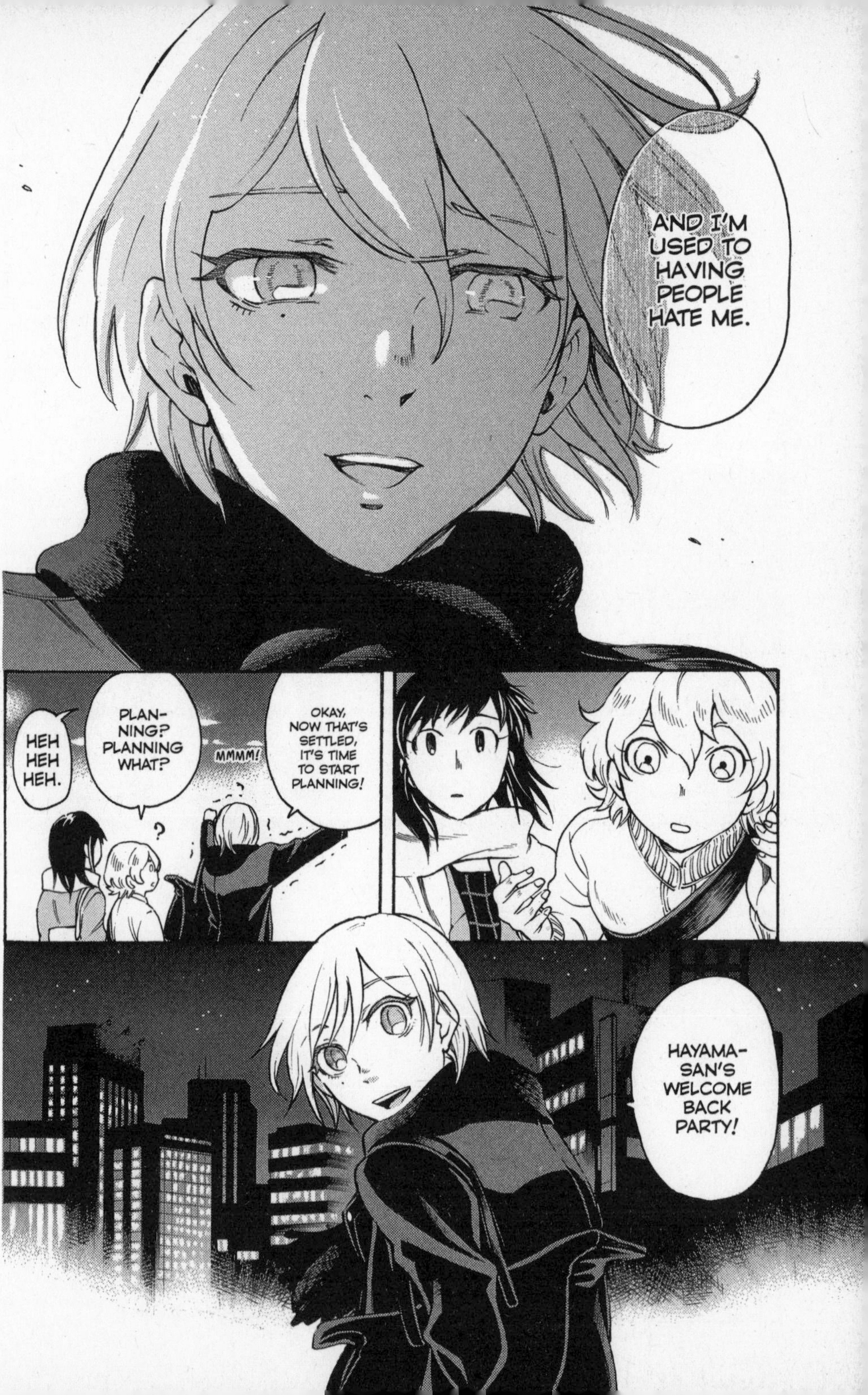
AND I'M USED TO HAVING PEOPLE HATE ME.
OKAY, NOW THAT'S SETTLED, IT'S TIME TO START PLANNING!
MMMM!
PLAN-NING? PLANNING WHAT?
HEH HEH HEH.
HAYAMA-SAN'S WELCOME BACK PARTY!

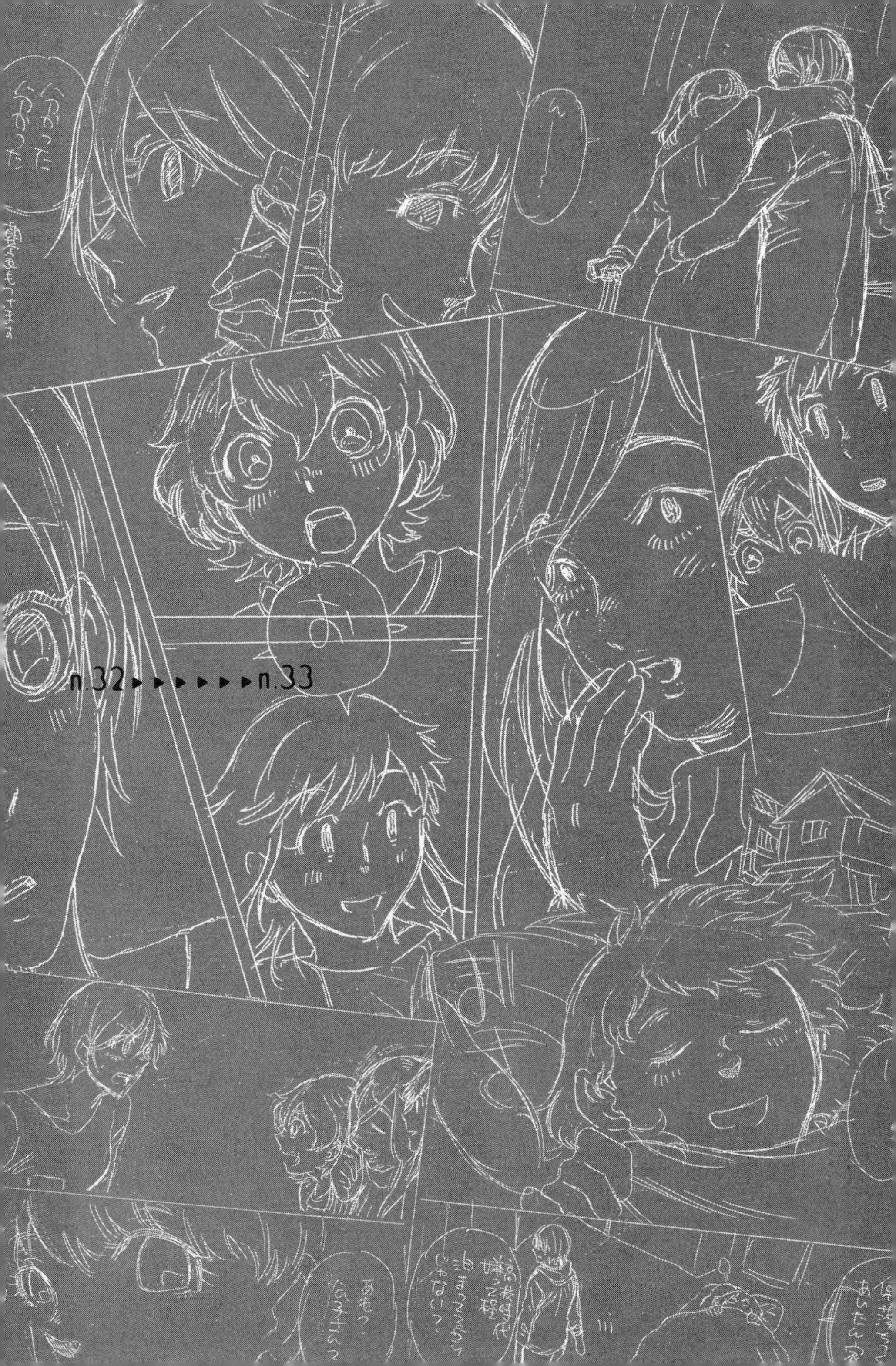
n.32▶▶▶▶▶▶▶n.33
おった おった

COSPLAY CARD
COLLECTION
BONUS

PROPS, ETC. USED IN MAKING THE CARDS.

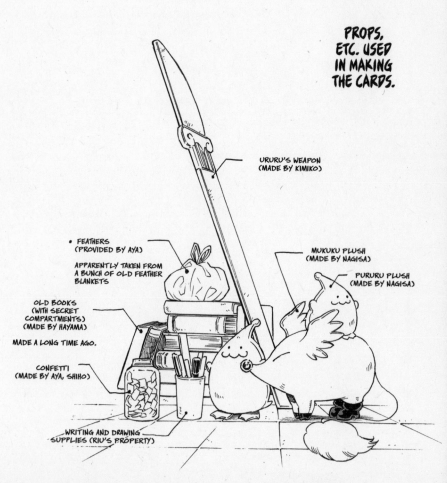

URURU'S WEAPON (MADE BY KIMIKO)
MUKUKU PLUSH (MADE BY NAGISA)
PURURU PLUSH (MADE BY NAGISA)
• FEATHERS (PROVIDED BY AYA)
APPARENTLY TAKEN FROM A BUNCH OF OLD FEATHER BLANKETS
OLD BOOKS (WITH SECRET COMPARTMENTS) (MADE BY HAYAMA)
MADE A LONG TIME AGO.
CONFETTI (MADE BY AYA, SHIHO)
WRITING AND DRAWING SUPPLIES (RIU'S PROPERTY)

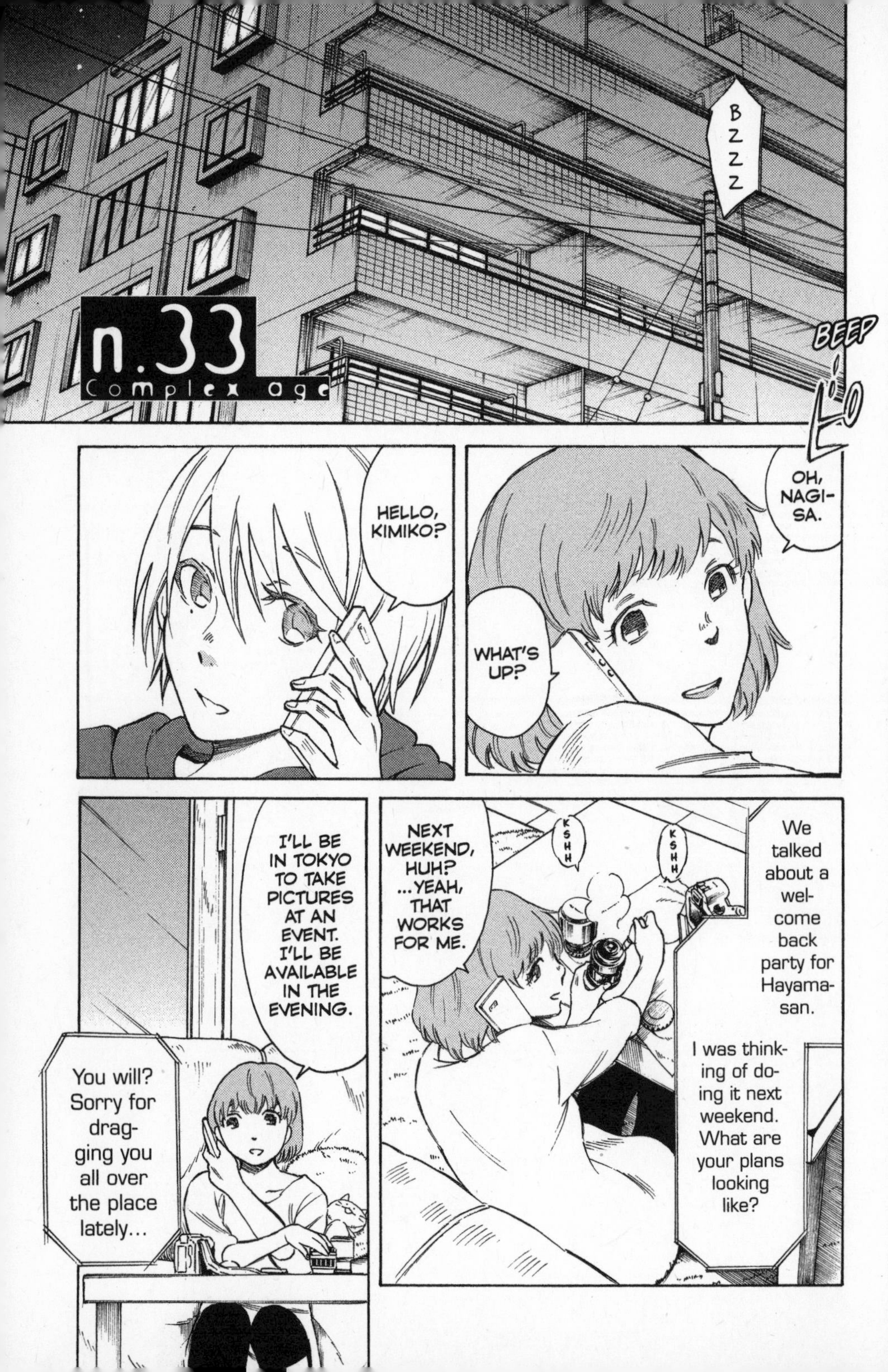
BZZZ
BEEP
n.33
Complex age
OH, NAGISA.
WHAT'S UP?
HELLO, KIMIKO?
We talked about a welcome back party for Hayama-san.
I was thinking of doing it next weekend. What are your plans looking like?
KSHH
KSHH
NEXT WEEKEND, HUH? ...YEAH, THAT WORKS FOR ME.
I'LL BE IN TOKYO TO TAKE PICTURES AT AN EVENT. I'LL BE AVAILABLE IN THE EVENING.
You will? Sorry for dragging you all over the place lately...

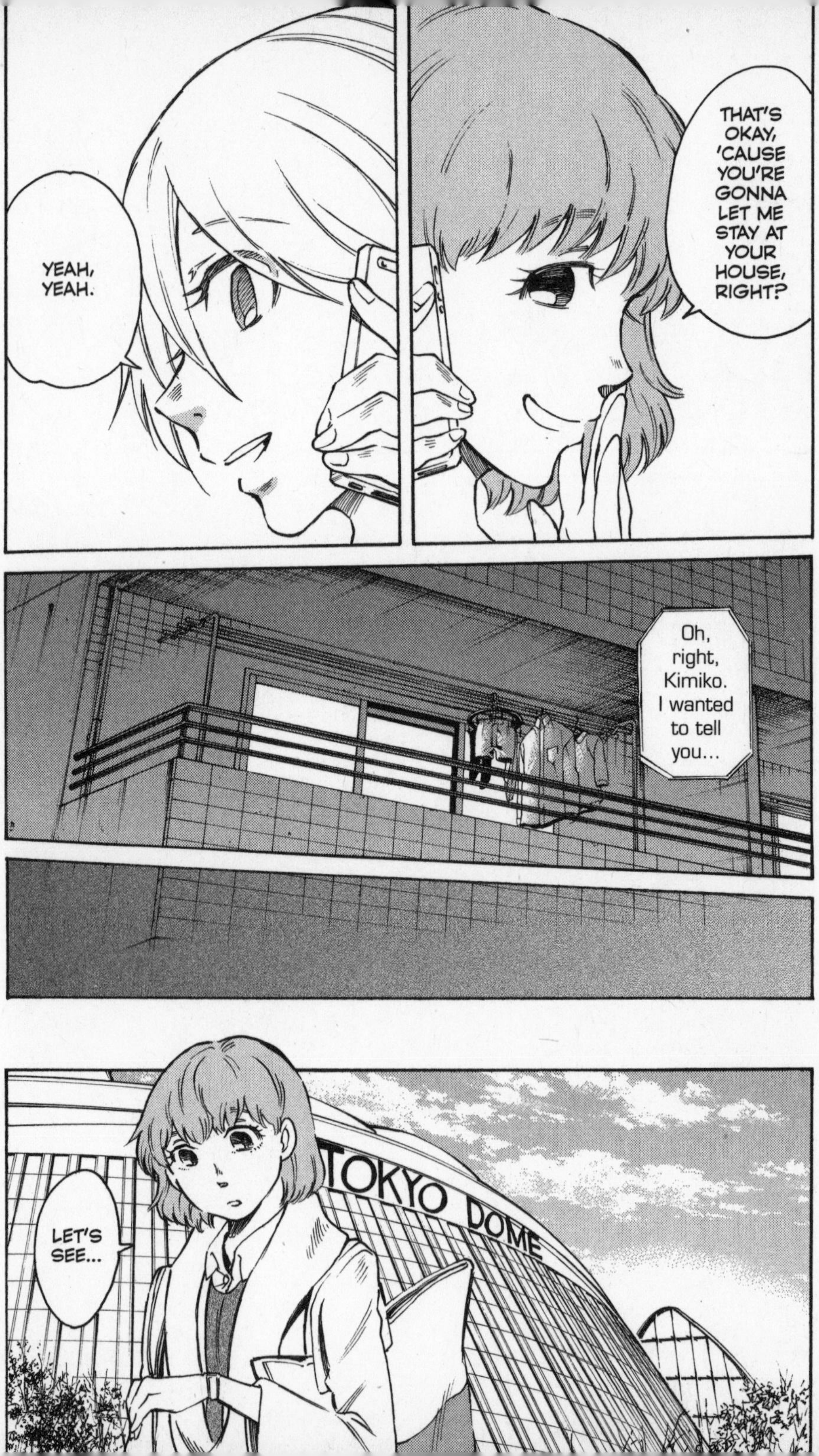
THAT'S OKAY, 'CAUSE YOU'RE GONNA LET ME STAY AT YOUR HOUSE, RIGHT?
YEAH, YEAH.
Oh, right, Kimiko. I wanted to tell you...
TOKYO DOME
LET'S SEE...

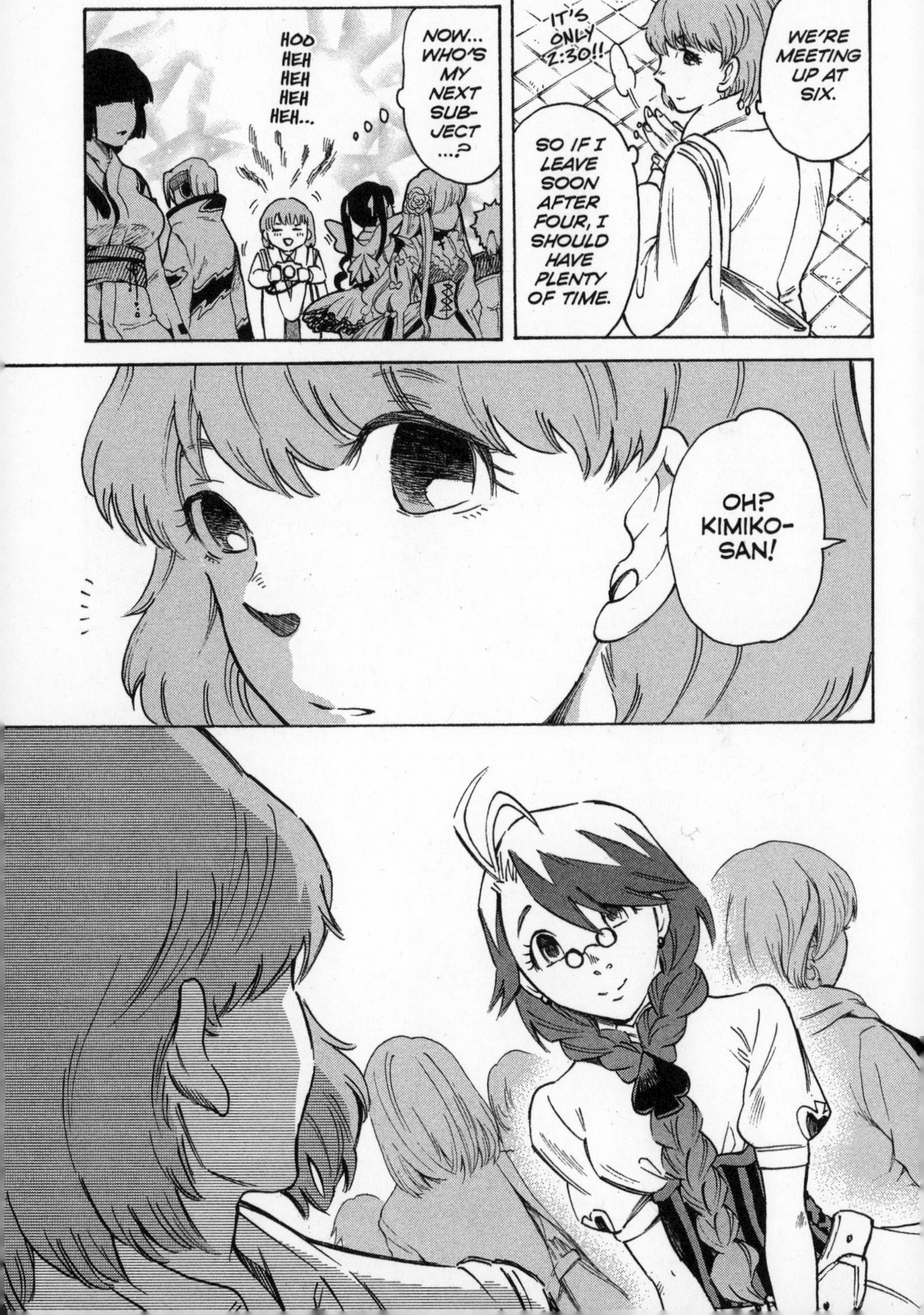
WE'RE MEETING UP AT SIX.
IT'S ONLY 2:30!!
SO IF I LEAVE SOON AFTER FOUR, I SHOULD HAVE PLENTY OF TIME.
NOW... WHO'S MY NEXT SUBJECT ...?
HOO HEH HEH HEH HEH...
OH? KIMIKO-SAN!

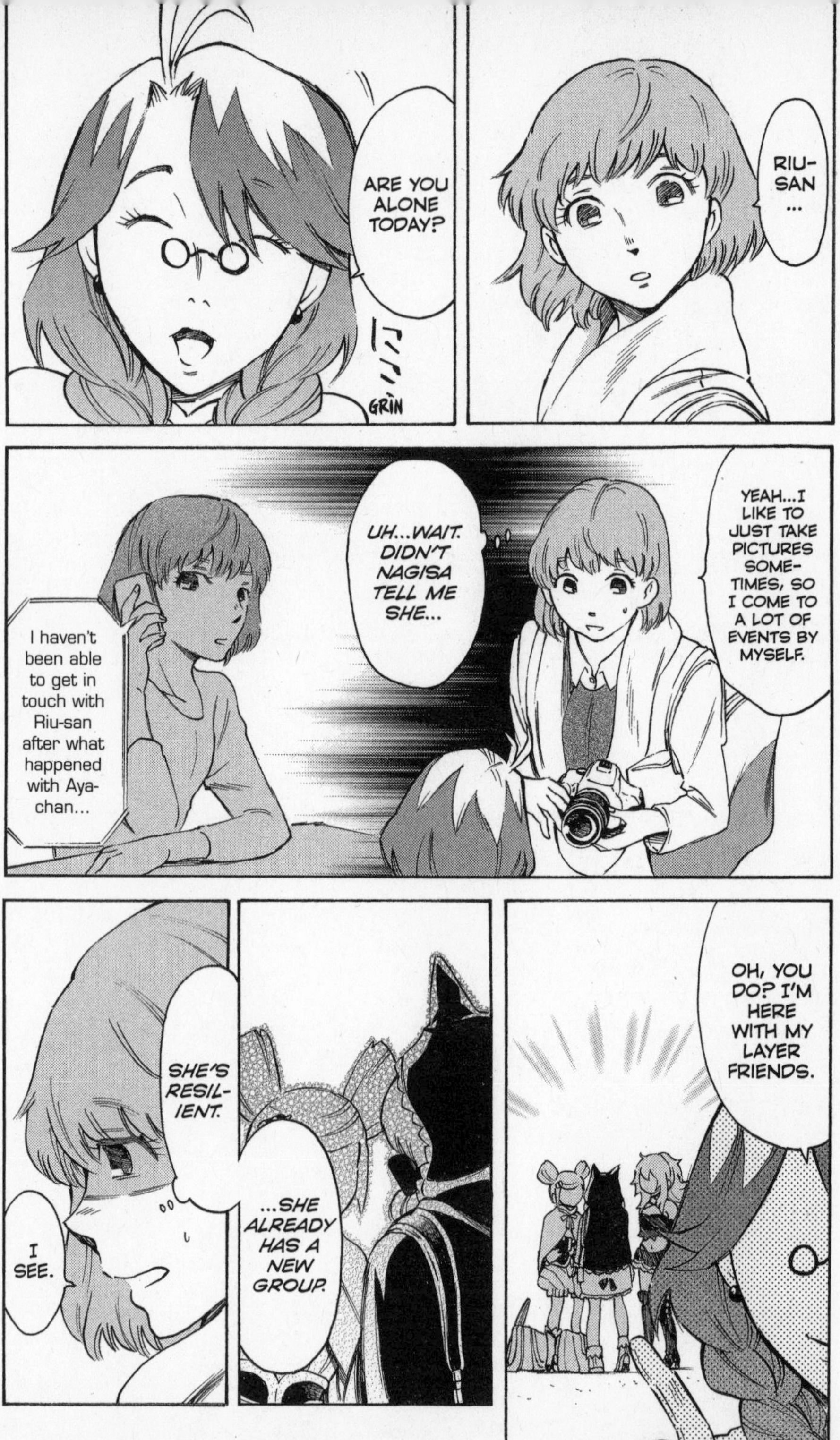
RIU-SAN...
ARE YOU ALONE TODAY?
GRIN
YEAH...I LIKE TO JUST TAKE PICTURES SOME-TIMES, SO I COME TO A LOT OF EVENTS BY MYSELF.
UH...WAIT. DIDN'T NAGISA TELL ME SHE...
I haven't been able to get in touch with Riu-san after what happened with Aya-chan...
OH, YOU DO? I'M HERE WITH MY LAYER FRIENDS.
...SHE ALREADY HAS A NEW GROUP.
SHE'S RESIL-IENT.
I SEE.

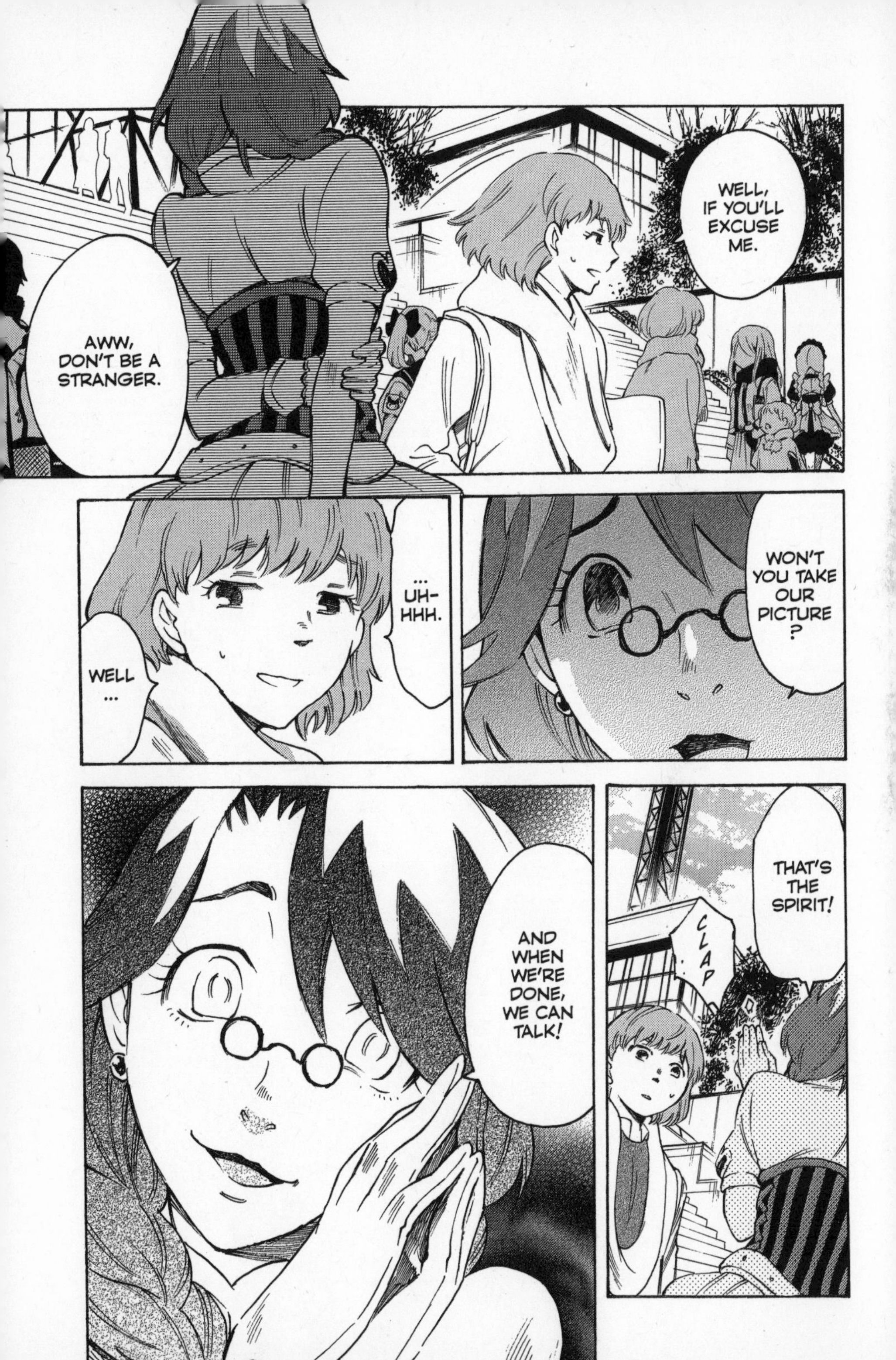
WELL, IF YOU'LL EXCUSE ME.
AWW, DON'T BE A STRANGER.
WON'T YOU TAKE OUR PICTURE?
... UH-HHH.
WELL ...
THAT'S THE SPIRIT!
CLAP
AND WHEN WE'RE DONE, WE CAN TALK!

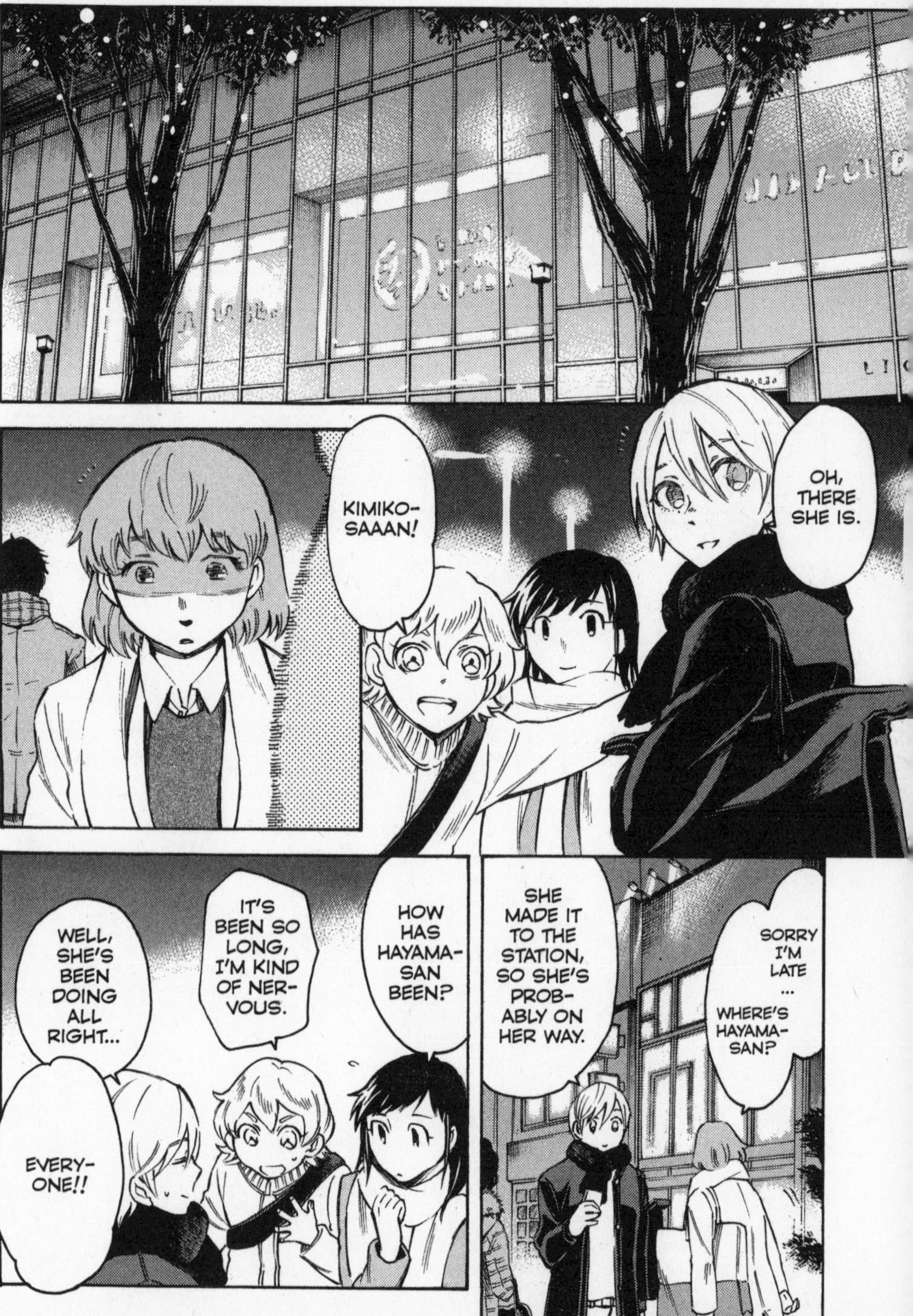
OH, THERE SHE IS.
KIMIKO-SAAAN!
SORRY I'M LATE ... WHERE'S HAYAMA-SAN?
SHE MADE IT TO THE STATION, SO SHE'S PROBABLY ON HER WAY.
HOW HAS HAYAMA-SAN BEEN?
IT'S BEEN SO LONG, I'M KIND OF NERVOUS.
WELL, SHE'S BEEN DOING ALL RIGHT...
EVERYONE!!

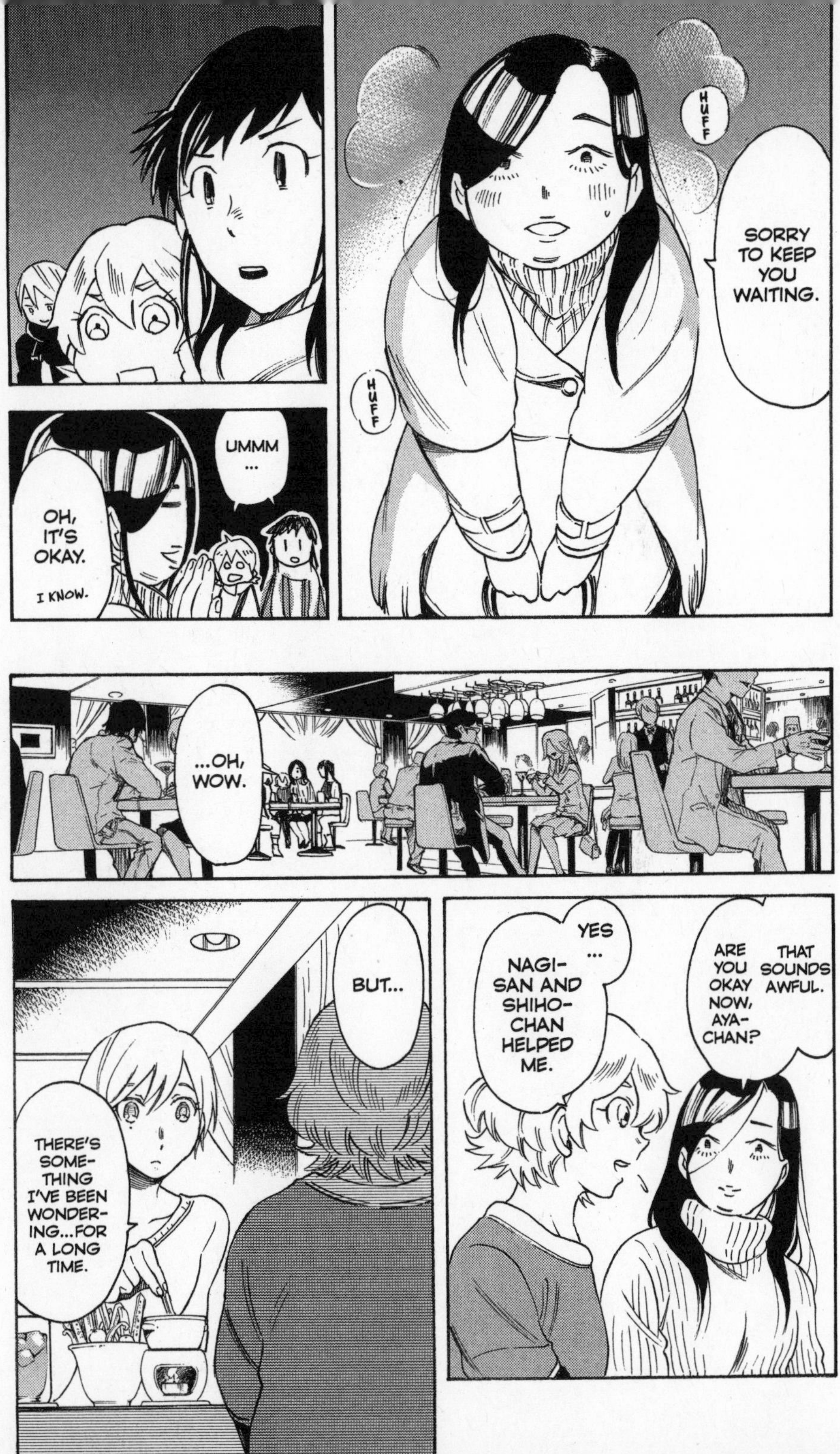
HUFF
SORRY TO KEEP YOU WAITING.
HUFF
UMMM ...
OH, IT'S OKAY.
I KNOW.
...OH, WOW.
THAT SOUNDS AWFUL.
ARE YOU OKAY NOW, AYA-CHAN?
YES ...
NAGI-SAN AND SHIHO-CHAN HELPED ME.
BUT...
THERE'S SOMETHING I'VE BEEN WONDERING...FOR A LONG TIME.

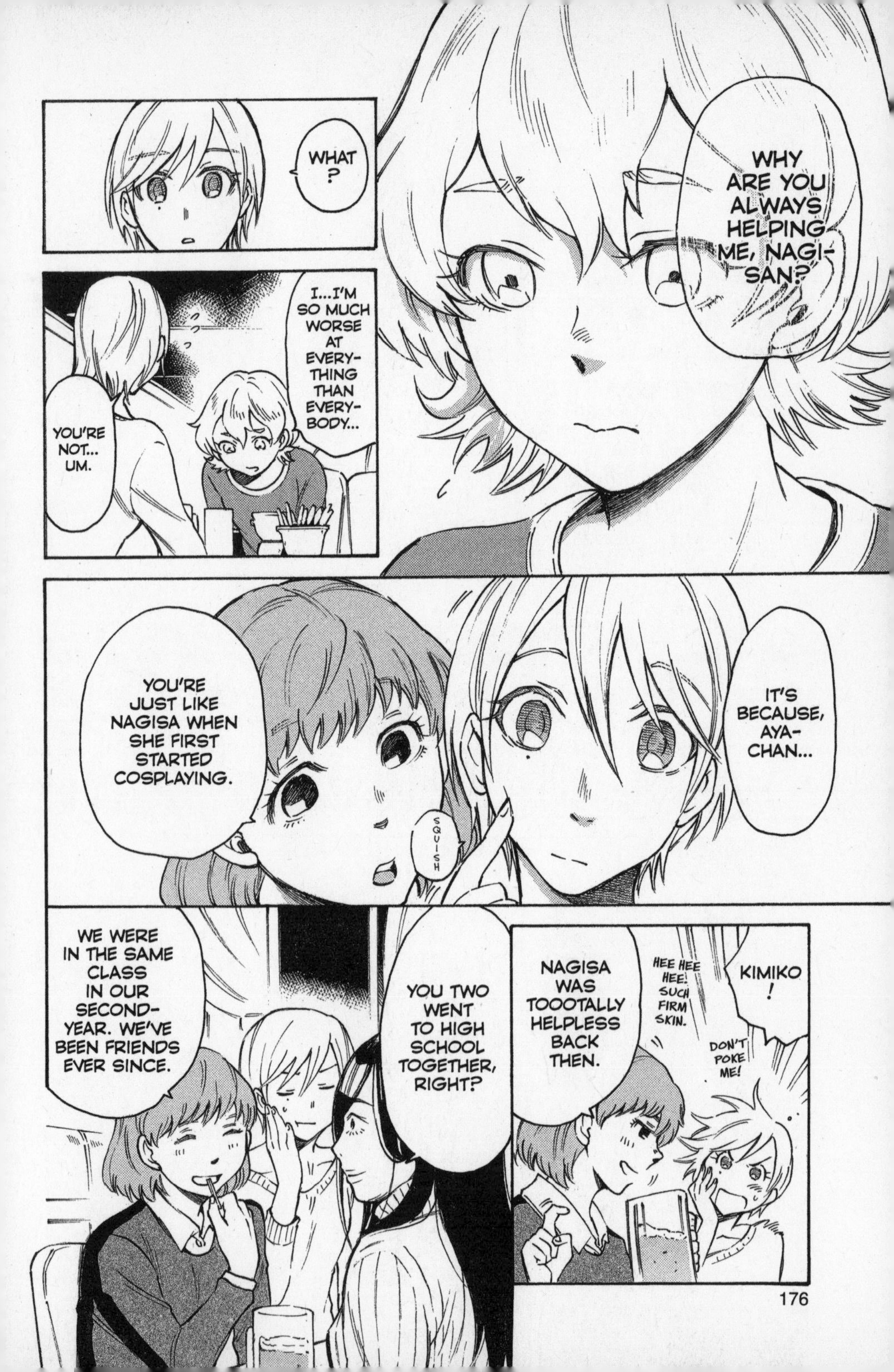
WHY ARE YOU ALWAYS HELPING ME, NAGI-SAN?
WHAT?
I...I'M SO MUCH WORSE AT EVERYTHING THAN EVERYBODY...
YOU'RE NOT... UM.
IT'S BECAUSE, AYA-CHAN...
SQUISH
YOU'RE JUST LIKE NAGISA WHEN SHE FIRST STARTED COSPLAYING.
KIMIKO!
HEE HEE HEE! SUCH FIRM SKIN.
NAGISA WAS TOOOTALLY HELPLESS BACK THEN.
DON'T POKE ME!
YOU TWO WENT TO HIGH SCHOOL TOGETHER, RIGHT?
WE WERE IN THE SAME CLASS IN OUR SECOND-YEAR. WE'VE BEEN FRIENDS EVER SINCE.

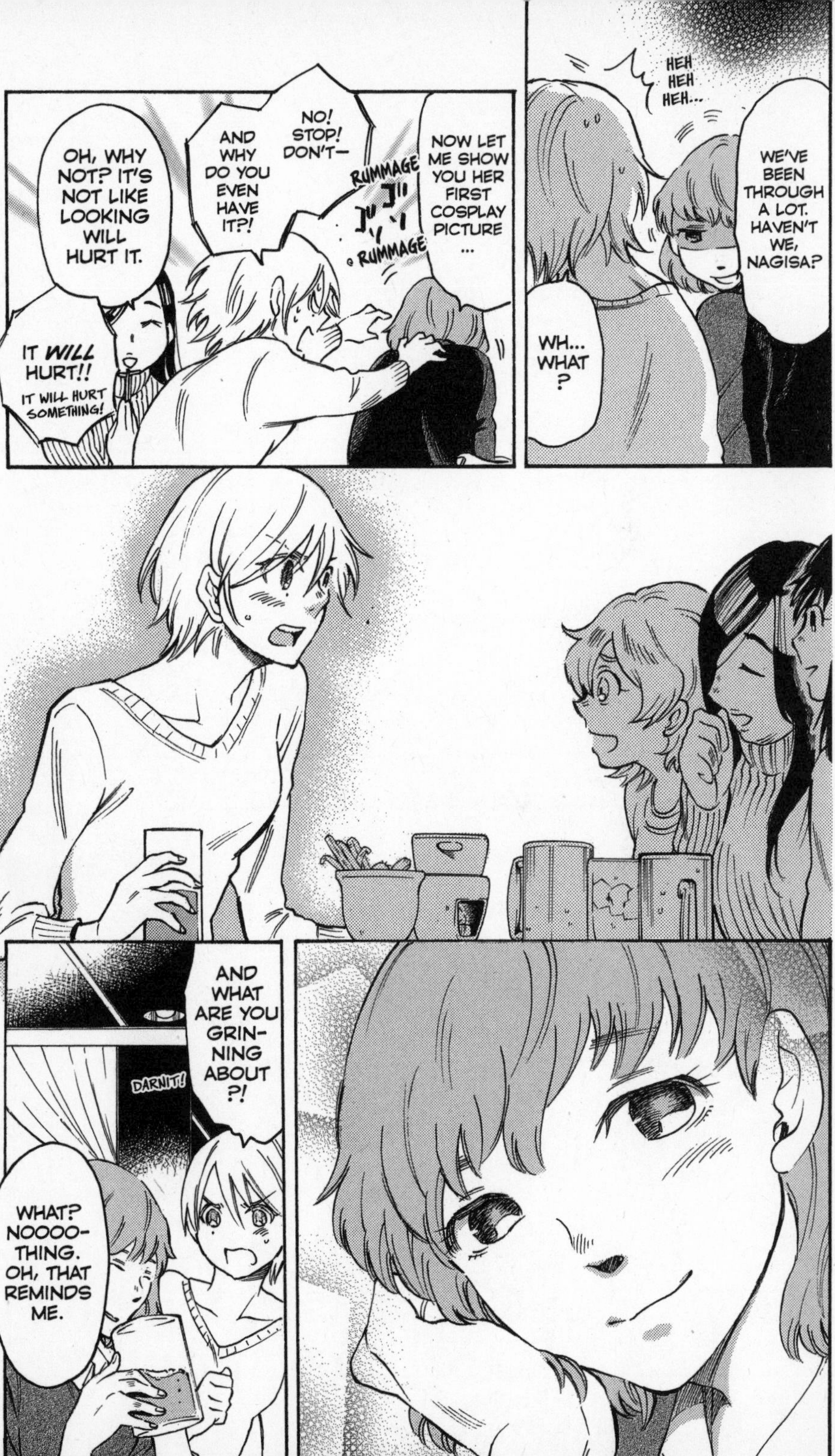
HEH HEH HEH...
WE'VE BEEN THROUGH A LOT. HAVEN'T WE, NAGISA?
WH... WHAT?
NOW LET ME SHOW YOU HER FIRST COSPLAY PICTURE ...
RUMMAGE
RUMMAGE
NO! STOP! DON'T—
AND WHY DO YOU EVEN HAVE IT?!
OH, WHY NOT? IT'S NOT LIKE LOOKING WILL HURT IT.
IT WILL HURT!! IT WILL HURT SOMETHING!
AND WHAT ARE YOU GRIN-NING ABOUT?!
DARNIT!
WHAT? NOOOO-THING. OH, THAT REMINDS ME.

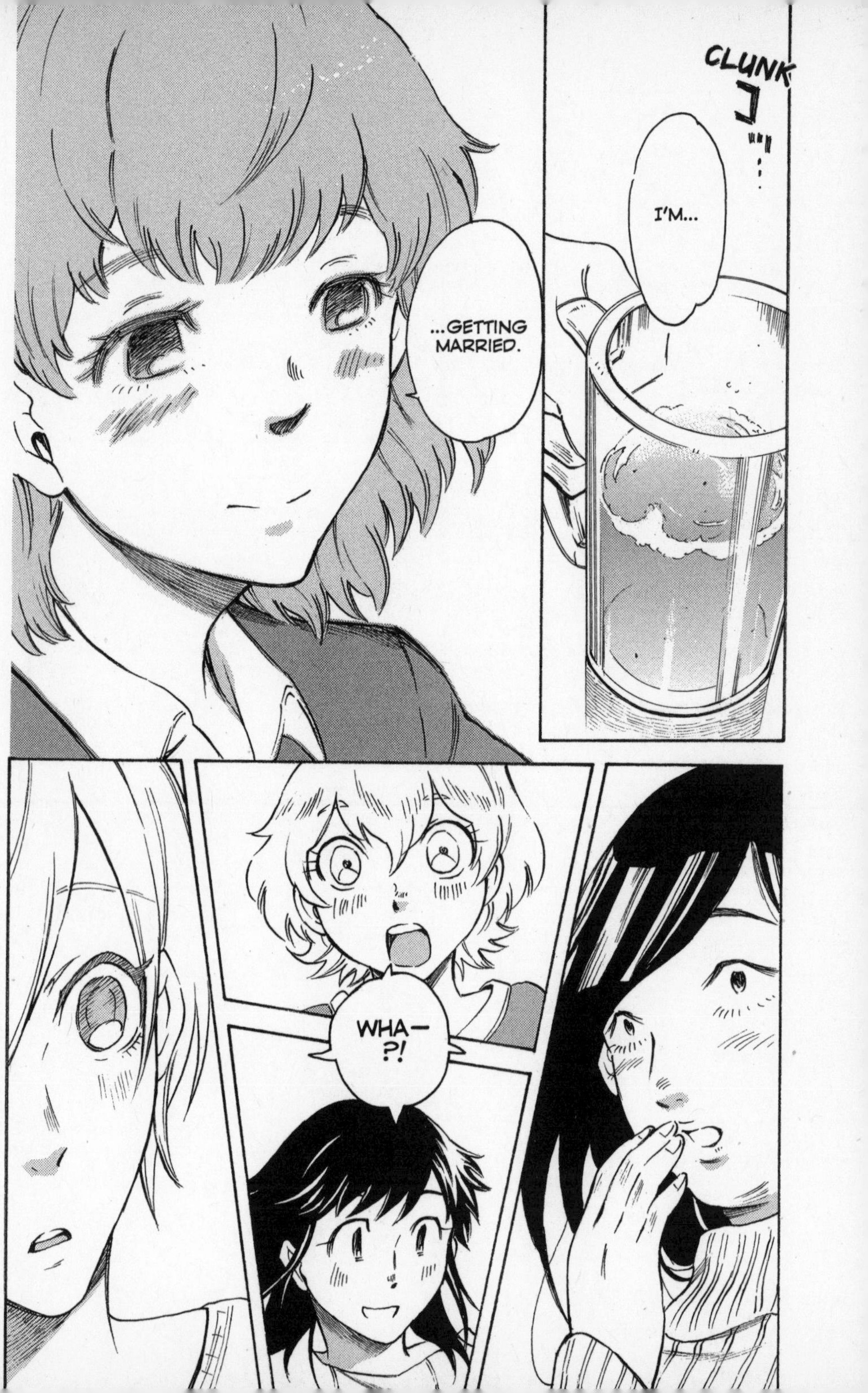
CLUNK
I'M...
...GETTING MARRIED.
WHA—?!

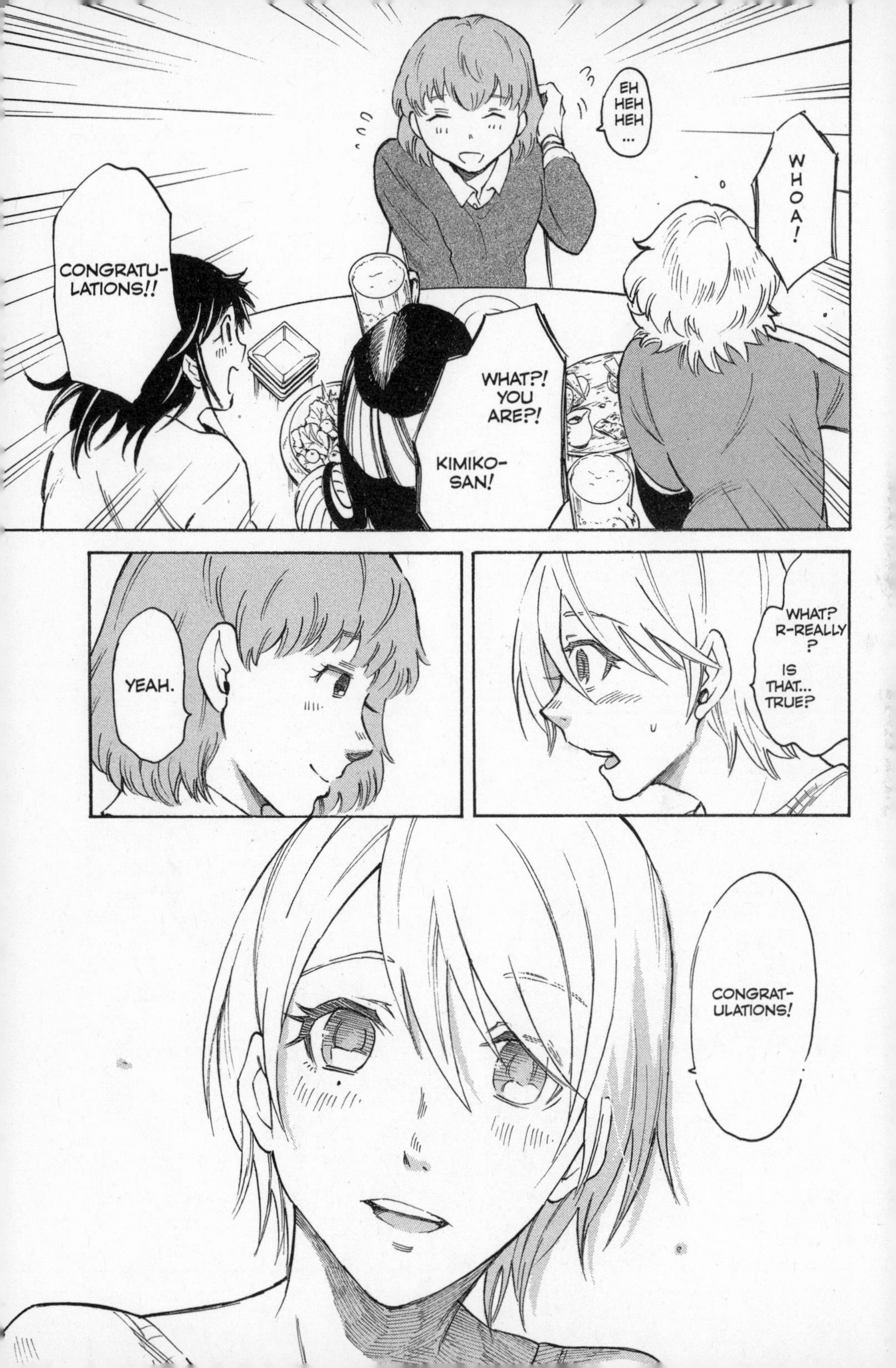
WHOA!
EH HEH HEH...
WHAT?! YOU ARE?!
KIMIKO-SAN!
CONGRATULATIONS!!
WHAT? R-REALLY?
IS THAT... TRUE?
YEAH.
CONGRATULATIONS!

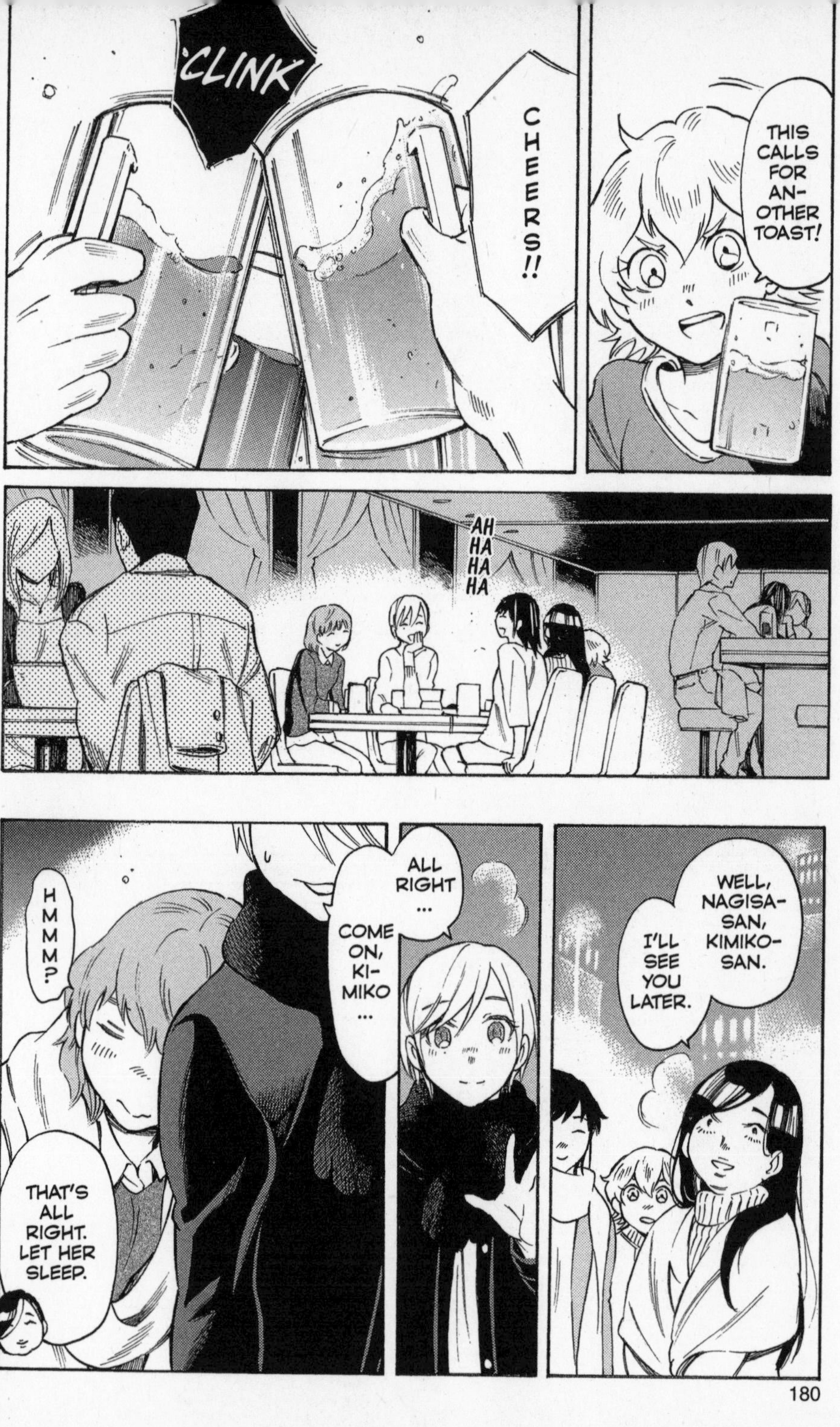
THIS CALLS FOR AN-OTHER TOAST!
CHEERS!!
CLINK
AH HA HA HA
WELL, NAGISA-SAN, KIMIKO-SAN.
I'LL SEE YOU LATER.
ALL RIGHT ...
COME ON, KI-MIKO ...
HMMM?
THAT'S ALL RIGHT. LET HER SLEEP.

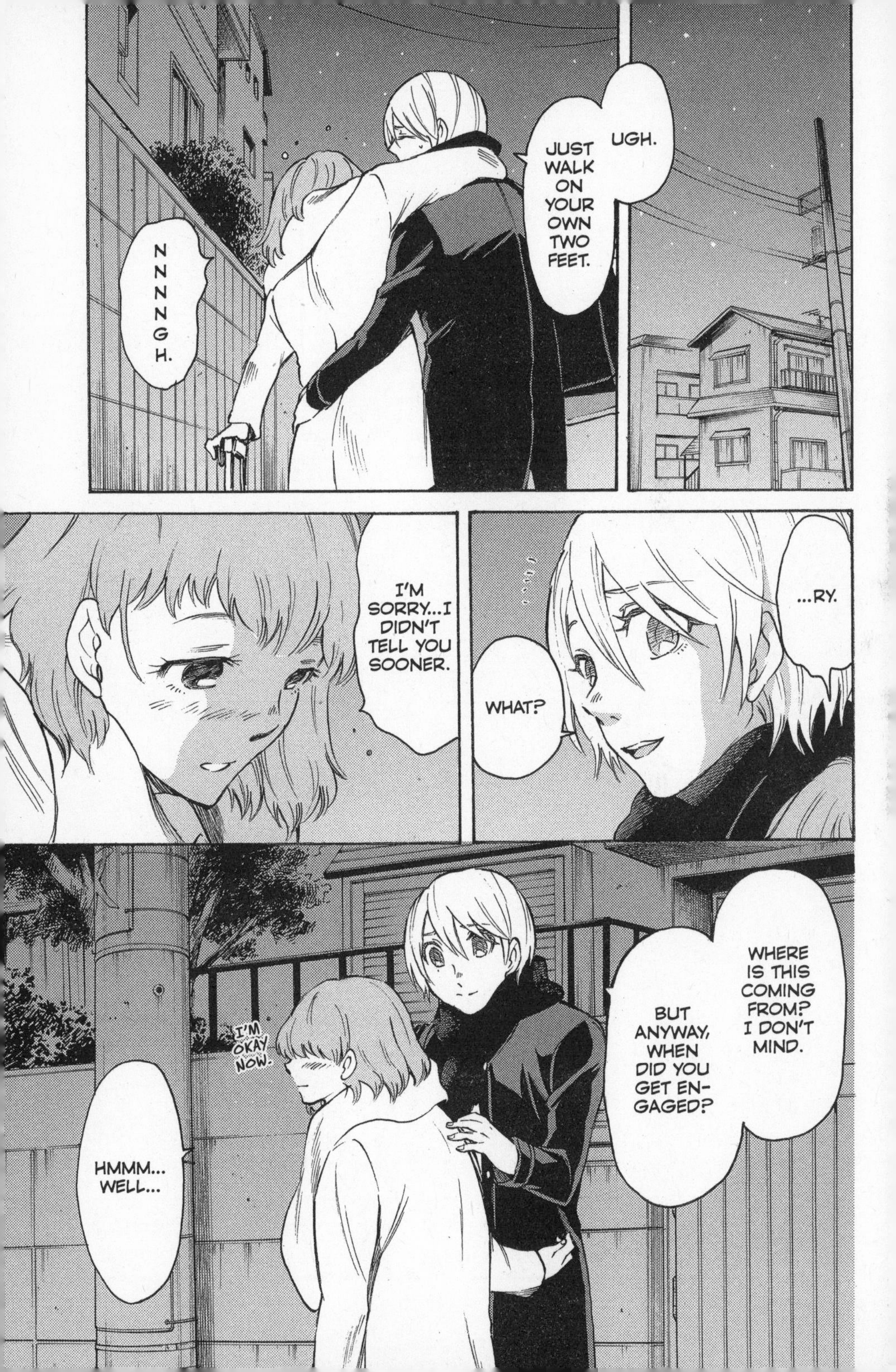
UGH.
JUST WALK ON YOUR OWN TWO FEET.
NNNNGH.
...RY.
WHAT?
I'M SORRY...I DIDN'T TELL YOU SOONER.
WHERE IS THIS COMING FROM? I DON'T MIND.
BUT ANYWAY, WHEN DID YOU GET EN-GAGED?
I'M OKAY NOW.
HMMM... WELL...

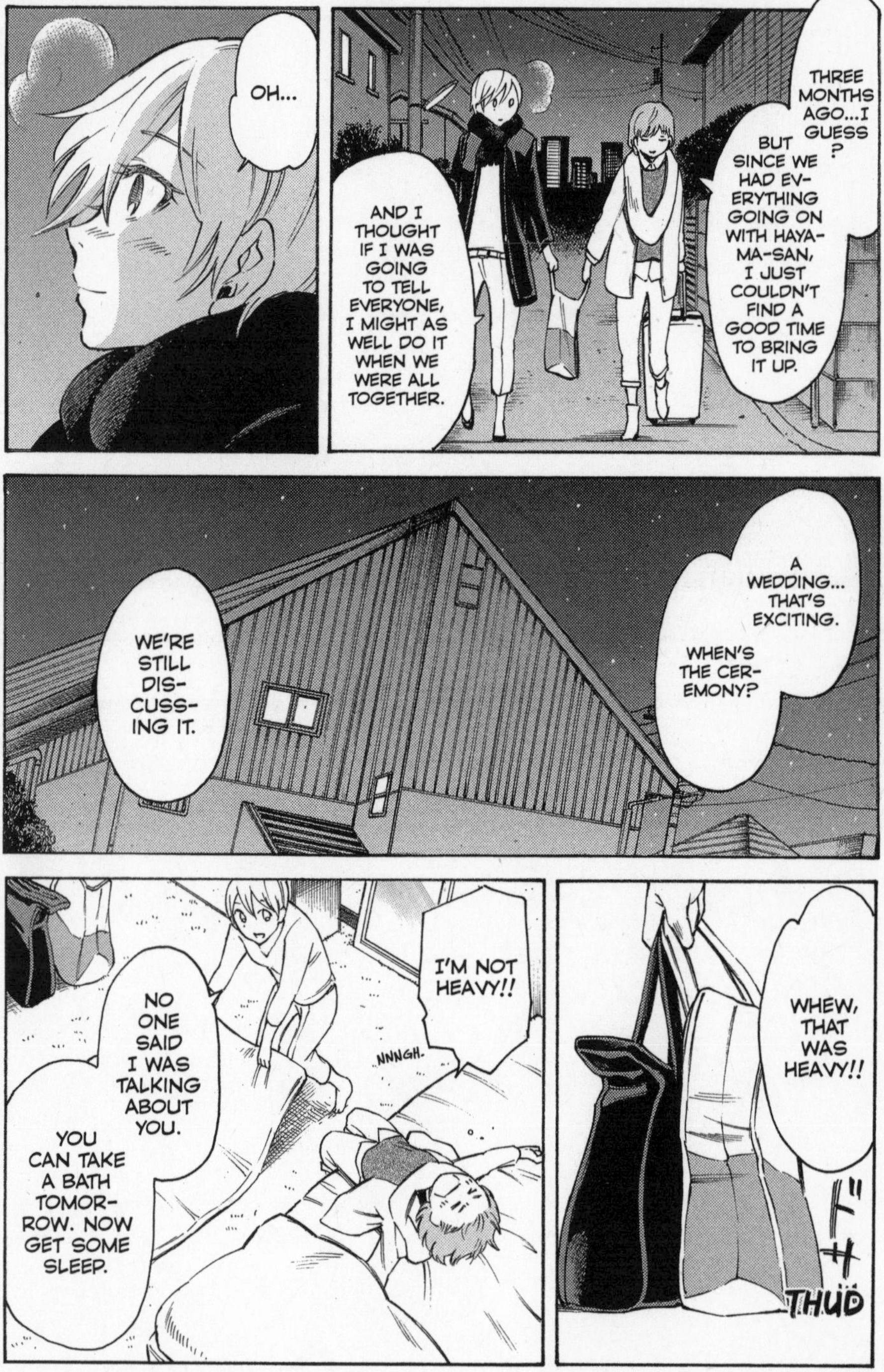
THREE MONTHS AGO...I GUESS?
BUT SINCE WE HAD EVERYTHING GOING ON WITH HAYAMA-SAN, I JUST COULDN'T FIND A GOOD TIME TO BRING IT UP.
AND I THOUGHT IF I WAS GOING TO TELL EVERYONE, I MIGHT AS WELL DO IT WHEN WE WERE ALL TOGETHER.
OH...
A WEDDING... THAT'S EXCITING.
WHEN'S THE CEREMONY?
WE'RE STILL DISCUSSING IT.
WHEW, THAT WAS HEAVY!!
ドサ
THUD
I'M NOT HEAVY!!
NNNGH.
NO ONE SAID I WAS TALKING ABOUT YOU.
YOU CAN TAKE A BATH TOMORROW. NOW GET SOME SLEEP.

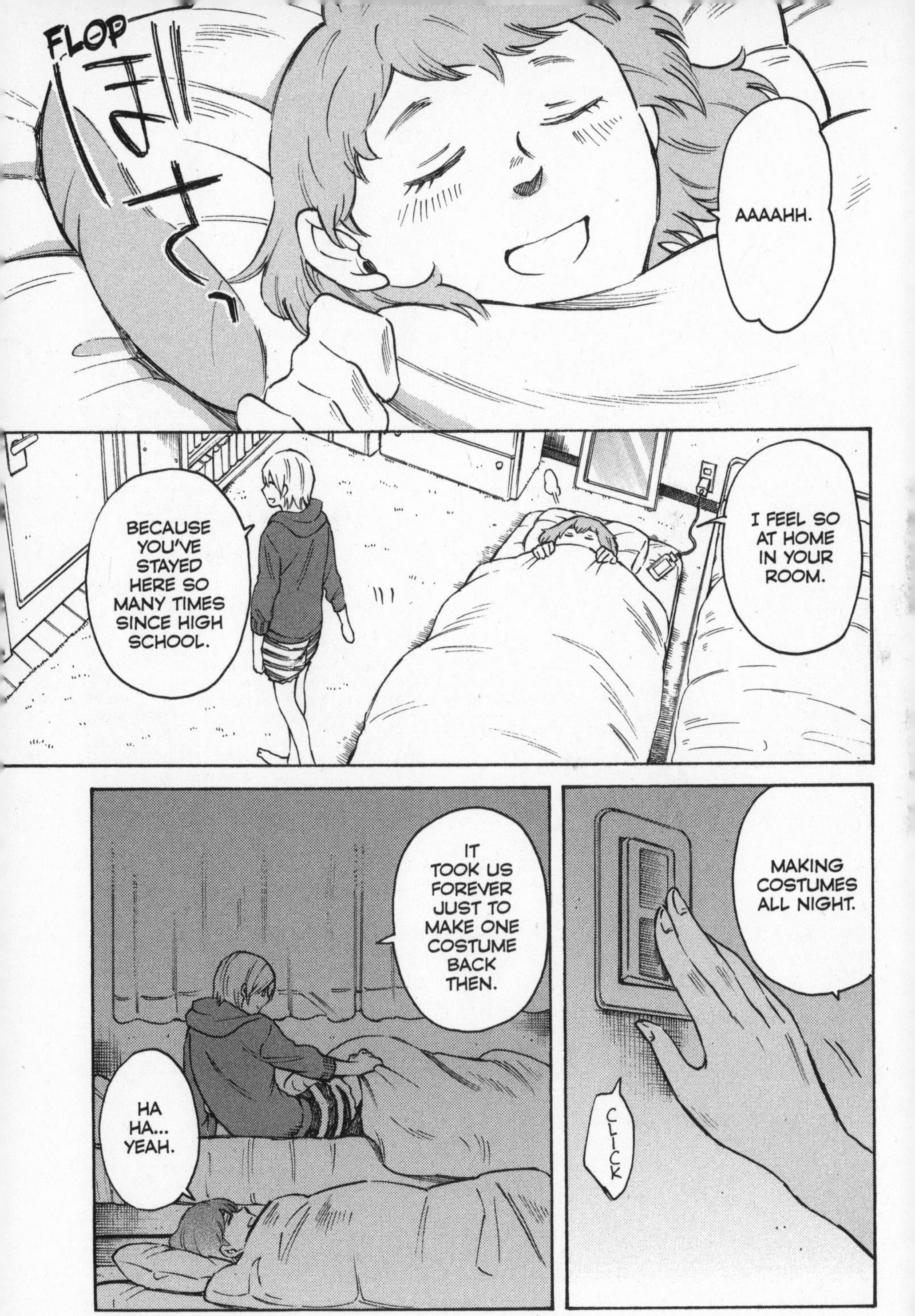
FLOP
AAAAHH.
I FEEL SO AT HOME IN YOUR ROOM.
BECAUSE YOU'VE STAYED HERE SO MANY TIMES SINCE HIGH SCHOOL.
MAKING COSTUMES ALL NIGHT.
CLICK
IT TOOK US FOREVER JUST TO MAKE ONE COSTUME BACK THEN.
HA HA... YEAH.

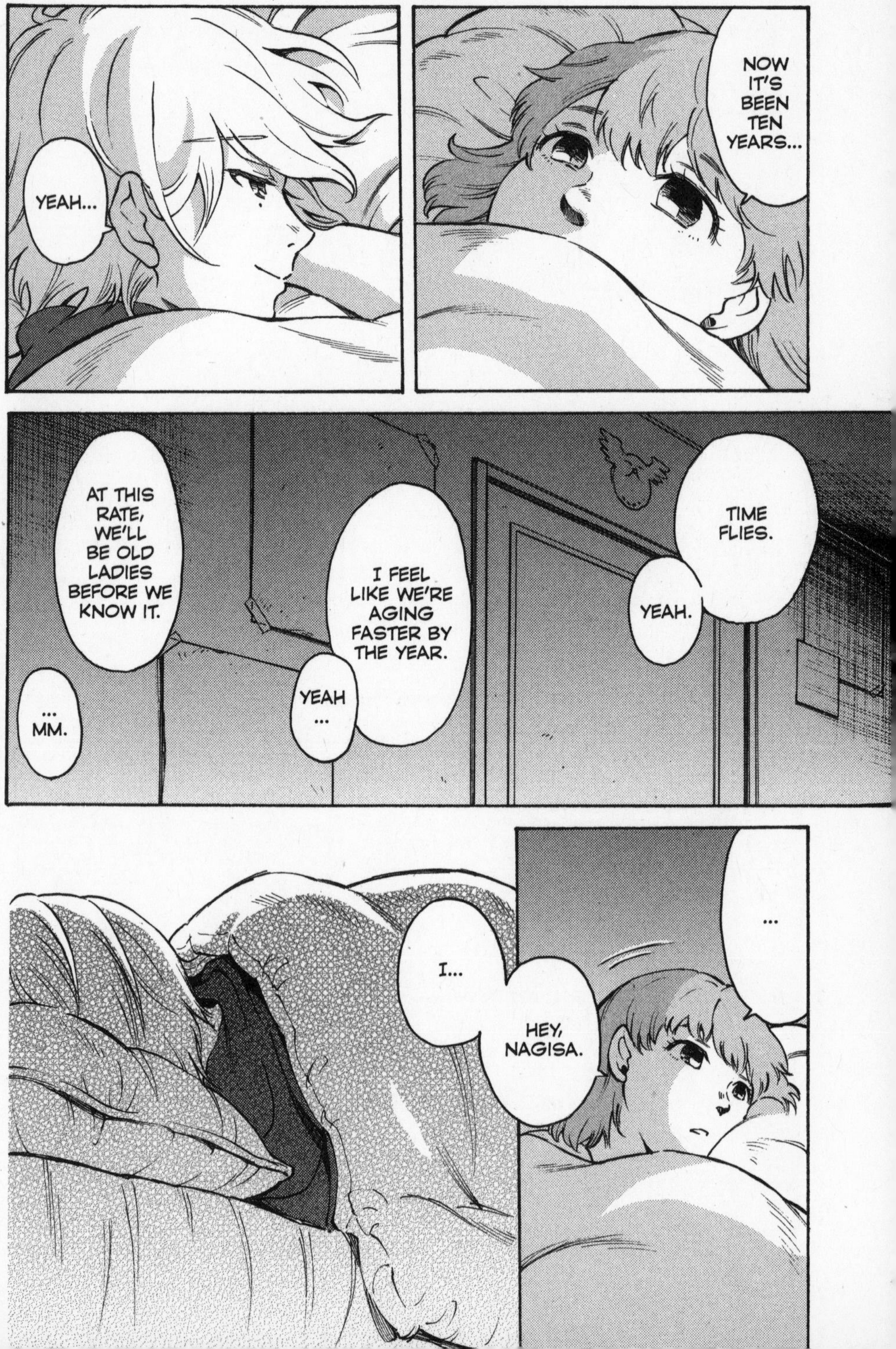
NOW IT'S BEEN TEN YEARS...
YEAH...
TIME FLIES.
YEAH.
I FEEL LIKE WE'RE AGING FASTER BY THE YEAR.
YEAH ...
AT THIS RATE, WE'LL BE OLD LADIES BEFORE WE KNOW IT.
... MM.
...
HEY, NAGISA.
I...

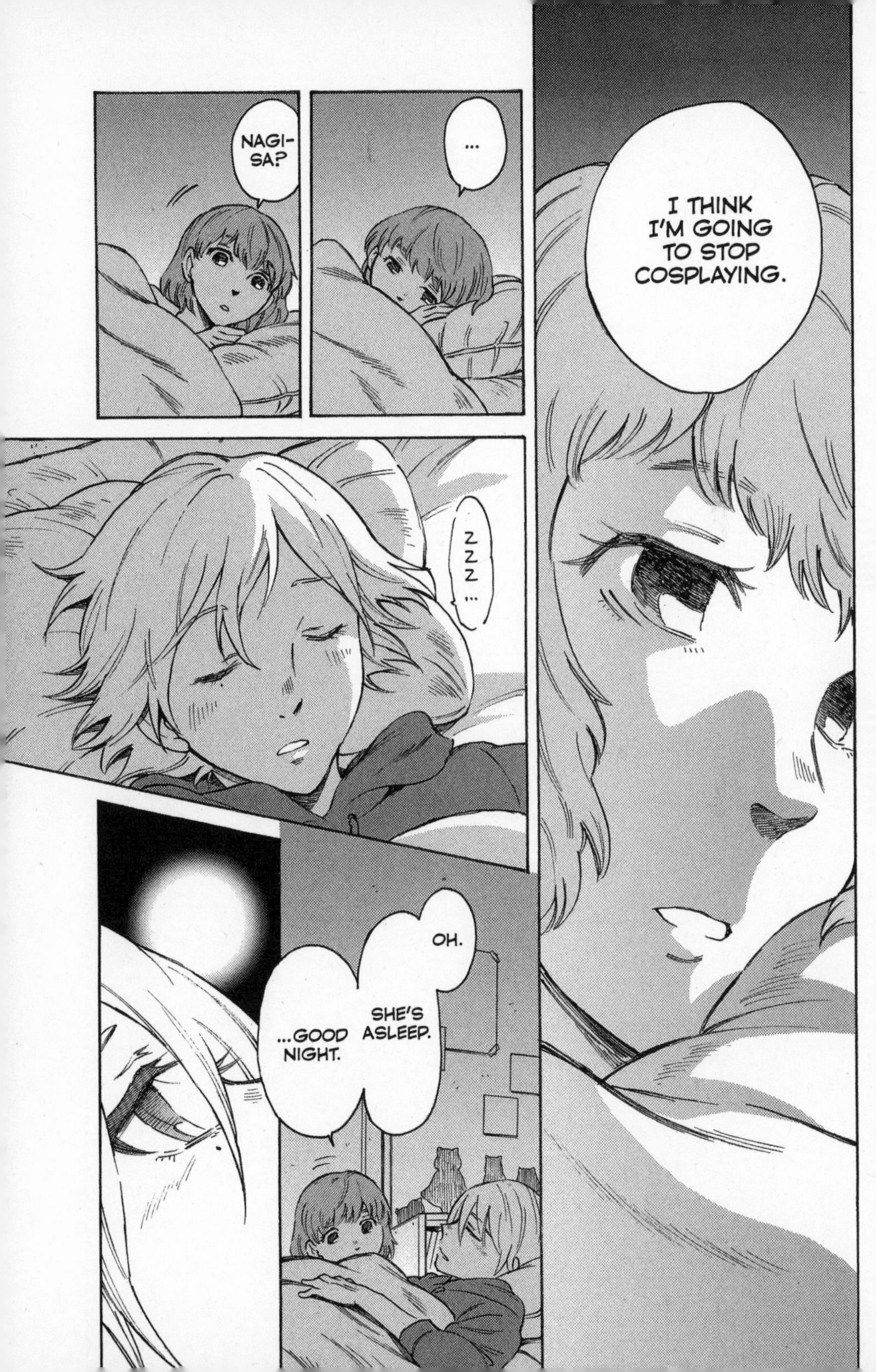
I THINK I'M GOING TO STOP COSPLAYING.
...
NAGI-SA?
ZZZ...
OH.
SHE'S ASLEEP.
...GOOD NIGHT.

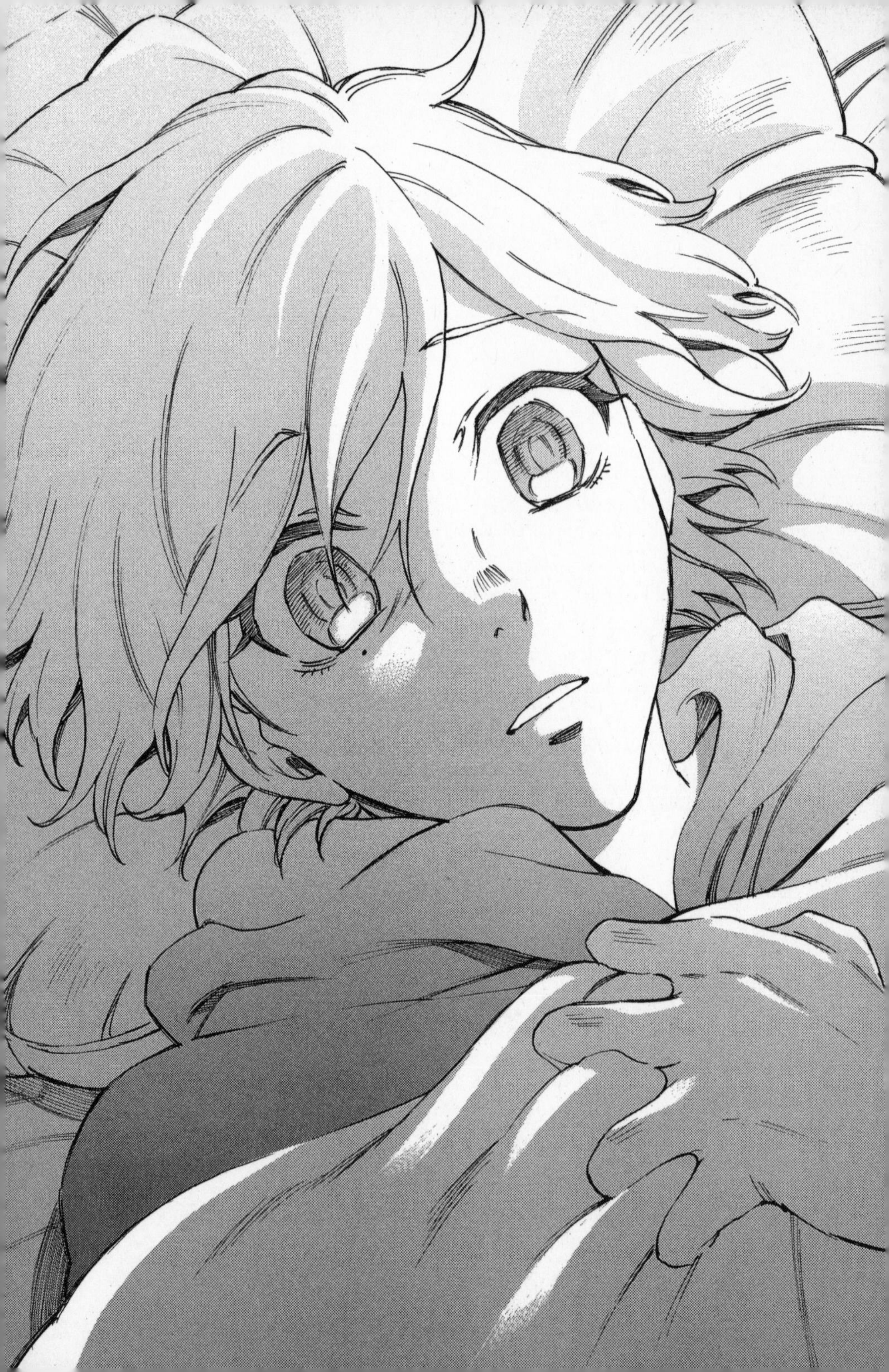

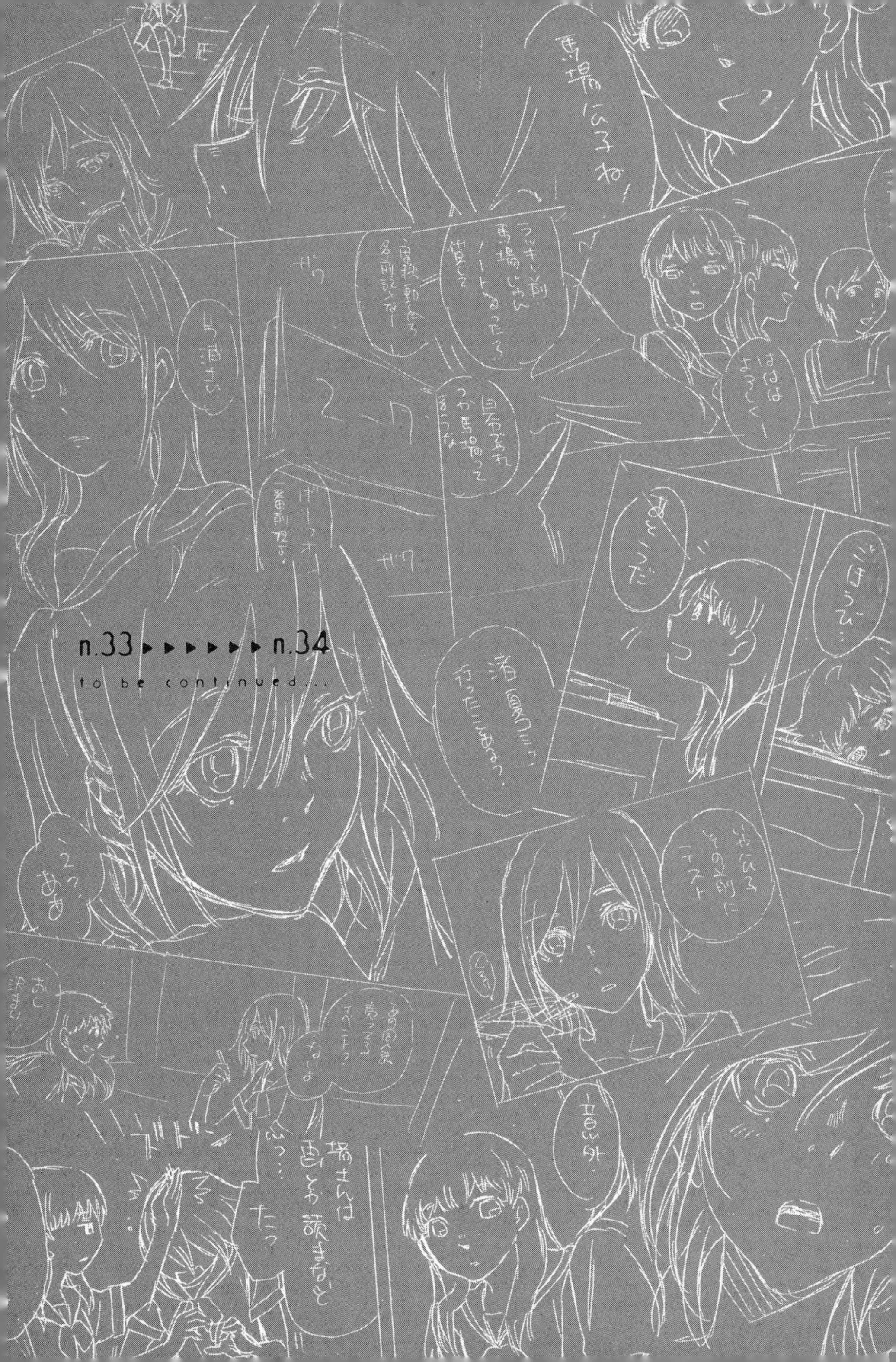
n.33 ▶▶▶▶▶▶▶ n.34
to be continued...

VOLUME FOUR, WHERE THE PEOPLE
IN THIS MANGA SHOWED US VARIOUS
DIFFERENT FACES.

I THINK IT'S BETTER NOT TO SEE TOO
MUCH OF SOMEONE'S INNER WORKINGS.

MY HEART KIND OF GOES OUT TO
PEOPLE WHEN I SEE THEM SPINNING
THEIR WHEELS, EXPOSING TOO MANY OF
THEIR FLAWS. THANKS FOR BEING HERE
FOR ANOTHER VOLUME.

NEXT IS THE BONUS MANGA.

VOLUME FOUR.

OH... UM... NEXT IS THE BONUS MANGA ...

...IT'S ALL RIGHT IF YOU DON'T READ IT, BUT IF... POS- SIBLE... UM

...I THINK I'D LIKE IT IF YOU WOULD... OH... BUT...

ORZ.4 BONUS ORIGINAL MANGA

CHARGE! RIU-TASO Q&A CORNER ☆

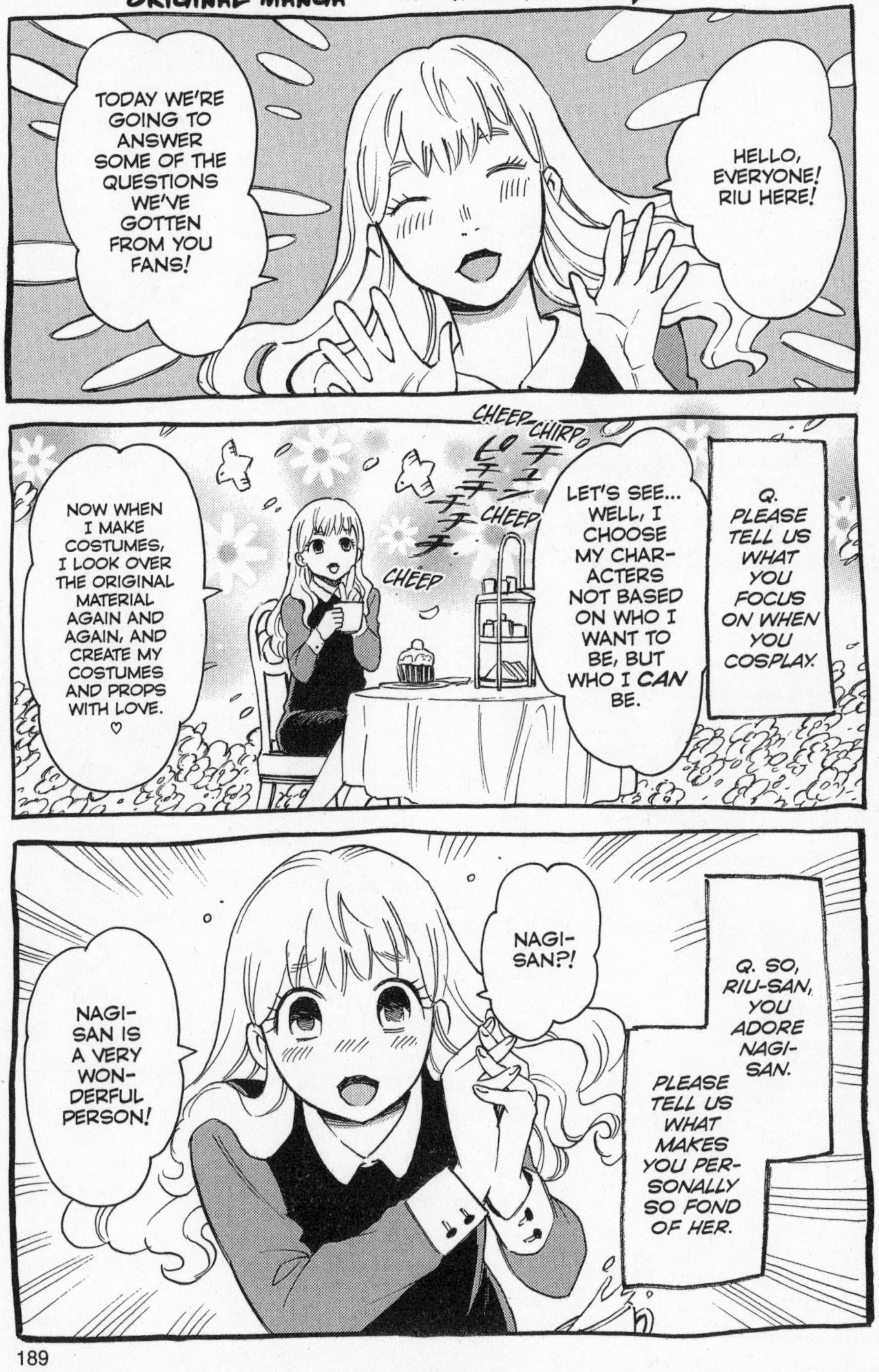

HELLO, EVERYONE! RIU HERE!
TODAY WE'RE GOING TO ANSWER SOME OF THE QUESTIONS WE'VE GOTTEN FROM YOU FANS!
Q. PLEASE TELL US WHAT YOU FOCUS ON WHEN YOU COSPLAY.
LET'S SEE... WELL, I CHOOSE MY CHAR-ACTERS NOT BASED ON WHO I WANT TO BE, BUT WHO I *CAN* BE.
チュン CHIRP CHEEP
ピチチチチ CHEEP CHEEP
NOW WHEN I MAKE COSTUMES, I LOOK OVER THE ORIGINAL MATERIAL AGAIN AND AGAIN, AND CREATE MY COSTUMES AND PROPS WITH LOVE. ♡
Q. SO, RIU-SAN, YOU ADORE NAGI-SAN. PLEASE TELL US WHAT MAKES YOU PER-SONALLY SO FOND OF HER.
NAGI-SAN?!
NAGI-SAN IS A VERY WON-DERFUL PERSON!

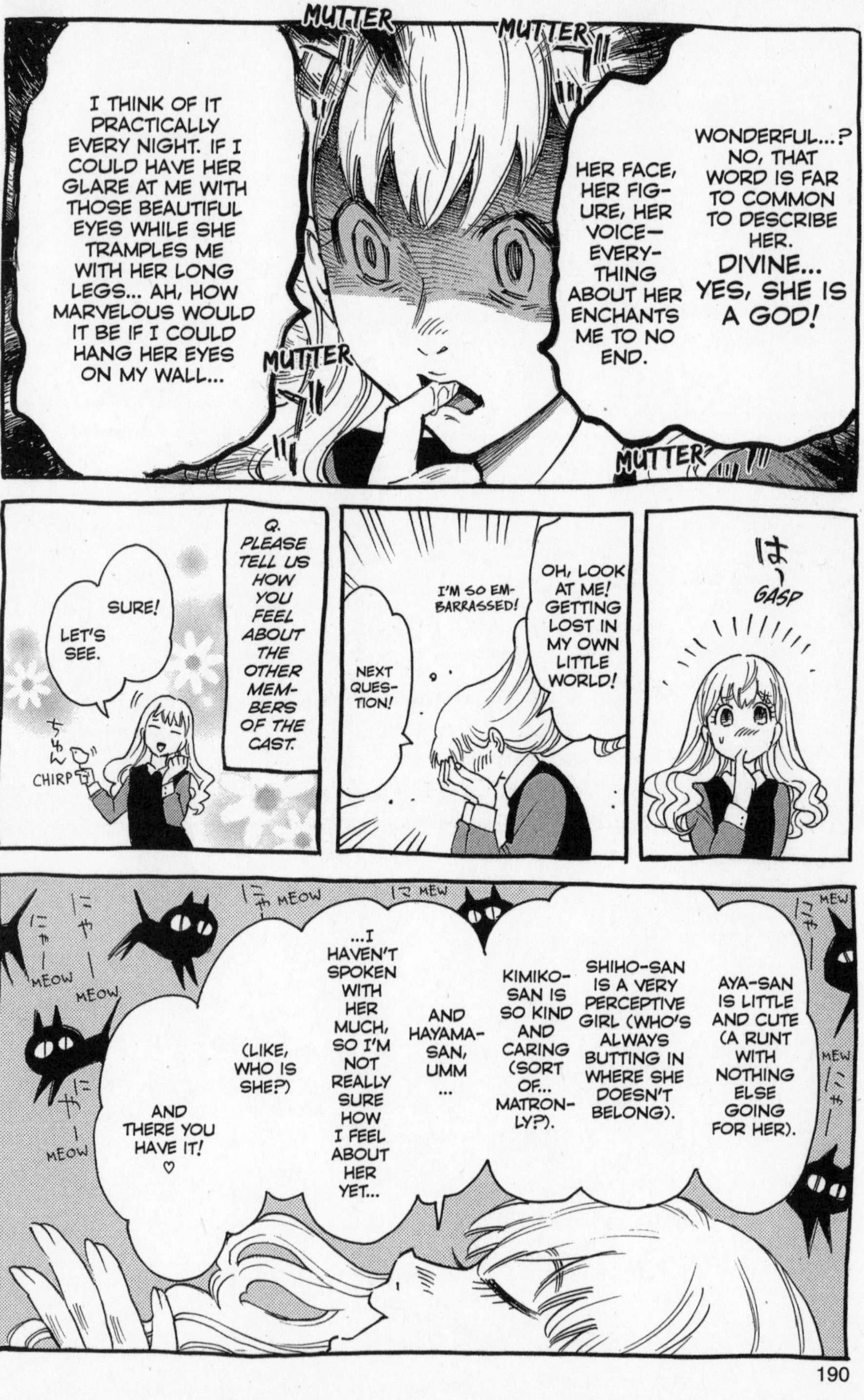
MUTTER
MUTTER
WONDERFUL...? NO, THAT WORD IS FAR TO COMMON TO DESCRIBE HER. DIVINE... YES, SHE IS A GOD!
HER FACE, HER FIG-URE, HER VOICE—EVERY-THING ABOUT HER ENCHANTS ME TO NO END.
I THINK OF IT PRACTICALLY EVERY NIGHT. IF I COULD HAVE HER GLARE AT ME WITH THOSE BEAUTIFUL EYES WHILE SHE TRAMPLES ME WITH HER LONG LEGS... AH, HOW MARVELOUS WOULD IT BE IF I COULD HANG HER EYES ON MY WALL...
MUTTER
MUTTER
は GASP
OH, LOOK AT ME! GETTING LOST IN MY OWN LITTLE WORLD!
I'M SO EM-BARRASSED!
NEXT QUES-TION!
Q. PLEASE TELL US HOW YOU FEEL ABOUT THE OTHER MEM-BERS OF THE CAST.
SURE! LET'S SEE.
ちゅん CHIRP
にゃー MEW
に MEW
にゃ MEOW
にゃー MEOW
にゃー MEOW
にゃー MEOW
にゃー MEW
AYA-SAN IS LITTLE AND CUTE (A RUNT WITH NOTHING ELSE GOING FOR HER).
SHIHO-SAN IS A VERY PERCEPTIVE GIRL (WHO'S ALWAYS BUTTING IN WHERE SHE DOESN'T BELONG).
KIMIKO-SAN IS SO KIND AND CARING (SORT OF... MATRON-LY?).
AND HAYAMA-SAN, UMM ...
...I HAVEN'T SPOKEN WITH HER MUCH, SO I'M NOT REALLY SURE HOW I FEEL ABOUT HER YET...
(LIKE, WHO IS SHE?)
AND THERE YOU HAVE IT! ♡

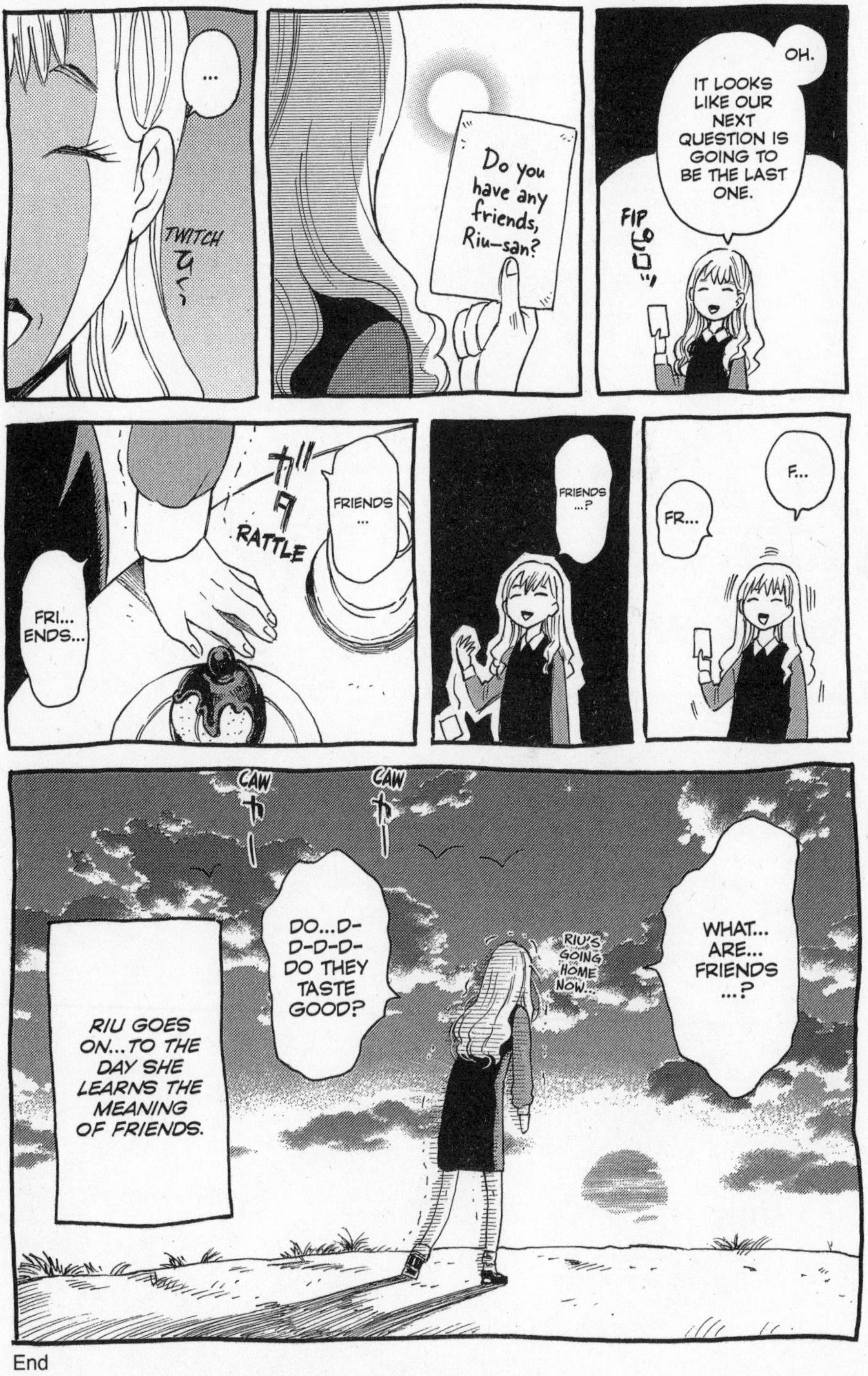
OH.
IT LOOKS LIKE OUR NEXT QUESTION IS GOING TO BE THE LAST ONE.
FIP
Do you have any friends, Riu-san?
...
TWITCH
F...
FR...
FRIENDS ...?
FRIENDS ...
RATTLE
FRI... ENDS...
CAW
CAW
WHAT... ARE... FRIENDS ...?
RIU'S GOING HOME NOW...
DO...D-D-D-D-DO THEY TASTE GOOD?
RIU GOES ON...TO THE DAY SHE LEARNS THE MEANING OF FRIENDS.

End

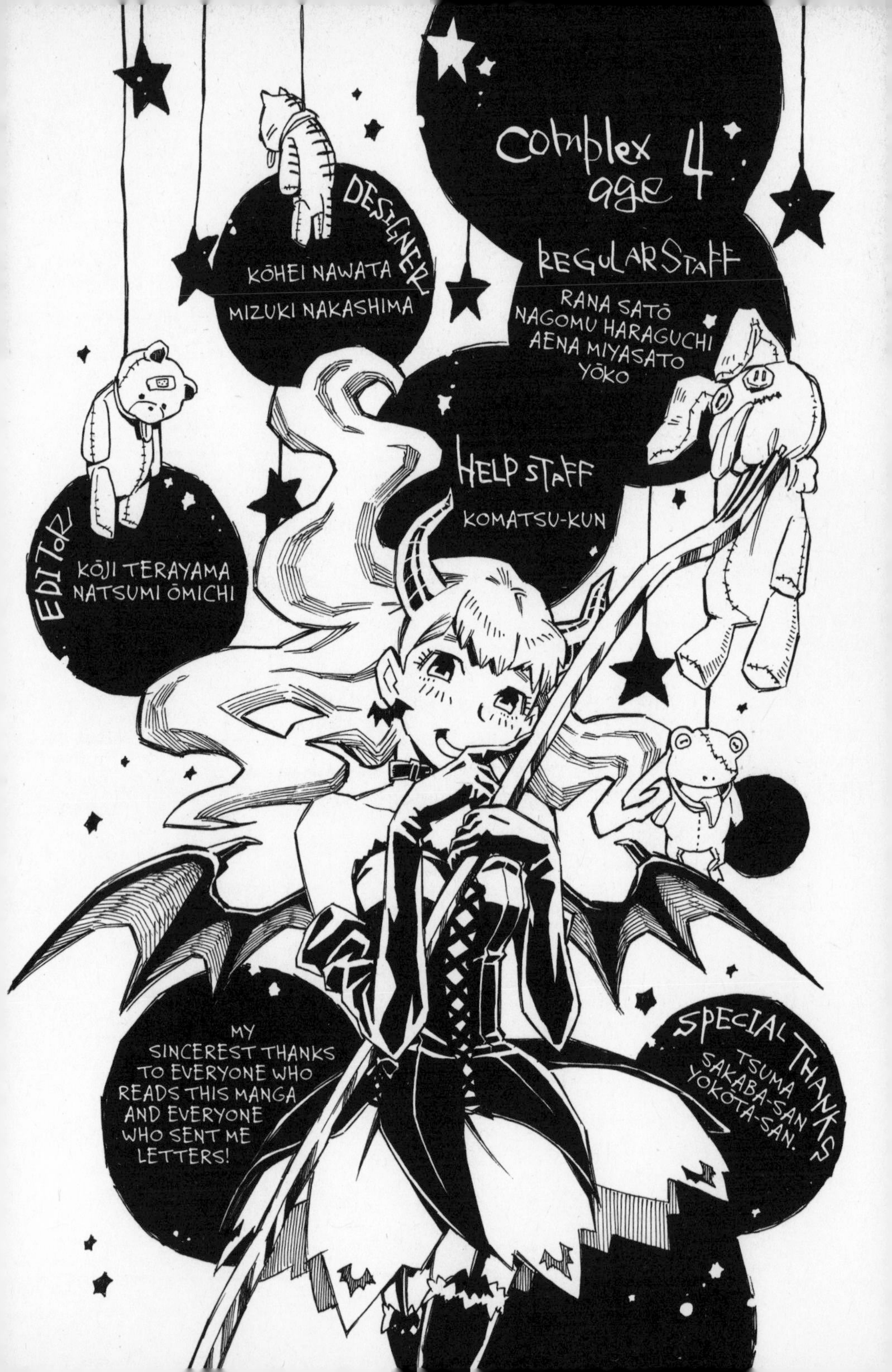
complex age 4
DESIGNER
KŌHEI NAWATA
MIZUKI NAKASHIMA
REGULAR STAFF
RANA SATŌ
NAGOMU HARAGUCHI
AENA MIYASATO
YŌKO
EDITOR
KŌJI TERAYAMA
NATSUMI ŌMICHI
HELP STAFF
KOMATSU-KUN
SPECIAL THANKS
TSUMA
SAKABA-SAN
YOKOTA-SAN.
MY SINCEREST THANKS TO EVERYONE WHO READS THIS MANGA AND EVERYONE WHO SENT ME LETTERS!

Cospedia

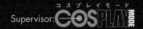

[GLOSSARY OF COSPLAY TERMS]

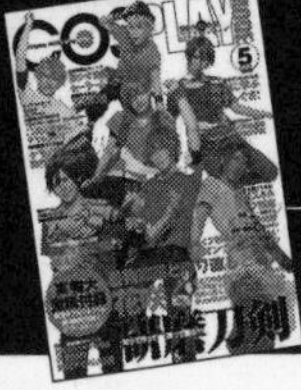

Supervisor: コスプレイモード COSPLAY MODE

The cosplay magazine that has taken over the reins of Cosmode magazine, which ran until spring 2014. It publishes everything related to cosplay, including pinup photos, fan-submitted cosplay photos, and information on costumes, makeup, photography, armor and prop building, and cosplay culture. Released on the 3rd of every even-numbered month. (Published by Famima.com)

n.25

► Page 12
Sunpu Castle
A castle that existed in Suruga Province (modern day eastern Shizuoka). It is also

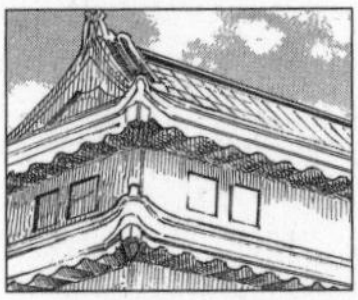

known as Fuchū Castle and Shizuoka Castle. It was built in 1585 (Tenshū 13) by Tokugawa Ieyasu, who ruled Suruga at the time, and is famous for being where he spent his final years. It has gone through several fires and large-scale renovations, so almost none of the original structure remains, but the bailey and the inner castle still remain as Sunpu Park, and other structures, such as the wooden East Gate, have been restored. In the past, cosplay events have been held there during the cherry blossom season.

► Page 22
Toshimaen
An amusement park often thought to be in Toshima, but actually located in Nerima, Tokyo. It was constructed around the ruins of Nerima Castle, which was built in the Muromachi Era by a member of the Toshima family, and that it where Toshimaen (Toshima Park) gets its name. It's famous for its unique

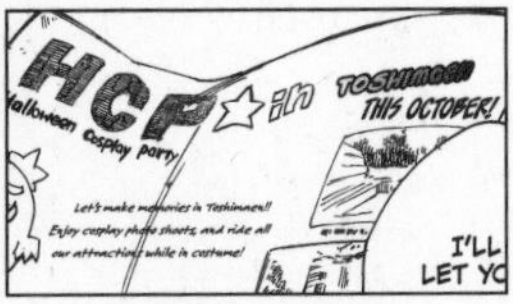
HCP☆in TOSHIMAEN THIS OCTOBER!!
Halloween Cosplay Party
Let's make memories in Toshimaen!! Enjoy cosplay photo shoots, and ride all our attractions while in costume!
I'LL LET YO

slogans, the most well-known being its 1986 slogan, *"Puuru hietemasu,"* which translates to, "Our pools are cool." In recent years, it's gained attention from the layer community for holding its Japan Cosplay Festival (JCF).

n.26

► Page 31
Thrill rides
The general term for thrilling theme park attractions that go so fast they make their riders scream. This includes roller coasters and water slides. At certain Toshimaen events, guests can ride in costume, but they must be careful how they handle their wigs, props, or anything else that might fly away while on the attraction.

► Page 32
Panda
Coin-operated moving animals are a common sight at theme parks. The panda at Toshimaen is popular among layers for its photogenicity, but if a child were to gaze

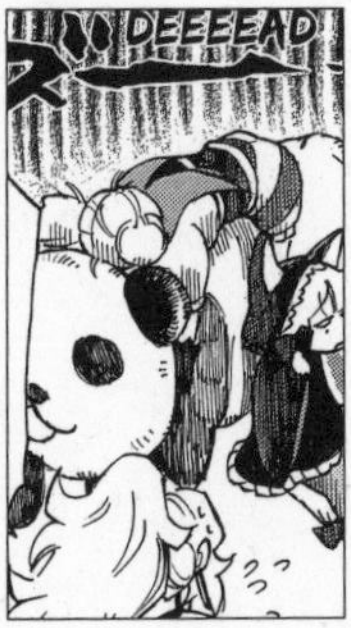
DEEEEAD

longingly at the panda, let us all be mature enough to let the child ride it without complaint.

n.27

► Page 53
"I don't want that girl over there to see."
When cosplaying characters from an anime for little girls, or superheroes from children's shows, cosplayers are very aware of the children who may be watching. For example, if the character wears a mask, it's basically considered taboo to take it off anywhere where people would see. Layers pay careful attention so as not to destroy the dreams of the children who see them as that character. Even if a precocious little tyke accuses them, "You're a fake!" they will carry on in character to the end. This is a beautiful custom that shows the kindness of layers and their dedication to their art.

n.28

► Page 69
A job managing cosplay events
Cosplay events are mainly run by staffers, whose job it is to run the event, and volunteers, who give freely of their time to help. In the case of staffers, it's extremely rare that they only work on cosplay events. In most cases, cosplay events are only some of the many events they have a hand in. Their duties include reserving the venue, securing the necessary items and equipment, and event publicity. As for volunteers, many also participate in the event—in other words, they are layers themselves. They support the event in various ways, such as setting up photo shoot equipment at the site and handling registration.

► Page 82
False eyelashes
Or eyelash extensions. In recent years, they've become a common part of a woman's makeup. In Japan, they were first sold in 1947 by the Kobayashi Koji Cosmetics Honpo (now Koji-Honpo). At the time, they were modeled after

the false eyelashes worn by the geisha in Asakusa, who wove them from their own hair. Nowadays, false eyelashes come in all shapes and colors, and some are even labeled "for cosplay."

▶ Page 84

Eyelash curler

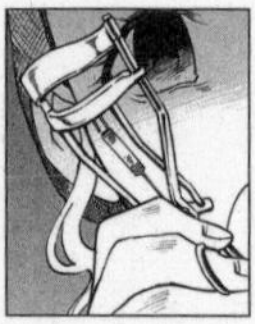

A cosmetic tool that pinches the upper eyelashes with the rubber (silicone) part and curls them upward. The purpose of this tool is to bring attention to the eyes by curling the lashes. In Japan, they are commonly known as beaula, from the eyelash curler first sold in Japan in 1930 by what is now the Keihodo Pharmaceutical Co. Ltd., which was trademarked as beaula, short for "beauty curler." Incidentally, the founder of this company, Yoshikatsu (Saburō) Nakashima joined the company Dai-Nippon Yūbenkai Kodansha (now Kodansha) at age 15 as a youth employee. At 18, he was put in charge of the mail-order department, which was responsible for obtaining and delivering import items requested by magazine readers in distant prefectures. After that, he left the company and started his own business.

n.29

▶ Page 91

Waterproof

A feature of certain cosmetics. It refers to makeup that has been treated to make it resistant to sweat and water, and does not come off easily. Primer, foundation, eyebrow pencil, mascara, etc. all come in waterproof varieties. While it can be beneficial to have water resistant makeup, this variety is difficult to remove with the average facewash or body soap, so some products come with their own removers.

▶ Page 103

Bitch

Originally meaning female dog, it came to be used to refer to a woman who wasn't chaste, and is now used as a pejorative against women. In Japan, it is mostly used in a sexual sense, to refer to a promiscuous woman, but in modern-day United States, it usually means "an unpleasant woman." In English, the words used to refer to a promiscuous woman include "slut" and "whore."

n.30

▶ Page 109

Forums (Computer Message Boards)

An internet website where members can post content and others can respond. Back in the 1990s, most users went by handles (see Volume 1: Handle), but when 2channel came onto the scene in 1999, there was a drastic increase in users who posted anonymously. While this has contributed to lively sharing of information and discussion, it has also caused various problems, such as users hiding behind anonymity to post slander and verbal abuse.

▶ Page 121

Photoshop

Short for Adobe Photoshop, an image editing software published by Adobe Systems. Many people use it to retouch their photos. There are many books on how to use Photoshop, and even amateurs can use it to alter their photos in many different ways. Changing the size of one's eyes or nose, and beautifying the skin are only the beginning—users can even change the background weather from rain to sun. Master the software, and one can turn pizza into a beautiful woman (there's a video online, so curious readers can search "pizza into woman").

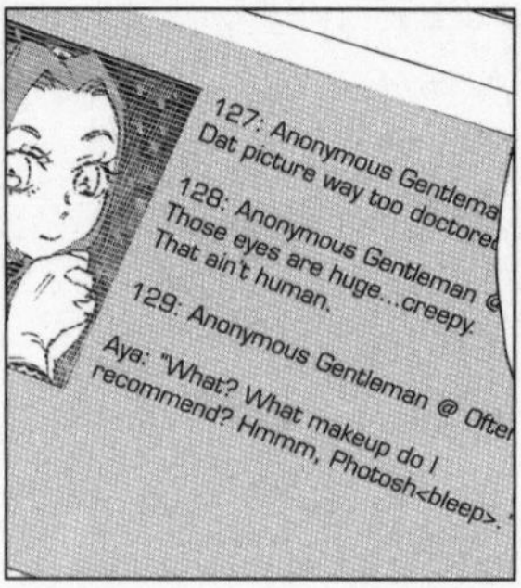
127: Anonymous Gentlema
Dat picture way too doctore
128: Anonymous Gentleman @
Those eyes are huge...creepy.
That ain't human.
129: Anonymous Gentleman @ Ofte
Aya: "What? What makeup do I
recommend? Hmmm, Photosh<bleep>.

n.31

▶ Page 137

Cos Photo

A mook (magazine book) published by Hobby Japan that specializes in cosplay photography techniques. It has features on everything from how to choose a camera, to settings for photo shoots, to lighting techniques. They also published *Cos Photo Beginners* for people just starting out.

n.32

▶ Page 155

"It's a stupid thing to get locked up for."

With the rise of internet forums came a noticeable increase in trolls who post slanderous, abusive, threatening messages. Under the protection of anonymity, some people write violent posts without even thinking about it, but posting baseless slander or obvious threats can lead to criminal charges. Anonymous posters have in fact used message boards to post death threats, and it has led to no end of arrests. In other incidents, users are manipulated by groundless information into lynching individuals over the internet.

n.33

▶ Page 170

Tokyo Dome City (TDC)

The common name for the entertainment complex run by the Tokyo Dome Corporation. It includes Tokyo Dome, Tokyo Dome City Attractions (formerly Kōrakuen), and Kōrakuen Hall. It is the forerunner of theme park based cosplay events, which have been growing more common since the Kōrakuen Halloween Fest in 1997. Currently, events held at TDC can generally be divided into two categories: Cosplay Fest and New Layers ☆ Paradise. During events, the venue is divided into areas that allow cosplay and areas that do not, so layers must proceed with caution.

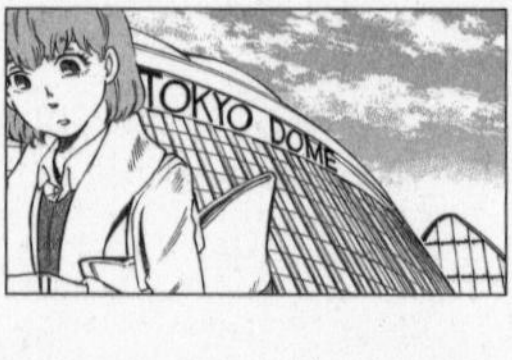
TOKYO DOME

I'm glad Nagisa didn't notice.

I'm so stupid. I'm so…so stupid.

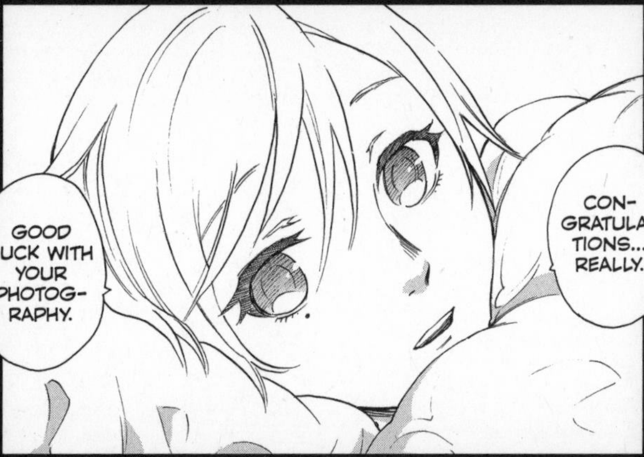
CON-GRATULA-TIONS… REALLY.
GOOD LUCK WITH YOUR PHOTOG-RAPHY.

The friend with whom she's cosplayed for the last ten years suddenly announces her retirement.

"Why…are you giving up cosplay?"

Kimiko, who has lived with her hobby for years, gives her answer at Nagisa's side.

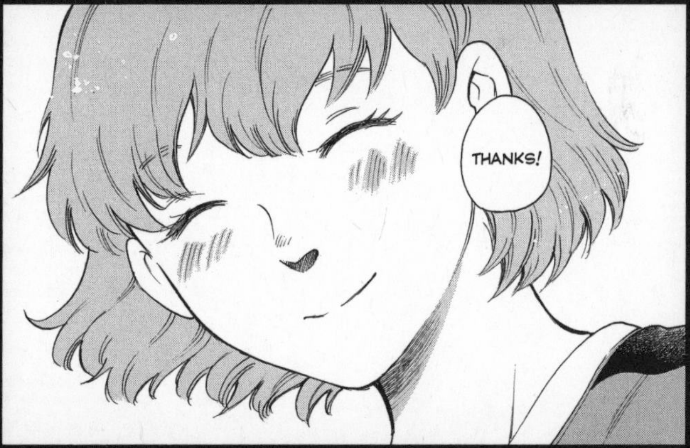
THANKS!

COMPLEX AGE 5

ON SALE SUMMER 2017

Translation Notes

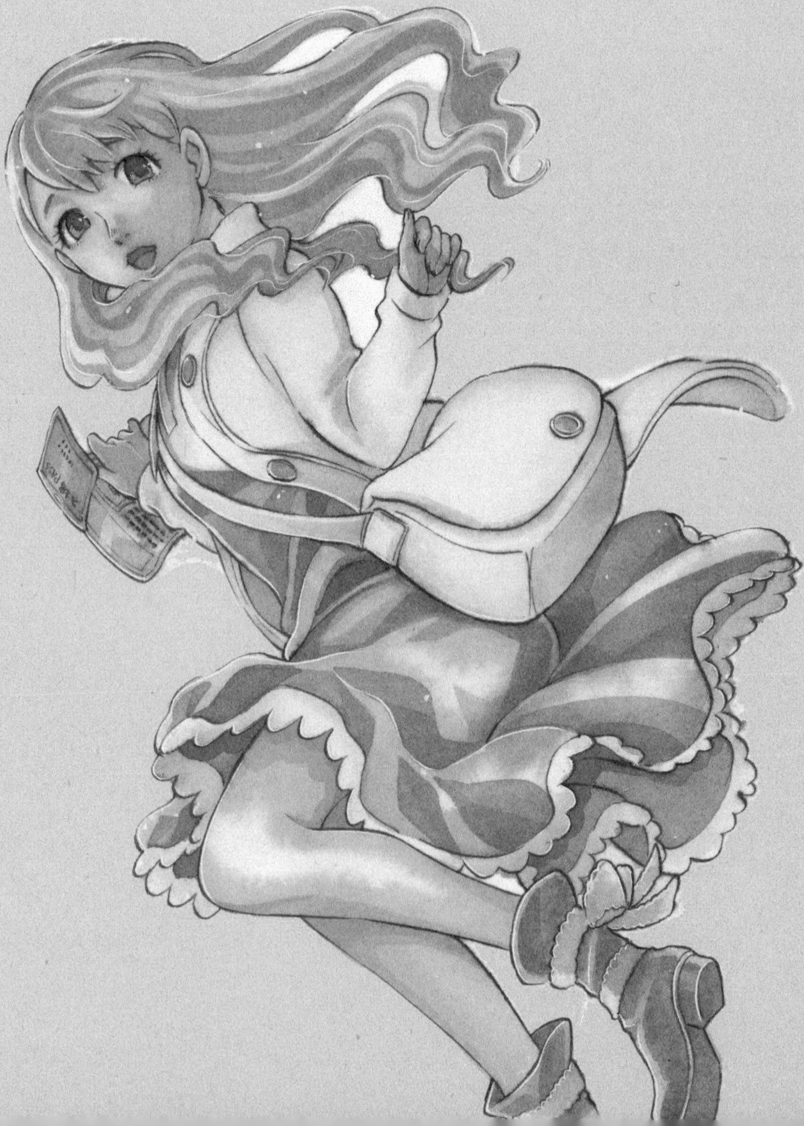

page 4

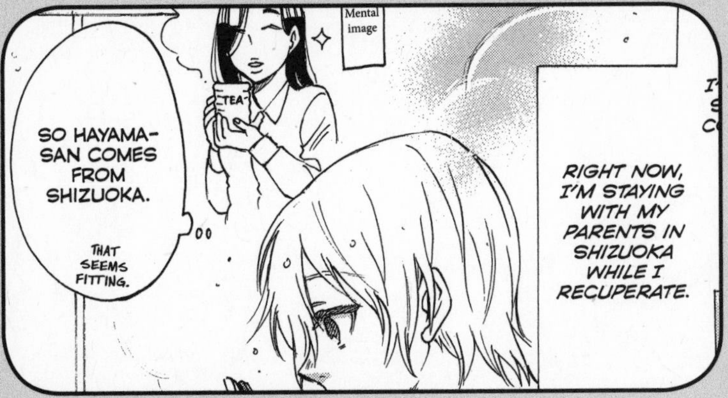
RIGHT NOW, I'M STAYING WITH MY PARENTS IN SHIZUOKA WHILE I RECUPERATE.
Mental image
TEA
SO HAYAMA-SAN COMES FROM SHIZUOKA.
THAT SEEMS FITTING.

HAYAMA IN SHIZUOKA

Shizuoka is the prefecture where Mt. Fuji is found, and people from there are known for being calm and agreeable. Shizuoka is also where most of Japan's green tea comes from, so when people hear Shizuoka, they think of tea.

---

page 69

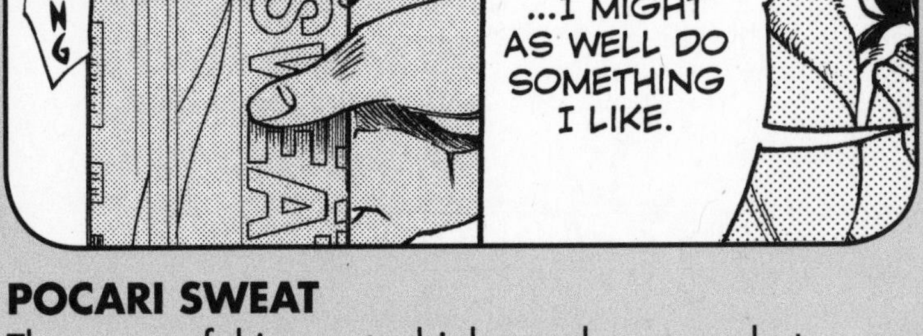
SO I FIGURE ...
...I MIGHT AS WELL DO SOMETHING I LIKE.
AND SO...
CLANG

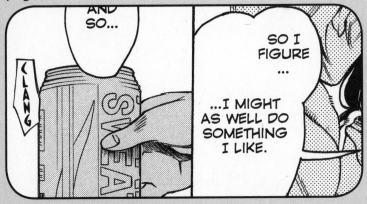

POCARI SWEAT

The name of this sports drink may be somewhat unappetizing, but it is not meant to imply that sweat is one of the ingredients. Rather, the drink is meant to supply the body with the nutrients and electrolytes lost by sweating.

page 76

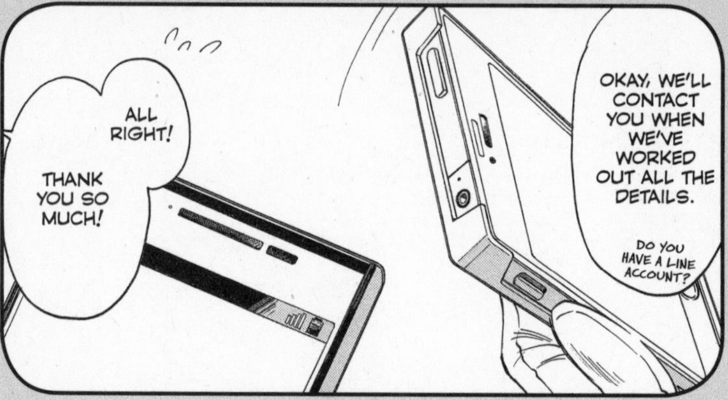
OKAY, WE'LL CONTACT YOU WHEN WE'VE WORKED OUT ALL THE DETAILS.
DO YOU HAVE A LINE ACCOUNT?
ALL RIGHT!
THANK YOU SO MUCH!

LINE

LINE is a social media app that allows its users to call and text each other, send videos and pictures, etc. It is Japan's largest social network, and is available for smartphones and tablets in the United States as well.

---

page 177

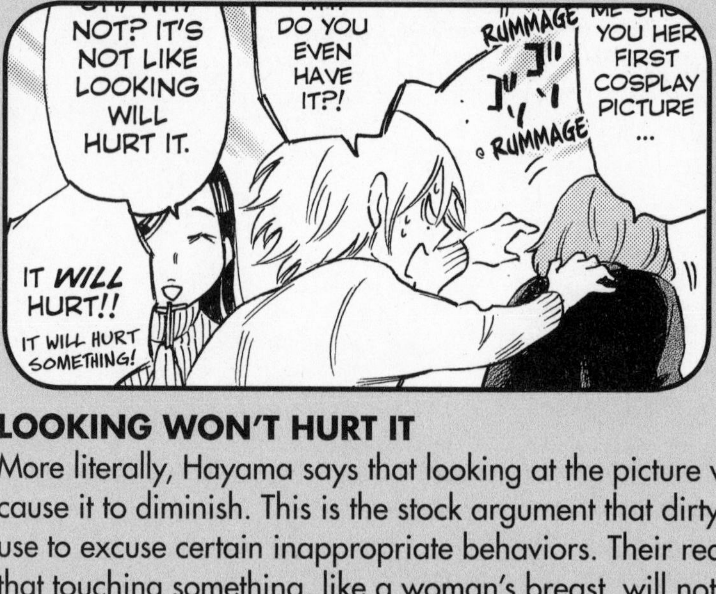
YOU HER FIRST COSPLAY PICTURE ...
RUMMAGE
RUMMAGE
DO YOU EVEN HAVE IT?!
NOT? IT'S NOT LIKE LOOKING WILL HURT IT.
IT WILL HURT!!
IT WILL HURT SOMETHING!

LOOKING WON'T HURT IT

More literally, Hayama says that looking at the picture will not cause it to diminish. This is the stock argument that dirty old men use to excuse certain inappropriate behaviors. Their reasoning is that touching something, like a woman's breast, will not cause any decrease in the supply. In this case, Hayama suggests that looking at the picture will not reduce the supply of old cosplay pictures of Nagisa.

page 189

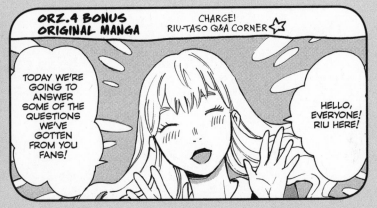

ORZ.4 BONUS ORIGINAL MANGA
CHARGE! RIU-TASO Q&A CORNER
HELLO, EVERYONE! RIU HERE!
TODAY WE'RE GOING TO ANSWER SOME OF THE QUESTIONS WE'VE GOTTEN FROM YOU FANS!

RUI-TASO

Taso is a suffix applied to names of two-dimensional characters to show endearment. The term derives from *chan*, which became the even cutesier *tan*, and then, because when written a certain way, the Japanese character for "n" looks like the character *so*, *tan* became *taso*.

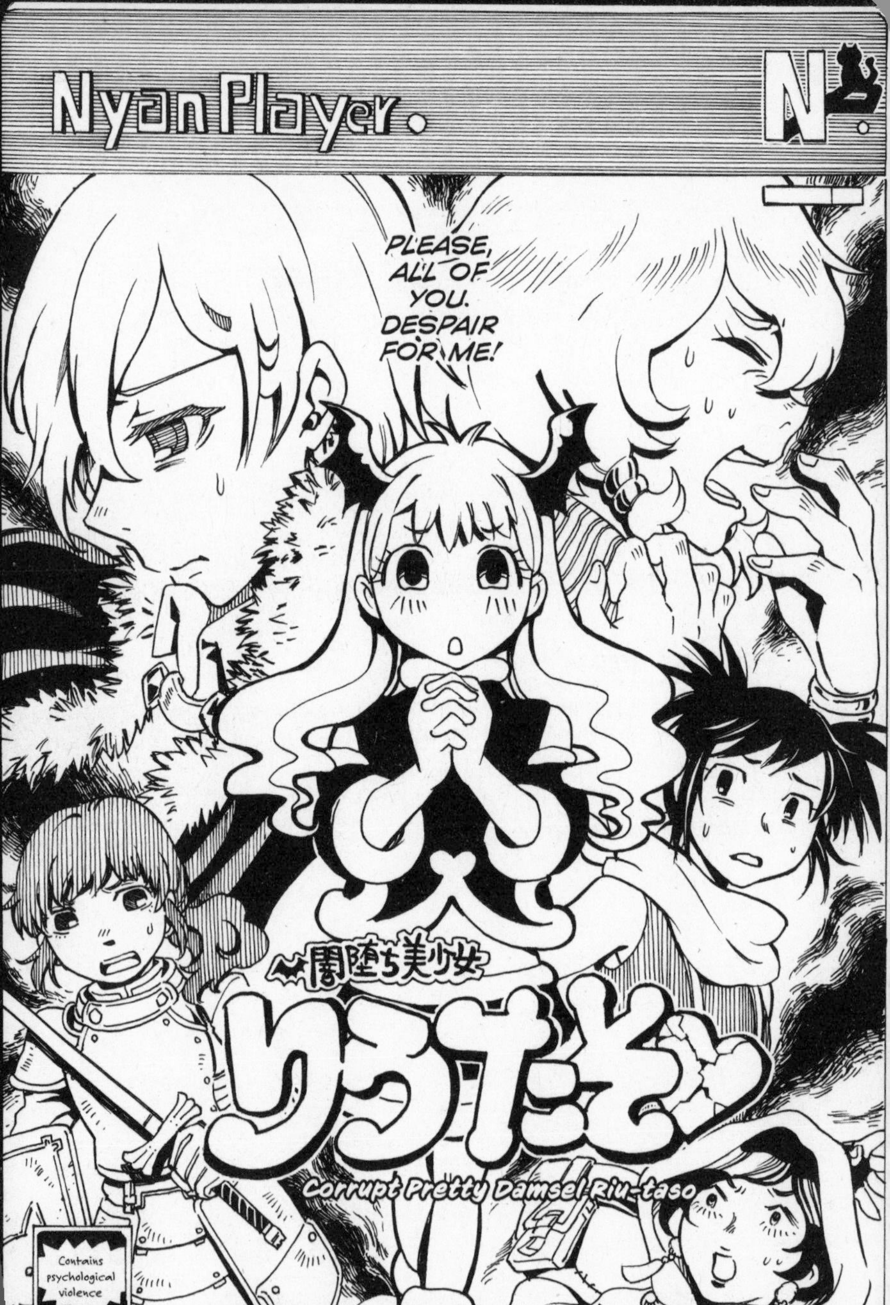
Nyan Player.
PLEASE, ALL OF YOU. DESPAIR FOR ME!
闇堕ち美少女
りうたそ
Corrupt Pretty Damsel Riu-taso
Contains psychological violence
PG-12

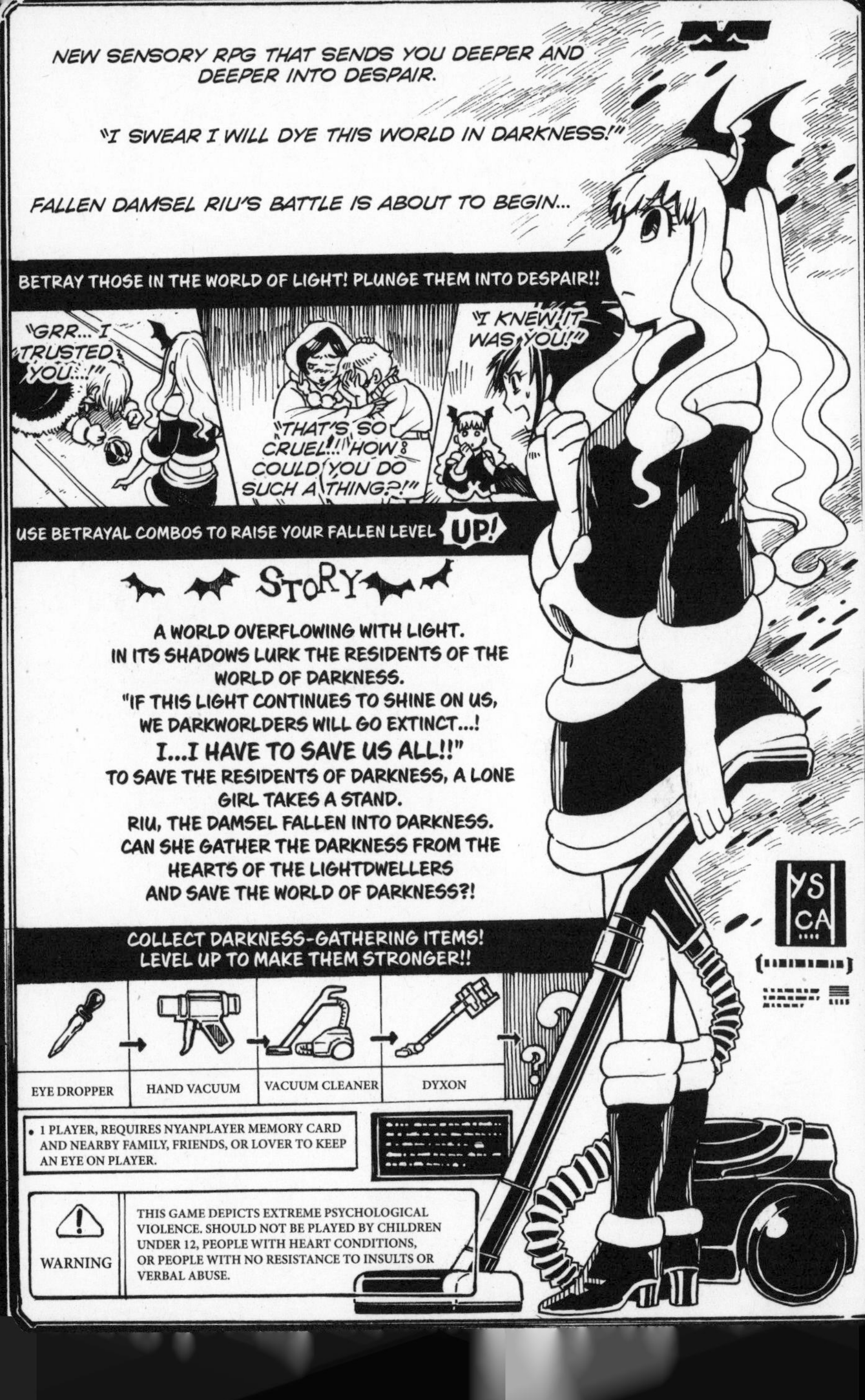

NEW SENSORY RPG THAT SENDS YOU DEEPER AND DEEPER INTO DESPAIR.
"I SWEAR I WILL DYE THIS WORLD IN DARKNESS!"
FALLEN DAMSEL RIU'S BATTLE IS ABOUT TO BEGIN...
BETRAY THOSE IN THE WORLD OF LIGHT! PLUNGE THEM INTO DESPAIR!!
"I KNEW IT WAS YOU!"
"THAT'S SO CRUEL!! HOW COULD YOU DO SUCH A THING?!"
"GRR... I TRUSTED YOU...!"
USE BETRAYAL COMBOS TO RAISE YOUR FALLEN LEVEL UP!
STORY
A WORLD OVERFLOWING WITH LIGHT.
IN ITS SHADOWS LURK THE RESIDENTS OF THE WORLD OF DARKNESS.
"IF THIS LIGHT CONTINUES TO SHINE ON US, WE DARKWORLDERS WILL GO EXTINCT...!
I...I HAVE TO SAVE US ALL!!"
TO SAVE THE RESIDENTS OF DARKNESS, A LONE GIRL TAKES A STAND.
RIU, THE DAMSEL FALLEN INTO DARKNESS.
CAN SHE GATHER THE DARKNESS FROM THE HEARTS OF THE LIGHTDWELLERS AND SAVE THE WORLD OF DARKNESS?!
COLLECT DARKNESS-GATHERING ITEMS!
LEVEL UP TO MAKE THEM STRONGER!!
EYE DROPPER
HAND VACUUM
VACUUM CLEANER
DYXON
?
• 1 PLAYER, REQUIRES NYANPLAYER MEMORY CARD AND NEARBY FAMILY, FRIENDS, OR LOVER TO KEEP AN EYE ON PLAYER.
WARNING
THIS GAME DEPICTS EXTREME PSYCHOLOGICAL VIOLENCE. SHOULD NOT BE PLAYED BY CHILDREN UNDER 12, PEOPLE WITH HEART CONDITIONS, OR PEOPLE WITH NO RESISTANCE TO INSULTS OR VERBAL ABUSE.

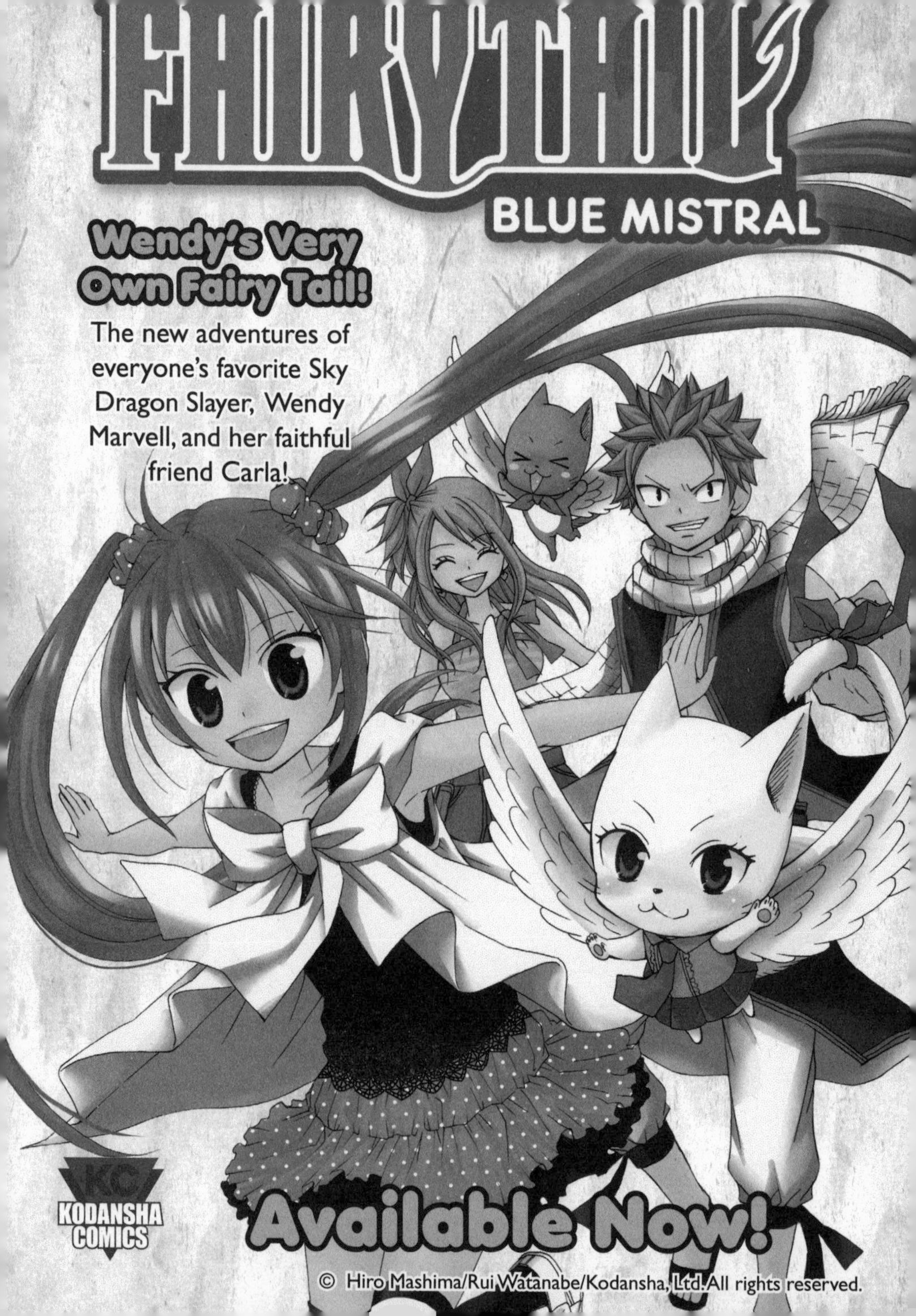
FAIRY TAIL
BLUE MISTRAL
Wendy's Very Own Fairy Tail!
The new adventures of everyone's favorite Sky Dragon Slayer, Wendy Marvell, and her faithful friend Carla!
KC
KODANSHA COMICS
Available Now!
© Hiro Mashima/Rui Watanabe/Kodansha, Ltd. All rights reserved.

FINALLY, A LOWER-COST OMNIBUS EDITION OF FAIRY TAIL! CONTAINS VOLUMES 1-5. ONLY $39.99!

-NEARLY 1,000 PAGES!
-EXTRA LARGE 7"x10.5" TRIM SIZE!
-HIGH-QUALITY PAPER!

Fairy Tail takes place in a world filled with magic. 17-year-old Lucy is a wizard-in-training who wants to join a magic guild so that she can become a full-fledged wizard. She dreams of joining the most famous guild, known as Fairy Tail. One day she meets Natsu, a boy raised by a dragon which vanished when he was young. Natsu has devoted his life to finding his dragon father. When Natsu helps Lucy out of a tricky situation, she discovers that he is a member of Fairy Tail, and our heroes' adventure together begins.

FAIRY TAIL

MASTER'S EDITION

Say I Love You.

KC KODANSHA COMICS

Mei Tachibana has no friends — and says she doesn't need them!
But everything changes when she accidentally roundhouse kicks the most popular boy in school! However, Yamato Kurosawa isn't angry in the slightest— in fact, he thinks his ordinary life could use an unusual girl like Mei. But winning Mei's trust will be a tough task. How long will she refuse to say, "I love you"?

"This series never fails to put a smile on my face."
-Dramatic Reviews

"A very funny look at what happens when two strange and strangely well-suited people try to navigate the thorny path to true love together."
-Anime News Network

My Little Monster

OPPOSITES ATTRACT...MAYBE?

Haru Yoshida is feared as an unstable and violent "monster." Mizutani Shizuku is a grade-obsessed student with no friends. Fate brings these two together to form the most unlikely pair. Haru firmly believes he's in love with Mizutani and she firmly believes he's insane.

KC
KODANSHA
COMICS

INUYASHIKI

A superhero like none you've ever seen, from the creator of "Gantz"!

Ichiro Inuyashiki is down on his luck. He looks much older than his 58 years, his children despise him, and his wife thinks he's a useless coward. So when he's diagnosed with stomach cancer and given three months to live, it seems the only one who'll miss him is his dog.

Then a blinding light fills the sky, and the old man is killed... only to wake up later in a body he almost recognizes as his own. Can it be that Ichiro Inuyashiki is no longer human?

Comes in extra-large editions with color pages!

DON'T MISS THE MOST ACCLAIMED ACTION MANGA OF 2013!

"Gripping doesn't begin to describe Vinland Saga. 5 stars."
—ICv2

"Deeply engrossing... If you have any interest at all in Vikings, the Medieval period, or pirates, this is not a series you want to miss."
—Anime News Network

"The art is gorgeous, a combination of beautiful cartooning and realistic backgrounds. Yukimura is also a master of pacing, both in frenetic battle scenes and charged emotional moments."
—Faith Erin Hicks, *Friends With Boys*

"For those who love Berserk, you'll love this too... Worth the long wait."
—A Case Suitable for Treatment

"It will be impossible to stop watching this story unfold."
—Japan Media Arts Awards jury

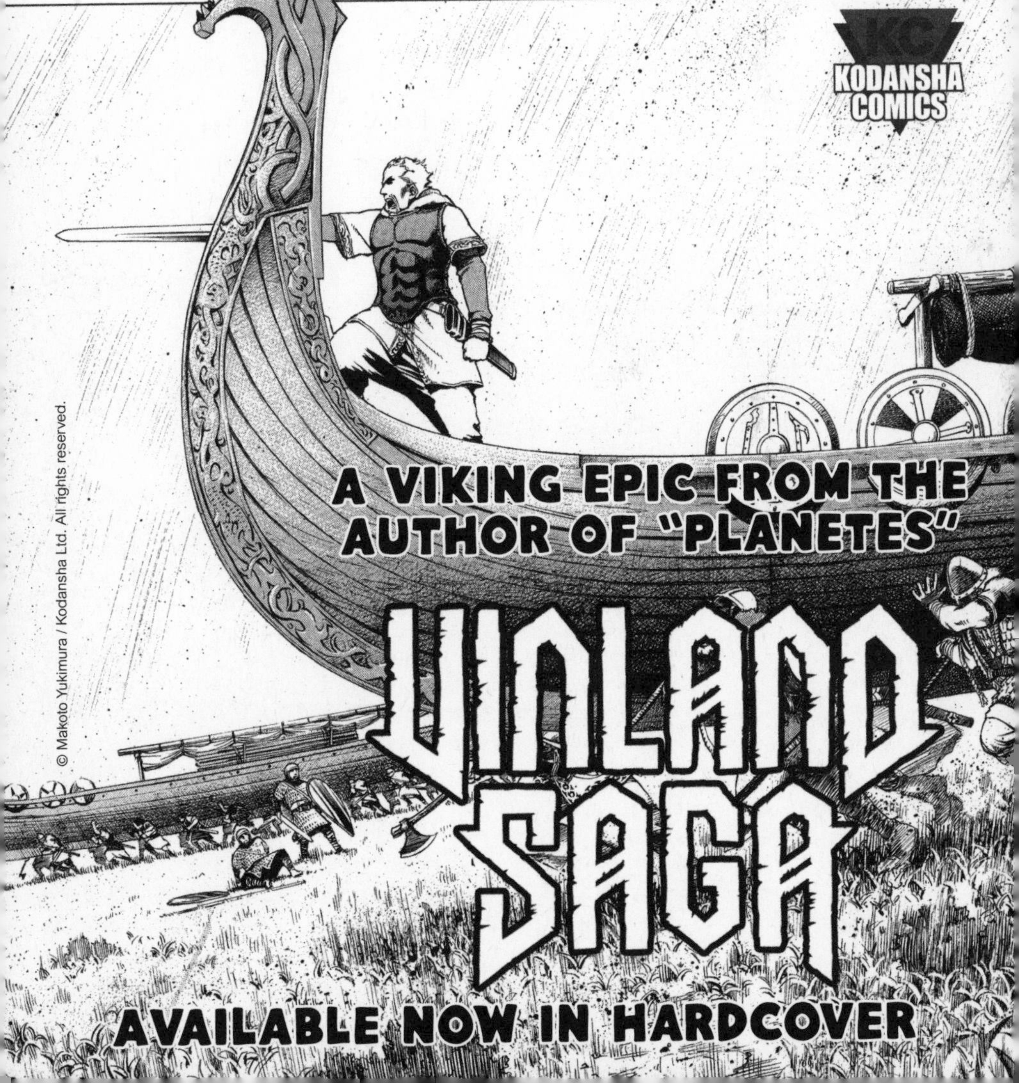
KC
KODANSHA COMICS
A VIKING EPIC FROM THE AUTHOR OF "PLANETES"
VINLAND SAGA
AVAILABLE NOW IN HARDCOVER

A Kodansha Comics Trade Paperback Original.

Published in the United States by Kodansha Comics,
an imprint of Kodansha USA Publishing, LLC, New York.

Publication rights for this English edition arranged through Kodansha Ltd.,
Tokyo.

First published in Japan in 2015 by Kodansha Ltd., Tokyo, as *Complex
Age* volume 4.

ISBN 978-1-63236-328-2

Printed in the United States of America.

www.kodanshacomics.com

9 8 7 6 5 4 3 2 1

Translation: Alethea Nibley & Athena Nibley
Lettering: AndWorld Design
Editing: Lauren Scanlan
Kodansha Comics edition cover design: Phil Balsman